CAMBRIDGE

Power Up 2

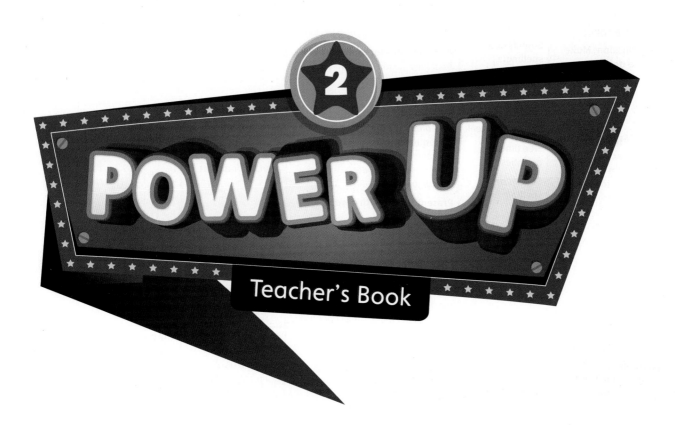

Teacher's Book

Lucy Frino

With Caroline Nixon and Michael Tomlinson

Map of the book

	Vocabulary	Grammar	Cross-curricular	Literature	Assessment
Meet the family Page 4	Character names	**Personal descriptions review** *How old is she? She's five.* *He's got long hair.*			
1 A day on the farm **Mission: Make a daily routine chart** Page 6	Countryside Daily routines **Sounds and spelling:** *r*	**Present continuous review** *Are you reading a book?* *No, I'm not. I'm doing my homework.* **Present simple for routines;** ***o'clock*** *What time do you get up?* *I get up at seven o'clock.* *What time does school finish?* *It finishes at four o'clock.*	***Look after our planet*** Learn about how to look after our planet	***The race*** A poem Social and emotional skill: Being supportive	A1 Movers Speaking Part 1
2 My week **Mission: Plan a fun activities timetable for two friends** Page 18	Days of the week Free time activities **Sounds and spelling:** *ay*	***How often … ?*** **and adverbs of frequency** *How often do you clean your teeth?* *Do you ever get up late?* *always, often, sometimes, never* **Present simple with** ***always, often, sometimes, never*** *He sometimes watches TV.* *They never play tennis.* ***must/mustn't*** *What must I do?* *You mustn't wear your skates in the house.* *You must put them in the cupboard.*	***Let's be healthy!*** Learn about being safe when doing exercise and sports	***A bad, bad Monday morning*** A narrative Social and emotional skill: Thinking about the consequences of our actions	A1 Movers Reading and Writing Part 1
3 Party time! **Mission: Plan and act out a scene** Page 30	Jobs and parties Physical descriptions **Sounds and spelling:** /ɑː/	**Present simple and present continuous** *I don't often listen to the radio.* *I'm not listening to it now.* ***Why … ?*** **and** ***Because …*** *Why are you asking a lot of questions?* *Because I love asking questions.*	***People who help us*** Learn about people who help us at home, at school and in the community	***The costume party*** A story Social and emotional skill: Asking for and offering help	A1 Movers Speaking Part 2
	Review units 1–3				
4 The family at home **Mission: Act out a visit to my cousins' new home** Page 44	Extended family In and around the home **Sounds and spelling:** /ʌ/	**Comparative adjectives with** ***-er/-ier*** **and** ***better/worse*** *My cousin's hair is longer/curlier than my uncle's.* *Shelly's singing is worse than Gracie's.* **Possessive pronouns** *Our car is smaller than my aunt and uncle's car, but ours is newer than theirs.*	***Machines in our homes*** Learn about machines at home and how they work	***Surprise!*** A story Social and emotional skill: Initiative and managing one's own emotions	A1 Movers Listening Part 3

	Vocabulary	Grammar	Cross-curricular	Literature	Assessment
5 Animal world **Mission: Plan an animal documentary** Page 56	Wild and domestic animals Action verbs **Sounds and spelling:** *g*	**Superlative adjectives** *This kitten's the prettiest/the fattest.* *These ice skates are the best.* **Prepositions: *above, below, near, opposite*** *The bat's above the tree.* *The snail's below the flower.* *The parrot's near the cage.* *The bus stop's opposite the zoo.*	***The animal kingdom*** Learn about animals and their food	***Why the kangaroo has a pouch*** An Australian dreamtime story Social and emotional skill: Helping others	A1 Movers Reading and Writing Part 2
6 Our weather **Mission: Make a weather map for a country** Page 68	The weather Clothes **Sounds and spelling:** *ee* **and** *y*	***was/were*** *Were your grandparents here last weekend? Yes, they were.* *Were you at school on Tuesday? No, I wasn't.* ***There was / There were*** *Was there a scarf in the bedroom? Yes, there was.* *Were there any boots in the bedroom? No, there weren't.*	***What's the weather like today?*** Learn about instruments to measure the weather	***Fun in all types of weather!*** A poem Social and emotional skill: Thinking positively	A1 Movers Listening Part 1 and Part 2
	Review units 4–6				
7 Let's cook! **Mission: Make a class recipe book** Page 82	Food Actions in the kitchen **Sounds and spelling:** *ch*	**Past simple: irregular verbs** *I went swimming last Saturday.* *I didn't go shopping yesterday.* *Did you go to the park? Yes, I did.* **Past simple: regular verbs** *I liked cooking them!* *I fried the onions.* *I stopped because you started asking me questions.*	***Plants are delicious!*** Learn about how we use plants in food	***Sonny's dream job*** A fantasy story Social and emotional skill: Perseverance	A1 Movers Speaking Part 3
8 Around town **Mission: Write a trip review** Page 94	A day trip Places in town **Sounds and spelling:** *ow* **and** *oa*	**Past simple: more irregular verbs** *I found my old hat.* *He bought it last year.* ***have to / don't have to*** *I have to see the eye doctor at the hospital.* *My brother has to wear glasses.* *Do you have to wear glasses? Yes, I do.*	***Road safety*** Learn how to be safe in town	***Tom's first day on the school bus*** A fantasy story Social and emotional skill: Being optimistic	A1 Movers Listening Part 4
9 A big change **Mission: Plan a holiday world tour** Page 106	Adjectives for opinions and feelings A new adventure **Sounds and spelling:** *ing* **or** *in*	**Comparative adjectives with *more*** *Circus clothes are more beautiful than these.* *The circus is more exciting than the farm!* **Superlative adjectives with *most*** *This city is one of the most beautiful in the world.* *In my family, my brother is the most frightened of spiders.*	***The wonders of the world*** Learn about natural and manmade wonders of the world	***The mystery picnic*** A counting poem Social and emotional skill: Pride in your work	A1 Movers Reading and Writing Part 3
	Review units 7–9				

Checklist for A1 Movers preparation

Paper	Part	Task	Practice
Listening 20 minutes	1	Draw lines to match names to people in a picture.	*Preparation*: Pupil's Book Unit 6 Page 78 *Practice*: Activity Book Unit 6 Page 78, Test Generator Unit 6 Movers Progress Test
	2	Write words or numbers in gaps.	*Preparation*: Pupil's Book Unit 6 Page 78 *Practice*: Activity Book Unit 6 Page 78, Test Generator Unit 6 Movers Progress Test
	3	Match pictures with illustrated words or names by writing letters in boxes.	*Preparation*: Pupil's Book Unit 4 Page 54 *Practice*: Activity Book Unit 4 Page 54, Test Generator Unit 4 Movers Progress Test
	4	Tick boxes under correct pictures.	*Preparation*: Pupil's Book Unit 8 Page 104 *Practice*: Activity Book Unit 8 Page 104, Test Generator Unit 8 Movers Progress Test
	5	Carry out instructions, locate objects, colour correctly and write.	See level 3
Reading and Writing 30 minutes	1	Match words to definitions.	*Preparation*: Pupil's Book Unit 2 Page 28 *Practice*: Activity Book Unit 2 Page 28, Test Generator Unit 2 Movers Progress Test
	2	Read a short dialogue and choose the correct responses from three options.	*Preparation*: Pupil's Book Unit 5 Page 66 *Practice*: Activity Book Unit 5 Page 66, Test Generator Unit 5 Movers Progress Test
	3	Read a gapped text, complete it with the correct words and choose the best title.	*Preparation*: Pupil's Book Unit 9 Page 116 *Practice*: Activity Book Unit 9 Page 116, Test Generator Unit 9 Movers Progress Test
	4	Read a gapped factual text and complete it with the correct words.	See level 3
	5	Read a story and complete sentences with one, two or three words.	See level 3
	6	Complete sentences, answer questions and write sentences about a picture.	See level 3
Speaking 5–7 minutes	1	Identify four differences between two pictures.	*Preparation*: Pupil's Book Unit 1 Page 16 *Practice*: Activity Book Unit 1 Page 16, Test Generator Unit 1 Movers Progress Test
	2	Describe a picture sequence.	*Preparation*: Pupil's Book Unit 3 Page 40 *Practice*: Activity Book Unit 3 Page 40, Test Generator Unit 3 Movers Progress Test
	3	Identify the odd one out in picture sets and give reasons.	*Preparation*: Pupil's Book Unit 7 Page 92 *Practice*: Activity Book Unit 7 Page 92, Test Generator Unit 7 Movers Progress Test
	4	Answer personal questions.	Embedded throughout the course and seen in full on the level 2 Test Generator

About *Power Up*

Power Up

What is *Power Up*?

Power Up is an engaging and effective approach to learning which uses:

- Lively activities with clear objectives
- Age-appropriate, engaging topics which support learner progress and collaborative learning
- Real-world contexts and language
- Development of life competencies and test skills
- Scaffolded tasks which support learners of all abilities
- A unifying learner-centred methodology which supports life-long learning.

Power Up provides both general English and comprehensive preparation for Cambridge English Qualifications, jointly published with Cambridge Assessment English. Student-centred learning is a core part of the course, with ongoing unit tasks giving ample opportunity for collaborative learning.

Key features of *Power Up*

Activities are based on real-world skills and situations that learners find engaging and fun. All four skills – reading, writing, listening and speaking – are used to explore interesting topics. The activities scaffold the learning to support both stronger and weaker learners. Grammar and vocabulary are developed through communicative activities which have a clear purpose and encourage learners to use language naturally. All new language is heard, read, written and spoken as learners acquire it and the language is then consolidated throughout, building as the units progress.

Power Up and the Cambridge Framework for Life Competencies

In addition to language learning, *Power Up* develops the life competencies of learners.

Power Up is one of the first generation of courses to integrate the Cambridge Framework for Life Competencies. This is an ongoing research initiative into how thinking and learning skills are developed over different life stages. Each unit of *Power Up* is mapped to a component within the Cambridge Framework for Life Competencies to ensure a wide range of skills are covered. This also provides opportunities for formative assessment and a broad view of each learner's development.

Missions

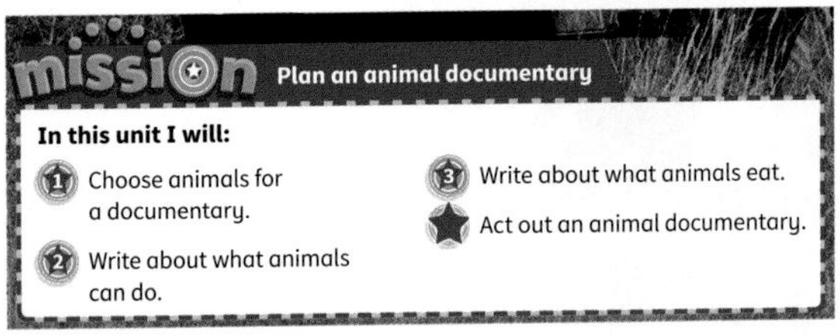
mission Plan an animal documentary

In this unit I will:

1 Choose animals for a documentary.

2 Write about what animals can do.

3 Write about what animals eat.

★ Act out an animal documentary.

The Life Competencies Framework is a key feature of the unit Missions, where learners are building on social skills by practising collaboration and communication. The enquiry-led approach used in the Missions also builds on learners' thinking and learning skills, through the creativity, critical thinking, problem solving and decision making employed in each stage of the Mission.

Each unit is structured around a 'Mission' which helps learners to set objectives at the beginning and understand their end goal and learning outcomes. Outcomes are also clearly stated at the beginning of each lesson so that learners can understand and think about them. The teaching notes suggest creative ways to share these with the learners. The Missions are based on real-world contexts with a focus on real English. They give learners the opportunity to build up a portfolio of their work as evidence of their learning and help them to reflect and evaluate their own learning even at a young age. As part of this approach, there are frequent opportunities for learners to reflect on what they have learnt, which helps them plan for the next stage of learning, with practical tips on how teachers can help learners to do this.

Literature

5

The kangaroo's kind to the old wombat all day. When it's late, she says goodbye to him and she looks for her baby. Where is he? She can't find him! 'Joey! Joey! Where are you?' the kangaroo shouts.

It's OK. He's asleep below the biggest tree. The kind kangaroo finds him and goes to sleep, too.

The next day she wakes up and sees a pouch. She puts her joey in the pouch. Then she sees the old wombat. 'Look! This pouch is brilliant, but where does it come from?'

'It's my present to you. You're the kindest kangaroo that I know,' the wombat says.

And from that day, all mummy kangaroos have pouches to carry their babies.

2 **Talk about the questions.**

1 How does the wombat feel at the start of the story?
2 How does the wombat feel when the kangaroo helps him?
3 Why does the wombat give her the pouch?
4 How does the kangaroo feel when the wombat gives her the pouch?

3 **Who's kind to you? Are you kind to people? What do you do?**

Social and emotional skill: Helping others 65

The Life Competencies Framework also features in the Literature spread, where learners are building on emotional skills and social responsibilities. Each story holds a message that learners can identify and explore, making it relevant to their own contexts. They learn about emotions, empathy and how to respond to others appropriately through identifying with the characters in the stories.

Cross-curricular learning

The **cross-curricular** sections also develop life competencies through critical thinking and wider world knowledge.

Cross-curricular learning is used in *Power Up* to refer to any teaching of a non-language subject through the medium of a second or foreign language. It suggests a balance between content and language learning. The non-language content such as Natural Science, Social Science or Arts and Crafts is developed through the second language, and the second language is developed through the non-language content. Cross-curricular learning can be seen as an educational approach which supports linguistic diversity and is a powerful tool that can have a strong impact on language learning.

Why cross-curricular learning is important for language learning

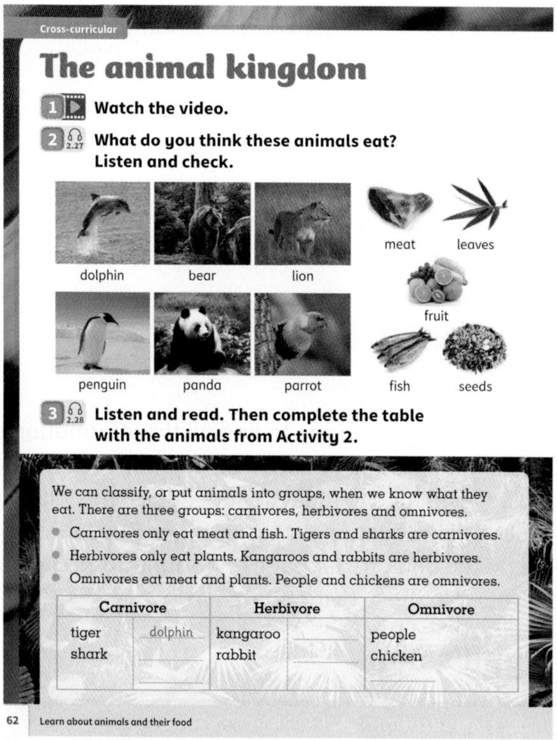

Cross-curricular

The animal kingdom

1 Watch the video.

2 2.27 What do you think these animals eat? Listen and check.

dolphin bear lion meat leaves fruit penguin panda parrot fish seeds

3 2.28 Listen and read. Then complete the table with the animals from Activity 2.

We can classify, or put animals into groups, when we know what they eat. There are three groups: carnivores, herbivores and omnivores.

- Carnivores only eat meat and fish. Tigers and sharks are carnivores.
- Herbivores only eat plants. Kangaroos and rabbits are herbivores.
- Omnivores eat meat and plants. People and chickens are omnivores.

Carnivore		Herbivore		Omnivore
tiger	dolphin	kangaroo		people
shark		rabbit		chicken

62 Learn about animals and their food

Research on second language acquisition has shown that exposure to naturally occurring language is necessary to achieve a good level of competence in the language. Acquiring a second language is a long and natural process. Learners need to have access to spontaneous speech in an interactive context and the cross-curricular lessons in *Power Up* provide learners with this access. Learners have to expand their linguistic resources in order to deal with the demands of content learning. Using a second language to grasp non-language content requires a depth of processing which leads to improved language acquisition. Learning is a problem-solving activity and cross-curricular learning requires learners to solve problems through a second language.

The benefits of using cross-curricular learning in the classroom

- Cross-curricular learning relies on intrinsic motivation, that is, the learners are involved in interesting and meaningful activities while using the language. Lessons provide opportunities for incidental language learning. Incidental learning has been shown to be effective and long lasting.
- Through exposure to interesting and authentic content, cross-curricular learning leads to greater involvement and helps increase learner motivation.
- Through the interactive and cooperational nature of the tasks, cross-curricular learning helps boost self-esteem, raise self-confidence, build learner independence and teach learner organisational skills.
- Through the integration of language and content, cross-curricular learning encourages creative thinking.
- Cross-curricular learning fosters learning to learn through the use of learning strategies and study skills.

Cross-curricular learning in *Power Up* levels 1 and 2

Every age has its own characteristics. In these first Primary stages, learners require longer input to be able to show production. The acquisition of the second language has to grow to allow them to understand and repeat the content. This can be achieved by following a communicative approach. In levels 1 and 2 we therefore mostly focus on oral skills in cross-curricular lessons in order to produce accurate reading and writing skills in the future. The topics covered in the cross-curricular lessons have been chosen to make the learners feel secure with the content in each lesson and to motivate them to use the English language.

Preparation for Cambridge A1 Movers in *Power Up 2*

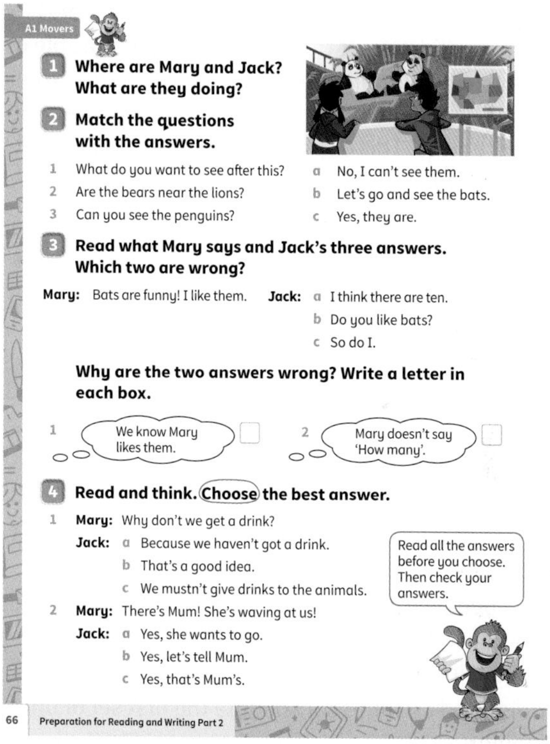

A1 Movers

1 Where are Mary and Jack? What are they doing?

2 Match the questions with the answers.

1 What do you want to see after this?
2 Are the bears near the lions?
3 Can you see the penguins?

a No, I can't see them.
b Let's go and see the bats.
c Yes, they are.

3 Read what Mary says and Jack's three answers. Which two are wrong?

Mary: Bats are funny! I like them.
Jack: a I think there are ten.
b Do you like bats?
c So do I.

Why are the two answers wrong? Write a letter in each box.

1 We know Mary likes them.
2 Mary doesn't say 'How many'.

4 Read and think. Choose the best answer.

1 Mary: Why don't we get a drink?
Jack: a Because we haven't got a drink.
b That's a good idea.
c We mustn't give drinks to the animals.

2 Mary: There's Mum! She's waving at us!
Jack: a Yes, she wants to go.
b Yes, let's tell Mum.
c Yes, that's Mum's.

Read all the answers before you choose. Then check your answers.

66 Preparation for Reading and Writing Part 2

Through a unique partnership between Cambridge Assessment and Cambridge University Press, *Power Up* is the first course to naturally integrate test preparation and formative assessment in a fun and effective English course. This well-rounded formula equips learners with the skills and abilities to approach Cambridge English tests with real confidence.

Power Up contains a motivating 'test builder' stage in each unit which develops the skills needed for test success and test strategies for younger learners. It familiarises learners with Cambridge test formats in a positive context which prioritises progress in learning and develops confidence. Learners are fully prepared for A1 Movers by the end of level 3 of *Power Up*.

The unique partnership between Cambridge University Press and Cambridge Assessment English means that *Power Up* has been developed with a new, integrated approach to the Cambridge exams.

Throughout *Power Up*, learners are given practice in Cambridge exam-style tasks, introduced by the YLE monkey.

In each unit of level 2, the Pupil's Book Exam preparation page focuses on one part of the A1 Movers test. It breaks down the task and focuses on the skills needed to complete it step by step. The lesson trains learners and provides tips and insights into what learners can do to achieve their best.

The Activity Book follows on by giving learners an opportunity to practise the task in full, building on what they have learnt in the Pupil's Book.

As a final step, the *Power Up* Test Generator includes full A1 Movers practice tests.

This fully-scaffolded approach prepares learners and gives them confidence. It trains them to be adaptable and think actively. It supports teachers with real exam training and it gives you an invaluable measurement of your learners' progress. This approach also gives *Power Up* its OFFICIAL badge.

A full set of flashcards and colouring-in sheets, which can be integrated into lessons for all the new vocabulary items in the 2018 revised tests, is available here: www.worldoffun.cambridge.org

Audio visual material

The audio visual material in *Power Up* serves both as a learning aid and as a tool to increase learner motivation.

Power Up level 2 features five videos per unit as well as video in each Review unit:

- A unit opener video to introduce the unit topic, activate prior knowledge and help establish both class and individual learning objectives
- An animated chant to consolidate the first set of unit vocabulary
- An animated story to preview the unit grammar
- An animated song, with optional karaoke, to consolidate the second set of unit vocabulary
- A presenter led documentary to facilitate cross-curricular learning
- There are also interactive review quizzes in our three Review units.

Components

Pupil's Book

Activity Book with online activities and Home Booklet

Teacher's Book

Teacher's Resource Book

Test Generator

Class Audio

Presentation Plus

Flashcards

Online wordcards

Posters

Visit cambridge.org/powerup to find all the information you need on the wide variety of *Power Up* components and how they can be combined to meet your needs. In the following section of this introduction we focus on the Pupil's Book followed by the unit opener page and sounds and spellings sections found in the Activity Book.

The Pupil's Book

The Pupil's Book features:

- An introductory unit, 'Meet the family'
- Nine core units with audio and audio visual content
- Sticker activities for each unit
- Three Review units.

Pupil's Book unit walk-through

Power Up levels 1 and 2 are based around life on a farm where the Friendly family live alongside the farm animals. Jim and Jenny live with their parents, Mr and Mrs Friendly, and their grandparents, Grandma and Grandpa Friendly. The family have a cat called Cameron and many farm animals who are friends: Harry the horse, Shelly the sheep, Gracie the goat, Rocky the rooster, and Rocky's mother Henrietta.

Power Up level 2 begins with a two-page introductory unit which reintroduces the Friendly family and the animals on their farm.

This is followed by nine core units, each with 12 lessons. The Teacher's Book contains a 'Warm-up' and an 'Ending the lesson' activity for each of the 12 lessons and the Review units. The 'Warm-up' is designed to prepare learners for the lesson and engage them fully. The 'Ending the lesson' activity is designed to consolidate what they have learnt in the lesson. The Review units appear after every three units.

The 12 lessons in each core unit are:

- Lesson 1 Unit opener and Mission set up
- Lesson 2 Vocabulary 1 presentation
- Lesson 3 Story with new language presented in context
- Lesson 4 Language practice 1 and Mission Stage 1
- Lesson 5 Vocabulary 2 presentation and song
- Lesson 6 Language practice 2 and Mission Stage 2
- Lesson 7 Cross-curricular presentation and video
- Lesson 8 Cross-curricular consolidation and Mission Stage 3
- Lesson 9 Literature – story focus
- Lesson 10 Literature – response to story and social and emotional skills
- Lesson 11 A1 Movers preparation
- Lesson 12 Unit review and Mission in action

Lesson 1

Unit opener and Mission set up

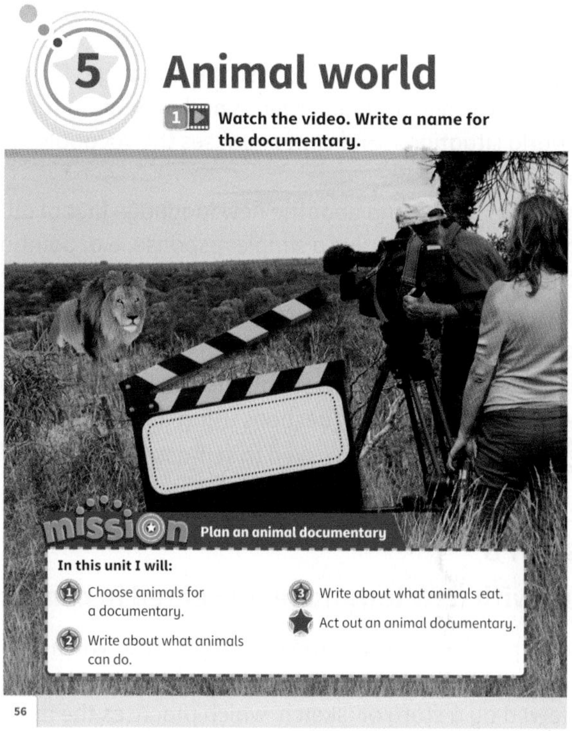

Lesson 1 opens the unit with a colourful illustrated page which sets up the context for the unit and introduces some of the core language that follows.

SA Learners are introduced to their first self-assessment in a self-assessment spot. They are invited to think about how much they can do at this stage of learning. This will allow them to see how much progress they have made by the end of the unit. At this stage:

  - learners have a chance to think about the topic and what they already know about it
  - they are asked to assess which language they know and what they can't say yet.

- Learners then complete a simple drawing or writing task to encourage them to think about what will follow in the rest of the unit. This task also personalises the learning and makes it relevant to their lives.
- The unit Mission is then set up. Three stages and a Mission completion activity are clearly outlined. The first page of each Activity Book unit includes a Mission diary section which is revisited as the learners progress through the Mission.

Lesson 2

Vocabulary 1 presentation

The first focus on vocabulary is presented and practised in Lesson 2 based on the topic of the unit and with a colourful cartoon illustration to contextualise the language. This shows the Friendly family and their friends and animals in typical real-world situations, and contextualises the vocabulary to present meaning.

- The learners see and hear the new language first of all and are required to give a simple response, e.g. pointing, colouring or numbering as they recognise the vocabulary.
- The learners are then encouraged to produce the language accurately in an engaging chant.
- This is followed by a consolidation task, usually requiring learners to respond to questions using the new vocabulary.
- **SA** Learners are then asked to self-assess their progress with the new language.

Lesson 3

Story with new language presented in context

Lesson 3 provides a song – the Friendly Farm – which is repeated in each unit so that learners can join in. The song is followed by a story or 'sketch' which practises the new vocabulary and introduces the language point to follow.

- Learners listen and read the language using the pictures to help them understand.
- The Teacher's Book provides comprehension checks for the teacher to use to support and check understanding.
- The sketch provides exposure to the new language in context. The storyline and pictures help to establish the meaning.

Lesson 4

Language practice 1 and Mission Stage 1

In Lesson 4, the new grammar point is practised and Mission Stage 1 is completed.

- Gracie's Grammar box highlights the target language which learners have heard in the sketch, and gives learners a chance to say and hear the language. It highlights key features of the language form in a simple, age-appropriate way. Pronunciation can also be corrected at this point.
- This is followed by a sticker activity using a picture. The picture helps the learners to understand the language through context. Learners listen to the language and give a response by choosing the correct stickers to add to the picture.
- The sticker activity is usually followed by a task requiring the learners to read and write using the new language.
- Learners then complete Mission Stage 1 using the language they have learnt so far in the unit. The Mission Stage 1 activities usually involve listening and speaking collaboratively to complete a topic-focused task. They require learners to make decisions and be creative in order to complete the task.
- **SA** Once Mission Stage 1 is completed, learners are directed to complete a reflection and self-assessment from the Mission diary section in the Activity Book.

Lesson 5

Vocabulary 2 presentation and song

This lesson uses a song to develop the topic and introduce further new vocabulary.

- Learners listen to the song and complete tasks such as numbering, colouring or choosing alternatives.
- Learners then sing the song with actions to consolidate the language.
- This is usually followed by an activity or game that provides further practice and develops one or more skills – listening, reading, writing or speaking.

Lesson 6

Language practice 2 and Mission Stage 2

This lesson begins with a listening task requiring learners to select a picture by understanding the new language.

- There is a second Gracie's Grammar box which again highlights the target language and gives learners a chance to hear the language and say it correctly.
- The task that follows provides further practice of the new language.
- In the final part of the lesson, learners use the new language to complete Mission Stage 2. This builds on Mission Stage 1 and again activities usually involve listening and speaking collaboratively to complete a topic-focused task.
- **SA** Once Mission Stage 2 is completed, learners are directed to complete a reflection and self-assessment from the Mission diary section in the Activity Book.

Lessons 7 and 8

Cross-curricular and video / Cross-curricular consolidation and Mission Stage 3

These two lessons introduce a topic which relates to the main focus of the unit, but which is linked to other subjects in the school curriculum. This encourages learners to think about other learning areas using English and develops their vocabulary further. It also develops critical-thinking skills and encourages broader knowledge of the world around them.

- In the first lesson, learners watch a video which introduces the topic and provides a context to use it.
- A task is provided to help learners focus on the video and understand the topic.
- A variety of practice activities follow: these can involve listening, reading, writing and speaking, and a range of different tasks including choosing pictures, matching, ordering, or following instructions. These tasks give learners the chance to practise language, develop their skills and improve their critical thinking.
- The next lesson offers more skills-based activities, developing the knowledge of the learners further and providing more practice of the target language.
- Learners now complete Mission Stage 3 which is the final scaffolded stage of the Mission. This builds on the first two stages and again uses the language and skills that have been practised so far. The activity involves further collaboration to complete a task.
- **SA** Once Mission Stage 3 is completed, learners are directed to complete a reflection and self-assessment in the Activity Book.

Lessons 9 and 10

Literature – story focus / response to story and social and emotional skills

In this section learners read and listen to a story and then respond to it. The story uses language from the unit in a context which learners can relate to. The pictures support understanding and help learners follow the story as they listen. It also helps them prepare for the activities that follow.

- Each story generally begins with an introductory speaking task which helps the learners to focus on the topic and encourages them to look at the title and pictures of the story before they read. Learners then listen to the story as they read, which helps bring it to life and aids understanding of the narrative.
- Teaching notes provide comprehension tasks to help support comprehension and to check understanding stage by stage as learners listen and read.
- In the second lesson learners complete follow-up activities using reading, speaking, writing and listening skills. Tasks include answering questions, talking about personal experience related to the topic, discussing ideas and identifying how characters feel. The activities help develop learners' emotional competences and encourage them to develop social and life skills such as kindness, sharing and politeness.

Lesson 11

A1 Movers skills builder

In Lesson 11 there is a focus on familiarising learners with the Cambridge A1 Movers test. Each lesson focuses on a part of the Listening, Speaking, or Reading and Writing test. It allows learners to develop test strategies and provides tips. It enables them to become familiar with the test rubrics and task types. It also allows both the learners and teacher to see how well they might perform in the A1 Movers test.

- Learners complete tasks typical of A1 Movers. These include matching words and pictures, reading and completing texts, and describing picture sequences.
- Notes in the Teacher's Book give advice on how to develop learners' test strategies, including confidence-building tips.

Lesson 12

Unit review and Mission in action

The final lesson reviews the language covered in the unit through the final Mission stage. This brings together all the previous stages in a collaborative and practical task. As such, it recycles all the language and skills developed in the unit.

- Learners are encouraged to follow all the stages of the Mission, which has a final outcome. This might be acting out a scenario, doing a presentation or showing a final piece of work.
- **SA** Once the Mission in action is completed, learners are directed to complete a final reflection and self-assessment from the Mission diary section in the Activity Book.

Review units

A Review unit is included every three units and appears after Units 3, 6 and 9. Each Review is two pages and recycles and consolidates the language from the preceding units. The topics are similar to those in the core units but encourage the learners to apply their new language and knowledge to new contexts.

- Each Review begins with an interactive video quiz which learners can do to see how much they can remember. This quiz can be repeated after the Review is completed to measure progress.
- This is followed by listening tasks, tasks based on pictures to encourage speaking practice, and personalised writing tasks.

Unit opener page in the Activity Book

The unit opener page in each unit of the Activity Book is actually a page for you and your learners to refer to *throughout* each unit. It has four key parts: My unit goals, a 'can do' statement sunflower, My mission diary and a page reference for the word stack. The following section provides you with the teaching notes for this page of the Activity Book, which you can return to as you progress through each unit.

My unit goals

Go through the unit goals with the learners. They circle the skills they want to work on and the number of new words they want to learn, and they draw something that they want to learn to say in English. Remember to go back to these at the end of each Mission stage during the unit and review them.

Sunflower

At the end of each unit ask learners to look at the sunflower leaves and read the 'can do' statements. Ask the learners to add a tick if they agree they have achieved the statement. They can colour the leaf green if they are very confident and orange if they think they need more practice. Quickly check what each learner is doing to get a sense of their own assessment.

My Mission diary

Tell the learners to think very carefully about how they did on each Mission stage. Ask them to think about the questions they answered, how much they understood and how confident they feel. Learners then choose an emoticon that shows how they feel about their work.

Word stack

The word stack is a personal record for each learner. At the end of each unit ask learners to spend a few minutes looking back at the unit and find a minimum of five new words they have learnt. **Fast finishers and stronger learners** can choose more. Learners write the new words into their word stack with an example sentence. **Extra support** – learners can draw pictures of words they have learnt and check back in their text books to copy the words they have chosen.

Practical techniques for using the word stack

1. Test yourself

- Learners go through their word stack and write a selection of words onto small cards. They can draw a picture on the other side of the card. Put the learners into pairs. Their partner holds up the card to show the picture and the learner says the word.
- Pairs then swap roles.

2. Test each other

- Learners choose a selection of words from their own word stack.
- Put the learners into pairs.
- Learners take it in turns to say a word to their partner. Their partner should draw, mime or give an example sentence of all the words they know. If they are asked a word they don't know, their partner should explain or show it to them.

3. K/M/F charts

- This is a play on the K/W/L chart. Learners go through their word stack and choose five words they feel confident about, three they think they know, and two they can't remember.
- They create a poster with the letters *K*, *M*, *F* at the top. *K* is for words they **know**; *M* is for words they **might** know, and *F* is for words they have **forgotten**. They can write the words into the columns or add sticky notes to each column.
- Learners then work in small groups of three or four and present their K/M/F charts to the rest of the group. Other learners in the group should remind them of the two words in the *F* list. If no-one can remember the words, they should check in their books.

4. Learner quiz

- Learners work in groups of four or five. They look at their word stacks and create three questions to ask the rest of the class about some of the words. The questions can be based on drawings (*What is this? / What are these?*) or on an action (*What do I feel?* – miming angry or happy) or a question (*Is Harry big or small?*).
- Once the learners have prepared their questions, they sit in their groups. Each group takes it in turns to ask one of their questions to the rest of the class.
- The first group to answer gains one point. If any group can ask a question the other learners don't know the answer to they get a bonus point.

Sounds and spelling in the Activity Book

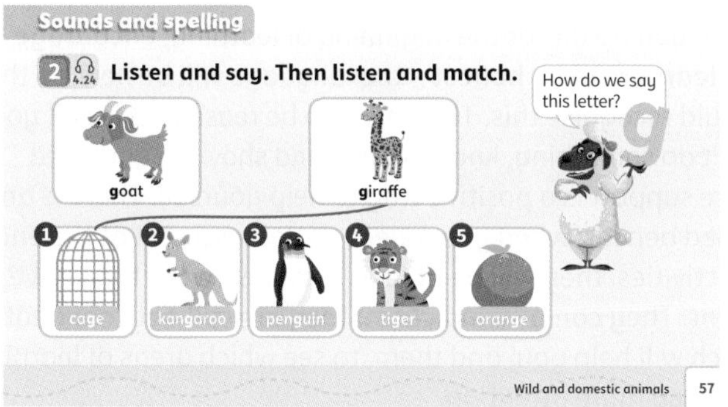

When learning another language, pronunciation and spelling are two of the most challenging aspects. English spelling can seem very complicated, but there are many patterns and rules which will help learners achieve success.

There are sounds and spelling practice activities in Lesson 2 of every unit in the Activity Book. The activities focus on particular sounds that learners often find challenging, or particular spelling patterns that sometimes pose difficulties, such as certain spelling patterns pronounced in different ways, as well as words pronounced the same but spelt differently.

The focus vocabulary used in these activities is drawn from the first vocabulary set of each unit, as well as any relevant revision vocabulary from prior units and levels where appropriate. The activities are designed to practise key sounds or spellings that occur in the words taught in the unit, so that the words and their meanings are already familiar to the learners, thereby making the focus more about sounds and spelling than reading and comprehension.

Power Up and its methodology

Power Up features a systematic approach to language learning in which the learner and teacher are in a partnership. It aims to develop the language and skills of the learner, but also helps them achieve better life-long progress in learning.

What does it involve? The *Power Up* methodology helps teachers and learners to plan learning effectively, measure progress and identify areas for improvement in learning. In practice this means that all activity, inside and outside the classroom, can be integrated with assessment. More traditional summative assessment still continues. External 'tests' can be used alongside the classroom-focused formative assessment activities. For teachers this should not feel strange: using external assessments to check progress and performance is familiar; monitoring learners' progress and adapting teaching to support them is also routine. *Power Up* simply combines these elements in a systematic way. In *Power Up* you will see that classroom activity is designed to allow the teacher to monitor for evidence to measure progress and also includes tasks that are similar to those in formal summative tests such as Cambridge English A1 Movers.

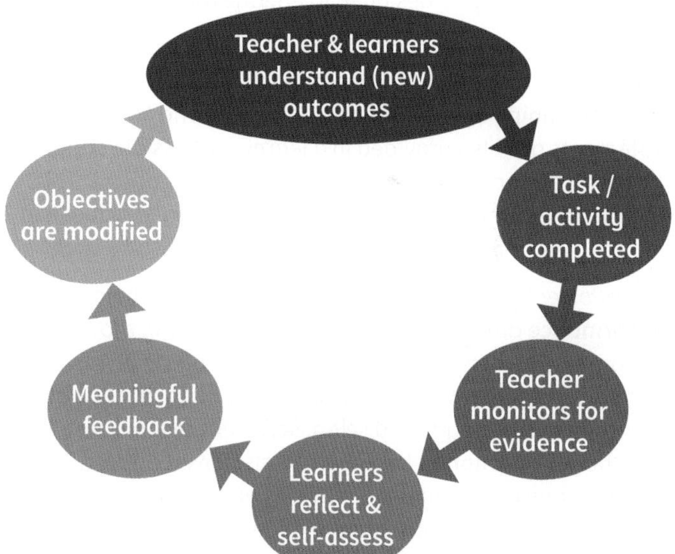

How does it work in the classroom? In *Power Up* learners are given more independence to understand their own strengths and weaknesses, both immediate (e.g. in a lesson) and longer term (e.g. over a school term). In the classroom this begins with making sure learning objectives are clear to both learner and teacher. In *Power Up* these are identified by the outcomes at the beginning of each lesson. Once outcomes are established, both the learner and the teacher think about how each activity can support a learning outcome. After the activity is finished they reflect on performance in relation to that outcome and use this evidence to adjust what happens in later lessons – this might be reviewing and practising some language again or moving on more quickly depending on the performance. Normal classroom activities therefore combine learning with assessment to provide meaningful feedback to learners. Being involved in the process helps learners improve outcomes and gain confidence. In addition, if the activities and content are linked to the language and skills of more formal language tests, classroom activities can also be benchmarked against formal tests.

No matter how young a learner might be, this process can help learners develop their skills and learn about the world around them. *Power Up* aims to develop skills such as collaboration and encourages learners to understand their own progress and think about how they can improve. Learners can begin to do this even when they are young. *Power Up* therefore includes multistage projects which encourage learners to collaborate and work together helping them develop better life skills, and regular self-assessment stages.

What kind of activities are used in class? *Power Up's* methodology can be integrated into everyday learning to support progress in different ways and these have been integrated into the course:

Power Up prioritises real-life language and activity. It therefore includes learning activities which reflect **real-world tasks** and offer topics designed to engage the learners.

Power Up asks teachers and learners to **understand objectives**. Expected outcomes for each lesson are shown at the beginning of each lesson in *Power Up* and Mission statements are also provided in a learner-accessible style; these can be shared in creative ways with the learners. This helps learners understand what they are trying to achieve in each activity they complete.

Using *Power Up*, learners begin to **reflect on their own performance and measure progress** in achieving those outcomes. Learners complete multistage projects in *Power Up* and consider how well they have done at each stage of the project using suggested self-assessment techniques. This encourages **autonomy**. Learners are also given opportunities to make choices during their activities and Missions, which encourages self-confidence and independence.

Teachers using *Power Up* can collect information about the learners through their classroom activities, completion of tasks and self-assessment, and this allows both teacher and learners to **plan learning** more effectively as they work through the material.

Links can be made between classroom activities and some of the performance measures of formal tests so that **formative and summative assessment are linked** together.

Self-assessment guide

It is important for learners to understand the purpose of lessons and to think about how well they achieve learning outcomes. They can begin to do this at a young age: their learning in all areas, not just language, will benefit. In this book, each unit of learning therefore includes stages:

- Asking learners to think about what they will learn – making the outcomes for each lesson clear to them
- Helping them to think about their progress – asking them to self-assess through simple activities.

When

These stages are labelled **Self-assessment**. You can use any of the techniques explained below at these stages. Choose one of the techniques each time. You can do this at the beginning and end of each lesson and/or at the beginning and end of each unit.

When you do this at the beginning of learning, **encourage the learners to be honest** – the language will be new, so they should recognise this. They need to be reassured that if you can't do something, knowing this and showing you need more support is a positive way to help yourself. There is an added benefit: when you repeat this assessment at the end of activities, they will be able to recognise what they have learnt. They can also indicate if they are still not confident, which will help you, and them, to see which areas of learning will need more attention.

Techniques for the classroom

1. Thumbs up

Tell the class to use their thumbs to demonstrate how they feel about what they are learning. They can use:

- Thumbs up (+ smiling) – 'I feel very confident'
- Thumbs mid position (+ neutral face) – 'I think I know this' (optional)
- Thumbs down (+ shaking head) – 'I'm not confident'.

2. Red and green cards

These cards can be prepared in advance. Although this takes preparation, these can be reused in class for a long time. Use thick green card and red card and cut these into squares approximately 12 cm x 12 cm. You will need one card of each colour per learner. If possible, laminate the cards. Punch a hole in the top left corner and tie together one red and one green card with string or a treasury tag.

Tell the class to use their cards to demonstrate how they feel about what they are learning. Hold up:

- Green for 'confident'
- Red for 'not sure'.

Learners can also leave these on their desks as they work, leaving red up if they want help from the teacher.

Variation:

If you don't have red/green cards ask learners to draw an empty square on a card and put it on their desk at the beginning of the lesson. During the lesson, stop at an appropriate point and ask them to colour in the square: red for 'I don't understand'; green for 'I understand'.

3. High fives

Tell the class to show how they feel about the learning using 'high fives' (the learner holding out their hand and slapping hands with another learner or the teacher):

- High five (holding the hand up high to slap) – 'I feel very confident'
- Low five (holding the hand lower near the waist) – 'I'm not confident'.

Even with a big class you can go around quite quickly to 'high five' or 'low five' each learner.

Alternatively you can ask them to go to one side of the room to 'high five' and to the other side of the room to 'low five' each other, giving you a quick visual of how learners are feeling.

4. K/W/L charts

Before beginning work on new language, create a poster with the letters *K*, *W*, *L* at the top. *K* is for words they **know**; *W* is for words they **would** like to know. Give the learners different words from the activities they are about to do. Ask them which words go into the *K* column and which go into the *W* column. If learners choose to put the words into the *K* column, they should explain or give an example using the word. After the lesson or activity sequence, go back to the poster and review the words in the *W* column. Learners can move them to the *L* column if they are confident (*L* is for words they have **learnt**) or leave them in the *W* column if not. You can ask them for examples of all the words in the *K* and *L* columns. If any words are left in the *W* column, you may need to teach them again.

Variations:

- Have one large poster and the words on cards. Use sticky tack and select learners to come up and stick them into the columns.
- Have several large posters. Divide learners into groups – one poster per group. Choose a group leader to stick the words up for the group or, for a more dynamic activity, allow all the learners to stick up some words. Words can be written on cards with sticky tape on the backs or onto sticky notes – ask the learners to copy the new words out themselves.
- Have several large posters. Divide learners into groups – one poster per group. Give each group a marker pen to write the words into the columns. (They can cross out the words at the end when they change position.)

5. Self-assessment cards

Create a simple self-assessment card and make a 'post box' by using a cardboard box with a 'letter box' cut in the lid. Learners complete their self-assessment and put it into the post box.

An example (which can be adapted for different tasks and activities) is below:

Ask learners which outcomes they are trying to achieve and help them complete the sentences, e.g. *I understand words about clothes.* Then tell them to think about how close they feel to achieving the outcome and to choose a face that shows this.

What we are doing	How I feel
I understand words about	☺ 😐 ☹
I can say	☺ 😐 ☹
I know	☺ 😐 ☹
I don't know	☺ 😐 ☹

6. Sticky notes

Put a large poster on one side of the room with *Hooray! It's OK.* ☺ at the top. Put another on the other side with a confused face (scratching its head) saying *Let's try again*. Learners write or draw something, e.g. a word or phrase they feel confident about and something they aren't sure about, on two different sticky notes. They add the first to the *Hooray* poster and the other to the *Let's try again* poster.

If many learners choose the same word to try again, you may need to revisit it with the whole class. You can ask learners to write their names on the sticky notes to help you identify individual learner's reactions.

7. Mini whiteboards

Give each learner a mini whiteboard if you have these.

Variation:

- You can make them by using laminated card which can be reused a few times.

At appropriate points, stop and ask learners to draw on the card to show how they feel. You can ask them to draw a smiley or frowning face.

Variation:

- Learners write *OK* / *Not OK* OR write a word/phrase they are confident about at the top and a word or phrase they don't fully understand at the bottom.

They can either hold up their mini whiteboard or leave it on the desk as they work so you can see them as you monitor.

8. Jump up / Sit down

Call out some of the words or language learners have been learning, and ask learners to jump up if they are confident but sit down if they aren't sure. You can do this with more than one item.

9. Paper planes

When looking at the outcomes of a lesson, ask learners to copy some of them, e.g. words, word categories or phrases, onto a piece of paper. Collect these in. After you have finished the activities, give the papers out again. Ask learners to read the lesson outcomes they have worked on. Then show them how to fold the paper into a paper aeroplane shape. (Simple instructions can be found on the Internet.) Put a bin or large box at the front of the class. If they are confident about what they have learnt, they should throw their planes into the box. If they are not confident, they should throw their planes onto your desk.

Variations:

- Learners screw their papers up into a ball.
- Use ping pong balls and write on them with indelible marker pens.

10. Baskets

Put three plastic baskets or boxes on your desk (a red, a yellow and a green one).

Learners write their names onto pieces of paper and drop their name into the basket that shows how they feel: red – not confident, yellow – OK, but need more practice, green – very confident.

Variations:

- If learners have completed a piece of writing or homework task, they can hand this in by placing it into the baskets to show how they feel they have done on that particular task.
- Just have red and green, without yellow, to keep reflection simple.
- Paint or colour three paper plates in the three different colours.
- Have three boxes or baskets, one with a smiley face on the front, one with a frowning face and one with a neutral face on it. Learners drop their names/work into these.

11. Traffic flags

Get learners to make flags. Give each learner paper. They cut out three large rectangles or triangles of paper and colour or paint them red, green and yellow. Give each learner three drinking straws and sticky tape. Ask them to stick the rectangles/triangles to the straws to make flags. When you complete an activity, the learners wave a flag according to how they feel.

12. Washing lines

Give each child two pegs – preferably one red and one green. Ask them to write their name on both using indelible marker pens. Set up two string lines at the front of the classroom (e.g. across a display board). After an activity, ask the learners to put either their red peg ('I don't understand') or their green peg ('I understand') on the line. If you can't find coloured pegs, use simple wooden ones for learners to write on; have two lines (one with the sign *I understand* and one with the sign *Let's try again* next to them).

13. Balloons

Get three balloons: one red, one yellow and one green. If you have a large group, you may need two or three of each colour.

After completing an activity, ask learners to write their names using a soft felt tip pen on the balloon that shows how they feel about the activity. Put the balloons to one side. After you have done some follow-up, e.g. re-teaching any difficult areas, bring the balloons out again and throw them back and forth asking questions about the words or language covered. At the end the learners can chant *We learnt the words!* and burst the balloons.

Variation:

- Have just two balloons, one red and one green, with no yellow.

14. Sticky spots

Create a poster divided into three columns. In the column headings, write *Hooray, it's OK / I'm not sure / It's not OK – let's try again*. At the end of any activity, give learners a sticky dot or sticky label. Ask them to write their name on it. As they leave the class, they stick their name into one of the columns.

15. Scales

Create a long arrow from cardboard and stick it on the side of the board or on the wall. Inside the very top, draw a smiley face and write *100%*. At the bottom draw a frowning face and write *0%*. (This is re-usable so you only need to prepare it once.) Give out slips of paper and paper clips to the learners. They write their name on the paper. At the end of an activity, ask them to bring up their name and to paper-clip it to the edge of the arrow showing where they think they are on the scale.

Teachers' classroom assessment

As we have seen, *Power Up* involves assessing learners during everyday activities along with more traditional types of assessment or test-type activities. This information will help the teacher adjust learning aims and lesson plans so that areas of difficulty can be reviewed and areas that are easy can be dealt with quickly. This responsive style of teaching allows better progress. The teacher will also take into account how the learners are feeling: even if a learner answers questions correctly, if they don't feel confident about a particular area they may still need some extra practice.

The teacher's role

To use this approach successfully, during teaching you need to:

a. identify language outcomes clearly at the start of lessons/tasks
b. use 'closing language' regularly to highlight the achievements made
c. monitor effectively during specific activities
d. keep formative assessment notes on the group and individual learners
e. alternatively use checklists to record assessment of skills and life skills (e.g. planning / collaborating / working autonomously / sharing)
f. encourage learners to engage in self-assessment.

After teaching you need to:

a. keep or update anecdotal records
b. use scoring rubrics to measure achievement against external scales
c. use 'portfolio' building / record keeping for individual learners.

This will give you a full record of assessment for each learner alongside any results from tests. This can help you when writing reports for learners, making them evidence-based and more detailed. It will give you an idea of how well learners are doing against external measures.

Practical techniques for the teacher's role: in class

a) Identifying outcomes

Each unit contains an opening stage which shows you how to set up the Mission clearly for learners. There is a Mission poster to help you track progress in the Activity Book. In this way setting outcomes and reviewing them are built into the materials.

You can:

- Tell learners what you will do at the beginning of the lesson
- Write the outcomes on the board
- Write the outcomes on a poster and stick it on the wall; at the end of the teaching cycle you can then return to this and tick the items, or encourage a learner to come up and tick them
- Put two posters on the wall: 'What we are learning', 'What we learnt'. Write each outcome for your lesson on a large card and stick it under the 'What we are learning' poster; at the end of the teaching cycle move the card or encourage a learner to move it to under the 'What we learnt' poster. All the outcomes from the term can gradually be added here giving a visual record for learners of what they have achieved.

b) Use 'closing language' regularly to highlight the achievement

- After the activity go back to the outcomes and use this to 'close' the task, e.g. *Well done. You have talked about school. You have listened and answered.*
- You can use the language from the outcomes to help close the task.
- If the learners have found something difficult make sure you praise their work even if you need to do more on this area, e.g. *Well done – you have worked hard. You talked about school. Let's try again later and do even better.*

c) Monitor effectively during specific activities

- Once you have set up an activity do a quick check around the room to make sure the learners are 'on task' and provide more guidance if any have not understood what to do. To keep the activity moving it might be necessary to use a little L1 to help them. Try to avoid doing this too much or you will find learners 'switch off' during English instructions as they know you will repeat in L1.
- Once all the learners are on task monitor the group, listening carefully to what they say and looking at their work especially if they are writing words. You may need to feed in words in English or answer questions if they ask you for help.
- If everything is going well you might want to praise their progress briefly in English, but don't step in too much. If you always step in, learners will stop doing tasks and expect you to be involved. This is fine sometimes but you want to see how they work and collaborate together and if you are involved all the time you can't do this. Learners will soon get used to you monitoring without intervening.
- Use this time to note how they are doing. If you have a large group make a list of all the learners and plan to monitor different members of the group closely during each activity, e.g. monitor learners 1–5 closely in Activity 1, monitor learners 6–10 closely in Activity 2 and so on. In this way over a few lessons you will have monitored each individual closely.

d) Keep formative assessment notes on the group and individual learners

- You can use monitoring, the activities learners complete and any classroom-based tasks and homework to gather evidence about learner progress.
- Keep a notebook and pen with you during lessons to make notes; alternatively use a mobile device, e.g. tablet.
- You can prepare your notebook in advance with a page or half page for each learner. This can be updated during and after activities. See below for examples of notes on language and the skills of speaking and writing (you could include listening and reading).

Example of notes:

Learner	Overall	Vocab	Grammar	Pron	Speaking	Writing
Maria	Good progress – motivated.	Fine. Good range. Tries new words quickly.	Good word order. Forgets 'am/is/are'.	✗ Word stress	✓ Fluency **?** Turn taking	✓ Spelling
Simone	Not doing homework. Progress limited.	**?** Uses a lot of L1.	✗ Tends to use single words not sentences.	✓ Accurate when using English. Uses L1 a lot.	**?** Lacks confidence.	✓ Strongest skill. Enjoys copying. Accurate.
Alex	Progress OK but not motivated.	Limited range but remembers.	Pres simp questions inaccurate.	**?** OK but problem with adding /ə/ before vowels.	✓ Fluent **?** Turn taking	**?** OK – has to check text book a lot for words.

e) Use checklists for skills and life skills (planning / collaborating / working autonomously / sharing, etc.)

- Alternatively – or in addition to notes – checklists can help you to keep evidence of progress. The lists need to be prepared in advance and can be based on outcomes and/or descriptors of level such as those in CEFR. See below for examples of a checklist for listening, reading and life skills. (You could include vocabulary, grammar, pronunciation, speaking and writing.) See the next section for information on CEFR.

Example of checklist:

	Maria	Simone	Alex
Listening – understanding gist	✓	✗ tries to understand everything	✓
Listening – understanding details	✓ some errors	**?** often incorrect	✓
Listening for specific information	✓ good at predicting strategies	**?** some errors	✓
Reading for gist	✓	✓ slow but can manage	✓
Reading for specific information		✓	✓
Collaborating for group work	✓	✓	✗ not motivated – doesn't do much
Sharing	✓	✓	✓
Working autonomously	✓	✗ tries but lacks confidence	✗ needs encouragement

f) Encourage students to engage in self-assessment

See notes on self-assessment.

Practical techniques for the teacher's role: after class

After teaching you can use the information and evidence you have collected to ensure you have full records for learners. This information can be reviewed, along with the learners' self-assessment, to decide on what kind of teaching and learning will follow, as well as to produce reports.

a) Keep or update anecdotal records

You can use your notes to add to any records you keep for learners. If you used a digital device you can cut and paste the notes you made. Along with formal test results, this will give you evidence and detailed information if you need to write reports for your learners.

b) Use scoring rubrics

You can combine in-class assessments with results of class tests, e.g. percentage scores, and all this information can be matched against external standards to give you an idea of how well learners are doing overall. For example, you can look at the 'can do' statements for each skill in CEFR scales.

We really hope you enjoy teaching with *Power Up* and look forward to supporting you throughout this journey with your learners.

Meet the family

1 1.02 **Listen. What's Jim and Jenny's mum doing?**

2 1.03 **Say the chant.**

3 1.04 **Listen and answer. Then ask and answer.**

Meet the family Unit learning outcomes

Learners learn to:

- introduce themselves
- talk about families and relationships
- ask and answer the question *How are you?*
- give personal information

New language *cook* (n), *How are you? I'm fine, thank you. Nice to meet you.*

Recycled language animals, character names, family, sports and hobbies, *farm, tractor, What's your name? My name's (Jim). How old are you? I'm (seven). Where do you live? I live in (London).* present continuous

Materials flashcards of Jenny and Jim, audio, video

Warm-up

- Say *My name's (Mrs Green). Nice to meet you.* Practise with the class. Repeat the greeting to different learners. Encourage them to respond *My name's (Mario). Nice to meet you.*
- Learners stand up and walk around. When you say *Stop* they introduce themselves to the nearest person.

Presentation

- Mime reading and say *Look! I'm … (reading a book).* Repeat with mimes for playing piano/football, taking photos, riding a bike, swimming, watching TV and writing.
  Stronger learners Learners play the mime game in pairs.

Self-assessment

- **SA** Say *Open your Pupil's Books at page 4. Where's this?* (*The Friendly Farm*) Point to the characters and ask *Who's this? (Jim) What animals can you see? (A goat, a horse,* etc.) Use self-assessment (see Introduction). Say *OK. Let's learn.*

Pupil's Book, page 4

1 1.02 Listen. What's Jim and Jenny's mum doing?

- Read the caption. Point to the characters and ask *What's his/her name?* Say *Listen. What's Jim and Jenny's mum doing?*

Track 1.02

Jim and Jenny are on the Friendly Farm.

Jenny:	I'm Jenny. I'm seven. This is my brother Jim.
Jim:	Hi. I'm seven too. We're both seven!
Jim and Jenny:	We're twins!
Jim:	I like music and I love playing the piano.
Jenny:	I like music too, but I don't like playing the piano. I love playing football and swimming.
Jim:	Look! This is a photo of our dad. He's a cook and he loves making food. Here he's making a cake. He's happy in the kitchen.
Jenny:	And this is our mum. She loves music and she enjoys playing the piano. Here she's writing a song.
Jim and Jenny:	We're the Friendly family!
Grandpa:	… and we live on Friendly Farm. These are our animals. Nice to meet you!

Key: She's writing a song.

- Point to each character and ask *Who's this? Is this Jenny's (dad)? No, it's her (grandpa). Is this Jim's (sister)? No, it's his (mum).* Say *Jim and Jenny's dad is a cook.* Mime cooking.
- Ask *How old are Jim and Jenny?* (*Seven*) Say *They're both seven. They're … (twins).*
- Point to the tractor. Ask *What's this?* Ask *Where's the small tractor?* Learners find the hidden tractor in the picture.

2 1.03 Say the chant.

- Ask a learner *How are you?* Help him/her reply *I'm fine, thank you.* Repeat with different learners.
- Stick flashcards of Jim and Jenny on the board. Play the audio or video, pointing to the flashcards. Hold up your fingers for *seven* and give a thumbs up for *I'm fine*. Learners chant and do the actions. Repeat in two groups (Jenny and Jim).

Track 1.03

Jenny:	What's your name? What's your name?
Jim:	My name's Jim.
Jim:	What's your name? What's your name?
Jenny:	My name's Jenny.
Jim:	How are you? How are you?
Jenny:	I'm fine, thank you.
Jenny:	How are you? How are you?
Jim:	I'm fine, thank you.
Jenny:	How old are you? How old are you?
Jim:	I'm seven.
Jim:	How old are you? How old are you?
Jenny:	I'm seven.

3 1.04 Listen and answer. Then ask and answer.

- Play the audio, pausing for learners to answer as a class.

Track 1.04

Jenny: What's your name?
Nice to meet you. How are you?
How old are you?
Where do you live?

- Learners ask and answer in pairs.

Activity Book, page 4

See pages TB120–132

Ending the lesson

- Make a sentence about someone in the picture, e.g. *He's Jenny's brother.* (*Jim*) *He's wearing a green hat.* (*Grandpa*) Learners say the name.
- Learners repeat the activity in pairs.

Learning outcomes By the end of the lesson, learners will be able to understand basic personal descriptions.

New language *asleep, good at …-ing, model, show* (n), *singer*

Recycled language adjectives, animals, family, *barn, book, ear, eat, fun, game, hair, paper, photo, sing, sleep, be* + adjective (*She's beautiful*), *Don't …*, *He's got (long hair). I like …-ing*, present continuous, *You can't …*

Materials Friendly Farm animal character flashcards, audio, video, coloured pens or pencils

Warm-up

- Show the flashcard of Shelly and say *This is Shelly.* Repeat with the other flashcards.
- Display the flashcards, point and ask *What's his/her name?* Stress the pronoun *his/her*. Say *Henrietta is Rocky's … (mum/mother)*.

  Extra support Write captions below the flashcards, e.g. *She's Shelly*. Point at random and learners say, e.g. *She's Shelly. / He's Rocky.* Once learners are familiar with the names and genders, erase the captions.
- Choose a flashcard, keeping it hidden. Make the appropriate animal noise and ask *What's his/her name?* Learners say *It's (Rocky).* Show the card and say *Yes, it's (Rocky).* Repeat with different flashcards. Call a learner to the front to lead the activity.
- Display all the flashcards again. Learners play the game in pairs, choosing a card from the board.

Pupil's Book, page 5

1.05 The Friendly Farm song

- Play the song at the beginning of the cartoon story. Learners listen. Repeat. Learners listen and sing. Tap out the rhythm on the table. Learners copy and tap.

Track 1.05

The Friendly Farm, the Friendly Farm,
Fun and games on the Friendly Farm,
With the animals in the barn,
Fun and games on the Friendly Farm.

1.05 The Friendly Farm

- Say *Open your Pupil's Books at page 5.* Ask *Who can you see in the pictures?* Learners name the characters. Ask *What happens in the story? Look at the pictures.* Give learners time to look.
- Ask *Who's in Harry's picture?* Write the question on the board. Play the audio or video. Learners listen and read. Check answers. (*His father*)

Track 1.05

The Friendly Farm song + see cartoon on Pupil's Book page 5

- Play the audio or video again. Pause after each picture and ask questions: 1: *Who's in the photo?* (*Shelly's sister*) 2: *How old is Shelly's sister?* (*She's five.*) *Is she ugly?* (*No, beautiful*) Use mime to show the meaning of *model.* 3: *Has Harry's father got short hair?* (*No, long hair*) *Is he sad?* (*No, happy*) 4: *Is Shelly a model?* (*No*) Say *She wants to be a model. She thinks her family is beautiful.* 5: *Who's sleeping?* (*Rocky's mum/mother / Henrietta*) 6: *Who's singing?* (*Shelly*) *Is her singing nice?* (*No*) Say *Point to your ears.*

  Extra support Say sentences for learners to complete, rather than asking questions, e.g. *Shelly's got a picture of her … (sister).*

  Extension Display the animal character flashcards and write their ages: Rocky 3, Shelly 3, Cameron 4, Henrietta 6, Harry 9, Gracie 11. Ask, e.g. *How old is Harry?* (*He's nine.*) Repeat for all the characters, making sure learners use *He/She* as appropriate. Learners ask and answer in pairs.

4 1.06 Who says it? Listen and say the name.

- Play the audio and pause for learners to say the name.

  Extra support Display the animal character flashcards with their names on the board.

Track 1.06

1 Harry: How old is she?
2 Henrietta: What … is … that?
3 Gracie: I like eating paper and books.
4 Rocky: That's a photo of Shelly's sister.
5 Shelly: We're a beautiful family.
6 Cameron: My ears, my ears …
7 Harry: Look! This is an old photo of my father.
8 Shelly: You can't eat my sister!

Key: See names in audioscript

Activity Book, page 5

See pages TB120–132

Ending the lesson

- Divide the class into two teams. Teams line up. Display the animal character flashcards at a height learners can reach. Say *Listen and touch the picture.*
- Say a sentence, e.g. *She's got a beautiful sister.* The two learners at the front of the lines race to touch the correct flashcard and win a point for their team. These two learners go to the back of the lines.
- Continue in this way, revising colours, families, ages and adjectives.

The Friendly Farm

1.05

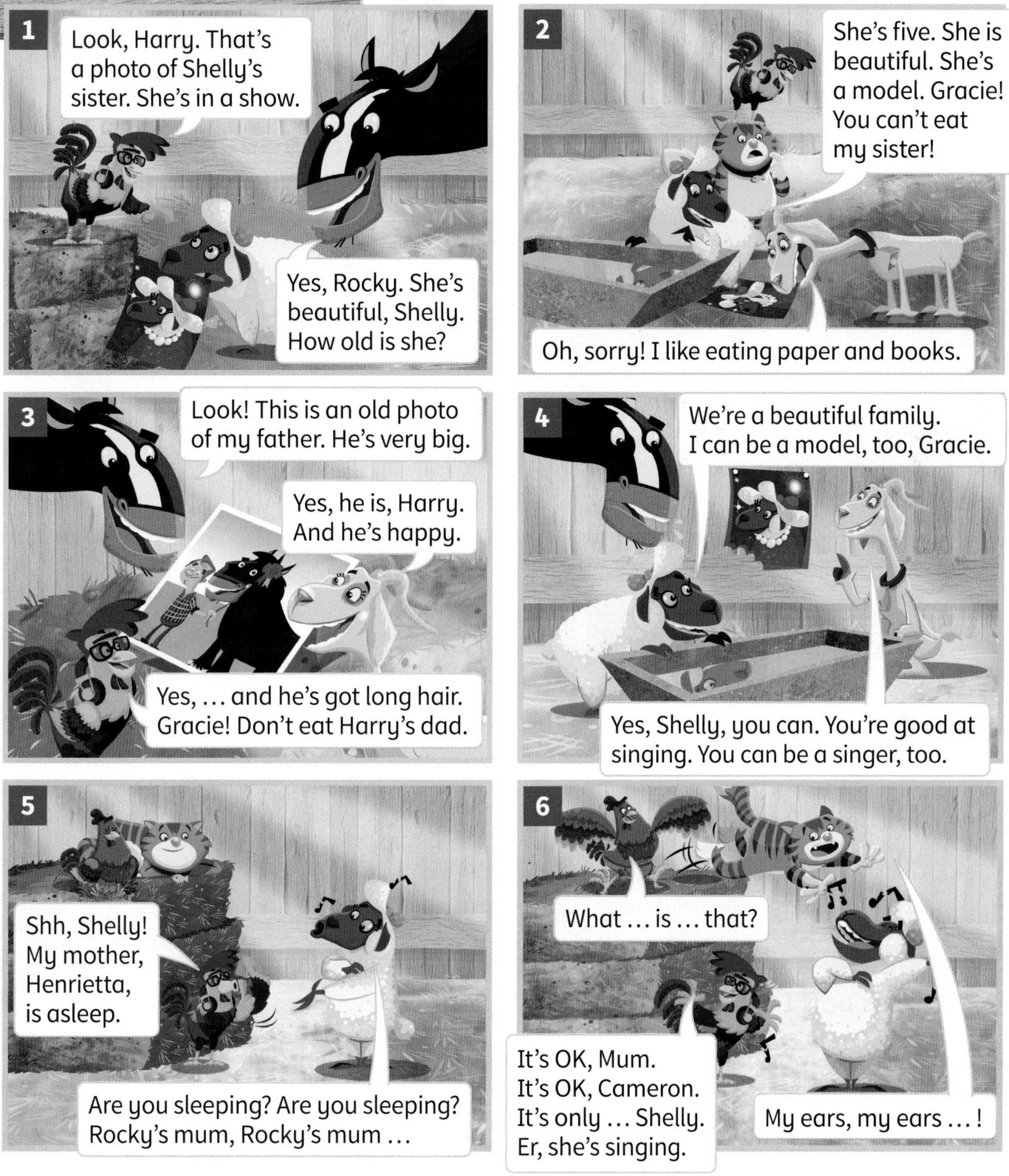
1
Look, Harry. That's a photo of Shelly's sister. She's in a show.
Yes, Rocky. She's beautiful, Shelly. How old is she?
2
She's five. She is beautiful. She's a model. Gracie! You can't eat my sister!
Oh, sorry! I like eating paper and books.
3
Look! This is an old photo of my father. He's very big.
Yes, he is, Harry. And he's happy.
Yes, … and he's got long hair. Gracie! Don't eat Harry's dad.
4
We're a beautiful family. I can be a model, too, Gracie.
Yes, Shelly, you can. You're good at singing. You can be a singer, too.
5
Shh, Shelly! My mother, Henrietta, is asleep.
Are you sleeping? Are you sleeping? Rocky's mum, Rocky's mum …
6
What … is … that?
It's OK, Mum. It's OK, Cameron. It's only … Shelly. Er, she's singing.
My ears, my ears … !

4 1.06 **Who says it? Listen and say the name.**

1 A day on the farm

1 Watch the video. Draw something you can see in the countryside.

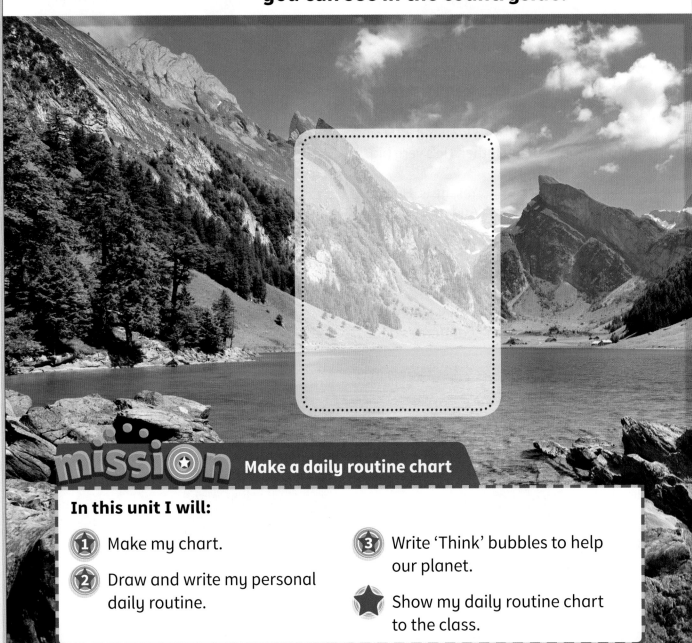

mission Make a daily routine chart

In this unit I will:

1. Make my chart.
2. Draw and write my personal daily routine.
3. Write 'Think' bubbles to help our planet.

★ Show my daily routine chart to the class.

Unit 1 learning outcomes

In Unit 1, learners learn to:

- talk about the countryside
- use the present continuous to talk about activities and actions happening now
- talk about daily routines
- use the present simple and times (*o'clock*) to ask and answer about routines
- learn about how to look after our planet
- read a poem and think about being supportive

Materials video, coloured pens or pencils, digital Mission poster, an example of a chart showing a plan for a day (optional), a copy of the Mission worksheet (Teacher's Resource Book page 14)

Self-assessment

- **SA** Say *Open your Pupil's Books at page 6. Look at the picture.* Ask, e.g. *What can you do here? Can you go for a swim? What colour is the lake? Is there a boat? Where are the houses? Are there lots of trees? Can you see a forest / a mountain / some rocks / some grass? Are there leaves on the trees?* Use self-assessment (see Introduction). Say *OK. Let's learn.*

Warm-up

- Hold up the picture. Ask *Are there lots of houses?* (*No*) *Are there lots of cars and people?* (*No*) Say *It's the countryside. It's quiet. It's beautiful.*
- Ask *What can we see in the countryside?* In pairs, learners think of five things they know in English, e.g. *bird, cow, sheep, flower, farm.* The first pair to think of five things are the winners.

Pupil's Book, page 6

1 Watch the video. Draw something you can see in the countryside.

- Say *In this unit we're talking about the countryside.* Say *Let's watch the video.* To introduce the topic of the unit, play the video.
- Say *Look at page 6.* Point to the empty box. Ask *What can you see in the countryside? Draw it here.* Learners draw. Monitor. Tell each learner the name of the item they have drawn.

mission Make a daily routine chart

- Point to the Mission box or the digital Mission poster and say *This is our Mission.* If learners completed level 1, remind them that they did a Mission in every unit.
- Say *Our Mission is: Make a daily routine chart.* Show learners an example of a chart or draw one. Say *A routine is something we do again and again. Every day.* Mime getting up and say *get up*. Mime eating breakfast and say *eat breakfast.*
- Say *Point to number 1. Make my chart.* Show the Mission worksheet, if available. Say *You draw a picture of you.* Draw a picture of yourself. Say *You write 'My daily routine chart' and your name.* Write these next to your picture. Say *Then you cut out cards for your chart.* Mime cutting out.
- Say *Point to number 2. Draw and write my personal daily routine.* Mime drawing and say *We draw pictures of things we do every day and we write them on the cards. Then we ask about the times.* Point to a clock or watch and say *What time do you get up? What time do you have breakfast?*
- Say *Point to number 3. Write 'Think' bubbles to help our planet.* Draw Earth on the board and say *This is our planet.* Write *planet.* Say *In our daily routines we can help the planet.* Give an example, e.g. *I come to school on my bike. I don't come in the car.* Draw a stick figure with 'Think' bubbles on the board. Explain that learners are going to write their ideas.
- Say *The last stage is 'Show my daily routine chart to the class.'* Hold up a piece of paper and start to talk about a daily routine, e.g. *I get up at seven o'clock.*
- Say *This is our Mission.* Go through the stages of the Mission again.
- For ideas on monitoring and assessment, see Introduction.

Activity Book, page 6

My unit goals

- Help learners to complete the unit goals. They circle the skills they want to work on and the number of new words they want to learn, and they draw something that they want to learn to say in English.
- You can go back to these unit goals at the end of each Mission stage during the unit and review them.

Ending the lesson

- Say *We have lots of routines in the classroom. What do we do in every lesson?* Mime how you begin the class, encouraging learners to help describe what you are doing, e.g. *I open the door. I write the date on the board. We get out our books. I say 'Good morning.' You say 'Good morning, (Mr Hill).'*
- Say *Let's act! You can be teachers!* Describe familiar routines in the classroom. Learners stand up and mime being the teacher. They speak as necessary, e.g. *I say 'Open your books!'* (Learners mime giving an instruction and say *Open your books!*) *I open my bag.* (Learners mime opening a bag.) etc.

Learning outcomes By the end of the lesson, learners will be able to talk about the countryside.

New language *countryside, field, forest, grass, ground, lake, leaf, leaves, mountain, outside, river, rock, tractor, farm, go for a swim/walk, move, pretty*

Recycled language colours, *afternoon, beautiful, behind, flower, garden, in front of, next to, nice, play, swim, tree, under, can* for requests, *have got, Let's ..., love ...-ing, There is/are*

Materials Countryside flashcards, coloured pens or pencils, audio, video

Warm-up

- Write on the board: *10 2 9 4 3 11 5 1 8 6 7*
- Write a 'secret code' on the board: *1=S 2=O 3=T 4=N 5=Y 6=D 7=E 8=I 9=U 10=C 11=R*
- Learners find the secret word (*countryside*).
  Stronger students Dictate the numbers/code.

Presentation

- Hold up each Countryside flashcard and say the word. Learners repeat. Display the flashcards in turn. Learners say the words.

Pupil's Book, page 7

1 1.07 Listen and point. Then listen again and colour.

- Say *Open your Pupil's Books at page 7. Who can you see?* (*Jim, Jenny, Grandpa*) Point to the new characters and say *This is Tom and this is Eva.* Ask *Where are they?* (*At the Friendly Farm*) Ask *Where's the small tractor? Can you find it?* Learners find the hidden picture of the tractor.
- Ask *Are they in the house?* (*No*) Say *No, they're outside.* Check understanding. Read the caption. Ask *Where's the (lake)? Where are the (leaves)?* Learners point.
- Play the audio. Learners point to the items in the picture.

Track 1.07

Grandpa, Jenny and Jim are outside, in the countryside, with their friends Eva and Tom.

Jenny:	Oh, this is nice, a walk in the countryside.
Jim:	Look, Tom. We can see our farm from here.
Tom:	Hmm, those purple flowers on the grass are beautiful.
Grandpa:	That's my garden.
Eva:	Oh, yes. It's very pretty.
Jenny:	Look, Eva! Grandpa's got a new blue tractor.
Eva:	Wooh! That's nice.
Grandpa:	Yes ... but ... there's a big grey rock in the field. That's a problem ... I want to move it.
Tom:	Look at that forest, with the mountains behind. There aren't many leaves on the trees ... and there aren't many leaves on that tree.
Eva:	No, there aren't, but there are a lot on the ground. They're red, yellow and brown. Look!
Tom:	I love playing with leaves.
Jenny:	So do I, and I love swimming. Grandpa, can you see that lake and the river? Can we go for a swim this afternoon?
Grandpa:	No, we can't go for a swim, but let's go for a walk in the forest.
Tom:	Great! We can play with the leaves.
Children:	Yoohoo!

Extra support Ask *What colour is the rock?* (*Grey*) Repeat with different items.

- Point to the tractor and the leaves and say *Listen and colour.* Play the audio again.

Key: tractor – blue leaves – red, yellow and brown

2 1.08 Say the chant.

- Play the audio or video. Learners point and chant.

Track 1.08

Countryside, countryside,
Forest and field,
Grass on the ground,
And leaves on the trees,
Mountains and rocks,
Rivers and lakes. [x2]

3 1.09 Listen and say *yes* or *no*.

- Say *Grandpa's got a red tractor. Yes or no?* (*No*)
- Play the audio. Pause for learners to say *yes* or *no*.

Track 1.09

1 Grandpa's got a new tractor.
2 His tractor's in his garden.
3 The purple flowers are in the forest.
4 Grandpa's garden is next to the forest.
5 There's a big rock behind the tractor.
6 There are a lot of leaves under the tree in Grandpa's garden.
7 The river's next to the lake.
8 They can go for a swim in the lake this afternoon.

Key: 1 yes 2 no 3 no 4 yes 5 no 6 yes 7 yes 8 no

Extension Learners ask and answer about the picture in pairs, e.g. *What colour are the flowers? Where's the rock?*

Activity Book, page 7

See pages TB120–132

Ending the lesson

- **SA** Say *We learnt about the countryside.* Show the flashcards. Ask *Do you know the words?* Use self-assessment (see Introduction). Learners show how they feel.

1 1.07 **Listen and point. Then listen again and colour.**

2 1.08 **Say the chant.**

3 1.09 **Listen and say *yes* or *no*.**

The Friendly Farm

1.10

1
Good morning, everyone.
Shh! Hi, Cameron. The farm cat's got some babies. Come and look at her kittens.
They're here. I think they're sleeping. They're beautiful.
2
Are they sleeping, Mum?
No, they aren't sleeping. I think they're awake.
That's right. They can't open their eyes because they're very young.
3
She's washing that kitten's face! The kitten's very pretty.
I'm pretty too … and my face isn't dirty.
Yes, Shelly, but come with me.
4
Look! There are three puppies. They're all happy.
The one with the short tail's playing with a ball.
It's playing with my ball!
5
Is that big puppy with the white ear drinking water?
No, it isn't. It's looking at its face … because it's a pretty puppy!
6
Look at that fat puppy. What's it eating?
It's naughty! It's eating Grandpa's old red sock.
Grandpa's old red sock?! That's my lunch!

1 1.11 **Listen and say the number.**

Learning outcomes By the end of the lesson, learners will be able to understand when they hear the present continuous.

New language *awake, fat, kitten, naughty, puppy (puppies), wash, the one with (the short tail)*

Recycled language adjectives, colours, parts of the body, *baby (babies), ball, drink, eat, look, lunch, open, play, sleep, sock, have got,* present continuous

Materials Countryside flashcards, paper, coloured pens or pencils, audio, video

Warm-up

- Practise the Countryside words with the flashcards. Put the flashcards away.
- Give out paper and coloured pens/pencils. Give instructions while learners draw, e.g. *Draw some mountains. Draw a river from the mountains to a lake.* Include all the countryside words. Learners compare pictures when they've finished.
- **SA** Use self-assessment to check how well learners think they understand the vocabulary. See Introduction.

Presentation

- Mime drinking and ask *What am I doing?* Help learners make the continuous form. (*Drinking / You're drinking.*) Repeat with different known verbs (e.g. *sleep, eat, play tennis, swim, ride a bike, run, throw a ball, watch TV*).

Pupil's Book, page 8

1.10 The Friendly Farm song

- Play the introductory song at the beginning of the cartoon story. Learners listen. Mime a happy face on the first line, do a thumbs up on the second line, and mime waving at the animals on the third line. Learners listen and copy.

Track 1.10
See The Friendly Farm song on page TB5

1.10 The Friendly Farm

- Say *Open your Pupil's Books at page 8.* Ask *Who can you see in the pictures?* Ask, e.g. *What is Cameron? Is he a horse? (No, a cat)*
- Point to the second picture and say *Look! The cat has got babies.* Mime holding a baby. Say *A baby cat is a kitten. A baby dog is a puppy.* Point to the rest of the story and ask, e.g. *Are the puppies old or young? What colour are the kittens? Has this puppy got a tail? Is it long or short?*
- Point to the red sock which the puppy is eating in picture 6 and ask *Whose sock is it?* Write the question on the board. Revise *Whose* by asking about learners' things. Play the audio or video. Learners listen and read. Check answers. (*It's Grandpa's sock.*)

Track 1.10
The Friendly Farm song + see cartoon on Pupil's Book page 8

- Play the audio or video again. Pause after each picture and ask questions: 1: *Are the kittens ugly? (No, they're beautiful.)* 2: *Are the kittens sleeping?* (No) *Why are their eyes closed?* (*Because they're very young / they can't open them*) Check understanding of *young.* 3: *What's the cat doing?* (*Washing the kitten's face*) Confirm the meaning of *wash* using mime. Check comprehension of *pretty.* 4: *How many puppies are there?* (*Three*) *What's the one with the short tail doing?* (*Playing with a ball*) Point to the puppy and say *This one* to show the meaning of *The one with the …* Ask *Whose ball is it?* (*Cameron's*) 5: *What's the big puppy with the white ear doing? Is it drinking?* (*No, looking at its face*) 6: *Why is Gracie angry?* (*Because the sock is her lunch*) Check learners understand *naughty* and *lunch.*

Extension Play the audio or video again. Mime the present continuous actions as you play it (sleeping, playing, washing, etc.). Learners copy.

1 (1.11) Listen and say the number.

- Play the first sentence. Learners find the correct picture, point and say the number. Play the rest of the audio. Pause after each sentence for learners to answer.

Track 1.11

a	Shelly:	It's eating Grandpa's old red sock. [6]
b	Harry:	The one with the short tail's playing with a ball. [4]
c	Gracie:	Is that big puppy with the white ear drinking water? [5]
d	Shelly:	It's looking at its face. [5]
e	Harry:	What's it eating? [6]
f	Rocky:	Are they sleeping, Mum? [2]
g	Harry:	She's washing that kitten's face! [3]
h	Henrietta:	No, they aren't sleeping. I think they're awake. [2]

Key: See numbers in audioscript

Activity Book, page 8

See pages TB120–132

Ending the lesson

- In pairs, learners take turns to make sentences about the pictures. The other learner points. They can talk about what the animals look like or what they are doing.

Learning outcomes By the end of the lesson, learners will be able to ask and answer questions and write about what people are doing, using the present continuous.

New language *Are you reading a book? No, I'm not. I'm doing my homework. Is she playing tennis? Yes, she is. She's playing tennis. Are they putting on their boots? No, they aren't. They're taking off their boots. clean* (v), *do homework, put on, scissors, take off*

Recycled language sports and hobbies, *boots, crayon, drink, eat, hand, ice cream, kitchen, lemonade, wash*

Materials Sports and hobbies flashcards from level 1, audio, Mission worksheets (Teacher's Resource Book page 14) or paper/card templates, scissors and an envelope for each learner, digital Mission poster, coloured pens or pencils

Warm-up

- Review sports and hobbies using the flashcards from level 1 or mime. Display flashcards or write sports and hobbies on the board. Ask different learners *Do you like (playing basketball)? Can you (play the piano)?*
- Learners ask and answer the same questions in pairs.
- Mime getting ready to do a sport and say, e.g. *I'm putting on a helmet. I'm getting something out of the garage. I'm getting on. What am I doing?* (*Riding a bike*) Encourage learners to make a complete sentence with *You're …-ing.* Repeat with different sports and hobbies.

Presentation

- Hold one of the sports and hobbies flashcards so learners can't see it. If you don't have flashcards, write the phrase (e.g. *playing tennis*) on a piece of paper.
- Say *There's a man in the picture. Is he swimming? No, he isn't. Now you guess.* Help learners make questions with *Is he/she … ?* Use short answers (*Yes, he is. / No, he isn't.*). Show the picture or words when learners guess correctly.

Pupil's Book, page 9

1.12 Gracie's Grammar

- Say *Open your Pupil's Books at page 9.* Point to Gracie's Grammar box. Write the same sentences on the board.
- Play the audio. Pause for learners to repeat.

Track 1.12
See Pupil's Book page 9

1 1.13 **Listen and stick. Then look, read and write.**

- Play the audio. Learners point to the correct sticker. Play the audio again. Learners stick in the stickers.

Track 1.13

1	Tom:	Is your mum eating some ice cream?
	Jim:	No, she isn't. My grandma's eating some ice cream.
2	Tom:	Is your grandma drinking lemonade?
	Jim:	No, she isn't. My mum's drinking lemonade.
3	Tom:	Is your grandpa washing his hands?
	Jenny:	No, he isn't. My dad's washing his hands.
4	Tom:	Is your dad cleaning the kitchen?
	Jenny:	No, he isn't. My grandpa's cleaning the kitchen.

- Ask *What's Grandma doing?* (*She's eating some ice cream.*) Point to the example sentence. Ask what word *'s* replaces. (*is*)
- Say *Now look, read and write.* Learners complete the sentences.

Extra support Ask about all four people before learners write. Write the infinitive of the verbs on the board to help learners with spelling.

Key: 2 's drinking 3 's washing 4 's cleaning

mission Stage 1

- Point to the Mission box or show learners the first stage of the digital Mission poster: *Make your chart.*
- Learners complete the worksheet task in the Teacher's Resource Book (page 14). See teaching notes on TRB page 7.
- Alternatively, if you do not have the Teacher's Resource Book, give out paper or card templates. Learners draw a small picture of themselves in one corner. Write *My daily routine chart, by …* on the board (or include it on the template). Learners copy this next to their picture and complete it with their name, then decorate it (e.g. with a colourful frame). They cut out the picture/title and then cut out 12 small cards.
- Learners put these into an envelope with their name on it. Collect the envelopes.

Activity Book, page 9

See pages TB120–132

Activity Book, page 6

- Review *My unit goals.* Ask *How is your Mission?* Learners reflect and choose a smiley face for *My mission diary 1.*

Ending the lesson

- **SA** Go back to Stage 1 on the digital Mission poster. Say *We made a chart.* Add a tick to the 'Make your chart' stage. Use self-assessment (see Introduction).
- Give out a completion sticker.

Gracie's Grammar

1.12

Are you read**ing** a book?	No, I**'m not**. I**'m** do**ing** my homework.
Is she play**ing** tennis?	Yes, she **is**. She's play**ing** tennis.
Are they put**ting** on their boots?	No, they **aren't**. They're tak**ing** off their boots.

1 1.13 **Listen and stick. Then look, read and write.**

1 Grandma's eating some ice cream.

2 Mum ______ lemonade.

3 Dad ______ his hands.

4 Grandpa ______ the kitchen.

mission STAGE 1

Make your chart.

- Write and decorate the title.
- Draw yourself and colour the picture.
- Cut up the little cards.

Are you using the red crayon?

No, I'm using the scissors.

My mission diary
Activity Book page 6

1 1.14 Listen and number. Then sing the song.

[1]**Wake up**, [2]**get up**.
Go and [3]**have a shower**.
Wake up, get up.
Time for us to run!

Get your [4]**towel**, get dry.
Now go and [5]**get dressed**.
Get your towel, get dry.
Time for us to run!

Sit down for breakfast.
Milk or juice for you?
Sit down for breakfast.
Time for us to run!

Clean your teeth.
[6]**Toothpaste** on your [7]**toothbrush**.
Clean your teeth.
Time for us to run!

Wake up, get up,
Go and have a shower.
Wake up, get up,
Get dressed, [8]**have breakfast**,
Clean your teeth and run!

Time for us to run! (x3)

2 Play the game.

What am I doing?

You're cleaning your teeth.

What do you do in the morning?

Learning outcomes By the end of the lesson, learners will have practised the language through song.

New language *get dressed, get up, have a shower, have breakfast, toothbrush, toothpaste, towel, wake up, clean your teeth, (get) dry, Time for us to …*

Recycled language food and drink, sports and hobbies, *get, go, run, sit down,* imperatives, present continuous, present simple

Materials Daily routines flashcards, a real toothbrush, toothpaste and towel (optional), audio, video, pieces of card/paper with phrases: *have breakfast, get dressed, get up, have a shower, clean your teeth, eat a mango, take a photo, play the guitar/piano, read a book, sing, catch/throw a ball,* etc. (optional)

Warm-up

- Review sports and hobbies. Give an instruction with 'Simon says', e.g. *Simon says 'Play the guitar.'* Learners mime. After a series of imperatives, give an instruction without saying 'Simon says'. Any learners who mime the action are 'out'. Revise *run, get, sit down* and *go* as well as sports and hobbies.

Presentation

- Mime switching off an alarm clock. Say *It's the morning. It's time for my alarm. Every day I do the same thing. I wake up.* Mime waking up and put the flashcard on the board. Repeat and encourage learners to copy you. Say *I get up.* Mime getting out of bed and put the flashcard to the right of the wake up flashcard. Continue with a morning routine in this way – *have a shower, get dressed, have breakfast.*
- Point to all the flashcards in order. Learners say the phrases. Say *Close your eyes.* Remove one flashcard. Say the routine up to the missing flashcard (*I wake up. I get up …*) and ask *What's missing?* Learners say, e.g. *I have a shower.*
- Use a real towel, toothbrush and toothpaste to teach the words, or use flashcards. Teach *tooth* and the plural *teeth.* Say *We use a towel to get dry.* Explain *dry*.
- **SA** Use self-assessment to check how well learners think they understand the vocabulary. See Introduction.

Pupil's Book, page 10

1 (1.14) Listen and number. Then sing the song.

- Say *Open your Pupil's Books at page 10. Who can you see?* (*Grandpa, Jenny, Jim*) Say *Find a towel.* Learners point. Repeat for *toothbrush, toothpaste, breakfast* and *shower.*
- Say *Wake up. Point to the picture*. Learners point. Say *Look at the number*. Show learners the number 1 next to the picture of Jenny waking up. Say *Let's listen and write the numbers.* Play the audio or video. Check answers.

Track 1.14

Rocky: I'm Rocky-Doodle-Doo and here's our song for today: *Wake up!*

Grandpa: Jim, are you awake? Oh dear, Jim's asleep and Jenny's asleep too. Wake up Jim! Wake up Jenny!

See song on Pupil's Book page 10

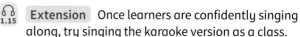

Key: a 5 b 4 (c 1) d 3 e 6, 7 f 8 g 2

- Learners stand up. Say each activity from the song and do the action. Learners repeat the words and actions.
- Play the audio or video again. Learners listen and sing, doing actions.

(1.15) **Extension** Once learners are confidently singing along, try singing the karaoke version as a class.

2 Play the game.

- Demonstrate the game. Show and read the cards with phrases for daily routines / sports and hobbies. Take a card without showing the class and mime the action. Ask *What am I doing?* Learners guess, e.g. *You're having breakfast.*
- Put learners into two teams. One learner comes to the front from each team. Show a different card to each of the learners at the front. They both ask *What am I doing?* and start miming at the same time. The first team to guess correctly wins a point. They must make a correct sentence in the present continuous. Two different learners come to the front and the game continues with new cards.

  Alternative Learners play the game in pairs.
- Show the picture of Rocky in the bottom right-hand corner. Read out the question. Put the daily routine flashcards on the board again (just the actions). Learners say the order in which they do things every day. Choose different learners. Then learners tell each other in pairs.

Activity Book, page 10

See pages TB120–132

Ending the lesson

- **SA** Repeat the self-assessment used at the start of the lesson to see how well learners think they understand the vocabulary. Is there any change?
- Play the song again. Learners join in and do the actions.

Learning outcomes By the end of the lesson, learners will be able to use the present simple for routines with times (*o'clock*).

New language *What time do you get up? I get up at seven o'clock. What time does school finish? It finishes at four o'clock. finish, go home, go to bed*

Recycled language daily routines, *at school, do homework, go to school, have lunch, lesson, start,* present simple questions and answers

Materials Daily routines flashcards, teaching clocks (optional), audio, envelopes with cards from Mission Stage 1 lesson, a piece of A4 card for each learner, coloured pens or pencils, glue, scissors, digital Mission poster

Warm-up

- Ask *What do you do in the morning on a school day?* The class say and mime verb phrases for a morning routine. Use the flashcards as prompts. When you get to *go to school,* describe a typical day, pausing for learners to supply words, e.g. *You go to school. You start school in the morning. You have …* (*lessons*) *and then in the middle of the day, you're hungry.* (Mime feeling hungry.) *You have …* (*lunch*). *In the afternoon you have more …* (*lessons*) *and then school finishes and you go …* (*home*).

Presentation

- Show a teaching clock with the hands set at seven o'clock or draw this on the board. Say *Seven o'clock. I have breakfast at seven o'clock.*
- Move the hands or draw different times (always *o'clock*) and say, e.g. *Nine o'clock*. Learners repeat. When they are confident, choose individual learners to say the times.

Pupil's Book, page 11

1 1.16 What time does he have lunch? Listen and tick ✓.

- Say *Open your Pupil's Books at page 11*. Point to the clock/watches. Learners say the times.
- Play the audio. Learners listen and tick. Check answers.

Track 1.16

Woman:	Tell me about your day. What time do you get up?
Boy:	I get up at seven o'clock and I have breakfast at eight o'clock.
Woman:	Do you have lunch at school?
Boy:	Yes, I do. I don't go home for lunch.
Woman:	What time do you have lunch? Is it 12 o'clock?
Boy:	No. I have lunch at one o'clock.
Woman:	Are there lessons in the afternoon?
Boy:	Yes. Lessons start at two o'clock.
Woman:	I see. And what time does school finish?
Boy:	It finishes at four o'clock.

Key: one o'clock – picture 2

Extension Write more questions on the board and play the audio again, e.g. *What time does he get up / have breakfast? What time do lessons start in the afternoon?*

1.17 Gracie's Grammar

- Write the questions and answers on the board.
- Play the audio, pausing so learners can repeat.

Track 1.17
See Pupil's Book page 11

- Ask different learners the questions. Tell them to 'round up' the times to the nearest hour.

2 Ask and answer.

- Read the phrases. Make an example sentence, e.g. *I go to bed at ten o'clock.* Ask a learner *What time do you go to bed?* Remind learners to use the nearest 'o'clock' time.
- In pairs, learners ask and answer.

mission Stage 2

- Show learners the second stage of the Mission poster: *Draw and write your personal daily routine*.
- Give learners their envelopes from Stage 1. Learners choose and write daily routines on six cards and draw pictures of these routines on the remaining six cards.
- In pairs, learners pick up their picture cards one by one and ask each other when they do the routines, e.g. *What time do you get up? I get up at seven o'clock.*
- Give each learner a piece of A4 card. They put the card in landscape position. They stick their picture/heading at the top. Along the bottom in a row, they stick the six daily routine word cards. Just above these, in a row, they stick the matching pictures. With scissors, learners cut up between each word card to create a row of flaps.

Activity Book, page 11

See pages TB120–132

Activity Book, page 6

- Review *My unit goals*. Ask *How is your Mission?* Learners reflect and choose a smiley face for *My mission diary 2*.

Ending the lesson

- **SA** Go back to Stage 2 on the digital Mission poster. Add a tick to the 'Draw and write your personal daily routine' stage. Use self-assessment (see Introduction).
- Give out a completion sticker.

1 1.16 What time does he have lunch? Listen and tick ✓.

1

2

3

1.17 Gracie's Grammar

What time do you get up? I get up at **seven o'clock**.

What time does school finish? It finishes at **four o'clock**.

2 Ask and answer.

get up go to school have lunch go home
do your homework have a shower go to bed

What time do you have lunch? I have lunch at one o'clock.

What time do you go home? I go home at four o'clock.

mission STAGE 2

Draw and write your personal daily routine.

- Draw a picture and write the name of each activity on a little card.
- Ask and answer with a friend about your routines.

What time do you get up? I get up at seven o'clock.

My mission diary
Activity Book page 6

Cross-curricular

Look after our planet

1 Watch the video.

2 Tick ✓ the activities that are good for our planet.

1

2
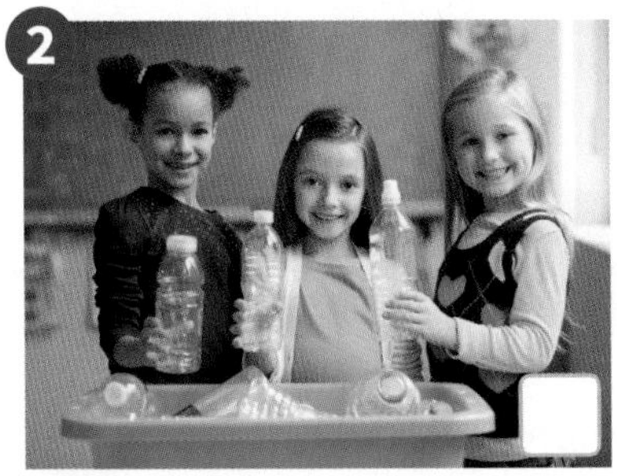

3

4

5
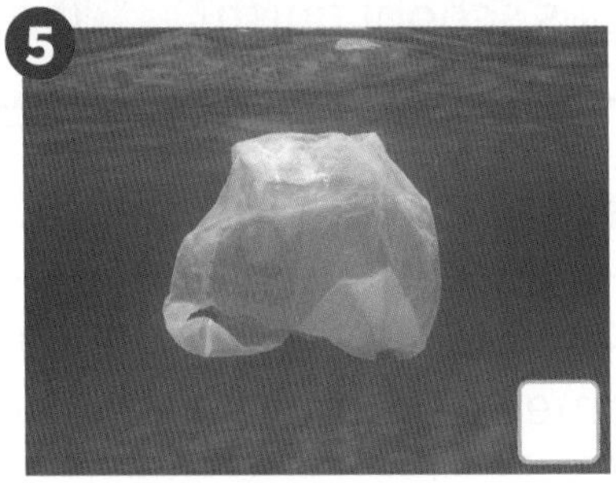

6

3 1.18 Listen and read. Answer the questions.

Our planet is called Earth. We can live on Earth because there is air around us. Air has oxygen and other gases. All plants and animals need oxygen. They need water too and there is water on Earth. Clean air and clean water keep us healthy, so it's important to look after our planet.

1 Which planet do we live on?
2 What do plants and animals need?
3 Why is it important to look after our planet?

Learning outcomes By the end of the lesson, learners will have learnt about how to look after our planet.

New language *air, Earth, gas, important, keep (someone) healthy, look after, need, oxygen, planet, plant* (n)

Recycled language daily routines, *animal, clean* (adj), *water*

Materials Daily routines flashcards, video, pictures from Digital photo bank of someone looking after the Earth (e.g. putting litter in a bin) and someone damaging the Earth (e.g. cutting down a tree) (optional), audio

Warm-up

- Show the Daily routines flashcards (just the verbs). Learners say the phrases. Draw two clocks with times to review *have lunch* and *have dinner*.
- Take one of the flashcards and look at it without showing the class. Say *What do I do? What time?* Mime the action and hold up your fingers to show the time you usually do it. The class make a sentence, e.g. *You have a shower at eight o'clock*. Repeat until learners get the idea.
- Mix up the flashcards and hand them out around the class. Choose a learner with a flashcard to mime their action and hold up his/her fingers to show the time.
- Repeat with the rest of the flashcards. Then collect them in, hand them to different learners and do the activity again.

  Extra support Write the phrases on the board.

  Stronger learners Write more prompts on the board or ask learners to think of their own actions, e.g. *get the bus, do homework, play football, have a snack, go home.*

Presentation

- Show the picture of Earth from Pupil's Book page 12 or draw it on the board. Say *This is a planet. We live on a planet.* Find out what learners already know about what living things need to live on our planet.
- Say *Let's find out more about our planet.*

Pupil's Book, page 12

1 Watch the video.

- Say *Let's watch the video.* Learners watch the video about looking after our planet and answer the questions at the end.

2 Tick ✓ the activities that are good for our planet.

- Put up two pictures on the board: one showing someone looking after the environment, and another showing someone damaging it. If you don't have pictures, act out dropping litter or putting litter in the bin.
- Ask *Which is good for our planet?* Learners point to the correct picture. Tick it.
- Say *Open your Pupil's Books at page 12. Look at the pictures. Which are good for our planet? Tick.* Put learners into pairs to do the activity. Check answers.
- Point to the correct pictures and say, e.g. *He's looking after our planet. When we look after something we do only good things. We look after our pets by giving them food and water. We can look after people in our family. And we need to look after our planet.* Point to the title of the page.

Key: Pictures 1, 2, 4, 6

Stronger learners Make sentences about the pictures.

3 1.18 Listen and read. Answer the questions.

- Read the questions with the class and check comprehension. Ask for examples of plants (*flowers, grass, trees*) and animals (*cats, dogs*, etc.). Make example sentences with *need*, e.g. *To do my homework I need a pen and some paper.*
- Play the audio. Learners listen and read. They talk about the questions in pairs. Check answers.

  Track 1.18

  See Pupil's Book page 12

  Extra support Read the text with the class, sentence by sentence, explaining new vocabulary. Answer the questions together.
- Check comprehension of *keep healthy*. Say *To keep healthy we need to do exercise* (mime exercising) *and eat good food. We need to drink clean water* (mime drinking) *and we need clean air* (mime breathing in deeply).

Key: 1 We live on Earth. 2 They need oxygen and water. 3 Because clean air and clean water keep us healthy.

Extension Ask *What things make the air dirty? What things make the water dirty?* Learners suggest ideas.

Activity Book, page 12

See pages TB120–132

Ending the lesson

- Show a line down the centre of the room and make one side 'True' and the other 'False'.
- Say sentences about the text. If learners think they are true, they jump on the true side; if not, they jump on the false side (e.g. *Our planet is called Venus* – false).

Learning outcomes By the end of the lesson, learners will be able to talk about looking after our planet.

New language *glass, go out, go shopping, have a bath, light* (n), *plastic, plastic bag, recycle, save (water), tap, turn off, use*

Recycled language daily routines, *at home, clean your teeth, look after, new, paper, water,* imperatives

Materials paper, coloured pens or pencils, audio, items which can be recycled made from paper, plastic and glass (e.g. old newspapers, empty plastic bottles and glass jars) (optional), daily routine charts from Mission Stage 2 lesson, sticky notes or paper and glue, digital Mission poster

Warm-up

- Show the picture of Earth from Pupil's Book page 12 or draw it on the board. Say *This is our planet. What's it called?* (*Earth*) *It's important to look after the Earth.* Remind learners of the meaning of *look after.*
- Hand out paper. Say *Draw a picture of someone looking after the Earth.* Monitor and ask questions about the pictures.
- Learners show their picture. Help them to say what the person is doing.
- Say *Let's think of how we can look after the Earth every day.*

Pupil's Book, page 13

4 1.19 Match the ideas with the photos. Listen and check.

- Say *Open your Pupil's Books at page 13. Look at the pictures. What can you see?* (*A plastic bag, bins, a shower, a tap, turning the light on/off*) Don't pre-teach new words at this stage, as learners can use known words to do the matching task.
- Read the instructions and the example sentence.
- Learners read and match individually, then listen and check.

  Track 1.19
  See Pupil's Book page 13
- Ask learners to find taps and lights in the pictures/classroom. Demonstrate turning the lights in the classroom on and off. Show examples of real items to confirm the meaning of *paper, glass* and *plastic*, or point to items in the classroom. Say *Turning off the taps saves water. Having a shower saves water.* Check learners understand the meaning of *save.*

Key: 2 c 3 e 4 b 5 a

5 What do you do to look after the planet? Tell a partner.

- Read the instructions. Tell learners which things you do from Activity 1. Ask individual learners.
- Learners talk in pairs, using the speech bubbles as models.

  Extension Learners think of something they do which is not in Activity 1. They tell the class. Help with new vocabulary and write ideas on the board.

mission Stage 3

- Mime thinking. Say *I'm thinking.* Draw your face and a 'Think' bubble coming from your head on the board. In the bubble write a phrase, e.g. *I want some tea.* Say *Look! I'm thinking 'I want some tea.' This is a 'Think' bubble.*
- Show the class the third stage of the Mission poster: *Write 'Think' bubbles to help our planet.*
- Put learners into small groups. They talk together to come up with ideas for helping save resources as part of their daily routine. Write daily routine phrases on the board as prompts: *have a shower, go to school, have lunch, go home, do my homework, go to bed.*
- Learners write 'Think' bubbles individually on pieces of paper or sticky notes. Hand out their charts. Learners cut out the bubbles and stick them on their chart at the appropriate point in their daily routine.

  Extra support Write sentence halves for learners to match on the board to make 'Think' bubbles:

I have a shower	*when I go to bed.*
I walk	*to save water.*
I recycle my plastic cup	*when I have a drink of water.*
I don't use lots of paper	*to school.*
I turn off the computer and TV	*when I do my homework.*

Activity Book, page 13

See pages TB120–132

Activity Book, page 6

- Review *My unit goals.* Ask *How is your Mission?* Learners reflect and choose a smiley face for *My mission diary 3.*

Ending the lesson

- **SA** Go back to Stage 3 on the digital Mission poster. Add a tick to the 'Write "Think" bubbles to help our planet' stage. Use self-assessment (see Introduction).
- Give out a completion sticker.

4 (1.19) Match the ideas with the photos. Listen and check.

Look after our planet … at home!

1 [d] Turn off the tap when you clean your teeth.
2 [ ] Have a shower and not a bath. Save water!
3 [ ] Turn off the lights when you go out.
4 [ ] Recycle paper, glass and plastic.
5 [ ] Don't use new plastic bags when you go shopping.

a
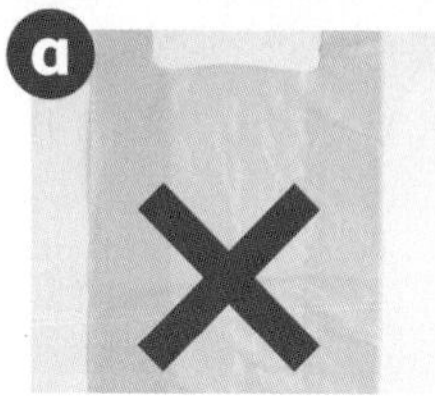
b

c

d
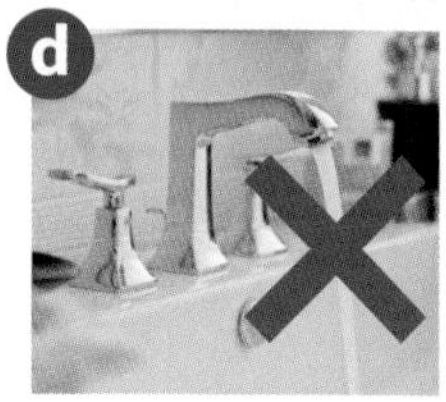
e

5 What do you do to look after the planet? Tell a partner.

We recycle paper, glass and plastic.

I have showers.

mission STAGE 3

Write 'Think' bubbles to help our planet.

- Say how you can look after our planet.
- Write 'Think' bubbles for your daily routines chart.

I turn off the tap when I clean my teeth.

My mission diary
Activity Book page 6

1 **Look at the pictures. Where are the girls? What are they doing?**

1.20

The race

'Get up! Have a shower!
Clean your teeth, get dressed!
Come on, Gwen!' says Beth.
'Let's go and see Jess!'

Jess is their puppy, with a little black nose.
She lives in the field where everyone goes
To be happy, not sad, to play and to run.
Today there are leaves on the ground – it's fun!

Every day Beth and Gwen run
to see Jess.
'I'm winning today,' says Beth.
'Oh yes!'
But then there's a rock in
the leaves and she falls!
And down on the ground
to her sister she calls.

Learning outcomes By the end of the lesson, learners will have read a poem about two sisters.

New language *come/go back, every day, fall, fast, feel (sad), last* (adj), *move, race* (n), *win*

Recycled language daily routines, *field, fun, ground, happy, help, leaves, leg, nose, play, puppy, river, rock, run, sad, sister, stand, stop, I'm sorry,* imperatives, *Let's …,* present continuous, present simple

Materials Daily routines flashcards, Countryside flashcards, word cards, audio

Warm-up

- Hand out the Daily routines and Countryside flashcards and the corresponding word cards so that each learner has a card (either a flashcard or a word card). Say *Stand up and find your partner!* Learners with a flashcard walk around saying, e.g. *I've got 'towel'.* until they find the learner with the matching word card. Then they give both cards back to you.

  Fast finishers When they have made a pair, learners make a sentence using the word/phrase.

Presentation

- Say *We're going to read a poem about two sisters. There's also an animal in the poem. What kind of animal do you think it is?* Learners guess.
- Write words from the poem on the board: *race, fast, win, last, fall.* Define each word or ask learners to help explain what it means (e.g. *People can run in a race. They swim. They ride bikes or horses or race in cars. They want to be fast. The person who is very fast finishes at the front. He or she wins the race.*). Use gesture and mime or draw a picture of a race with someone clearly winning. Ask questions, e.g. *Do you like racing? What type of race? Running? Swimming? Who wins when you race in your family? Who is last?*

Pupil's Book, pages 14 and 15

1 Look at the pictures. Where are the girls? What are they doing?

- Say *Open your Pupil's Books at page 14. Look at the pictures. Where are the girls? What are they doing?* Learners suggest ideas. Encourage them to use the vocabulary on the board.

Key: (possible answers) They're at home. They're cleaning their teeth. They're in the countryside. They want to see a puppy. They're racing/running. One girl falls. The other girl wants to win/run but she goes back. She helps the other girl. They go to see the puppy.

Extra support Ask questions about each picture, e.g. 1: *Are the girls friends?* (*No, sisters*) *Where are they?* (*In the bathroom*) *Are they having a bath?* (*No, cleaning their teeth*) 2: *Are the girls in a forest?* (*No, near some fields*) *Which animal do you think is in the field?* (*A dog/puppy*) *What are the girls doing? Are they walking?* (*No, they're running/racing.*) 3: *What's happening?* (*One girl is falling.*) 4: *Has the girl got a problem with her head?* (*No, her leg*) *What's the other girl thinking?* (*She wants to run/win.*) 5: *What's happening?* (*One girl is helping the other girl.*)

1.20 The race

- Say *Let's listen and read.* Play the audio. Learners listen and read. Pause the audio after the first verse. Ask *What are the girls' names?* (*Beth and Gwen*) *What's the dog's name?* (*Jess*)

  Track 1.20
  See poem on Pupil's Book pages 14–15
- Play the next verse. Learners listen and read. Ask *What colour is Jess's nose?* (*Black*) *Where does she live?* (*In a field*) *What's on the ground?* (*Leaves*)
- Play verse three. Ask *Who's winning the race?* (*Beth*) *Why does she fall?* (*Because there's a rock in the leaves*)
- Play verse four. Ask *What's the problem with Beth's leg?* (*She can't move it.*) *What does Gwen think?* (*'I don't want to be last.'*)
- Play the last verse of the poem. Ask *How does Gwen feel?* (*Sad*) *What does she do?* (*She goes back and helps her sister – then they go to see the puppy.*)

  Extra support Instead of asking questions, make sentences about the poem, pausing for learners to say key words, e.g. *The girls' names are Gwen and* (*Beth*). *The puppy's name is* (*Jess*).

  Extension Play the whole poem again, without pauses, for learners to listen and read.

Activity Book, page 14

See pages TB120–132

Ending the lesson

- Place Daily routines and Countryside flashcards on the floor like a winding river. Say *It's a river.* Show the river flashcard. Say *Let's cross the river.*
- Choose a learner to stand at the beginning of the river. The other learners watch and answer. Point to the first flashcard and ask a question, e.g. *Is he having a shower? / Is it a mountain?* If learners answer correctly, the learner crossing the river can step on the first flashcard. Continue to ask questions about the flashcards, e.g. *What's she doing? What colour is the tractor?*

Learning outcomes By the end of the lesson, learners will have acted out a poem and thought about being supportive.

New language *support, supportive*

Recycled language language from the poem

Materials audio, pictures of people supporting or helping others (optional)

Social and Emotional Skill: Being supportive

- After reading the poem, say the following sentences and ask learners to complete them: *Gwen and Beth have a …* (*race*) *every day. Gwen and Beth run and run, but then Beth …* (*falls*). *Gwen feels …* (*bad*). *Gwen goes to …* (*help*) *Beth.*
- Say *Yes, Gwen helps Beth when she falls in the leaves. She is being supportive.*
- Point out that we can be supportive to people in different ways. Sometimes we can help them to carry something and sometimes we can be supportive by talking to someone and helping them with a problem.
- Write on the board *I can support people …* and a list of ways:
  - *I can help carry books or bags.*
  - *I can help someone who falls in the playground.*
  - *I can talk to someone who is sad or scared.*
  - *I can talk to someone who's got a problem.*
- Read them aloud and learners put up their hands to show which they do.
- Ask learners *Who is supportive to you? What do they do?*
- Learners think about who supports them. It can be their parents, grandparents, friends, teachers, etc.
- They think of all the things these people do. They work in pairs and think of three ways people support them. Then, in their pairs, they act out one situation (e.g. *When I'm sick, my dad looks after me.*).
- Optional: Learners make a card to thank a family member or friend for everything they do to support them.

Warm-up

- Write *Beth* and *Gwen* on the board. Ask *Who are Beth and Gwen?* (*Sisters*) *Where does the story happen?* (*In the countryside*) *What animal do they go to see?* (*A puppy*)
- Say *Listen. Who says it? 'Let's go and see Jess!'* (*Beth*) *'I'm winning the race!'* (*Beth*) *'I don't want to be last!'* (*Gwen*) *'Come back!'* (*Beth*) *'I'm sorry.'* (*Gwen*)

Pupil's Book, pages 14 and 15

- Say *Open your Pupil's Books at pages 14 and 15.* Play the audio. Learners read and listen to the poem again.

  Track 1.20

  See poem on Pupil's Book pages 14–15

2 Act out the poem.

- Read the instructions and the speech bubbles.
- Put learners into pairs. They act out the story, using the pictures in the Pupil's Book to help them. Encourage them to say lines, such as *Let's go and see Jess. I'm winning*. etc. Write key words and phrases on the board, if necessary. When they have acted the story once all the way through, get them to swap roles.

  Extra support Summarise the story, sentence by sentence, as learners act. Say *Gwen and Beth have a shower. They clean their teeth. They get dressed. Beth says 'Let's go and see Jess.' The girls run to see Jess. Beth says 'I'm winning.' Oh, no! Beth falls on a rock. Gwen looks back but she doesn't stop. She says 'I don't want to be last.' Beth says 'Ow! Gwen, can you come?' Gwen feels sad. She stops running. She goes back and says 'I'm sorry.' She helps Beth stand up. The two girls go and see Jess.*

  Extension Pairs continue acting out the story, after the end of the poem. They make up lines for the girls to say (e.g. *Let me help you, Beth. / Thanks, Gwen.*). They can act out the girls going home. Monitor and help with vocabulary. Pairs act out their stories for the class.

3 Gwen goes to help Beth. When do you support people like this?

- Check understanding of *support.* Show learners pictures of people helping others. Give examples, e.g. *This woman is helping someone who can't walk very well.*
- Ask *Who do you support? How?* If possible, talk about ways in which you support people. Say, e.g. *I support my son. I help him when he doesn't want to go to the dentist.*
- Put learners into small groups of three or four. Each learner tells the group about what they do to support people.

Activity Book, page 15

See pages TB120–132

Ending the lesson

- **SA** Use self-assessment to see how well learners think they understand the story. See Introduction.

1

‘Where are you going,
Gwen? Come back to me!
I can’t move my leg.
Please come and see!’
But Gwen’s winning the race.
She’s running so fast.
She looks, but she thinks,
‘I don’t want to be last’.

‘Owwww, my leg!’ says Beth.
‘Gwen, can you come?’
Gwen starts to feel sad
And she stops her run.
She goes back and she says,
‘I’m sorry, Beth.’
She helps her to stand
And they go and see Jess.

2 Act out the poem.

Are you OK, Beth?

Owwwww, my leg.

Can you stand up?

3 Gwen goes to help Beth. When do you support people like this?

1 Practise with a friend.

What's your name?

How old are you?

2 Look at this picture. What can you see?

A

3 Look at this picture. How is it different from picture A? Read and correct.

B

1 In picture B, there are four sheep in the field.
2 In picture B, there are some leaves on the grass.

In picture B, there are …

4 Look and say.

1 I can see orange juice in picture A. Here, it's …

2 In picture A, she's washing her hands. In this picture, she's washing …

3 There's a lizard on the rock. In picture B, there's …

You can say *Here, there's / there are* … and *There isn't/aren't*.

Learning outcomes By the end of the lesson, learners will have practised answering basic personal questions and talking about the differences between two pictures (A1 Movers Speaking Part 1).

Test skills Describing two pictures by using short responses

New language *farmer, have a picnic, sandwich(es)*

Recycled language animals, countryside, food and drink, *tap, tree, wash (her) hands/boots, have got, Here …,* prepositions of place, present continuous, *There is/are*

Materials paper, coloured pens or pencils (optional), practice paper for Movers Speaking Part 1 (optional), Countryside and Daily routines flashcards

Warm-up

- Draw a landscape on the board with mountains, a lake, a forest and a river. Draw flowers, rocks and grass. Draw animals, e.g. a dog swimming in the river, a cat on a rock.
- Ask *What can you see?* Learners make as many sentences as they can with *There is/are*.
- Ask about positions: *Where's the (bird)?* (*In the tree*)

  Extension Learners draw their own picture with different details/animals. They swap pictures and talk about their partner's picture in the same way.

  Extra support Practise prepositions by asking about objects in the classroom or giving instructions (e.g. *Put your book under your chair. Put one pen on your desk.*).

Presentation

- Say *Let's practise for a speaking exam.* Write *Speaking exam* on the board. Say your name in a quiet/unclear voice. Ask *Is that good for a speaking exam?* (*No*) Say your name clearly and ask *Is this good?* (*Yes*) Say *Speak clearly in the exam. At the beginning of the exam, the examiner asks questions about you. What are the questions?* Write learners' suggestions on the board (e.g. *What's your name? Where are you from?*).

Pupil's Book, page 16

1 Practise with a friend.

- Say *Open your Pupil's Books at page 16. Look at the questions from the exam.* Choose two or three learners to answer. Learners practise in pairs. Tell learners the examiner only asks these two questions. Learners can also role play the exam – with someone taking them to meet the examiner and exchanging greetings before the questions.

2 Look at this picture. What can you see?

- Show an example of the Movers Speaking paper (Part 1), if possible. Say *Part 1 of the exam has two pictures. You need to look for four differences between the pictures.*
- Focus on picture A. Point and ask *Who's this?* Teach *farmer*.
- Learners work in pairs to say as much as they can about the picture / name as many items as they can. Teach/Revise *have a picnic* and *sandwiches*.
- Learners share ideas with the class. Encourage them to use different structures (*I can see … There is/are … have got …* present continuous and prepositions of place) and expand on their first sentence, e.g. say *Yes, there's a farmer. What's she doing? / Yes, there's an orange fish. Where is it?*

Key: (possible answers) There's a farmer. She's washing her hands under a tap. She's got two children, a boy and a girl. They're having a picnic. There are sandwiches, orange juice and apples. There's an orange fish in the river. There's a lizard on a rock. There are three cows.

3 Look at this picture. How is it different from picture A? Read and correct.

- Read the instructions and the sentences. Learners look carefully at picture B and correct the sentences individually or in pairs. Check answers. Note that in the exam, the pictures are not labelled A and B.

Key: 1 In picture B, there are four cows in the field. 2 In picture B, there are no leaves on the grass / there aren't (any) leaves on the grass.

4 Look and say.

- Say *Now look at the pictures again.* Focus on the first speech bubble and ask a learner to complete it.
- Learners talk about how to complete the other sentences in pairs. Check answers.

  Extra support Do all three sentences as a class.

Key: 1 water 2 her boots 3 a duck

-  Point to the monkey at the bottom of the page and read the sentence. Ask learners to look at another picture with lots of details, e.g. Pupil's Book page 4 or 9. In pairs, they make as many sentences as they can.

Activity Book, page 16

See pages TB120–132

Ending the lesson

- Show some Countryside and Daily routines flashcards. Ask learners *What is it? What colour is it? What's he/she doing? Tell me about it.* Put learners into groups of four. Each learner chooses and describes one of the flashcards. Other learners try to guess which it is.

Learning outcomes By the end of the lesson, learners will have revised the language in the unit and presented their daily routine chart to the class.

Recycled language unit language

Materials teaching clock (optional), Daily routines flashcards, daily routines charts from Mission Stages 1–3 lessons (with a completed example for you), dice and counters (for Activity Book game), coloured pens or pencils, digital Mission poster

Warm-up

- Show a teaching clock or draw a clock with an 'o'clock' time. Ask *What time is it?* Repeat with different times.
- Show the Daily routines flashcards for actions (not *towel, toothbrush* or *toothpaste*). Learners say the phrases.
- Put one of the flashcards on the board. Then show or draw a clock with a different time. Make a sentence, e.g. *I have breakfast at eight o'clock.* Learners repeat. Change the flashcard and the time to prompt different sentences. Write key words to prompt other phrases, e.g. *'lunch' (have lunch), 'teeth' (clean my teeth), 'home' (go home).*

  Extension Clear a space or move to the playground. Learners stand at one side. Stand at the other side and say *I'm Mr Wolf. I want to eat you.* Mime to demonstrate how the game works.
- Learners ask *What time is it, Mr Wolf?* when you turn your back to them. This starts the game. Say a time with *o'clock*, e.g. *It's three o'clock.* Learners take three steps towards you. They ask *What time is it, Mr Wolf?* Say a time, e.g. *It's six o'clock.* Learners take six steps.
- Continue in this way, with the learners getting closer. At a certain point, when they ask *What time is it, Mr Wolf?*, say *It's dinner time!* and turn around. Run after the learners and try to 'catch' one. If you catch a learner, he/she becomes 'Mr Wolf' and the game starts again.

Pupil's Book, page 17

mission in action!

Show your daily routine chart to the class.

- Say *Open your Pupil's Books at page 17.* Point to the Mission box or show learners the last stage of the digital Mission poster. Say *Let's put our Mission in action!* Say *Show your daily routine chart to the class.*
- Read the instructions. Hold up your example chart and do a presentation yourself, stage by stage.
- Give learners time to practise in pairs. Monitor and help. Ask learners questions to prepare them for the last part of the presentation, e.g. *Do you have a shower or a bath?*
- Learners take turns to present their charts to the class or to a group of classmates. Encourage other learners to ask questions at the end.
- Learners take their charts home and can use them to help organise their day. When they have completed each activity in their daily routine, they can fold up the flap. (They may like to draw a tick on the back of each flap.)

  Note: You may want to spread the presentations over several lessons.

Self-assessment

- **SA** Say *Did you like our 'Make a daily routine chart' Mission? A lot?* (cheer) *It's OK?* (smile) *Or not much?* (shake your head and shrug) Encourage learners to show how they feel.
- Ask *Which was your favourite stage of the Mission? Making the chart? Writing? Thinking about our planet? Showing the class?* Learners respond.
- Say *Our next Mission is 'Plan a fun activities timetable for two friends'.* Explain the meaning of *timetable*. Say *How can we do better? Shall we learn more words?* Say *Put your hand up if you want to learn more words.* (Learners can raise hands.) *More speaking? Writing? Reading? Listening?*

Activity Book, page 17

See pages TB120–132

Activity Book, page 6

- Review *My unit goals*. Ask *How is your Mission?* Learners reflect and choose a smiley face for *My mission diary* the final stage.
- Point to the sunflower. Learners read the 'can do' statements and tick them if they agree they have achieved them. They colour each leaf green if they are very confident or orange if they think they need more practice.
- Point to the word stack sign. Ask learners to look back at the unit and find at least five new words they have learnt. They write them in their word stack.

Ending the lesson

- **SA** Go back to the completion stage on the digital Mission poster. Add a tick or invite a learner to do it. Use self-assessment (see Introduction).
- Give out a completion sticker.
- Tell learners *You have finished your Mission! Well done!*

mission in action!

Show your daily routine chart to the class.

My mission diary
Activity Book page 6

★ **Say 'Hello' and show your chart.**

Hello. I'm Alicia and this is my daily routine chart.

★ **Talk about your daily activities.**

I get up at seven o'clock.

★ **Point to your 'Think' bubbles and say what you do.**

I turn off the tap when I clean my teeth.

★ **Answer questions.**

What time do you have lunch?

I have lunch at one o'clock.

2 My week

1 **Watch the video. Draw an activity which you like doing.**

mission **Plan a fun activities timetable for two friends**

In this unit I will:

1. Work with a partner to talk to two friends about free time activities.
2. Make a fun activities timetable for a week.
3. Write important information about the activities.

★ Give our timetable to our two friends.

Unit 2 learning outcomes

In Unit 2, learners learn to:

- talk about the days of the week and free time activities
- ask and answer questions using *How often … ?* and adverbs of frequency
- use *must* and *mustn't*
- learn about being safe when doing exercise and sports
- read a personal narrative and think about the consequences of their actions

Materials items needed for hobbies (e.g. swimming goggles) (optional), paper, video, coloured pens or pencils, digital Mission poster, an example of a timetable for a week with free time activities marked (optional), a copy of the Mission worksheet (Teacher's Resource Book page 24)

Self-assessment

- **SA** Say *Open your Pupil's Books at page 18.* Read the title and check comprehension of *week.* Focus on the pictures and say *These are all activities we can do in our free time. What are the children doing?* (e.g. *Reading / listening to music / watching television / shopping*) *What do you like doing?* Learners suggest activities, e.g. *riding my bike, playing basketball, going to the beach.* Use self-assessment (see Introduction). Say *OK. Let's learn.*

Warm-up

- Show an object used for a free time activity, e.g. swimming goggles, or draw a picture on the board. Say *I use these in my free time. Free time is when you don't need to go to work or school. What do I like doing?* (*Swimming*) Repeat with different items.
- Give out paper. Learners quickly draw an object used for an activity they know in English. They play the game in pairs or as a class.

Pupil's Book, page 18

1 Watch the video. Draw an activity which you like doing.

- Say *In this unit we're talking about activities.* Say *Let's watch the video.* To introduce the topic of the unit, play the video.
- Say *Look at page 18.* Show the space on the page. Say *Draw an activity which you like doing*. Monitor and check. Tell each learner the name of their activity in English if they haven't learnt the word yet.

Fast finishers Learners write a short sentence for their activity, e.g. *I like skateboarding (in my free time).*

mission Plan a fun activities timetable for two friends

- Point to the Mission box or the digital Mission poster and say *Our Mission is: Plan a fun activities timetable for two friends.* Show learners an example of a timetable or draw one on the board. Say *A timetable has days and times. We can plan a week. I look and ask 'What am I doing today in the morning?' 'What am I doing in the afternoon?' It helps us. 'Oh! Look! On Tuesday I play tennis.'*
- Say *Point to number 1. Work with a partner to talk to two friends about free time activities.* Show the Mission worksheet, if available, or draw a three-column table on the board with two or three activities in the left column (e.g. *play football, ride your bike, watch TV*) and the names of two learners at the top of the columns on the right. Say *You ask two friends about their free time and complete the table.*
- Say *Point to number 2. Make a fun activities timetable for a week.* Explain that learners will make a timetable for the friends they talked to in Stage 1.
- Say *Point to number 3. Write important information about the activities.* Say *In my free time I ride my bike. What do I need to wear? I need a helmet.* Tell learners they are going to think about the activities in the timetable and give their friends information about what to do/wear to be safe.
- Say *The last stage is 'Give our timetable to our two friends.'* Say *You need to give your friends the timetable and talk about it.*
- Say *This is our Mission.* Go through the stages of the Mission again.
- For ideas on monitoring and assessment, see Introduction.

Activity Book, page 18

My unit goals

- Help learners to complete the unit goals. See notes on page TB6.
- You can go back to these unit goals at the end of each Mission stage during the unit and review them.

Ending the lesson

- Say *Listen and mime.* Say a free time activity. Learners do the action. Hobbies and sports to revise (from level 1): *play football/tennis/badminton/basketball/baseball/hockey, ride a bike, play the piano/guitar, swim, watch TV, listen to music, run, skateboard.*

Stronger learners Repeat the activity in pairs.

Learning outcomes By the end of the lesson, learners will be able to talk about days of the week.

New language days of the week, *week, after, before, book club, feed, on (Wednesday(s)), swimming pool, swimsuit, take turns, (at the) weekend*

Recycled language sports and hobbies, *at home, classroom, day, favourite, fish, go for a swim, need, outside, play, read, school, sport, today, towel, write, have got, I love …-ing, So do I.*

Materials Days of the week flashcards, audio, video

Warm-up

- Write *My week* on the board. Tell learners they have 30 seconds to think of four things they do in their free time every week. Check ideas and write them on the board.

Presentation

- Say *There are seven days in a week.* Hold up each flashcard and say the day. Learners repeat. Display them in turn. Learners say the words.
- Put the flashcards on the board in order. Ask *Which is the first day of the week? Which is the last?* Say *Monday comes before Tuesday. Tuesday comes before Wednesday. Which day comes before Friday?* (*Thursday*) Ask more questions with *before*, then present *after* in the same way.

Pupil's Book, page 19

1 1.21 Listen and point. Draw a happy face on Jim's favourite school days.

- Say *Open your Pupil's Books at page 19. Who can you see?* (*Jim, Jenny, Tom, Eva and a teacher*) *Where are they?* (*In the classroom*) *What are they looking at?* (*A timetable*) *Who's in the small picture?* (*Cameron and a fish*) Ask *Where's the small tractor? Can you find it?* Learners point.
- Read the caption. Ask *Where's Monday?* Learners point. Say *Listen and point to the days.* Play the audio.

Track 1.21

Jim, Jenny, Tom and Eva are at school. They're talking about their school week.

Teacher: Good morning. Let's look at our school week for this year. Today's Monday and we haven't got any activities outside school today.
Jim: We're in the classroom all day.
Jenny: Hmm. We've got sport on Tuesdays and Thursdays. We can play badminton or basketball. I love playing basketball.
Tom: So do I! And look! We go for a swim at the swimming pool on Wednesdays.
Eva: Great!
Teacher: That's right, on Wednesdays you need your swimsuit and a towel.
Eva: Do we need our swimming caps too?
Teacher: Yes, I think that's a good idea.
Tom: Look, Jim! On Fridays we've got book club. You love reading.
Teacher: Yes, in book club we write about our book of the week.
Jim: Fantastic! Mondays and Fridays are my favourite school days.
Teacher: We haven't got school on Saturdays and Sundays and we need to feed Fred the fish every day.
Eva: Do we take turns to feed him at home at the weekend?
Teacher: Yes, please.
Jenny: I can take Fred home on Friday. We can feed him this weekend.
Jim: What about Cameron? Our cat loves eating fish!

- Say *Your favourite day is the day you like more than the other days. What's your favourite day? Why?*
- Point to the partially drawn faces and say *Listen and draw a happy face on Jim's favourite school days.* Play the audio again. Check answers.
- Point to the swimming pool. Ask *What do the children need on Wednesday?* Revise *towel* and teach *swimsuit.*

Key: Monday, Friday

2 1.22 Say the chant.

- Say *Listen and say the chant.* Play the audio or video. Learners point and chant. Then divide the class into groups to do the chant as a round.

Track 1.22

Monday, Tuesday, [x2]
Wednesday, Thursday, [x2]
Friday! Friday!
Saturday, Sunday. [x2]

3 1.23 Listen and say the days.

- Focus on the timetable and ask, e.g. *When do they swim?*
- Play the audio. Pause for learners to say the day(s).

Track 1.23

1 They can play badminton or basketball.
2 They write about the book of the week.
3 They don't go to school.
4 They need a swimsuit and a towel.
5 They're in the classroom.
6 They go for a swim.

Key: 1 Tuesday, Thursday 2 Friday 3 Saturday, Sunday 4 Wednesday 5 Monday 6 Wednesday

Activity Book, page 19

See pages TB120–132

Ending the lesson

- **SA** Show the Days of the week flashcards. Ask *Do you know the words?* Use self-assessment (see Introduction). Learners show how they feel.

1 1.21 **Listen and point. Draw a happy face on Jim's favourite school days.**

2 1.22 **Say the chant.**

3 1.23 **Listen and say the days.**

The Friendly Farm

1.24

1
Friday afternoon and we're home from school! Let's put Fred here on the table.
Cameron can get on the table! Let's put him up there on the shelf.
2
Jim and Jenny have got a new pet … but only for the weekend. It's the school fish, but it needs food on Saturdays and Sundays too.
3
How often do they feed it?
Once a day, … in the evening.
Hmm, they feed us twice a day: in the morning and the evening.
4
How often does this fish wash its face?
It never washes its face, Shelly. It …
Fish live in water, Shelly. They're always in water.
5
Hmm. Fish are always in water. Can they talk?
Birds often talk. Cameron, does the fish ever talk?
I don't know. No, I don't think so.
6
So, fish. Do you ever talk?
Yes, I do … I sometimes talk, but I never talk to cats.

1 1.25 **Who says it? Listen and say the name.**

Learning outcomes By the end of the lesson, learners will be able to understand when they hear *How often … ?* and adverbs of frequency.

New language *shelf, How often … ?, once/twice a day, always, often, sometimes, never, Do you ever … ?, I don't think so.*

Recycled language days of the week, *at home/school, bird, face, feed, fish, food, here, live, (in the) morning/afternoon/evening, need, on, pet, put, table, talk, wash, weekend, I don't know, can, Let's …*, present simple

Materials Days of the week flashcards, audio, video

Warm-up

- Practise the days of the week with the flashcards. Mix them up and hand them to seven learners. They come to the front and arrange themselves in order. The others help.
- Put the flashcards away and ask, e.g. *Which day comes before Thursday? Which day comes after Saturday? Which day is between Tuesday and Thursday?*

  Extra support Leave the flashcards on the board while you ask questions.
- **SA** Use self-assessment to check how well learners think they understand the vocabulary. See Introduction.

Presentation

- Write *always, often, sometimes, never* on the board. Mime and say *I brush my hair on Monday, Tuesday, Wednesday, Thursday, Friday, Saturday and Sunday. Every day. I* ***always*** *brush my hair.* Write the sentence next to *always*. Say *I walk to school four days a week – Tuesday, Wednesday, Thursday and Friday. I* ***often*** *walk to school.* Present *sometimes* and *never* in the same way.
- Say *These words tell us how often we do things. How often do you brush your hair? How often do you walk to school?* Write *How often?* on the board.

Pupil's Book, page 20

1.24 The Friendly Farm song

- Play the introductory song at the beginning of the cartoon story. Learners listen and sing.

Track 1.24
See The Friendly Farm song on page TB5

1.24 The Friendly Farm

- Say *Open your Pupil's Books at page 20.* Ask *Where are they? (In the living room) What can you see? (A table, a TV,* etc.*) Where's Cameron? (On a chair)* Use the picture to teach *shelf*.
- Point to the fish and ask *What's this? (A fish) What's his name? (Fred) Is Fred at school? (No, at home with Jim and Jenny)* Say *The children need to look after Fred at the weekend.* Ask *Have you got any animals at home? How do you look after your pets?* Revise *feed*.
- Point to the rest of the story and ask, e.g. *Where's Cameron now? (On the farm) Who is he talking to? (The other animals)*
- Ask *Does the fish talk?* Play the audio or video. Learners listen and read. Check answers and explain the meaning of *ever* (*Do you ever talk?*). Check comprehension of *sometimes*.

Track 1.24
The Friendly Farm song + see cartoon on Pupil's Book page 20

- Play the audio or video again. Pause after each picture and ask questions: 1: *Which day is it? (Friday) Is it the morning? (No, the afternoon) Why can't they put Fred on the table? (Because Cameron can get on the table – and he loves eating fish!)* 2: *When does Fred need food? (Every day)* 3: *When do Jim and Jenny feed Fred? (Once a day / In the evening) When do they feed the other animals? (Twice a day / In the morning and the evening)* Explain the meaning of *once/twice a day*. 4: *Does the fish wash its face? (No – it lives in water)* 5: *Do birds talk? (Yes, often)* 6: *Why doesn't Fred talk to cats? (Because cats want to eat him)*

1 1.25 Who says it? Listen and say the name.

- Say *Listen and say the name.* Play the audio and pause for learners to say the name.

Track 1.25

1	Henrietta:	How often do they feed it?
2	Fred/fish:	I sometimes talk, but I never talk to cats.
3	Harry:	Fish are always in water. Can they talk?
4	Jim:	Cameron can get on the table!
5	Gracie:	Fish live in water, Shelly. They're always in water.
6	Cameron:	It's the school fish, but it needs food on Saturdays and Sundays too.
7	Shelly:	How often does this fish wash its face?
8	Rocky:	Birds often talk. Cameron, does the fish ever talk?

Key: See names in audioscript

Activity Book, page 20

See pages TB120–132

Ending the lesson

- Put learners into pairs to role play picture 1. Play the audio. Learners repeat the speech bubbles for Jim and Jenny and act deciding where to put Fred.

Learning outcomes By the end of the lesson, learners will be able to ask and answer questions using *How often … ?* and adverbs of frequency.

New language *How often do you clean your teeth? I always clean them after breakfast, lunch and dinner. Do you ever get up late? No, I never get up late. always, often, sometimes, never, at night, late*

Recycled language daily routines, days of the week, sports and hobbies, *breakfast, burger, clean your teeth, dinner, feed, fish, go for a swim, lunch, once/twice a (week)*

Materials pieces of paper with adverbs of frequency, audio, Sports and hobbies flashcards from level 1, Mission worksheets (Teacher's Resource Book page 24), digital Mission poster

Warm-up

- Revise *always, often, sometimes* and *never.* Put pieces of paper with the four adverbs on different walls. Say a sentence, e.g. *I do my homework.* Learners decide how often they do that thing and go to the right wall (or point).

Presentation

- Mime and say *Look! I'm sleeping. It's seven o'clock … It's eight o'clock … Oh, no!* Mime waking up. Point to a clock. Say *It's time for school! I'm late!*
- Ask *Do you ever get up late for school? How often do you get up late? Sometimes? Never?*

Pupil's Book, page 21

1.26 Gracie's Grammar

- Say *Open your Pupil's Books at page 21.* Write the questions and answers on the board.
- Play the audio. Pause for learners to repeat.

Track 1.26
See Pupil's Book page 21

1 1.27 Listen and stick. Then look, read and write.

- Play the audio. Learners point to the correct sticker.
- Check they understand what the ticks and crosses mean. Play the audio again. Learners stick in the stickers.

Track 1.27

1 Woman: Do you ever go for a swim, Peter?
Peter: Yes, I go with my class on Mondays, Wednesdays and Fridays. On Saturdays I go to the swimming pool with my parents.
Woman: Yes, I see! You often go for a swim!
2 Man: How often do you feed your fish, Clare?
Clare: I feed it once a day, every day, in the evening.
Man: Do your mum or dad, or your brother, sometimes feed it?
Clare: No, they don't. I always feed it. It's my fish.
3 Woman: Do you always have a shower in the morning, Peter?
Peter: No, I don't. I sometimes have a shower in the morning, before school, on Mondays, Tuesdays, Wednesdays and Thursdays, but I have a shower at night on Fridays, Saturdays and Sundays.
4 Man: How often do you have burgers for breakfast, Clare?
Clare: I never have burgers for breakfast. I always have cake and milk.

- Say *Now look, read and write*. Check answers.

Key: 2 always 3 sometimes 4 never

mission Stage 1

- Point to the Mission box or show learners the first stage of the digital Mission poster: *Work with a partner to talk to two friends about free time activities.*
- Review hobbies and sports and write them on the board.
- Learners complete the worksheet task in the Teacher's Resource Book (page 24). See teaching notes on TRB page 17.
- Alternatively, if you do not have the Teacher's Resource Book, draw a three-column table on the board with activities in the first column and names of two learners at the top of the other columns. Ask these learners, e.g. *How often do you (play basketball)?* Note their answers in the second and third columns.
- Put learners into groups of four (two pairs in each group). Pairs choose activities to write in their table and write the names of the other learners.
- Pairs take turns to ask and answer and complete their table.

Activity Book, page 21

See pages TB120–132

Activity Book, page 18

- Review *My unit goals*. Ask *How is your Mission?* Learners reflect and choose a smiley face for *My mission diary 1.*

Ending the lesson

- **SA** Go back to Stage 1 on the digital Mission poster. Say *We talked about free time activities.* Add a tick to the 'Work with a partner … ' stage. Use self-assessment (see Introduction).
- Give out a completion sticker.

Gracie's Grammar

1.26

How often do you clean your teeth?

I **always** clean them after breakfast, lunch and dinner.

Do you **ever** get up late?

No, I **never** get up late.

always ✓✓✓ often ✓✓ sometimes ✓✗ never ✗

1 Listen and stick. Then look, read and write.

1.27

always ✓✓✓

often ✓✓

sometimes ✓✗

never ✗

1 Peter ___often___ goes for a swim.

2 Clare ________ feeds her fish.

3 Peter ________ has a shower at night.

4 Clare ________ has burgers for breakfast.

mission STAGE 1

Work with a partner to talk to two friends about free time activities.

- In pairs, write free time activities.
- Ask two friends how often they do each activity.

How often do you play basketball?

I play basketball on Tuesdays and Thursdays.

My mission diary
Activity Book page 18

1 1.28 Listen and number. Then sing the song.

How often … how often …
do you [1]listen to music?
How often … how often …
do you [2]write an email?

Do you ever … do you ever …
[3]**go skating** in the park?
Do you ever … do you ever …
[4]**read a comic** in the car?

How often … how often …

Do you ever … do you ever …
[5]**go shopping** with your dad?
Do you ever … do you ever …
[6]**watch films** that are bad?

A CD, a CD –
do you ever [7]**listen to a CD**?
DVD, DVD –
do you ever [8]**watch a DVD**?

How often … how often …

2 Ask and answer. Use *often*, *sometimes* or *never*.

How often do you go skating? ________
How often do you write emails? ________
How often do you go shopping? ________
How often do you watch films? ________
How often do you listen to CDs? ________

How often do you read comics?

Learning outcomes By the end of the lesson, learners will have practised the language through song.

New language *go skating/shopping, listen to a CD / music, read a comic, watch a DVD/film, write an email*

Recycled language sports and hobbies, adverbs of frequency, *Do you ever … ?, How often do you … ?*, present simple

Materials six or seven questions with *How often … ?* on pieces of paper (e.g. *How often do you wear sunglasses? How often do you listen to the radio? How often do you go swimming? How often do you eat chocolate?*), Free time activities flashcards, a real comic (optional), audio, video

Warm-up

- Pick ten learners to stand in a line at the front of the class. Choose a question from the ones you have prepared on paper, e.g. *How often do you go to the countryside?*
- Whisper it to the first learner in the line. The learner whispers it to the next learner. They continue whispering down the line. The last learner asks the question out loud.
- See if it is the same as the original question. Show learners the question and say it aloud so they can hear if it is correct. Say *Well done!* or *Let's try again.* When the learner says the question correctly let him/her choose a classmate to answer.
- Repeat with new learners and questions.

  Alternative Write *How often do you … ?* on the board. Say *watch TV* and point to a learner. He/She asks a classmate *How often do you watch TV?* The second learner answers. Say a different prompt, e.g. *wear jeans* for the second learner to make a *How often … ?* question. Weave the question around the class, changing the prompt each time (e.g. *wear a hat, play badminton, eat fruit, help at home*).

Presentation

- Introduce the new free time activities using the flashcards. Show a real comic, if possible.
- Show the flashcards. Learners do appropriate mimes. Do a mime. Learners say the activity.
- Ask *Which film do you often watch? Which type of music do you never listen to? Where can you go skating in (name of town)? Who do you write emails to? Do you like going shopping?*
- **SA** Use self-assessment to check how well learners think they understand the vocabulary. See Introduction.

Pupil's Book, page 22

1 (1.28) Listen and number. Then sing the song.

- Say *Open your Pupil's Books at page 22.* Say a sentence and learners point to the correct picture, e.g. *She's listening to music. / She's skating. / She's watching a DVD.*, etc.
- Say *Look at number 1.* Point and show learners that number 1 is written next to the picture of the girl listening to music. Say *Let's listen and write the numbers.*
- Play the audio or video. Learners listen and write numbers in the boxes. Check answers.

Track 1.28

Rocky: I'm Rocky-Doodle-Doo and here's our song for today: *How often?*

See song on Pupil's Book page 22

Key: a 6 b 3 (c 1) d 8 e 2 f 4 g 5 h 7

- Say each activity from the song and do the action. Learners repeat the words and actions.
- Play the audio or video again. Learners listen and sing, doing actions. Once they have practised the song, ask them to stand up and perform it.

(1.29) **Extension** Once learners are confidently singing along, try singing the karaoke version as a class.

2 Ask and answer. Use *often, sometimes* or *never*.

- Demonstrate doing a survey. Pretend you have a clipboard and ask a learner *How often do you go to the beach?* Mime writing down the answer.
- Focus on the clipboard in the Pupil's Book and say *Ask and answer.* Put learners into pairs. They write their partner's answers on the lines.

  Stronger learners Write *once/twice a week, once/ twice a month, once/twice a year* on the board. Check comprehension. Learners can answer with these time phrases as well as the adverbs.
- Show the picture of Rocky in the bottom right-hand corner. Read out the question. Ask for a show of hands for each answer*: I often read comics. / I sometimes read comics. / I never read comics.* Repeat for different materials: *How often do you read a book / an e-book / a magazine?*

  Fast finishers Write sentences about how often they read the different materials.

Activity Book, page 22

See pages TB120–132

Ending the lesson

- **SA** Repeat the self-assessment used after the Presentation to see how well learners think they understand the vocabulary. Is there any change?
- Play the song again. Learners join in and do the actions.

Learning outcomes By the end of the lesson, learners will be able to use *must* and *mustn't*.

New language *What must I do? You mustn't wear your skates in the house. You must put them in the cupboard. helmet, roller skating, rules, skate* (n, v)

Recycled language days of the week, free time activities, *birthday, cupboard, do (your) homework, go shopping, listen, park, present, put, street, swimming pool, talk, wear,* adverbs of frequency, *can/can't*

Materials Free time activities flashcards, cycling helmet (optional), audio, worksheets/tables from Mission Stage 1 lesson, an example weekly timetable, paper, digital Mission poster

Warm-up

- Mime a free time activity. Learners guess. Show the flashcard to confirm the answer.

Presentation

- Say *I sometimes ride my bike to school. When I ride my bike there are rules.* Write *rules* on the board. Say *When I'm on my bike I must wear a helmet.* Mime or show a real helmet. Say *I mustn't ride on the pavement. I must ride in the street.* Draw a picture to show the meaning. Say *Rules are things we must or mustn't do.*

Pupil's Book, page 23

1 (1.30) Where can Jack go with his birthday present? Listen and tick ✓.

- Say *Open your Pupil's Books at page 23.* Ask *Where's this?* (*Street, park / skate park, swimming pool*)
- Play the audio. Learners listen and tick. Check answers.

Track 1.30

Jack: Mum, can I have some roller skates for my birthday … please?
Mum: Hmm … that's a nice idea, but first we must talk about the rules.
Jack: The rules? What must I do?
Mum: You mustn't skate in the street.
Jack: OK. I must skate in the park.
Mum: That's right, but in the roller skating area in the park, OK? And remember, you must wear a helmet on your head.
Oh, and you mustn't wear your skates in the house. You must put them in the cupboard.
Jack: All right. So, can I have some skates, please, Mum?
Mum: OK, but you must remember they're for your birthday, not for now.
Jack: Yes, of course, thanks, Mum.

Key: Picture 2

- Ask *What is Jack's birthday present?* (*Skates / Roller skates*) Draw a picture of some roller skates. Ask different learners *Do you ever go roller skating?*

(1.31) Gracie's Grammar

- Write the questions and answers on the board.
- Play the audio. Pause for learners to repeat.

Track 1.31
See Pupil's Book page 23

2 Read and circle to make class rules.

- Say *Let's think about rules in the classroom. What must you do? Must you put up your hand to speak?* (*Yes, we must.*) Learners suggest rules with *must/mustn't*.
- Learners read and circle. Check answers.

Key: 2 mustn't 3 must 4 mustn't

3 Talk to your friends. Make more class rules.

- In pairs, learners write more class rules in their notebooks.
  Extension Make a poster with the rules.

mission Stage 2

- Show learners the second stage of the Mission poster: *Make a fun activities timetable for a week*. Show learners an example of a weekly timetable.
- Learners work in their Stage 1 pairs. They draw a weekly timetable on a piece of paper and add activities for the pair of learners they worked with in Stage 1. They should put some activities that the other learners already do (referring to their Stage 1 tables) and some new. Make sure they leave space for adding safety information (see Stage 3).
  Extra support Write the days of the week and possible activities on the board.

Activity Book, page 23

See pages TB120–132

Activity Book, page 18

- Review *My unit goals*. Ask *How is your Mission?* Learners reflect and choose a smiley face for *My mission diary 2*.

Ending the lesson

- **SA** Go back to Stage 2 on the digital Mission poster. Add a tick to the 'Make a fun activities timetable' stage. Use self-assessment (see Introduction).
- Give out a completion sticker.

1 1.30 Where can Jack go with his birthday present? Listen and tick ✓.

1

2

3

1.31 Gracie's Grammar

What **must** I do? You **mustn't** wear your skates in the house.
You **must** put them in the cupboard.

2 Read and circle to make class rules.

1 We **must** / **mustn't** listen to the teacher.
2 We **must** / **mustn't** talk when the teacher is talking.
3 We **must** / **mustn't** do our homework.
4 We **must** / **mustn't** put our feet on the chairs.

3 Talk to your friends. Make more class rules.

mission STAGE 2

Make a fun activities timetable for a week.

STAGE 2

- In pairs, make a timetable for a week.
- Talk about your friends' answers. Write a fun activity for each day.

They never go roller skating.

Let's write 'skate' on Sunday.

My mission diary
Activity Book page 18

Let's be healthy!

1 **Watch the video.**

2 **Tick ✓ the activities that you do.**

1

2

3

4

5

6

3 1.32 **Read, look and complete. Then listen and check.**

helmet

elbow and knee pads

Exercise is good for us, but sometimes there are accidents. It's very important to wear the correct clothes to protect our bodies.

We wear [1] elbow and knee pads to protect our elbows and knees.

We wear [2] ____________ to protect our hands.

We wear a [3] ____________ to protect our head.

We wear [4] ____________ to protect our eyes.

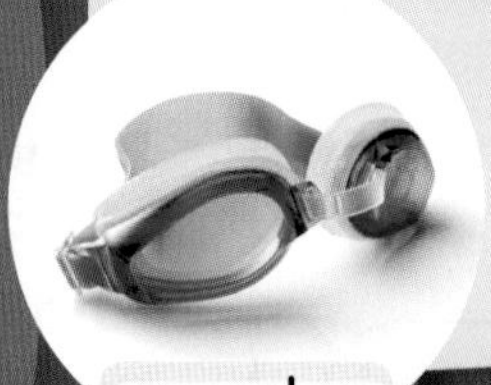
goggles

gloves

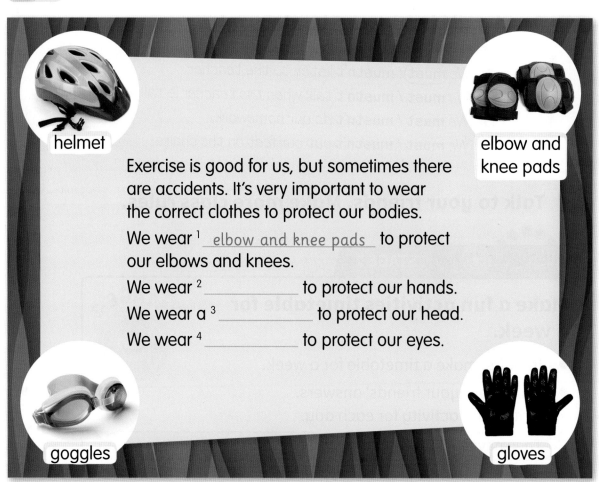

Learning outcomes By the end of the lesson, learners will have learnt about being safe when doing exercise and sports.

New language *accident, body (bodies), elbow/knee pads, exercise* (n), *gloves, goggles, healthy, protect, safe*

Recycled language free time activities, parts of the body, *clothes, helmet, wear,* adverbs of frequency

Materials video, audio, pictures from Digital photo bank of people wearing protective clothing for hobbies, e.g. a beekeeper, an ice-hockey player, a climber (optional)

Warm-up

- Review parts of the body by giving instructions and doing actions for learners to follow. Say *Stand up. Touch your head. Wave your hand. Shake your arm. Stamp your feet. Close your eyes. Open your eyes. Touch your ears. Lift your leg. Put your arms up. Put your arms down. Touch your nose.* Practise several times. Then give instructions without doing the actions yourself, getting faster and faster.

  Alternative Make this a competitive game. The learner who is last to do the correct action is 'out'.

  Stronger learners Play the same game in pairs.

Presentation

- Ask *What do you like doing in your free time? Do you wear special clothes to do it? Why?*
- Say *Let's find out more about special clothes and equipment.*

Pupil's Book, page 24

1 Watch the video.

- Say *Let's watch the video.* Learners watch the video about being safe when doing exercise and sports and answer the questions at the end.

2 Tick ✓ the activities that you do.

- Say *Open your Pupil's Books at page 24. Look at the pictures. What are these free time activities? (1: Riding a bike, 2: swimming, 3: playing tennis, 4: roller skating, 5: playing basketball, 6: playing football) Which do you do? Tick.* Learners look and tick. Check answers. Learners say, e.g. *I ride a bike and play basketball.*

  Extension List the activities on the board, and for each one ask *Who likes (riding a bike)?* Learners put up their hands. Count hands with the class. Write the results on the board. Ask different learners *Which day(s) do you (ride a bike)?*

  Stronger learners Say or write sentences about how often they do each of the activities, with adverbs of frequency or *once/twice a (week/month/year).*

3 1.32 Read, look and complete. Then listen and check.

- Focus on the photos. Learners practise saying the words. Ask *Which part of the body does a helmet protect?* (*Head*) Say *It protects your head.* Repeat with the other items. Teach *elbows* and *knees.* Ask different learners *Have you got a helmet? When do you wear it? Have you got any (gloves / elbow pads / knee pads / goggles)? When do you wear them?*
- Read the text and the sentences with the class and go through the example. Check comprehension of *accidents* and *bodies.* Learners complete the sentences individually.
- Play the audio. Learners listen, read and check their answers.

Track 1.32
See Pupil's Book page 24

Key: 2 gloves 3 helmet 4 goggles

Extension Ask about different items of clothing: *Why do we wear sunglasses?* (*To protect our eyes*) *Why do we wear caps or sun hats?* (*To protect our heads*) *Why do we wear walking boots?* (*To protect our feet*) Show pictures of people wearing different protective clothing, for example a beekeeper, an ice-hockey player, a climber. Point to different items and ask *Why is he/she wearing this?* (*To protect his/her (face).*)

Activity Book, page 24

See pages TB120–132

Ending the lesson

- Give instructions for learners to get ready for a sport or hobby which requires protective clothing. Mime as you do so. They stand up and follow your instructions/mimes, then tell you which activity they are ready for, e.g. *Put on your trainers. Put on some long shorts. Put on elbow pads, knee pads and big shoulder pads. Put on a helmet. Put in a mouth guard. Pick up the ball.* (*American football*)

  Alternative Learners work in pairs. They write the days of the week on small pieces of paper. They mix them up and practise putting them in order. Monitor and ask *Which day comes after (Saturday)? What do you do on (Sunday)?*

Learning outcomes By the end of the lesson, learners will be able to talk about being safe when doing exercise and sports.

New language *bones, do exercise, exercise* (v), *horse riding, (get) hot, hurt, muscles, skin, sun cream, sweat* (v), *warm up*

Recycled language days of the week, free time activities, parts of the body, *beach, body, boots, drink, helmet, help, look after, move, outside, play (sport), protect, remember, safe, sun, use, water, must*

Materials cue cards with the name of an activity and items needed (optional), audio, timetables from Mission Stage 2 lesson, paper, coloured pens or pencils, scissors, glue, digital Mission poster

Warm-up

- Draw pictures of a helmet, goggles, elbow and knee pads and gloves on the board (or mime putting on each item). Learners say the words. Write them on the board.
- Learners work in pairs. One learner gives the other learner instructions for putting on items of clothing for a sport/ hobby, e.g. *Put on a helmet. Put on elbow and knee pads. Get your skateboard.* The other learner mimes and then acts out playing the sport / doing the activity.

  Extra support Provide cue cards with the name of the activity and the items needed.

Pupil's Book, page 25

4 1.33 Listen and read. Then read and say *yes* or *no*.

- Say *Open your Pupil's Books at page 25. Look at the pictures. What are they doing*? Teach *warm up* (*He's warming up.*) and *sun cream* (*She's putting on sun cream.*). Revise *drink water.*
- Ask *What happens to our bodies when we exercise?* (*We get hot.*) Teach *sweat.* Say *We get sweat on our skin.* Teach *skin.*
- Read the instructions and sentences 1–4.
- Play the audio. Learners listen and read and decide if the answer to each sentence is *yes* or *no*. Check answers. Check comprehension of *bones* and *muscles.*

  Track 1.33
  See Pupil's Book page 25
- Ask *Do you use sun cream when you do sport? Do you always drink when you do exercise? Do you warm up?*

  Extension Ask learners to show you some of the warm-up exercises they do.

Key: 1 no 2 yes 3 no 4 yes

5 Talk to a partner about your favourite sport or activity.

- Read the instructions and the speech bubble. Check comprehension of *horse riding.* Learners plan what to say using the speech bubble sentences as a model.
- Learners take turns to tell each other about their favourite activity.
- Ask learners to tell the class about their partner's activity.

  Extra support Write the prompts on the board (*I like … I go on … I must wear/use/drink …*) and give more examples before the pair work.

mission Stage 3

- Show the class the third stage of the Mission poster: *Write important information about the activities.*
- Put learners into the same pairs as for Stage 2. They look at the timetable they made for the other pair and think about important information/advice they can give their friends. Say *Write three sentences.* Focus on the example in the Pupil's Book and ask learners to complete it. (*For skating, they must wear knee pads, elbow pads, gloves and helmets.*)
- Hand out paper, scissors and glue and say *Write your sentences. Cut them out and stick them on the timetable.* Monitor and help. Learners may like to draw pictures or write their sentences in a shape (e.g. a helmet). Check learners' sentences before they stick them on their timetables.

  Extra support Ask for examples for different activities and write them on the board, e.g. *play tennis – You must use sun cream and drink water.*

Activity Book, page 25

See pages TB120–132

Activity Book, page 18

- Review *My unit goals.* Ask *How is your Mission?* Learners reflect and choose a smiley face for *My mission diary 3.*

Ending the lesson

- **SA** Go back to Stage 3 on the digital Mission poster. Add a tick to the 'Write important information about the activities' stage. Use self-assessment (see Introduction).
- Give out a completion sticker.

4 1.33 Listen and read. Then read and say *yes* or *no*.

Let's warm up!
Our bones and muscles help us move. Before we play a sport or do exercise, it's important that we warm up our muscles so we don't hurt them.

Drink water!
When we exercise, we get hot and we sweat. Our body loses water when we sweat. Remember to drink water when you exercise.

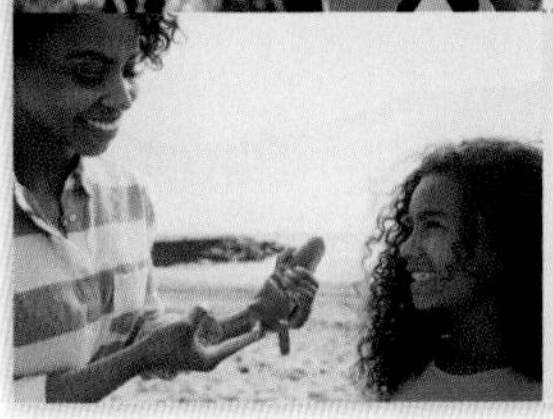

Use sun cream!
You put on sun cream when you go to the beach. But do you use it when you play sport? Protect your skin from the sun when you're outside. It's important to put on sun cream when it isn't a very hot day too.

1 We warm up before exercise to look after our skin.
2 We drink water when we get hot.
3 We use sun cream when we play inside.
4 Sun cream is always important when you're outside.

5 Talk to a partner about your favourite sport or activity.

I like horse riding. I go on Saturdays. I must wear a helmet and boots.

mission STAGE 3

Write important information about the activities.

- In pairs, think about the activities. What must your friends do to be safe?
- Write three ideas for their timetable.

For skating, they must wear knee pads, …

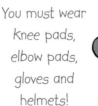

You must wear knee pads, elbow pads, gloves and helmets!

My mission diary
Activity Book page 18

1 **Read the question at the start. Tell a classmate your answer and say why.**

A bad, bad Monday morning

1.34

How often do you want to sleep and not get up for school?

I sometimes do that. I turn off my alarm and go to sleep. I want to tell you about a very bad Monday morning …

Suddenly, Mum's standing over me.

She's shouting and she's pulling off my blanket.

'Alex! It's eight o'clock. We mustn't be late! You have a presentation at school today!'

I jump out of bed and get dressed.

Then I run to the bathroom, but my big sister's using it.

I run downstairs to the other bathroom. My dad's using it.

Learning outcomes By the end of the lesson, learners will have read a personal narrative.

New language *alarm, assembly hall, blanket, downstairs, drive, go to sleep, leave (= go out), lights (= traffic lights), mirror, now, presentation, shout, suddenly*

Recycled language daily routines, days of the week, family, parts of the body, time (o'clock), *bathroom, breakfast, chocolate, classmate, fruit, happy, kitchen, late, milk, shirt, turn off, use,* adverbs of frequency, *How often … ?, must/mustn't,* present continuous, present simple, *want to*

Materials Daily routines flashcards, Free time activities flashcards, pieces of paper with verb phrases for each pair of learners, an alarm clock (optional), audio

Warm-up

- Revise daily routines and free time activities with the flashcards.
- Write a sentence with an adverb about yourself on paper, but keep it secret, e.g. *I never eat cake.* Ask *How often do I eat cake?* Learners guess, e.g. *You sometimes eat cake.* until someone gets it right. Show them your sentence to confirm. Repeat with a different sentence.
- Learners play the game in pairs using pieces of paper with verb phrases (e.g. *write emails, go shopping*). They put the pieces of paper in a pile face down and take turns to take one and guess.

  Stronger learners Use time expressions as well, e.g. *once a week / twice a year / every day.*

Presentation

- Say *We're going to read a story called 'A bad, bad Monday morning'.* Write the title on the board. Ask *Why do you think the morning is bad?* Learners guess.
- Ask *What wakes you up in the morning? Do you have an alarm clock?* Draw an alarm clock or set off a real alarm. *Why do people need alarms? (So they aren't late)* Say *There's an alarm in today's story. Let's find out what happens.*

Pupil's Book, pages 26 and 27

1 Read the question at the start. Tell a classmate your answer and say why.

- Say *Open your Pupil's Books at page 26. Read the question. Tell your friend the answer.* Learners talk in pairs. The class share ideas. Encourage them to make full sentences and explain, e.g. *I often want to sleep because I don't like getting up in the morning.*

1.34 A bad, bad Monday morning

- Look at each picture and ask questions, e.g. Picture 1: *Where is the boy? (In his bedroom / In (his) bed) What does he like? (Football) Has he got an alarm clock? (Yes, he has.) What's the time? (Seven o'clock)* Picture 2: *Who's the woman? (The boy's mum)* Picture 3: *What does the boy want to do? (Open the door) Why do you think he can't get in? (Maybe someone is in the bathroom.)* Picture 4: *Where is the boy? (In the kitchen) What's his mum giving him? (An apple and a drink)* Picture 5: *Where are they now? (In the car)* Teach *traffic lights.* Explain that sometimes people call them *lights.* Picture 6: *Is the boy happy? (No)* Teach *mirror.*
- Say *Read and listen to the first part.* Play the audio. Pause after *at school today!* Ask *What's the boy's name? (Alex) What time is it? (Eight o'clock) Why mustn't they be late? (Because he has a presentation at school)* Check comprehension of *presentation.*

  Track 1.34
  See story on Pupil's Book pages 26–27
- Say *Read and listen to the next part.* Play the audio. Pause after the third paragraph. Ask *What does Alex do after he jumps out of bed? (He gets dressed.) Who's in the bathroom? (His big sister) Who's in the bathroom downstairs? (His dad)* Check comprehension of *downstairs.*
- Play the next part. Pause after *Now, Alex!* Ask *What does Alex have for breakfast? (Chocolate milk and fruit) Does he always have that? (No) Why doesn't he have breakfast at home? (There's no time.)*
- Play the rest of the story. Ask *Why are they in the car for a long time? (Because all the traffic lights are red) Where does Alex go at school? (The assembly hall) Do we have an assembly hall? Where is it? Is his presentation OK? (Yes, it's good.) What does he see in the mirror? (He's wearing his sister's shirt, his hair is bad and he has chocolate milk around his mouth.)*

  Extra support Instead of asking questions, make sentences, pausing for learners to say key words, e.g. *The boy's name is … (Alex).*

  Extension Play the whole story again, without pauses, for learners to listen and read.

Activity Book, page 26

See pages TB120–132

Ending the lesson

- Ask *Do you sometimes wake up late? What happens? Can you always get into the bathroom at home? Who is in the bathroom for a long time in your house?*

Learning outcomes By the end of the lesson, learners will have thought about the consequences of actions.

New language *action, consequence*

Recycled language language from the story, days of the week, *favourite*

Materials audio

Social and Emotional Skill: Thinking about the consequences of our actions

- After reading the story, ask learners *What time do you get up to go to school? Do you sometimes get up late? What do you do before you go to school? Why is Monday morning bad for Alex?* (*He gets up late.*)
- Explain that Alex has a bad Monday morning because he gets up late. There are consequences to his action.
- Tell learners that they must think of the consequences of their actions. Explain the word *consequences*. Write two lists on the board:

  Actions
  I don't do my homework.
  I don't get dressed.
  I don't have breakfast.
  I break my tablet.
  Consequences
  My parents are angry.
  I go to school in pyjamas.
  I'm hungry.
  I don't understand in class.
- The learners work in groups and match the action and the consequence. They share their ideas with the class.

Warm-up

- Write phrases from the story on the board:

turn off	*the bathroom*
jump out	*to school*
run to	*breakfast*
have	*the alarm clock*
drive	*the mirror*
look in	*of bed*

- Learners match in pairs. Check answers (*turn off the alarm clock, jump out of bed, run to the bathroom, have breakfast, drive to school, look in the mirror*).
- Ask *Why does Alex have a bad, bad Monday morning?* Learners use the phrases to help them recall the story.

Pupil's Book, pages 26 and 27

- Say *Open your Pupil's Books at pages 26 and 27.* Play the audio. Learners read and listen to the story again.

  Track 1.34
  See story on Pupil's Book pages 26–27

2 What bad things happen to Alex in the story? Why?

- Learners share ideas. Write sentences on the board and ask for reasons, e.g. *He wakes up late. Why? Because he turns off his alarm. He gets to school late. Why? Because the traffic lights are red.*

  Extra support Write the bad things that happen in the story on the board (as below, but in random order). Learners talk in pairs and number them in order.

  Alex wakes up late.
  He can't use the bathroom upstairs.
  He can't use the bathroom downstairs.
  He doesn't have his usual breakfast.
  He arrives at school late.
  He's very surprised when he looks in the mirror.
- Check answers and ask about the reasons, e.g. *Why can't Alex use the bathroom upstairs?* (*Because his sister is using it*) *Why doesn't he have his usual breakfast?* (*Because there's no time*)

  Extension Learners act out the story in pairs – one is Alex, one is Mum. Play the audio. They do the actions and join in with their characters' lines.

3 Ask and answer.

- Read the speech bubbles. Explain that in the Movers Speaking exam, the examiner may say *Tell me about …* or *Let's talk about …*
- Put learners into pairs. They each say their favourite day and explain why. Share ideas as a class.

Activity Book, page 27

See pages TB120–132

Ending the lesson

- **SA** Use self-assessment to see how well learners think they understand the story.
- Play 'The photo game'. Choose a confident learner to come to the front. Ask him/her to mime an activity from the story or a daily routine. If he/she can't think of one, whisper an idea, e.g. *Clean your teeth.*
- Explain that when you take the photo, he/she should 'freeze'. Let the learner begin their mime and then, as he/she moves, act taking a photo, aiming and clicking your camera.
- When the learner freezes, ask the other learners *What's he/she doing?* Repeat with other learners.

2

Then Mum calls, 'Breakfast!'

I run to the kitchen.

'Here's some chocolate milk and some fruit,' Mum says.

'But for breakfast, I always have ... '

'No time for that today!' Mum says. We must leave now!'

I start to say 'I must ... ', but Mum says, 'Now, Alex!'

We run to the car and drive to school. All the lights are red.

When we get to school, I run to the assembly hall. All my classmates are there. They're smiling.

My presentation is good.

I'm very happy ... but then I go to the bathroom and look in the mirror.

I'm wearing my sister's shirt, my hair is going in all directions and I have chocolate milk around my mouth!

2 What bad things happen to Alex in the story? Why?

3 Ask and answer.

Tell me about your favourite day of the week.

I love Fridays. We play games in our English class.

1 Look at the pictures. What can you see? Copy a word or words from the box.

a comic   breakfast   skates   a lake
an email   toothpaste   leaves   a tractor

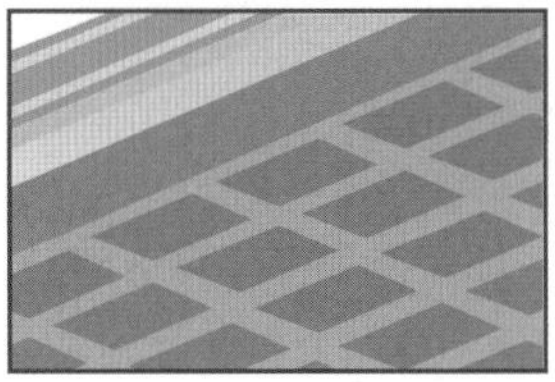

1 leaves   2 ________   3 ________   4 ________

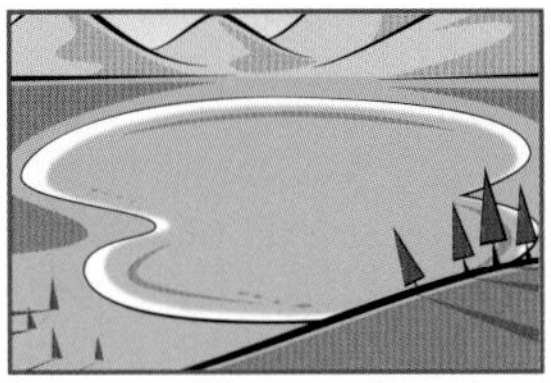

5 ________   6 ________   7 ________   8 ________

2 Read and think. Circle the correct answer.

1 You find these on trees and they're green. **a leaf / leaves**
2 Most people eat this in the morning. **breakfast / breakfasts**
3 You can use these in the park. It's fun! **skate / skates**
4 You write this on a computer or phone. **emails / an email**

3 Look at the answers. Read and complete.

1 You use this to clean your t _ _ _ _. toothpaste
2 There are lots of different st _ _ _ _ _ in this. a comic

4 Look at Units 1 and 2. Write five sentences like Activity 3. Can your friend say the words?

Circle the words which help you choose the answer.

Learning outcomes By the end of the lesson, learners will have practised interpreting and writing definitions (A1 Movers Reading and Writing Part 1).

Test skills Reading short definitions and matching to words; Writing words

Recycled language vocabulary from Units 1 and 2, *breakfast, lunch, dinner, morning, afternoon, evening,* adverbs of frequency, present simple

Materials flashcards from Units 1 and 2, practice paper for Movers Reading and Writing Part 1 (optional)

Warm-up

- Stick eight flashcards on the board (not from Pupil's Book page 28).
- Put the class into teams of six to eight learners. Teams stand in lines facing the board. Define one of the words, e.g. *There are lots of trees here.* (*Forest*) The learners at the front of their line race to take the correct flashcard from the board.
- Repeat with the next two learners. The team with the most flashcards wins.

Presentation

- Say *Let's practise for a reading and writing exam.* Show the Movers Reading and Writing paper Part 1. Say *Part 1 of the exam has eight pictures. On the next page are five sentences. You need to match each sentence with a picture and copy the word carefully. So there are three pictures that you don't use (one is the example). Let's practise!*

Pupil's Book, page 28

1 Look at the pictures. What can you see? Copy a word or words from the box.

- Say *Open your Pupil's Books at page 28.* Read the instructions. Learners work in pairs to choose words. Remind them to copy carefully and use the articles where they are given. Explain that in all parts of the Reading and Writing exam they must spell correctly.
- Check answers. Ask *How many words have articles?* (*Four*)

Note: Candidates often lose marks because they do not write words or letters clearly. It is often better not to use joined-up writing, as letters can become confused and unclear.

Key: 1 leaves 2 a comic 3 an email 4 toothpaste 5 a lake 6 breakfast 7 a tractor 8 skates

Extension In pairs, one learner closes his/her book. The other learner asks him/her to spell one of the words in Activity 1 (e.g. *How do you spell 'breakfast'?*). The first learner writes the word. They check and then swap roles.

2 Read and think. Circle the correct answer.

- Point to each picture in Activity 1 and say *This is a/an …* or *These are …* Learners practise doing the same.
- Read the first sentence, exaggerating the words *these* and *they're.* Show learners they need to circle the plural answer (*leaves*). Learners read the rest of the sentences and circle individually. Check answers.

Extra support Read each sentence out, exaggerating pronouns and helping learners choose the correct answer.

Key: 2 breakfast 3 skates 4 an email

3 Look at the answers. Read and complete.

- Learners read the words on the right and complete the definitions. If necessary, help learners form the plural of *story*. Check answers. Point out that *toothpaste* uses the singular form *tooth* not *teeth.*

Key: 1 teeth 2 stories

4 Look at Units 1 and 2. Write five sentences like Activity 3. Can your friend say the words?

- Read the instructions. Look back at the sentences in Activity 3. Write *You can …* and *There is/are …* on the board. Add *This is …* and *These are …* Learners write five definitions using the prompts on the board.
- Learners swap their sentences with a partner, who writes the word. Remind learners to think about whether they need to write the singular form (with *a/an*) or the plural.

Extra support Learners write three sentences, instead of five. Alternatively, they write their definitions in pairs, then swap with another pair.

- Point to the monkey at the bottom of the page and read the sentence. Ask learners to look back at the sentences in Activity 2 and circle the words that help them choose the answer (e.g. *these, trees, they're, green* in the example, *leaves*). They can do the same with the sentences from Activity 4.

Activity Book, page 28

See pages TB120–132

Ending the lesson

- In pairs, learners test each other on spelling words from the unit. This can also be done as a team game.

Learning outcomes By the end of the lesson, learners will have revised the language in the unit and described their timetable of fun activities.

Recycled language unit language, *scene*

Materials a large piece of paper and pen for each group of four/five learners, a watch or timer, a bell or whistle (optional), surveys from Mission Stage 1 lesson, timetables from Mission Stages 2 and 3 lessons, dice and counters (for Activity Book game), coloured pens or pencils, digital Mission poster

Warm-up

- Put learners into groups of four or five. Give each group a large piece of paper. Choose a strong learner in each group and give them a pen.
- Say *Let's remember!* Tell them they have one minute for each part of the game. Show your watch or, if you have a timer, set the timer. Ask *How many words can you remember?* Check learners understand they have to write as many words as they can. The learner with the pen in each group writes. The other learners in the group say words.
- Say *Write down things you do every day. You have one minute.* After a minute, ring a bell or blow a whistle (or call *Stop!*). Check with each group how many things they wrote. Repeat with *Write down free time activities*.
- Pick out two or three words from each list. Ask learners to cover their lists. Say the words slowly. Learners try to write the words with the correct spelling.
- To check, ask learners to spell out the words and write them on the board, correcting any errors.
- **SA** Use self-assessment techniques to check how well learners think they understand and can write the vocabulary. See Introduction.

Pupil's Book, page 29

mission in action!

Give your timetable to your two friends.

- Say *Open your Pupil's Books at page 29.* Point to the Mission box or show learners the last stage of the digital Mission poster. Say *Let's put our Mission in action!* Say *Give your timetable to your two friends.*
- Read the instructions and demonstrate. First hold up an example survey from Stage 1 for two learners and talk to them about the activities which they do every week now, e.g. *You play basketball twice a week. You never skate.* Then hold up an example timetable from Stages 2 and 3. Describe the learners' new timetable day by day, giving some safety advice with *must/mustn't*.
- Put learners into their pairs from Stages 1–3. Give them time to practise talking about the other pair's current activities and the new timetable they have made for them. Monitor and help. Make sure both learners in each pair are talking.
- Pairs join with the pair they worked with in Stage 1. They talk about current activities before presenting their new timetable.

  Fast finishers Write a response to the pair who prepared the timetable, e.g. *We like the timetable of fun activities. We want to try horse riding and hockey. Our favourite day on the timetable is Friday.*

Self-assessment

- **SA** Say *Did you like our 'Plan a fun activities timetable' Mission? A lot?* (cheer) *It's OK?* (smile) *Or not much?* (shake your head and shrug) Encourage learners to show how they feel.
- Say *Write down one thing you know now about your classmates. Write one fun activity you want to try. Write a rule for an activity or sport with 'must' or 'mustn't'.* Learners think and write individually or in pairs. Ask different learners to share with the class.
- Say *Our next Mission is 'Plan and act out a scene'.* Explain the meaning of *scene*. Ask *Do you like acting? Do you think you need to practise speaking in class?* Learners share their expectations and concerns.

Activity Book, page 29

See pages TB120–132

Activity Book, page 18

- Review *My unit goals*. Ask *How is your Mission?* Learners reflect and choose a smiley face for *My mission diary* the final stage.
- Point to the sunflower. Learners read the 'can do' statements and tick them if they agree they have achieved them. They colour each leaf green if they are very confident or orange if they think they need more practice.
- Point to the word stack sign. Ask learners to look back at the unit and find at least five new words they have learnt. They write them in their word stack.

Ending the lesson

- **SA** Go back to the completion stage on the digital Mission poster. Add a tick or invite a learner to do it. Use self-assessment (see Introduction).
- Give out a completion sticker.
- Tell learners *You have finished your Mission! Well done!*

mission in action!

Give your timetable to your two friends.

My mission diary

Activity Book page 18

★ **Talk about the activities which they do every week now.**

You play basketball twice a week. You never skate.

★ **Tell them the activity for each day.**

You skate on Sunday.

★ **Tell them how to be safe.**

You must wear knee pads, elbow pads, gloves and helmets.

★ **Do your friends like the timetable?**

Do you like the activities?

Yes, thank you. It's a fun week!

COMPLETE

3 Party time!

1 **Watch the video. Draw yourself at the costume party.**

mission **Plan and act out a scene**

In this unit I will:

1. Choose a job and draw my character.
2. Describe my character.
3. Write a scene with my group where someone is helping.
★ Act out our scene for the class.

Unit 3 learning outcomes

In Unit 3, learners learn to:

- talk about jobs and parties
- use the present simple and the present continuous
- describe people (physically)
- ask and answer questions with *Why … ?* and *Because …*
- learn about people who help them at home, at school and in the community
- read a story about a costume party and think about asking for and offering help

Materials Friendly family and animal character flashcards, paper, video, coloured pens or pencils, digital Mission poster, a printed script for a play or a video clip of a play (optional), a copy of the Mission worksheet (Teacher's Resource Book page 34)

Self-assessment

- **SA** Say *Open your Pupil's Books at page 30. Look at the picture.* Ask *What's happening?* (*A party*) Point to the unit title and say *Yes, it's party time! Look, everyone's wearing costumes at the party*. Check comprehension of *costume.* Ask *Do you like wearing costumes? Which costumes do you wear / can you see?* Use self-assessment (see Introduction). Say *OK. Let's learn.*

Warm-up

- Show the Friendly family and animal character flashcards. Learners say the names. Say *Imagine it's your birthday. Who's at your party? Let's see!*
- Put learners into groups of five and give each learner a number 1 to 5. Each group sits in a circle with a sheet of paper in the middle. Call out *One!* Learner 1 from each group comes up and looks at a flashcard. They go back to their group and sketch or mime the character. The group guess the name. Continue until all flashcards have been drawn/mimed and named.

Pupil's Book, page 30

1 Watch the video. Draw yourself at the costume party.

- Say *In this unit we're talking about parties.* Say *Let's watch the video.* To introduce the topic of the unit, play the video.
- Say *Look at page 30.* Point to the empty box. Ask *What are you wearing at the costume party? Draw yourself here.* Learners draw themselves in a costume. Tell each learner the name of the animal/job/character they draw.

mission Plan and act out a scene

- Point to the Mission box or the digital Mission poster and say *This is our Mission.*
- Say *Plan and act out a scene.* Show learners a copy of a play script or a video clip of a scene from a play (with the stage visible). Say *A play is a story you can watch in a theatre. Actors speak the lines. A scene is part of the story.* Ask learners if they have ever seen or acted in a play.
- Say *Point to number 1. Choose a job and draw my character. A character is one of the people in a play.* Ask learners for examples of characters they know (from films, TV or plays). Write them on the board. Say *These are all characters.* Choose a character who has a job and ask *What's his/her job? What does he/she do every day?* Check comprehension of *job.* Say *In Stage 1 of the Mission, you choose a job for your character and you draw a picture.*
- Say *Point to number 2. Describe my character.* Choose one of the characters from the board and describe what he/she looks like. Learners should be familiar with descriptions of hair and eye colour (e.g. *He's got brown eyes and black hair.*). Use gesture to show the meaning of any new vocabulary (*tall, thin,* etc.). Say *In Stage 2 you think about your character and write a description.*
- Say *Point to number 3. Write a scene with my group where someone is helping.* If possible, show a scene in the script of a play or write a few lines on the board, with the speakers' names on the left. Say *In a group, you write a short scene for a play. Something happens and someone helps.*
- Say *The last stage is 'Act out our scene for the class.'* Say *You need to act and the rest of the class watch.*
- Say *This is our Mission.* Go through the stages of the Mission again.
- For ideas on monitoring and assessment, see Introduction.

Activity Book, page 30

My unit goals

- Help learners to complete the unit goals. See notes on page TB6.
- You can go back to these unit goals at the end of each Mission stage during the unit and review them.

Ending the lesson

- Ask *Who's this?* Describe a learner, e.g. *She's got long, brown hair. She's got blue eyes. She's wearing a blue T-shirt today. She's sitting next to the cupboard.* Learners say his/her name. Repeat, describing different learners.

  Stronger learners Repeat the activity in pairs.

Learning outcomes By the end of the lesson, learners will be able to talk about jobs and parties.

New language *clown, cook, costume, dentist, doctor, farmer, film star, nurse, party, pirate, pop star, present, surprise, treasure, everyone, invite, job, only, Happy Birthday!*

Recycled language clothes, eye/hair colour, *have got*

Materials Friendly Family flashcards, Jobs and parties flashcards, music, audio, video, coloured pens or pencils

Warm-up

- Hold up the Friendly Family flashcards and ask, e.g. *What colour's his hair? What's she wearing?*
- Learners sit in a circle. Hand out the flashcards. Play some music. Learners pass the cards around. Stop the music. Choose a learner with a flashcard. He/She says, e.g. *This is Grandma Friendly. She's got grey hair.*

Presentation

- Say *I'm a teacher. It's my job.* Ask *Is Mr Friendly a teacher?* (*No, a cook*) Say *Let's learn some more jobs.*
- Show the Jobs and parties flashcards and say the words. Learners repeat.
- Put the flashcards for the jobs on the board and number them 1 to 9. Say *He's a farmer.* Learners say the number. Say a number. Learners say the job or *He's/She's a (nurse).*

Pupil's Book, page 31

1 (1.35) Listen and point. Then listen again and colour.

- Say *Open your Pupil's Books at page 31*. Ask *What's happening?* (*A (birthday) party*) *Whose birthday is it?* (*Grandpa's*) *Can you see a present? Who's a pirate?* (*Grandma*) *What's Grandma got?* Teach *treasure. Where's the small tractor? Can you find it?*
- Read the caption. Teach *surprise*. Say *Listen and point.*

Track 1.35

It's Grandpa's birthday today. The Friendly family are having a surprise costume party.

Eva:	Hi, everyone! Look, Jenny, we've got the same costumes. We're both pop stars.
Jenny:	Yes, that's right, we are. I love your costume, Tom. What are you?
Tom:	I'm a film star. I'm Craig Daniels.
Eva:	Can we invite Cameron?
Jim:	Cameron's here. Look! He's wearing a clown's costume. He loves it!
Tom:	Oh, yes! And there's Grandpa's present, the purple box on the table. I like your grandma's costume.
Jim:	Yes, she's a great pirate. There's treasure in her orange box. It's chocolate.
Eva:	Hmm! Fantastic! We can see you're a doctor, Jim.
Jim:	Yeah, and Mum's a nurse. She always helps me.
Mrs Friendly:	Well, you can help me now, Jim. I must go and look at the cake.
Jim:	Dad can go and look at the cake, Mum! He's only a dentist for the costume party. He's a cook really.
Mr Friendly:	Yes, I am … and you can help me with the food, Jim.
Grandpa:	Hello?
Everyone:	Surprise! … Happy Birthday, Grandpa!
Grandpa:	Ooh! Oh, I say! Where's *my* costume? What am *I*?
Jenny:	It's OK, Grandpa … you're a farmer!
Grandpa:	Oh, yes, of course I am!

- Say *Listen again and colour*. Play the audio.

Key: present – purple treasure box – orange

2 (1.36) Say the chant.

- Play the audio or video. Learners point and chant. Check comprehension of *invite*.

Track 1.36

It's Farmer Friendly's costume party!
Wear a costume, bring a present.
A clown, a doctor, a pirate with treasure,
A pop star, a film star, a dentist and a nurse.
Mr Friendly's a cook and he's cooking for the party.
Invite everyone to a costume party! [x2]

3 (1.37) Listen and answer.

- Say *Who is it?* Play the audio. Pause for learners to say the name(s).

Track 1.37

1 Who's the pirate?
2 Who's the film star?
3 Who are the pop stars?
4 Who's the nurse?
5 Who's the farmer?
6 Who's the clown?
7 Who's the doctor?
8 Who's the dentist and the cook?

Key: 1 Grandma 2 Tom 3 Eva and Jenny 4 Mrs Friendly 5 Grandpa 6 Cameron 7 Jim 8 Mr Friendly

Activity Book, page 31

See pages TB120–132

Ending the lesson

- **SA** Show the Jobs and parties flashcards. Ask *Do you know the words?* Use self-assessment (see Introduction). Learners show how they feel.

1 1.35 Listen and point. Then listen again and colour.

2 1.36 Say the chant.

3 1.37 Listen and answer.

The Friendly Farm

1.38

1
Oh, Cameron! What are you wearing?
I'm wearing a clown's costume, from the party.
Oh, we never dress up. Can we have a costume party too?
2
There's a box of costumes here … with Farmer Friendly and Grandma's old clothes.
OK, but ... where is Farmer Friendly?
He's outside feeding the cows. He always feeds them in the evenings.
3
I'm a pop star.
Oh, I don't want to be a pop star … I want to be a famous film star. Film stars often go to parties.
4
I'm a nurse. I help people … hmm, we need a doctor.
Rocky! What are you doing?
I'm calling Gracie. She likes studying. She can be a doctor.
5
Are you calling me? What do you want?
Put these on, Gracie. You're our doctor.
Remember – doctors help other people.
6
Harry! I'm a doctor! I must look at your eye. I'm … helping … you.
No, you aren't. It's my costume. I'm a pirate. Please stop! … Ow!

1 1.39 **Listen and complete. Use one word.**

Learning outcomes By the end of the lesson, learners will be able to understand when they hear the present simple and present continuous.

New language *call, dress up, famous, other people, study, work, be* + *a(n)* + job (*I'm a pop star*)

Recycled language jobs and parties, *box, cow, eye, feed, help, in the evenings, need, put on, stop, want to (be),* adverbs of frequency, *must,* present continuous, present simple

Materials Jobs and parties flashcards, audio, video

Warm-up

- Put the flashcards on the board and say, e.g. *She's a nurse* for each one. Learners practise.
- Learners open their Pupil's Books at page 31. Ask, e.g. *Who's a nurse?* (*Mrs Friendly*) Tell learners they have 30 seconds to look and remember all the jobs.
- They close their books and write the names and jobs individually or in pairs.

  Alternative Learners work in pairs. One closes his/her book and the other says the jobs, e.g. *Cameron's a clown.* Then they swap.
- **SA** Use self-assessment to check how well learners think they understand the vocabulary. See Introduction.

Presentation

- Write *I work in this school. I'm working now.* on the board. Point to the first sentence and say, e.g. *I work here on Monday, Tuesday, Wednesday, Thursday and Friday. And today is (Tuesday), so I'm working now. I'm talking to you!*
- Underline *'m* and *ing* in the second sentence.

Pupil's Book, page 32

1.38 The Friendly Farm song

- Play the introductory song at the beginning of the cartoon story. Learners listen and sing.

  Track 1.38
  See The Friendly Farm song on page TB5

1.38 The Friendly Farm

- Say *Open your Pupil's Books at page 32.* Ask *Who can you see?* Learners name the characters. Teach *dress up.* Ask *Do you like dressing up? What do you dress up as?*
- Point to the pictures and ask *What are the animals doing?* (*Dressing up*) *Who puts on a film star costume?* (*Shelly*)
- Ask *What costume does Gracie put on?* Write the question on the board. Play the audio or video. Learners listen and read. Check answers. (*A doctor costume*) Check comprehension of *help other people*. Ask *Does Harry need a doctor?* (*No*) *Why not?* (*He doesn't have a problem with his eye – it's his pirate costume.*) Draw a pirate with an eye patch on the board (or point to picture 4).

  Note: *a (clown's) costume* and *a (clown) costume* are both correct usage.

  Track 1.38
  The Friendly Farm song + see cartoon on Pupil's Book page 32
- Play the audio or video again. Pause after each picture and ask questions: 1: *How often do the animals wear costumes?* (*Never*) *What does Shelly want to do?* (*Have a costume party*) 2: *Whose clothes are in the box?* (*Grandma and Grandpa's clothes*) *Where's Grandpa?* (*He's feeding the cows*) 3: *What costume is Rocky wearing?* (*Pop star*) *Why does Shelly want to be a film star?* (*Because they go to lots of parties*) Explain the meaning of *famous* and ask different learners *Do you want to be famous?* 4: *What costume is Henrietta wearing?* (*Nurse*) *What does Gracie like doing?* (*Studying*) Explain the meaning of *call.* 5: *What must Gracie remember?* (*Doctors help other people*) 6: *What does Gracie want to look at?* (*Harry's eye*) *Is she helping Harry?* (*No, she isn't.*)

1 1.39 Listen and complete. Use one word.

- Books closed. Play the audio and pause for learners to complete the questions and sentences.

  Extra support Write the missing words in random order on the board.

Track 1.39

1	Harry:	Oh, Cameron! What are you …
2	Shelly:	Oh, we never dress …
3	Harry:	He's outside feeding the …
4	Shelly:	I want to be a famous film …
5	Harry:	Rocky! What are you …
6	Rocky:	I'm calling Gracie. She likes …
7	Gracie:	Are you calling me? What do you…
8	Gracie:	Harry! I'm a doctor! I must look at your …

Key: 1 wearing? 2 up. 3 cows. 4 star. 5 doing? 6 studying. 7 want? 8 eye.

Activity Book, page 32

See pages TB120–132

Ending the lesson

- **SA** Repeat the self-assessment technique used at the start of the lesson to see how well learners think they understand the vocabulary. Is there any change?
- Put the flashcards on the board and number them. Learners work in pairs to ask and answer, e.g. *Number 3. What does he do? / He's a …*

Learning outcomes By the end of the lesson, learners will be able to use the present simple and present continuous appropriately.

New language *He never works at the weekend. It's Friday. He's working today. I don't often listen to the radio. I'm not listening to it now. Do you eat meatballs? What are you eating at the moment? at the moment, work* (v)

Recycled language adverbs of frequency, free time activities, jobs, *eat, every day, field, make a cake, meatballs, now,* present continuous, present simple

Materials four pieces of paper, each with an adverb of frequency, Jobs and parties flashcards, audio, Mission worksheets (Teacher's Resource Book page 34) or paper, coloured pens or pencils, digital Mission poster

Warm-up

- Put pieces of paper with *always/often/sometimes/never* on different walls. Say a sentence, e.g. *I do my homework.* Learners decide how often they do that thing and go to the right wall (or point). Ask some learners to make a sentence (e.g. *I always do my homework.*).

Presentation

- Show the flashcard for *pop star*. Ask *What does he do?* (*He's a pop star.*) *What's he doing in this picture?* (*He's singing.*)
- Ask different learners questions in the present simple and continuous, e.g. *Are you wearing pink socks today? How often do you wear pink socks? Who are you sitting next to at the moment? Do you always sit next to (name)?*

Pupil's Book, page 33

1.40 Gracie's Grammar

- Say *Open your Pupil's Books at page 33.* Point to Gracie's Grammar box. Write the sentences on the board. Underline the *s* in *works* and remind learners that in the third person singular we add *s* to the verb.
- Play the audio. Pause for learners to repeat.

Track 1.40
See Pupil's Book page 33

1 1.41 Listen and stick. Then look, read and write.

- Play the audio. Learners point to the correct sticker.

Track 1.41

1 Harry: What's Jenny doing this morning?
Cameron: She's watching TV.
Harry: Does she always watch TV in the morning?
Cameron: No, she goes to school in the morning, but today's Saturday.

2 Cameron: What's Grandpa doing?
Harry: He's working in the field.
Cameron: But today's Saturday.
Harry: Yes, Grandpa works every day. He's a farmer.

3 Harry: What's Jim doing?
Cameron: He's making a cake.
Harry: That's good. Does he often make cakes?
Cameron: Yes, he does. He enjoys cooking.

4 Harry: That's nice music. Who's playing the piano?
Cameron: Mrs Friendly is.
Harry: Does she always play the piano?
Cameron: No, she sometimes plays the piano and she sometimes plays the guitar.

- Play the audio again. Learners stick in the characters. Check answers by asking, e.g. *Who's making a cake?*
- Ask *What's Jenny doing now?* (*Watching TV*) Point to the example sentence and explain that because the sentence is about what is happening *now*, it is in the present continuous.
- Learners complete sentences 2 to 4. Check answers.
  Extra support Do all three sentences as a class.

Key: 2 works 3 making 4 play

mission Stage 1

- Point to the Mission box or show learners the first stage of the digital Mission poster: *Choose a job and draw your character.* Check comprehension of *character*. Explain that learners will choose characters for their scene.
- Put learners into groups of four. They each choose a different job and a name for their character.
- Learners complete the worksheet task in the Teacher's Resource Book (page 34). See teaching notes on TRB page 27.
- Alternatively, if you do not have the Teacher's Resource Book, learners write the names and jobs of their group's characters. They draw their own character and then present the character to their group.

Activity Book, page 33

See pages TB120–132

Activity Book, page 30

- Review *My unit goals.* Ask *How is your Mission?* Learners reflect and choose a smiley face for *My mission diary 1.*

Ending the lesson

- **SA** Go back to Stage 1 on the digital Mission poster. Say *We chose jobs and drew characters.* Add a tick to the 'Choose a job ...' stage. Use self-assessment (see Introduction).
- Give out a completion sticker.

Gracie's Grammar

1.40

He **never works** at the weekend.

I **don't** often **listen** to the radio.

Do you **eat** meatballs?

It's Friday. He**'s working today**.

I**'m not listening** to it **now**.

What **are you eating at the moment**?

1 Listen and stick. Then look, read and write.

1.41

1 Jenny's watching TV now.

2 Grandpa ______________ every day. He's a farmer.

3 Jim's ______________ a cake at the moment.

4 Does she always ______________ the piano?

mission STAGE 1

Choose a job and draw your character.

STAGE 1

- In groups, choose a different job each.
- Draw your character for the scene.
- Talk about your character.

She helps other people. She's a doctor.

My mission diary

Activity Book page 30

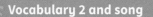

1 1.42 Listen and colour. Then sing the song.

Her scarecrow's **thin**
And she's very **tall** too.
She's got **straight**, **blonde** hair
And her hat is blue.
Scarecrow! Scarecrow!

His scarecrow's **short**.
He's also **fat**.
He's got a long, black **beard**
And a big **moustache**.
Scarecrow! Scarecrow!

Their scarecrow's ugly.
He's got a purple nose.
He's got **fair**, **curly** hair
And he's wearing dirty clothes!
Scarecrow! Scarecrow!
Scarecrow! Scarecrow!
Scarecrow!

2 1.44 Listen and say the number. Then play the game.

1

2

3

4

Learning outcomes By the end of the lesson, learners will have practised the language through song.

New language *beard, blonde, curly, fair, fat, moustache, short, straight, tall, thin, scarecrow*

Recycled language clothes, colours, hair and eye colour, *dirty, ugly, He's/She's* + adjective, *He's/She's got (brown) hair/eyes. His/Her (hat) is (blue).* possessive pronouns, *Whose … ?*

Materials items of clothing in different colours and pairs of dice (optional), Clothes flashcards from level 1 (optional), Physical descriptions flashcards, coloured pens or pencils, audio, video, paper (optional)

Warm-up

- Show some real clothes and ask *What's this? / What are these? What colour is it / are they?*
- Hand out pairs of dice and tell learners to throw them and then pass them along. Whoever throws a double number (e.g. two fives) comes to the front of the class.
- Tell the learner at the front, e.g. *Put on the blue T-shirt.* The learner chooses the correct item of clothing and puts it on over his/her own clothes. Repeat instructions to this learner until someone else throws a double number, in which case the first learner takes off the items and you give instructions to the new learner. The rest of the class continue throwing the dice.
  Alternative Revise items of clothing and colours with flashcards from level 1 / pictures, or by pointing to things you/learners are wearing.

Presentation

- Teach the words for descriptions using the flashcards.
- Ask *Has anyone in your family got a beard/moustache? Is your mum/dad (tall)? Who's got curly hair in your family?*
- **SA** Use self-assessment to check how well learners think they understand the vocabulary. See Introduction.

Pupil's Book, page 34

1 1.42 Listen and colour. Then sing the song.

- Say *Open your Pupil's Books at page 34.* Ask *Who can you see? (Eva, Tom, Jim and Jenny)* Point to the scarecrows and ask *Where can you see these? (On a farm / in a field) Why do farmers need them? (To make birds go away)* Say *They scare birds. They're scarecrows.* Explain the meaning of *crow*.
- Ask *Whose scarecrow 's got curly hair? (Jim and Jenny's) Whose scarecrow's tall? (Eva's) Whose scarecrow's short? (Tom's)*, etc.
- Say *Listen and colour.* Point to the blank areas.
- Play the audio or video. Learners listen and colour the hair blonde (yellow), the beard black and the nose purple. Check answers by asking, e.g. *What colour hair has she got? (Blonde)* Make sure learners don't say *yellow hair*.

Track 1.42

Rocky: I'm Rocky-Doodle-Doo and here's our song for today: *Scarecrow*

See song on Pupil's Book page 34

- Learners stand up. Practise the song in sections.
- Play the audio or video again. Make three groups. One group sings each verse.

1.43 **Extension** Once learners are confidently singing along, try singing the karaoke version as a class.

2 1.44 Listen and say the number. Then play the game.

- Point to scarecrow 1 and ask *Has he got a beard? (No, he hasn't.) Is he fat? (Yes, he is.) Has he got blonde hair? (No, black)*, etc.
- Say *Listen and say the number.* Play the audio.

Track 1.44

There's a tall scarecrow in the field. It hasn't got a moustache, but it's got a beard. It's wearing a small, green hat, it's got curly, blonde hair, and it's thin. Which one is it?

Key: 3

- Learners work in pairs. One learner chooses a scarecrow and describes it. The other says the letter. Then they swap.
  Stronger learners One learner chooses a scarecrow and the other learner asks questions to guess which one it is, e.g. *Has it got a beard? Is it fat?*
- Show the picture of Rocky in the bottom right-hand corner. Read out the instruction. Ask a strong learner to describe his/her hair, e.g. *I've got short, black hair. It's curly.*
- Learners talk in pairs about their hair.
  Fast finishers Learners write sentences about what they look like and what they are wearing on a piece of paper. Collect the paper and read a description, without saying the name. The class guess who it is.

Activity Book, page 34

See pages TB120–132

Ending the lesson

- **SA** Repeat the self-assessment used after the Presentation to see how well learners think they understand the vocabulary. Is there any change?
- Play the song again. Learners join in.

Learning outcomes By the end of the lesson, learners will be able to ask and answer questions with *Why … ?* and *Because …*

New language *Why are you asking a lot of questions? Because I love asking questions.*

Recycled language jobs, parties, physical descriptions, *read a (big) book, show* (n), *wash (his) hands, wear (a helmet)*

Materials paper, coloured pens or pencils, audio, worksheets/notes and pictures from Mission Stage 1 lesson, digital Mission poster

Warm-up

- Learners draw an adult in their family. Ask *Is he or she thin? Has he or she got long hair? Has he got a beard?*
- Learners show their picture to a partner, say who the person is and describe him/her.

Presentation

- Ask *Why are you listening to me?* (*You're a teacher.*) Say *Because I'm your teacher.* Ask different *Why* questions in the present continuous about school / the classroom / what learners are doing, e.g. *Why are we speaking English?* Encourage learners to use *Because* before their answers. Say *We use 'why' when we want to know the reason for something and 'because' to give a reason.*

Pupil's Book, page 35

1 1.45 What's Dad doing? Listen and tick ✓.

- Say *Open your Pupil's Books at page 35.* Point to each picture. Ask *What's he doing?* (*Watching TV / listening to music / cleaning his shoes*)
- Play the audio. Learners listen and tick. Check answers.

Track 1.45

Clare:	Charlie, why's Julia watching TV?
Charlie:	Because it's Saturday morning and she hasn't got school.
Clare:	Hmm … And why's Dad cleaning his new shoes?
Charlie:	Because they're dirty and he needs them for a party this evening.
Clare:	Hmm … I like parties … And why's Mum listening to music in the kitchen?
Charlie:	Because she likes listening to music when she cooks. Why are you asking a lot of questions?
Clare:	Oh! … Because I love asking questions.

Key: He's cleaning his shoes. (picture 3)

Extension Write *Why?* on the board. Ask *Why's Julia watching TV? Why's Dad cleaning his shoes? Why's Mum listening to music?* Play the audio again.

1.46 Gracie's Grammar

- Write the questions and answers on the board.
- Play the audio. Pause for learners to repeat.

Track 1.46
See Pupil's Book page 35

- Mime an activity, e.g. running. Encourage learners to ask you *Why are you running?* Give them a reason (funny if possible), e.g. *Because there's a tiger behind me.*

2 Ask and answer with your own ideas.

- Point to the first picture and the examples. Ask learners for more ideas, e.g. *Because they live in a circus.*
- Learners ask and answer about the other pictures in pairs.
- Ask pairs to share the best reasons they came up with.

Key: (possible answers) 2 Because they're dirty / it's lunchtime 3 Because he likes reading / he's doing his homework 4 Because she's skating / riding a bike

mission Stage 2

- Show learners the second stage of the Mission poster: *Describe your character.* Remind learners of the characters they created for Stage 1.
- Learners complete the second worksheet task in the Teacher's Resource Book (page 34). See teaching notes on TRB page 27.
- Alternatively, if you do not have the Teacher's Resource Book, go through the examples in the Pupil's Book. Learners work individually to think about a description, then get together in their Mission groups from Stage 1. They pretend to 'be' their character and introduce themselves to the rest of the group. Monitor and encourage learners to use an appropriate voice/act.
- Learners write a description of their character.

Activity Book, page 35

See pages TB120–132

Activity Book, page 30

- Review *My unit goals.* Ask *How is your Mission?* Learners reflect and choose a smiley face for *My mission diary 2.*

Ending the lesson

- **SA** Go back to Stage 2 on the digital Mission poster. Add a tick to the 'Describe your character' stage. Use self-assessment (see Introduction).
- Give out a completion sticker.

1 1.45 What's Dad doing? Listen and tick ✓.

1 

2 

3 

1.46 Gracie's Grammar

Why are you asking a lot of questions?

Because I love asking questions.

2 Ask and answer with your own ideas.

1 
wear / clown costumes?

2 
wash / his hands?

3 
read / a big book?

4 
wear / a helmet?

Why are they wearing clown costumes?

Because they're going to a party.

Because they like dressing up.

Because they're in a show.

mission STAGE 2

Describe your character.

- In groups, say who you are and describe your character.

  Hi! I'm Daisy. I'm a doctor. I'm tall with long …

- Write about your character.

  Daisy's a doctor. She's tall with long …

STAGE 2

My mission diary

Activity Book page 30

People who help us

1 Watch the video.

2 1.47 **These people help us. Where do they work? Look and write the number. Then listen and check.**

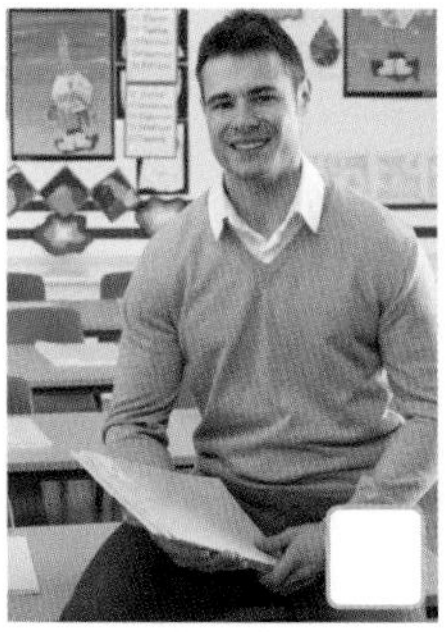

a teacher

a firefighter

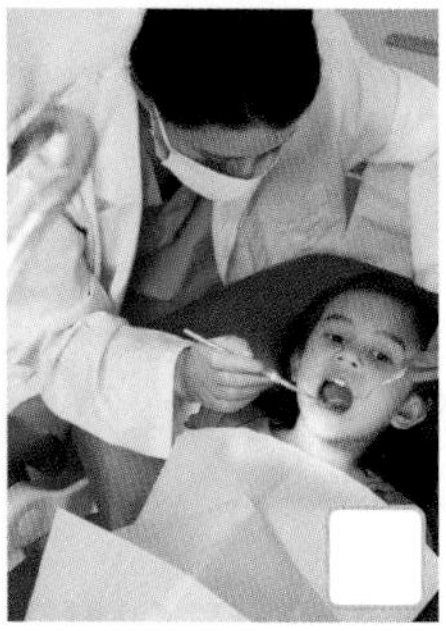

a dentist

a doctor / a nurse

a police officer

1

2

3

4
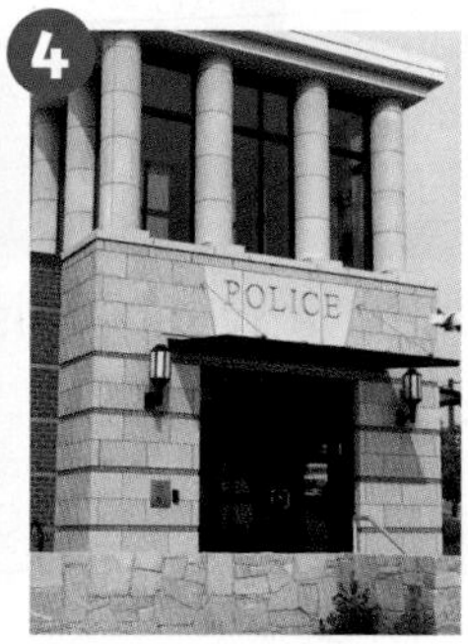

5
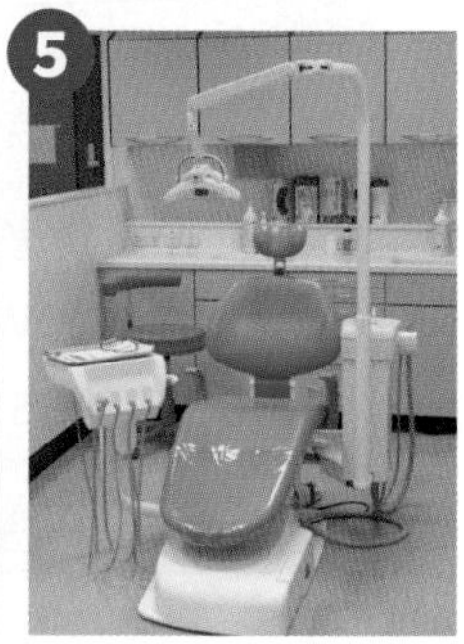

3 **Look at the pictures. Who can help?**

1
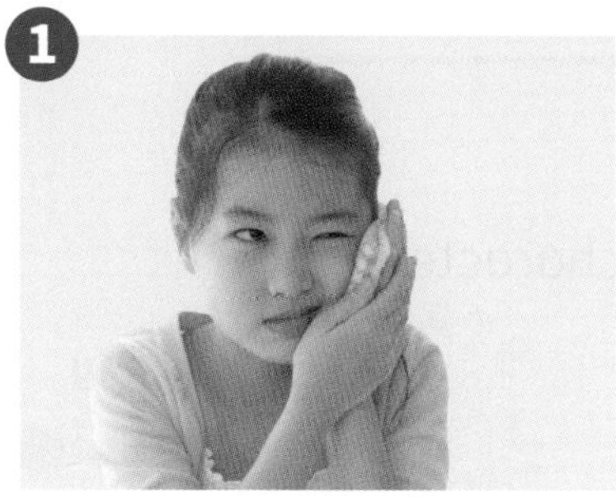

2

3

Learning outcomes By the end of the lesson, learners will have learnt about people who help us at home, at school and in the community.

New language *fire station, firefighter, hospital, police officer, police station, surgery*

Recycled language jobs, *help, school, work* (v), present simple

Materials Jobs and parties flashcards, video, audio

Warm-up

- Review jobs with the flashcards. Stick them on the board. Learners practise making sentences, e.g. *He's a farmer.*
- Mime doing one of the jobs and ask *What's my job?* Learners answer, e.g. *You're a cook.*
- Learners play the same mime game in pairs or groups.
- After the game, ask *What do you want to be when you grow up?* Help with new vocabulary.

  Stronger learners Ask follow-up questions about what learners want to be: *Why do you want to be a (vet)? Is anyone in your family a (taxi driver)?*

Presentation

- Stick the flashcards for doctor, dentist and nurse together on the board and ask *What's the same about these people?* Learners suggest ideas. Say *They all help people.*
- Say *Let's find out more about people who help us.*

Pupil's Book, page 36

1 Watch the video.

- Say *Let's watch the video.* Learners watch the video about people who help us and answer the questions at the end.

2 1.47 These people help us. Where do they work? Look and write the number. Then listen and check.

- Say *Open your Pupil's Books at page 36. Look at the pictures of the people. Point to the (doctor).* Practise the new jobs *firefighter* and *police officer.* Ask *What does a firefighter do? (Fights fires, rescues people, helps people when there's bad weather) What does a police officer do? (Keeps us safe, catches criminals) Is anyone in your family a firefighter / police officer?*
- Point to the picture of the firefighter and then the pictures of places and ask *Where does she work?* Learners point to the picture of the fire station. Show how the number 1 is written next to the picture of the firefighter. Learners work in pairs to number the rest of the people. Play the audio. Learners listen and check.

Track 1.47

Man:	a teacher
Woman:	Picture 3. He works in a school.
Man:	a firefighter
Woman:	Picture 1. She works in a fire station.
Man:	a dentist
Woman:	Picture 5. She works in a dentist's surgery.
Man:	a doctor
Woman:	Picture 2. He works in a hospital.
Man:	a nurse
Woman:	Picture 2. She works in a hospital.
Man:	a police officer
Woman:	Picture 4. He works in a police station.

- Learners work in pairs. One learner points to a person and asks, *Where does he/she work?* The other learner points to the correct place. Remind them to use *Where do they work?* for the picture of the doctor and nurse.

Key: a teacher – 3 a firefighter – 1 a dentist – 5 a doctor / a nurse – 2 a police officer – 4

Note: *firefighter* is acceptable written as one or two words in YLE exams.

3 Look at the pictures. Who can help?

- Say *Listen. Which picture? He's fallen off his bike. Ouch!* Learners point to the correct picture.
- Point to the first picture and ask *Who can help? (A dentist)* Repeat for the other pictures.
- Learners ask and answer the same question in pairs, then write the words under the pictures.

Key: 1 a dentist 2 a firefighter 3 a doctor or a nurse

Activity Book, page 36

See pages TB120–132

Ending the lesson

- Say *What do I do? Listen and guess.* Make sentences about a job, stopping after each one for learners to guess, e.g. *I don't help people. I can work in a theatre or on TV. I love music. I wear beautiful costumes. (Pop star)* You can make the game competitive – give learners five points if they guess after one sentence, four points after the second sentence, and so on.
- Once learners have got the idea, call on volunteers to lead the activity. Help the learner at the front with ideas/ prompts.
- **SA** Use self-assessment to see how well learners think they understand any new vocabulary from the lesson. See Introduction.

Learning outcomes By the end of the lesson, learners will be able to talk about people who help us.

New language *near, restaurant, teach, work* (n)

Recycled language days of the week, jobs, time (*o'clock*), *animal, children, finish, fire, fun, hospital, kitchen, listen, plant* (n), *scary, scene, start, street, tell, work* (v), *I'm a …, I like …-ing, My name's …*, present simple

Materials Jobs and parties flashcards, a picture of someone in your family dressed for work (optional), audio, worksheets/notes from Mission Stages 1 and 2 lessons, digital Mission poster

Warm-up

- Review jobs with the flashcards.
- In pairs, learners spell out jobs on one another's backs and guess the words.
- Show a picture of someone doing their job and say, e.g. *This is my sister. She's a nurse. She works in a hospital. She sometimes works at night or early in the morning. She helps people every day.*

  Stronger learners Think about the working day of someone in their family and tell a partner / the class.
- Say *Let's learn more about different jobs.*

Pupil's Book, page 37

4 Read the sentences. Who is it?

- Say *Open your Pupil's Books at page 37.* Read the jobs in the box and check comprehension.
- Say *Read the sentences. Who is it?* Learners read and match individually, then compare answers in pairs. Check answers.

  Extra support Read each sentence and match with a job as a whole class. Follow up by asking *Who stops fires?* (*A firefighter*) *Who works in a restaurant?* (*A cook*), etc.

Key: 1 a police officer 2 a doctor 3 a firefighter 4 a cook 5 a teacher 6 a farmer

5 1.48 Listen and read. Answer the questions.

- Read the questions with the class. Review *scary.* Play the audio. Learners listen and read, and answer the questions in pairs. Check answers.

  Track 1.48
  See Pupil's Book page 37

Key: 1 She's a teacher. 2 She works in a school. 3 No, she doesn't. 4 No, it isn't. 5 Yes, she does. (She loves it.)

Extension Ask more questions about Sally: *What's her surname?* (*Green*) *Where's the school?* (*Near her house*) *When does she start/finish work?* (*Nine/Four o'clock*) *Why does she love her job?* (*Because she likes helping children*)

Stronger learners In pairs, one learner thinks of someone in their family who works outside the home. The other learner asks the same questions as in Activity 5. Learners tell the class what they found out.

mission Stage 3

- Show the class the third stage of the Mission poster: *Write a scene where someone is helping.* Remind learners of the meaning of *scene* and show an example or draw their attention to the example lines in the box.
- Learners complete the third worksheet task in the Teacher's Resource Book (page 34). See teaching notes on TRB page 27.
- Alternatively, if you do not have the Teacher's Resource Book, tell learners that they need to write a scene for the four characters in their group, with the names of the speakers before the lines.
- Put learners into their Mission groups. They look at their characters, think of a setting for their scene and a situation where one or more of their characters can help. Read through the example in the Pupil's Book. Write *Where?* on the board and a list of places (with learners' help), e.g. *school, street, park, home*. Write *What's happening?* and some ideas for incidents, e.g. *someone falls off their bike, there's a fire, someone can't find their little brother*.
- Groups work together to write the lines of their scene and think of a title for their scene. Monitor and help. Make sure each learner has something to say in the scene. Encourage them to use *Why … ? Because …*

  Extra support Write some useful lines learners can include in their scene on the board, e.g. *Help! / Can you help me? / What's the problem? / Can I help you? / I can help. / Thank you very much.*

Activity Book, page 37

See pages TB120–132

Activity Book, page 30

- Review *My unit goals*. Ask *How is your Mission?* Learners reflect and choose a smiley face for *My mission diary 3*.

Ending the lesson

- **SA** Go back to Stage 3 on the digital Mission poster. Add a tick to the 'Write a scene where someone is helping' stage. Use self-assessment (see Introduction).
- Give out a completion sticker.

4 Read the sentences. Who is it?

a cook | a teacher | a doctor | a farmer | a firefighter | a police officer

1 This person tells people what to do in the street. We must listen.
2 This person works in a hospital.
3 This person stops fires.
4 This person works in a school kitchen or in a restaurant.
5 This person teaches children.
6 This person works with animals and plants.

5 1.48 Listen and read. Answer the questions.

Hello. My name's Sally Green and I'm a teacher. I work in a school near my house. I work from Monday to Friday. I start work at nine o'clock and finish at four o'clock in the afternoon. My job is fun and I love it because I like helping children.

1 What's her job? __________
2 Where does she work? __________
3 Does she work at the weekends? __________
4 Is her job scary? __________
5 Does she like her job? __________

mission STAGE 3

Write a scene where someone is helping.

- In groups, think of a scene. What's happening?
- How can someone help? Write the scene.

Fred: Oh no! Look at the clown's leg!
Daisy: I can help because I'm a doctor!

My mission diary
Activity Book page 30

1 **Do you like costume parties? Talk about your favourite costumes.**

1.49 The costume party

It's Emily's birthday and there's a costume party on Saturday. Matt's thinking about his costume. 'Mum, I want to be a superhero. But Harry wants to be a superhero and he's got a superhero costume.'

'Then what about a pirate costume?' his mum asks. 'You can make a short beard and a moustache with black paper and you've got a pirate hat!'

'No,' Matt says. 'I can't be a pirate. Dan and Zoe have got pirate costumes!'

At school the next day, everyone's talking about their costumes for the party. Emily's got a pop star costume. Julia's got a farmer costume. 'And I'm taking Ludo as a sheep!', she says. Ludo's her little white dog. Only Matt hasn't got a costume.

After school, Matt asks his mum for help. 'Go as a clown,' she says, but Matt says, 'No. A clown's silly. I want a great costume like Harry's or Dan's!' Then his mum has an idea!

Learning outcomes By the end of the lesson, learners will have read a story about helping others.

New language *have an idea, laugh, superhero, be good at …-ing, What about … ?*

Recycled language clothes, jobs, parties, physical descriptions, *birthday, dog, everyone, help, listen, meet, open, paper, sheep, silly, sing, smile, start, stop, wear, want to (be), can/can't, have got,* present continuous, present simple

Materials Jobs and parties flashcards, word cards, a photo of yourself in fancy dress (optional), audio, coloured pens or pencils

Warm-up

- Practise the Jobs and parties words with the flashcards and word cards, e.g. by asking learners to come and match flashcards with word cards (if you don't have word cards, write the words – learners draw lines to match).
- Ask *How do you spell (dentist)?* The class practise spelling the words. Leave the words on the board.
- Divide the class into two teams. Two learners from each team stand at the front with their backs to the board. Ask one learner to spell a word from the board, e.g. *How do you spell 'present'?* He/She spells the word without looking. If he/she is right, the team get a point. Then it is the turn of the other team. Learners swap so everyone gets a turn. The team with the most points wins.
  Stronger learners Add more vocabulary, e.g. *police officer, firefighter, hospital, school.*

Presentation

- Ask *Who helps you?* Learners tell you people who help them. They share stories of when someone has helped them.
- Say *We're going to read a story about someone who needs help.*

Pupil's Book, pages 38 and 39

1 Do you like costume parties? Talk about your favourite costumes.

- Say *Open your Pupil's Books at page 38.* Read the instructions. Learners talk in pairs. Ask extra questions, e.g. *Do you wear a hat for your favourite costume? Does anyone dress up with a beard?* Show a photo of yourself in fancy dress, if possible, and describe the outfit (e.g. *I'm wearing my favourite costume. I'm a cat! I've got a long tail and black ears. I've got a white face.*).
- Ask *Does anyone dress up as a superhero? Who's your favourite superhero?* Write some famous superheroes on the board.

1.49 The costume party

- Look at each picture and ask questions, e.g. Picture 1: *Is the boy happy?* (*No*) *What's on the walls of his bedroom?* (*Posters of superheroes*) *Who's the woman?* (*The boy's mum*) Picture 2: *What does the picture in the 'Think' bubble mean?* Say *She has an idea.* Picture 3: *Where's the boy?* (*At a party*) *Is he happy now?* (*Yes*) *Which costumes can you see?* (*A pirate,*
  a pop star, a dentist, a superhero, a farmer, a clown, a nurse, a police officer)
- Say *Read and listen to the first part.* Play the audio. Learners listen and read. Pause after *superhero costume.* Ask *What's the boy's name?* (*Matt*) *Whose birthday is it?* (*Emily*) *Which costume does Matt want to wear?* (*A superhero costume*) *Why can't he wear it?* (*Because Harry wants to be a superhero*)
  Track 1.49
  See story on Pupil's Book pages 38–39
- Say *Read and listen to the next part.* Pause after *pirate costumes!* Ask *What can Matt make for a pirate costume?* (*A beard and a moustache*) *Has he got a pirate hat?* (*Yes, he has.*) *Why can't he wear a pirate costume?* (*Because Dan and Zoe have got pirate costumes*)
- Play the next part. Pause after *has an idea!* Ask *What is everyone talking about at school?* (*Their costumes*) *Who's got a farmer costume?* (*Julia*) *What kind of animal is Ludo?* (*A dog*) *Is Ludo a dog at the costume party?* (*No, a sheep*) *Who hasn't got a costume?* (*Matt*) *Why doesn't Matt want to be a clown?* (*Because he thinks it's silly*) Check comprehension of *silly.*
- Play the rest of the story. Ask *What's Emily wearing?* (*A pop star costume*) *What's she doing?* (*Singing*) *What is Matt's costume?* (*A superhero pirate clown*) *Why is everyone laughing?* (*Because his costume is funny*) Explain the meaning of *good at* and ask *What is Matt's mum good at?* (*Helping*)
  Extra support Instead of asking questions, make sentences, pausing for learners to say key words, e.g. *The boy's name is (Matt).*
  Extension Play the whole story again, without pauses, for learners to listen and read.

Activity Book, page 38

See pages TB120–132

Ending the lesson

- Ask *How do your family help you? Make a list of ways.* Learners work in pairs to write sentences, e.g. *My parents cook every day. My dad takes me to football.* Monitor and help with vocabulary. Learners share their ideas. Write the sentences on the board.

Learning outcomes By the end of the lesson, learners will have thought about asking for and offering help.

New language *choose*

Recycled language language from the story, adverbs of frequency

Materials A4 paper, coloured pens or pencils, audio

Social and Emotional Skill: Asking for and offering help

- After reading the story, say to learners *Matt asks his mother for help. Why does he need help? (He needs a costume for Emily's birthday party. He doesn't know what he can wear.) Does his mother help him? (Yes) How? (She gives him an idea for a great costume.)*
- Ask *What do your parents do for you?* Learners say one thing their mother or father does for them (e.g. *my father makes my breakfast* or *my mother takes me to school*).
- Point out that it's good that learners do things themselves, but sometimes we need to ask for help. Ask learners in what situations they ask for help. Write some prompts on the board (e.g. *when I can't do my homework, when I can't find something, when I …*).
- Explain that it's important to ask for help in class too (e.g. *when I don't understand a word, when I don't know how to do an activity, when I can't remember a word …*).
- Write a list of ways of asking for help in class:
  - *What does … mean?*
  - *Can you repeat that, please?*
  - *How do I do this?*
  - *How do you say … ?*
- Hand out A4 paper. Learners copy down the questions and decorate the card. In pairs, they role play using the questions in class.

Warm-up

- Write sentences about the story on the board, with names on the right.

1	*It's her birthday.*	*Ludo*
2	*He needs a great costume.*	*Emily*
3	*They've got pirate costumes.*	*Harry*
4	*She's got a pop star costume.*	*Matt's mum*
5	*He's a dog, but he's a sheep at the party.*	*Matt*
6	*He's got a superhero costume.*	*Emily*
7	*She has a good idea.*	*Dan and Zoe*

- In pairs, learners read and match. Check answers. (*1 Emily, 2 Matt, 3 Dan and Zoe, 4 Emily, 5 Ludo, 6 Harry, 7 Matt's mum*)
- Ask *What is Matt's costume at the end of the story? Do you remember? (Superhero pirate clown)*

Pupil's Book, pages 38 and 39

- Say *Open your Pupil's Books at pages 38 and 39.* Play the audio. Learners read and listen to the story again.

  Track 1.49

  See story on Pupil's Book pages 38–39

2 Answer the questions.

- Read the questions and check comprehension of *choose*. Learners think about the answers and talk in pairs. Check answers.

Key: 1 No, he doesn't. 2 His mum has the idea. 3 Yes, he does. 4 Because he's very happy at the end of the story.

Extra support Say *Act out the story*. Summarise the story, sentence by sentence, and mime, e.g. *There's a costume party for Emily's birthday. Matt's thinking about his costume*. Mime thinking. Say *He wants to be a superhero*. Make a superhero flying pose. *But Harry's got a superhero costume. Matt can be a pirate.* Mime swordfighting. *But Dan and Zoe have got pirate costumes. Emily's got a pop star costume*. Mime singing into a microphone. *Julia's got a farmer costume*. Mime driving a tractor. *Matt's sad. He hasn't got a costume. Then his mum has an idea*. Mime having an idea. *It's the day of the party. Matt opens the door.* Mime opening the door. *Matt says 'Meet the superhero pirate clown!'* Mime being a superhero, then a pirate, then a clown.

- Repeat and encourage learners to act the story with you.
- Repeat and this time encourage learners to complete some of your sentences.

3 Ask and answer.

- Read the speech bubbles. Put learners into pairs to talk about helping.

  Extra support Write some prompts on the board, e.g. *wash the car, do the shopping, clean my bedroom, look after my brother*.

Activity Book, page 39

See pages TB120–132

Ending the lesson

- **SA** Use self-assessment to see how well learners think they understand the story. See Introduction.

It's the day of the party. Emily's wearing her pop star costume and she's singing. Everyone's listening to her, but who's this? The door opens and Matt comes in.

'Hello, everyone,' he says. 'Meet the superhero pirate clown!'

Emily stops singing. Everyone starts laughing because Matt's costume's so funny!

Matt smiles. 'Thank you, Mum,' he thinks. 'You're good at helping!'

2 Answer the questions.

1 Does Matt choose his costume?

2 Who has the idea for his costume?

3 Does Matt like the idea?

4 How do you know?

3 Ask and answer.

Tell me about when you help someone.

I sometimes help my grandma with her dog. I feed him when she isn't well.

1 Look and read. Tick ✓ the sentences which describe the picture.

1 Jim is going to a costume party. ☐
2 Jim's having a party at his house. ☐
3 He's got a present for his friend, Zoe. ☐
4 He's opening a present. ☐

2 Look at pictures 2–4. What's the story called? Circle the answer.

Jim's kitten / Zoe's present / Jim's party

The examiner can ask questions to help you, for example *What's the kitten doing?*

3 Make sentences about the pictures. Use some of these words.

Zoe's/Jim's … Zoe's/Jim's got …
The kitten's walking … … 's happy/sad.
… are looking/pointing. There's / There are …

Learning outcomes By the end of the lesson, learners will have practised talking about a picture story (A1 Movers Speaking Part 2).

Test skills Understanding the beginning of a story and then continuing it based on a series of pictures

Recycled language jobs, parties, physical descriptions, *describe, happy, kitten, look, open, point, sad, walk, have got,* present continuous, present simple, *There is/are …*

Materials paper, coloured pens or pencils, practice paper for Movers Speaking Part 2 (optional)

Warm-up

- Give out paper and say *Let's draw a party! Think of a room before the party starts. What do you need?* Set a time limit so this stage doesn't take too long. Monitor and ask questions, e.g. *Is it a costume party? Is it someone's birthday? What about a cake? What's this on the table?*
- Draw your own picture. Show it to the class, point and say, e.g. *At my party there are balloons on the wall. There's a big table with drinks and food. There's a lovely chocolate cake!*
- Learners describe their picture to a partner.

  Fast finishers Label items in their picture. Monitor and check spelling.

Presentation

- Say *Let's practise for a speaking exam.* Show an example of the Movers Speaking paper (Part 2): the four pictures and the story title. Say *Part 2 of the exam has four pictures that make a story. The name of the story is at the top. You need to look and think about the story and then tell the examiner. The name of the most important character is there. Let's practise looking at pictures and making a story.*

Pupil's Book, page 40

1 Look and read. Tick ✓ the sentences which describe the picture.

- Say *Open your Pupil's Books at page 40.* Ask questions about picture 1, e.g. *What's the boy's name? (Jim) What has he got? (A present) What's he wearing? (A pirate costume) Whose birthday is it? (Zoe's)* Read the instructions. Learners work in pairs to read and tick. Check answers.

  Extra support Read the sentences as a class and decide together which to tick.

Key: 1, 3

2 Look at pictures 2–4. What's the story called? Circle the answer.

- Point to picture 2 and ask *Who's this girl? (Zoe)* Say *Jim's giving his present to Zoe.* Ask *Is Zoe wearing a costume? What costume is it? (Pop star)* Say *Look at pictures 3 and 4. What's happening? What's the story about?*
- Read the possible titles and ask *What's the story called?* Ask learners to vote for each title.

Key: Zoe's present

3 Make sentences about the pictures. Use some of these words.

- Read the instructions. Read the phrases in the box and check comprehension. Point to the first picture and ask for some example sentences, e.g. *There's a party at Zoe's house. Jim's wearing a pirate costume. There are balloons.*
- Put learners into pairs to describe pictures 2 to 4 in the same way. Monitor and help.

  Extra support Write more example sentences on the board for learners to match with the correct picture before the pair work.

Key: (possible answers) Zoe's wearing a pop star costume. She's got long, pink hair. Zoe likes the present. Zoe's happy. It's a comic (book). The comic book's on the table. The window's open. There's a kitten. The kitten's walking on Zoe's present. Zoe's sad. The other children are looking at the kitten. A girl is pointing at the kitten.

Extension Hand out paper. Learners imagine what happens next in the story about Zoe's party (or invent a story of their own). They draw four pictures and give the story a title. Monitor and help. In pairs, learners show their pictures and explain what is happening in the first picture. Their partner tells the rest of the story.

Point to the monkey at the bottom of the page and read the sentence. Tell learners not to worry if they don't follow the story at first, or can't find the words they need. The examiner has words which can help.

Activity Book, page 40

See pages TB120–132

Ending the lesson

- Write the following questions on the board:

  When do you read stories?
  Where do you like to read?
  What type of stories do you like?
  Who reads stories with you?
- Learners ask and answer in pairs. Discuss answers with the whole class.

Learning outcomes By the end of the lesson, learners will have revised the language in the unit and acted out a scene for the class.

Recycled language unit language

Materials Jobs and parties and Physical descriptions flashcards, worksheets/notes from Mission Stages 1–3 lessons, props and costumes for the scenes (optional), dice and counters (for Activity Book game), coloured pens or pencils, digital Mission poster

Warm-up

- Put learners into groups. Say *Let's do a quiz.*
- Put the flashcards from the unit on the board. Ask for examples of the following and give a point for each correct answer:
  Someone who works with animals
  Hair men sometimes have above their mouths
  Two jobs which help us
  Two words for hair colour
  Someone who likes treasure
  Something we give at a birthday party
  Alternative Play 'Hangman'. Draw a picture of a cliff dropping down to the sea. Draw a shark fin in the sea. Write the numbers 1–6 spaced out along the top of the cliff.
- Choose a word from the unit and write up a line for each letter in the word, e.g. *costume* would be _ _ _ _ _ _ _.
- Learners call out letters. If they say a letter that is in the word, write it in the relevant space. If the letter is not in the word, tick one of the numbers, starting with 1, at the top of the cliff.
- Learners try to fill in all the letters and guess the word before they reach 6 and lose.
- Write the letters they have said at the side of the board.

Pupil's Book, page 41

mission in action!

Act out your scene for the class.

- Say *Open your Pupil's Books at page 41.* Point to the Mission box or show learners the last stage of the digital Mission poster. Say *Let's put our Mission in action!* Say *Act out your scene for the class.*
- Read the instructions. Say *First you tell the class about your scene and the characters.* Show learners what to do: pretend you are presenting a scene, tell them a title and mime showing a picture of your character and describing yourself. Say *Then you say 'Here is our scene' and you act out your scene.*
- Put learners into their Mission groups. Give them time to practise presenting their scene and characters and then time to rehearse the scene itself. If possible, learners use props/costumes. Monitor and help.
- Groups take turns to present their scene and act it out. Remind them to thank the audience (*Thank you for watching and listening!*).

Self-assessment

- **SA** Say *Did you like our 'Plan and act out a scene' Mission? Think and draw a face.* Learners draw a happy face, neutral face or sad face and then hold it up in the air.
- Ask *Was this Mission better than the last Mission* (do a 'thumbs up' gesture) *or worse* (do a 'thumbs down' gesture)*?* Check comprehension of the question. Learners show you what they think.
- Say *Our next Mission is 'Act out a visit to my cousins' new home.'* Explain the meaning of *cousin*. Ask *Have you got any cousins? How many have you got? How old are they? Do you often visit them? What kind of things do you do?*
- Ask *What can you do better in the next Mission? Choose one thing and write.* Monitor and help learners write a simple sentence, e.g. *I can talk more in groups. I can use my imagination more*. They compare sentences in pairs. Make notes of their ideas.

Activity Book, page 41

See pages TB120–132

Activity Book, page 30

- Review *My unit goals*. Ask *How is your Mission?* Learners reflect and choose a smiley face for *My mission diary* the final stage.
- Point to the sunflower. Learners read the 'can do' statements and tick them if they agree they have achieved them. They colour each leaf green if they are very confident or orange if they think they need more practice.
- Point to the word stack sign. Ask learners to look back at the unit and find at least five new words they have learnt. They write them in their word stack.

Ending the lesson

- **SA** Go back to the completion stage on the digital Mission poster. Add a tick or invite a learner to do it. Use self-assessment (see Introduction).
- Give out a completion sticker.
- Tell learners *You have finished your Mission! Well done!*

Review

3

mission in action!

Act out your scene for the class.

My mission diary
Activity Book page 30

★ Tell the class the name of your scene.

Hello, everyone! This is 'What a silly clown!'

★ Say your character names and describe yourselves.

Hi! I'm Daisy. I'm a doctor. I'm tall with long, blonde hair.

★ Act out your scene.

Oh no! Look at the clown's leg!

I can help because I'm a doctor!

★ Thank the class.

Thank you for watching and listening!

Review ●●● Units 1–3

1 Watch the video and do the quiz.

2 1.50 Listen and circle the activities you hear. Then listen and complete.

	Jack	Zoe
FRI	watch a [1] ________	go [2] ________
SAT	go to the *forest* go for a [4] ________	play [3] ________
SUN	Kim's party at [5] ______ o'clock Costume [6] ________	Costume [7] ________

3 Choose a person. In pairs, ask, answer and guess who.

How often do you watch TV?

I sometimes watch TV.

What time do you wake up?

I wake up at seven o'clock.

Are you … ?

✓✓✓ always ✓✓ often ✓✗ sometimes ✗ never

Name	watch TV	play football	read comics	have lunch	wake up	go shopping
Sally	✓✗	✓✓✓	✗	12 o'clock	8 o'clock	✗
Peter	✗	✓✓	✓✗	1 o'clock	7 o'clock	✓✗
Clare	✓✗	✓✓✓	✗	12 o'clock	7 o'clock	✗
Jane	✗	✓✓	✓✗	1 o'clock	8 o'clock	✓✗

Learning outcomes By the end of the lesson, learners will have consolidated language from Units 1–3.

Recycled language countryside, daily routines, days of the week, free time activities, parties, times (*o'clock*), *afternoon, morning,* adverbs of frequency, *How often ... ?,* present simple for routines

Materials flashcards from Units 1 and 2, word cards (optional), video, audio, teaching clock(s) (optional)

Warm-up

- Revise the Countryside and Daily routines words using the flashcards.
- Divide learners into two groups and ask them to stand in two lines at the front of the class. Draw a line down the centre of the board and write each team's name (or number) as a heading on the side nearest to them.
- Place a selection of flashcards on the floor or on a table at the back of the classroom. Define one of the words, e.g. *This is something you need after you have a shower*. The two learners who are at the front of their teams race to find the correct flashcard (towel) and stick it on the board.
- The team with the most flashcards on their side of the board wins.

  Stronger learners Use word cards instead of flashcards.

Pupil's Book, page 42

1 Watch the video and do the quiz.

- Show the video to learners.
- Ask learners to do the quiz. Check their answers to see how much learners can remember.
- Repeat this at the end of the Review unit and compare the results to measure progress.

2 1.50 Listen and circle the activities you hear. Then listen and complete.

- Say *Open your Pupil's Books at page 42.* Give learners time to look at the small pictures. Then say an activity at random (*play football, go for a swim, watch a DVD, go shopping, go to a costume party, write an email, go to the forest, go to the mountains*). Learners point to the correct picture. They do the same in pairs.
- Read the instructions. Play the audio for learners to listen and circle the pictures of the activities they hear.

Track 1.50

Zoe: Hello, Jack!
Jack: Hi, Zoe! Hey, do you have any plans for Saturday morning?
Zoe: Why?
Jack: Because I want to go to the forest with my family. Do you want to come?
Zoe: I'm sorry, I can't. I always play football on Saturday morning. I can come after lunch.
Jack: Oh, I always go for a swim on Saturday afternoon. How about Friday after school? Do you want to watch a DVD with me?
Zoe: Oh, I must go shopping with my mum on Friday. Mum always works on Saturdays and I must buy a present for Kim's birthday on Sunday.
Jack: Oh, yes! When is it?
Zoe: At five o'clock.
Jack: That's right. What's your costume? I want to be a pirate!
Zoe: My costume's a clown!
Jack: Great! See you on Sunday!

Key: Learners circle the pictures of shopping, swimming, costumes, football, forest and DVD.

- Play the audio again for learners to complete the chart.

Key: 1 DVD 2 shopping 3 football 4 swim 5 five 6 pirate 7 clown

3 Choose a person. In pairs, ask, answer and guess who.

- Revise free time activities with the flashcards.
- Make sure learners understand the table by making sentences, e.g. *She wakes up at eight o'clock and she never reads comics.* Learners say the name (e.g. *Sally*).
- Read the instructions and the speech bubbles. Model the activity with a learner (he/she chooses a person and you make the questions).
- Put the class into pairs. Learners take it in turns to choose a person. Monitor and support.

  Extra support Show a time (*o'clock* only) on a teaching clock or draw a clock on the board. Ask *What time is it?* Learners answer, e.g. *Eight o'clock.* Repeat with different times.
- Set the clock so learners can't see (or draw a clock). Say *On Saturdays I play tennis at ... What time do I play tennis? Guess!* Learners say, e.g. *Two o'clock.* When they guess correctly, show the clock to confirm. You can make this competitive by giving them only three guesses and scoring a point when they don't manage to guess / awarding them a point when they do.

  Stronger learners Play the same game in pairs.

Activity Book, page 42

See pages TB120–132

Ending the lesson

- In pairs, learners ask and answer *How often ... ?* questions using the pictures in Activity 2 as prompts, e.g. *How often do you play football?*

Learning outcomes By the end of the lesson, learners will have consolidated language from Units 1–3.

Recycled language jobs, physical descriptions, *feed, help, kitten, make a cake, puppy*, adverbs of frequency, *How often … ?, must,* present continuous, present simple

Materials Friendly family flashcards, Jobs and parties flashcards, paper, coloured pens or pencils, video

Warm-up

- Show the Friendly family flashcards and Jobs and parties flashcards (human characters only). Each time you show one, ask questions, e.g. *Has he got straight or curly hair? Is he tall? Has he got a beard? What about a moustache? Has he got blonde hair? What colour is his hair? What does he do? What's he doing in the picture?* Learners answer.
- Display flashcards and say *Look and remember*. Give learners two minutes to look at the pictures and then take them off the board.
- Hide one of the flashcards behind your back without showing learners which one, e.g. the pirate. Ask *Which picture have I got? Ask me questions.* Choose a learner. Say *Have you got a man, a woman or a child?* The learner repeats. Say *It's a man*. Choose another learner. Say *Has he got black hair?* The learner repeats. Say *Yes, he has.* Ask another learner *Can you ask about a beard?* (*Has he got a beard?*) Encourage learners to ask more questions in this way until they guess *pirate*.
- Continue with other flashcards. Encourage learners to ask questions until they guess who the person is each time. Learners say, e.g. *Jim* or *the pop star*.

  Extension Put learners into groups of six. Give them a selection of flashcards face down. Learners take it in turns to pick up a flashcard without showing the group. The other learners ask them questions about their flashcard following the same sequence.

Pupil's Book, page 43

4 Look and read. Correct the sentences.

- Say *Open your Pupil's Books at page 43.* Focus on the pictures. Ask *Where's the (cook)?* Learners point.
- Read the instructions and go through the example.
- Learners work in pairs to read and correct the sentences. Monitor and support. Check answers.

  Extra support Ask questions about all the pictures before learners read and correct, e.g. *Has the farmer got curly hair? Is it blonde? What's she doing?*

Key: 2 The doctor's got short, curly hair. She's listening to music. 3 The pirate's got a long beard. He's (roller) skating. 4 The farmer's got straight, brown hair. She's feeding a kitten. 5 The nurse's got a moustache. He's helping a girl.

Extension Learners find a picture of a person in the book and write two sentences about him/her. One sentence must have a mistake. They show the picture and their sentences to a partner, who corrects the mistake.

5 Write about you.

- Read the questions and check comprehension. Ask two or three learners to give answers to the first two questions.
- Learners write their answers individually. Monitor and help.

  Extra support Write model answers / prompts on the board.
- Put learners into pairs with someone they don't know very well. They ask and answer the questions. Ask different learners to tell the class the best answer their partner gave.

  Stronger learners Write three more questions for their partner beginning *How often do you … ? When do you … ?* and *What do you do … ?*

Activity Book, page 43

See pages TB120–132

Ending the lesson

- Hand out paper and ask learners to draw a picture of a person – full length. Set a time limit so this stage doesn't take too long.
- Put learners in pairs with someone who hasn't seen their picture. One learner describes his/her person for the other learner to draw, e.g. *My person's a man. He's short and fat. He's got short, straight, red hair. He's got green eyes and a small nose. He's got a beard*. The other learner can ask questions, e.g. *Has he got a moustache?* but mustn't look at the picture. When the first learner has finished describing, they compare pictures. Then they swap roles.

Repeat the video and quiz.

4 Look and read. Correct the sentences.

1 The cook's got straight hair. He's making a cake.

The cook's got curly hair. He's reading a comic.

2 The doctor's got long, straight hair. She's helping a girl.

3 The pirate's got a long moustache. He's looking at his treasure.

4 The farmer's got curly, blonde hair. She's feeding a puppy.

5 The nurse's got a beard. He's reading a book.

5 Write about you.

What are you doing now?

When do you clean your teeth?

What do you do at the weekend?

How often do you visit the doctor?

What must you do after school?

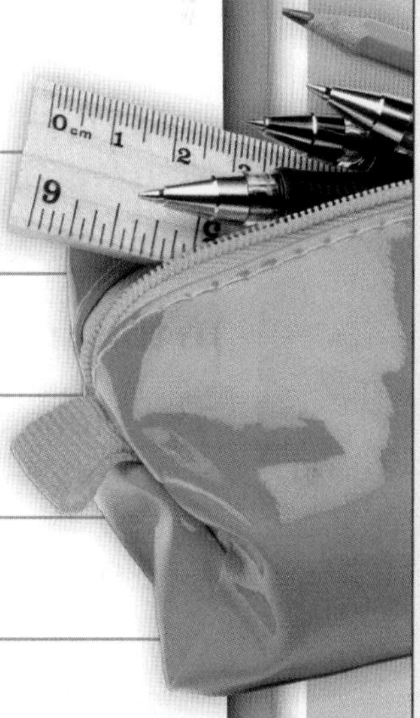

4 The family at home

1 Watch the video. Draw something which you do at home.

mission Act out a visit to my cousins' new home

In this unit I will:

1. Make a family and talk to my cousin.
2. Draw our family's home and talk to my cousin.
3. Invent a machine for our home.
★ Act out a visit to my other cousins' new home.

Unit 4 learning outcomes

In Unit 4, learners learn to:

- talk about extended family and homes
- make comparisons
- use possessive pronouns
- learn about machines at home
- read a story about a surprise party and think about initiative and managing their own emotions

Materials video, coloured pens or pencils, digital Mission poster, a copy of the Mission worksheet (Teacher's Resource Book page 44)

Self-assessment

- **SA** Say *Open your Pupil's Books at page 44. Look at the picture. Who can you see? (A family) Where are they? (In their home)* Point and ask *Who's this? Is she the children's mum? (Yes, or big sister) Is she in the bathroom? (No, in the kitchen) Who's got (curly) hair? (The man) Is this his son/daughter? Can you see a (table)?* Use self-assessment (see Introduction). Say *OK. Let's learn.*

Warm-up

- Say *Look at the picture and remember.* Time one minute, then say *Close your books!* Ask, e.g. *Are there any paintings on the wall? Is there a sofa? What colour is the man's T-shirt?* You can play this as a team game, asking each team a question in turn.

Pupil's Book, page 44

1 Watch the video. Draw something which you do at home.

- Say *In this unit we're talking about families and homes.* Say *Let's watch the video.* To introduce the topic of the unit, play the video.
- Say *Look at page 44.* Talk about what the family are doing in the picture. Encourage learners to suggest things they often do in their own homes. Show the space on the page. Say *What do you do at home? Draw it here.* Monitor and check. Help each learner to make a sentence about what they are doing, e.g. *I'm playing with my sister.*
  Fast finishers Learners write a sentence about what they are doing in their picture.

mission Act out a visit to my cousins' new home

- Point to the Mission box or the digital Mission poster and say *Our Mission is: Act out a visit to my cousins' new home.* Remind learners of the meaning of *cousin.*
- Say *Point to number 1. Make a family and talk to my cousin.* Tell learners that they are going to work in groups to draw an imaginary family: grandparents, mum, dad and two children. Each group makes a family. Then they talk to a learner in another group (their cousin) and compare the people in their families.
- Say *Point to number 2. Draw our family's home and talk to my cousin.* Explain that learners design a new home for their 'family'. Draw a simple house on the board and ask *What do you need to put in the house?* Revise names of rooms and features (*door, window, garden*) and add them to your picture. Say *After you draw the house you describe it to your cousin.*
- Say *Point to number 3. Invent a machine for our home. There are lots of machines in our homes. They can help us with washing, cooking and cleaning, or they can be for watching films and listening to music.* Check comprehension of *invent.* Say *In Stage 3 you invent a new machine for your new home.*
- Say *The last stage is 'Act out a visit to my other cousins' new home.'* Ask *What happens when you visit a new home? (People show you the house.) The people say 'This is the living room. The windows are very big. We like it because …'*
- Say *This is our Mission.* Go through the stages of the Mission again.
- For ideas on monitoring and assessment, see Introduction.

Activity Book, page 44

My unit goals

- Help learners to complete the unit goals. See notes on page TB6.
- You can go back to these unit goals at the end of each Mission stage during the unit and review them.

Ending the lesson

- Write a sentence about your home on the board, e.g. *My house has got a red door.* Ask the class *Whose house has got a red door too?* If no-one puts up their hand, try another sentence.
- Say *Now write one sentence about your home.* Write some useful words on the board (names of rooms, *hall, clock, mirror, window*, etc.). Monitor and help.
- Learners stand up and say their sentence to other learners until they find someone who says *Me too!* Help pairs make a sentence about what they have in common, e.g. *There's a clock in the kitchen.*

Learning outcomes By the end of the lesson, learners will be able to talk about extended family.

New language *aunt, cousin, daughter, granddaughter, grandparents, grandson, grown-up* (n), *parents, son, uncle, at the front*

Recycled language *baby, brother, children, (grand)father, (grand)mother, sister, smile, stand, tall,* imperatives, prepositions of place, present continuous

Materials Friendly family flashcards, Extended family flashcards, audio, video, coloured pens or pencils

Warm-up

- Show the Friendly family flashcards and ask *Who's this? Who's Jenny's brother? Who's Mr Friendly's father?* etc.

Presentation

- Make the Friendly family tree on the board with flashcards. Add *uncle* and *aunt* (holding *cousin*). Use the family tree to teach the new extended family words.

Pupil's Book, page 45

1 1.51 1.52 Listen and point. Then listen and number.

- Say *Open your Pupil's Books at page 45. Who can you see?* Learners say the characters. Say *Point to Jim and Jenny's cousin. Point to their aunt. Point to their parents.*
- Ask *Where's the small tractor? Can you find it?*
- Ask *Who are the children in the picture? (Jenny, Jim, Zoe) Who's the baby? (Zoe)* Say *The other people are grown-ups.* Write *grown-up* on the board and practise.
- Say *Listen and point to the people*. Play Track 1.51.

Tracks 1.51 and 1.52

(1) Today, there's a family photo. The children are at the front and the grown-ups are behind.

Photographer: Excuse me, everyone! Please listen. OK. Jenny and Jim, come and sit on the grass at the front, please.
Jenny: OK. Can Cameron sit between us? He's part of the family.
Photographer: Yes, of course. Now, let's have the grandparents behind their big grandchildren. …
(2)Photographer: … Grandpa Friendly, sit behind your granddaughter, please, …
(3)Photographer: … and Grandma Friendly, can you sit behind your grandson, please?
(4) Jim: Can our cousin Zoe sit here, …
(5) Jim: … with Aunt Julia, behind Cameron?
(6) Photographer: Good idea! Yes, that's nice. We can see the baby in the photo.
Jenny: Where's Uncle Jack standing?
(7) Photographer: He's tall, so he's standing behind your Aunt Julia and between your parents.
(8) Grandma: That's right. I'm sitting in front of my son.
(9) Grandpa: And I'm sitting next to my daughter.
Photographer: OK, that's nice. The children are smiling … and the grown-ups … can you all smile too, please? OK, that's lovely. Don't move!
Grandpa: Oh, Rocky!

- Say *Listen and number*. Play Track 1.52. Learners write numbers 2–9 in the boxes. (Note that Track 1.52 omits the last two lines.)
- Ask *What's number (2)?* Learners say the word/name.
- Ask *Who's sitting at the front? Who's sitting next to Grandpa? Who's sitting in front of Grandma? Who's standing behind Aunt Julia?*

Key: 2 granddaughter 3 grandson 4 cousin Zoe 5 Aunt Julia 6 Uncle Jack 7 parents 8 son 9 daughter

2 1.53 Say the chant.

- Play the audio or video. Learners point and chant.

Track 1.53

Aunt, uncle, cousin,
Parents, daughter, son,
Granddaughter, grandson,
Grandparents, grown-ups. [x2]

3 1.54 Listen and say the name.

- Play the audio. Pause for learners to say the name(s).

Track 1.54

1 She's Jim and Jenny's cousin.
2 He's sitting behind his granddaughter.
3 She's holding her baby daughter.
4 They're sitting in front of their grandparents.
5 She's sitting behind her grandson.
6 She's sitting in front of her son.
7 He's standing behind his baby daughter.
8 She's sitting between her parents.

Key: 1 Zoe 2 Grandpa Friendly 3 Aunt Julia 4 Jim and Jenny 5 Grandma Friendly 6 Grandma Friendly 7 Uncle Jack 8 Aunt Julia

Activity Book, page 45

See pages TB120–132

Ending the lesson

- **SA** Show the Extended family flashcards. Ask *Do you know the words?* Use self-assessment (see Introduction). Learners show how they feel.

Vocabulary 1

4

1 1.51 1.52 Listen and point. Then listen and number.

2 1.53 Say the chant.

3 1.54 Listen and say the name.

The Friendly Farm

2.02

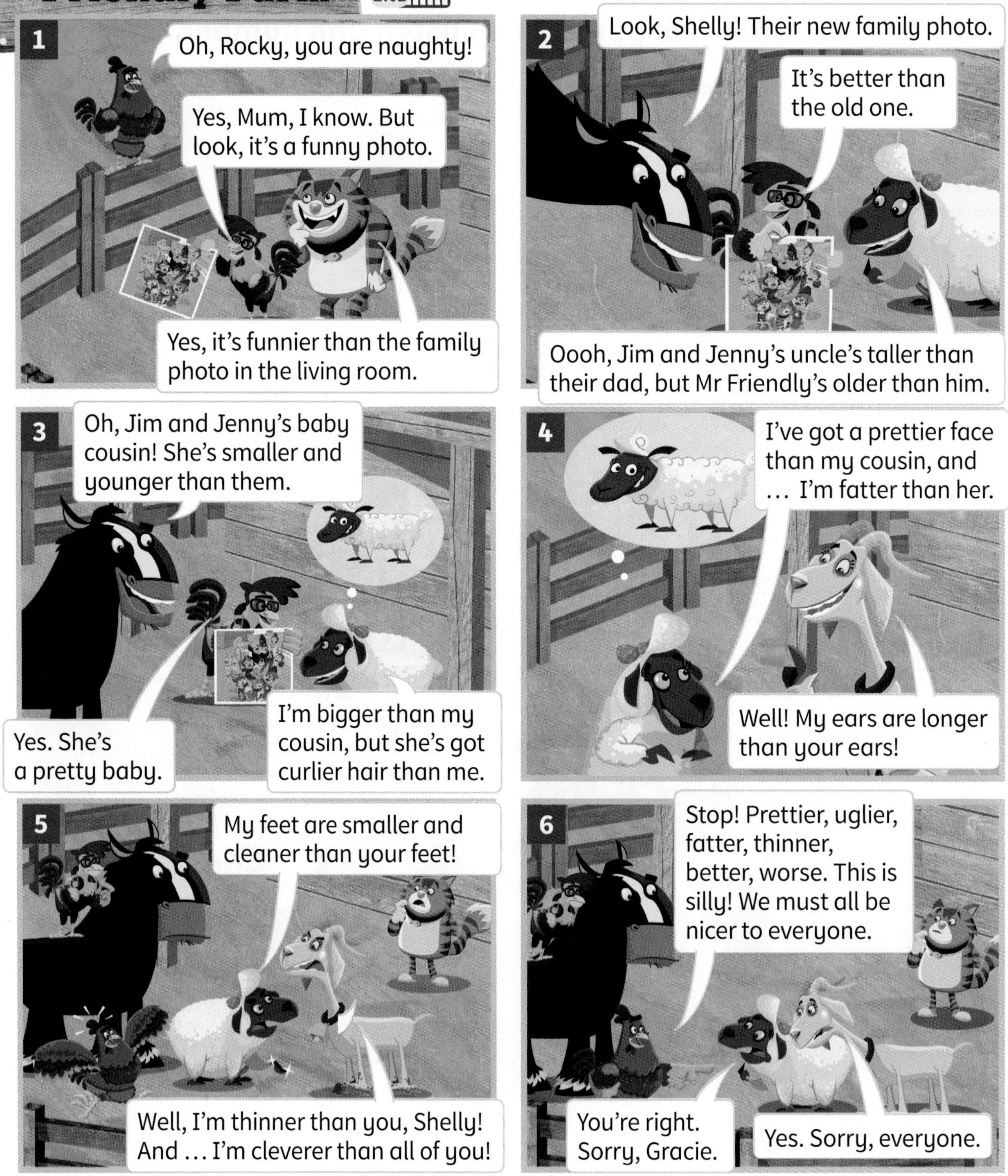

1
Oh, Rocky, you are naughty!
Yes, Mum, I know. But look, it's a funny photo.
Yes, it's funnier than the family photo in the living room.
2
Look, Shelly! Their new family photo.
It's better than the old one.
Oooh, Jim and Jenny's uncle's taller than their dad, but Mr Friendly's older than him.
3
Oh, Jim and Jenny's baby cousin! She's smaller and younger than them.
Yes. She's a pretty baby.
I'm bigger than my cousin, but she's got curlier hair than me.
4
I've got a prettier face than my cousin, and … I'm fatter than her.
Well! My ears are longer than your ears!
5
My feet are smaller and cleaner than your feet!
Well, I'm thinner than you, Shelly! And … I'm cleverer than all of you!
6
Stop! Prettier, uglier, fatter, thinner, better, worse. This is silly! We must all be nicer to everyone.
You're right. Sorry, Gracie.
Yes. Sorry, everyone.

1 2.03 **Listen and say the number.**

Learning outcomes By the end of the lesson, learners will be able to understand when they hear comparative adjectives.

New language *clever, You're right.* comparative adjectives

Recycled language adjectives, extended family, parts of the body, physical descriptions, *baby, living room, photo, Sorry*

Materials sticky notes or slips of paper, photos of you and your family (optional), audio, video

Warm-up

- Say *Tell me a word we can use for a description, a word like 'old'.* Brainstorm adjectives and write them on the board. Give or ask for example sentences. Learners can also match opposites (*small/big*, etc.). Teach *clever* and revise *clean, pretty* and *naughty*.
- Give each learner a sticky note or slip of paper. Divide the class into two groups and ask one group to write an adjective on their note. The other group write a noun (give some examples first). Monitor and support.
- Learners stand up and walk around. Learners with an adjective find a partner who has a noun that their adjective can describe (e.g. *pretty* and *kitten*). Pairs tell you their combination or stick their words on the board.
- **SA** Use self-assessment to check how well learners think they understand the adjectives. See Introduction.

Presentation

- Use items in the classroom or photos of your family to present comparative adjectives, e.g. *This blue pencil is shorter than the red pencil. The red pencil is longer. This book is newer than this one. I'm older than my sister. My brother is taller than me.* Then hold up the items/photos and ask *Which pencil is shorter? Which book is newer? Who is taller, me or my brother?*

Pupil's Book, page 46

2.02 The Friendly Farm song

- Play the introductory song at the beginning of the cartoon story. Learners listen and sing.

Track 2.02
See The Friendly Farm song on page TB5

2.02 The Friendly Farm

- Say *Open your Pupil's Books at page 46.* Ask *What are the animals looking at?* (*The Friendly family photo*) *Who's in the photo?* Learners name the characters.
- Ask *Why do the animals say 'Sorry'?* Write the question on the board. Play the audio or video. Learners listen and read. Check answers. (*Because they must be nicer / they mustn't talk about others*) Explain the meaning of *better* and *worse* and check understanding of *silly*.

Track 2.02
The Friendly Farm song + see cartoon on Pupil's Book page 46

- Play the audio or video again. Pause after each picture and ask questions: 1: *Does Rocky like the photo?* (*Yes, he thinks it's funny.*) 2: *Is it an old photo?* (*No, it's new.*) *Who's taller, Uncle Jack or Mr Friendly?* (*Uncle Jack*) 3: *Is Shelly bigger than her cousin?* (*Yes, she is.*) *Who's got curlier hair, Shelly or her cousin?* (*Shelly's cousin*) 4: *Who's fatter, Shelly or her cousin?* (*Shelly*) 5: *Who's got smaller feet, Shelly or Gracie?* (*Shelly*) *Whose feet are cleaner?* (*Shelly's*) *Who says she's cleverer than the other animals?* (*Gracie*) 6: *Is Henrietta happy?* (*No, she's angry.*)

1 2.03 Listen and say the number.

- Play the first sentence as an example. Learners find the correct picture, point and say the number. Play the rest of the audio. Pause after each sentence for learners to answer.

Track 2.03

a	Shelly:	I'm bigger than my cousin, but she's got curlier hair than me. [3]
b	Henrietta:	Prettier, uglier, fatter, thinner, better, worse. This is silly! [6]
c	Cameron:	Yes, it's funnier than the family photo in the living room. [1]
d	Gracie:	I'm cleverer than all of you! [5]
e	Henrietta:	We must all be nicer to everyone. [6]
f	Harry:	She's smaller and younger than them. [3]
g	Rocky:	It's better than the old one. [2]
h	Gracie:	My ears are longer than your ears! [4]

Key: See numbers in audioscript

Activity Book, page 46

See pages TB120–132

Ending the lesson

- **SA** Use self-assessment to see how well learners think they understand the adjectives in the story. See Introduction.
- Say *Stand up.* Make a comparison, e.g. *Grandpa Friendly's older than Jim. Yes or no?* Learners jump to the left or right (or give a 'thumbs up' or a 'thumbs down'). Repeat with different comparative adjectives.

Learning outcomes By the end of the lesson, learners will be able to use comparative adjectives to describe people and things.

New language *Gracie's ears are long. They're longer than Shelly's ears. Those puppies are both fat, but the brown puppy's fatter than the white one. My cousin's hair is curly. It's curlier than my uncle's. Shelly's singing is bad. It's worse than Gracie's singing.*

Recycled language adjectives, extended family, physical descriptions, *better, puppy, worse*

Materials Extended family flashcards, Friendly family and Friendly Farm animal character flashcards, audio, Mission worksheets (Teacher's Resource Book page 44), digital Mission poster

Warm-up

- Show the Friendly family flashcards and ask *Who's this?* (*Julia*) Encourage learners to ask, e.g. *Is she Jim's cousin?* (*No, his aunt*) *What's her daughter's name?* (*Zoe*) *Has she got straight hair?* (*No, curly*)

Presentation

- Put flashcards of Gracie and Shelly on the board. Say and write *Gracie is taller than Shelly. Gracie's legs are longer than Shelly's.* Explain comparatives with *-er*.
- Ask *Who's prettier – Shelly or Gracie?* Say and write *Shelly is prettier than Gracie.* (or the other way round, depending on what the class decides). Explain the spelling for comparative adjectives ending in *-y*, e.g. *prettier, happier, dirtier, curlier.*
- Add a flashcard of Harry. Say and write *Harry is bigger than Gracie and Shelly.* Explain the spelling for comparative adjectives ending in some consonants, e.g. *bigger, sadder, fatter*.

Pupil's Book, page 47

2.04 Gracie's Grammar

- Say *Open your Pupil's Books at page 47.* Write the sentences on the board. Revise *better* and *worse*.
- Play the audio. Pause for learners to repeat.

Track 2.04
See Pupil's Book page 47

1 2.05 Listen and stick. Then look, read and write.

- Describe the stickers, e.g. *long, straight hair*. Learners point.
- Play the audio. Learners point to the correct sticker.
- Play the audio again. Learners stick on the hair.

Track 2.05

1 Man: In this photo you can see my son with his family, and my daughter with her family. Those two children are my grandchildren. They're cousins.
Woman: Which is your son?
Man: Here he is. My son's got short, brown hair. His hair's shorter and straighter than my daughter's.

2 Woman: So your daughter hasn't got red hair?
Man: No, this is my daughter. My daughter's hair's short and curly. It's curlier than my granddaughter's hair.

3 Woman: Yes, I see. Your granddaughter has got long, straight hair.
Man: That's right. She's got longer hair than her cousin.

4 Woman: Yes, but your grandson's hair is longer than some boys' hair.
Man: Yes, it is. But it's shorter than his cousin's.

- Point to the example sentence. Remind learners to use the correct spelling for the comparative forms.

Key: 2 curlier 3 longer 4 shorter

mission Stage 1

- Point to the Mission box or show learners the first stage of the digital Mission poster: *Make a family. Then talk to your cousin.*
- Learners complete the worksheet task in the Teacher's Resource Book (page 44). See teaching notes on TRB page 37.
- Alternatively, if you do not have the Teacher's Resource Book, ask learners to make a family of six together – grandma and grandpa, mum, dad and two children (a boy and a girl). They decide what each person will look like. Each learner draws a picture of the whole family.
- Put two groups together. Explain that the children are cousins. Each learner takes the role of one of the children, and they compare families, e.g. *Your brother is shorter than my brother.*

Activity Book, page 47

See pages TB120–132

Activity Book, page 44

- Review *My unit goals*. Ask *How is your Mission?* Learners reflect and choose a smiley face for *My mission diary 1*.

Ending the lesson

- **SA** Go back to Stage 1 on the digital Mission poster. Say *We made a family and talked to our cousins.* Add a tick to the 'We made a family …' stage. Use self-assessment (see Introduction).
- Give out a completion sticker.

2.04 Gracie's Grammar

Gracie's ears are **long**. They're **longer** than Shelly's ears.

Those puppies are both **fat**, but the brown puppy's **fatter** than the white one.

My cousin's hair is **curly**. It's **curlier** than my uncle's.

Shelly's singing is **bad**. It's **worse** than Gracie's singing.

1 2.05 Listen and stick. Then look, read and write.

1 His son's hair is shorter and straighter than his daughter's.

2 His daughter's hair is ________ than his granddaughter's.

3 His granddaughter's hair is ________ than her cousin's.

4 His grandson's hair is ________ than his cousin's.

mission STAGE 1

Make a family. Then talk to your cousin.

- In groups, decide what each person looks like.
- Draw your family.
- Talk to your cousin in another group.

Your brother is shorter than my sister.

My mum's hair is curlier than your mum's hair.

My mission diary
Activity Book page 44

Vocabulary 2 and song

1 2.06 Listen and complete. Then sing the song.

Town centre, in the town centre,
town centre.
Our Uncle Paul lives on the third floor.
His flat's got a balcony
and a [1] green door.
There are plants on his balcony
and a garden on the roof.
His car's in the basement
and his guitar's in his [2] ________.
There's a lift that goes up and down
To his flat in the centre of town.

Small village, in the small village,
small village.
We live in a village outside town.
We've got stairs that go up and down.
Outside in the garden
there are lots of [3] ________.
Inside our house
we've got two showers.
One's upstairs, on the first floor.
One's downstairs,
with a [4] ________ door.

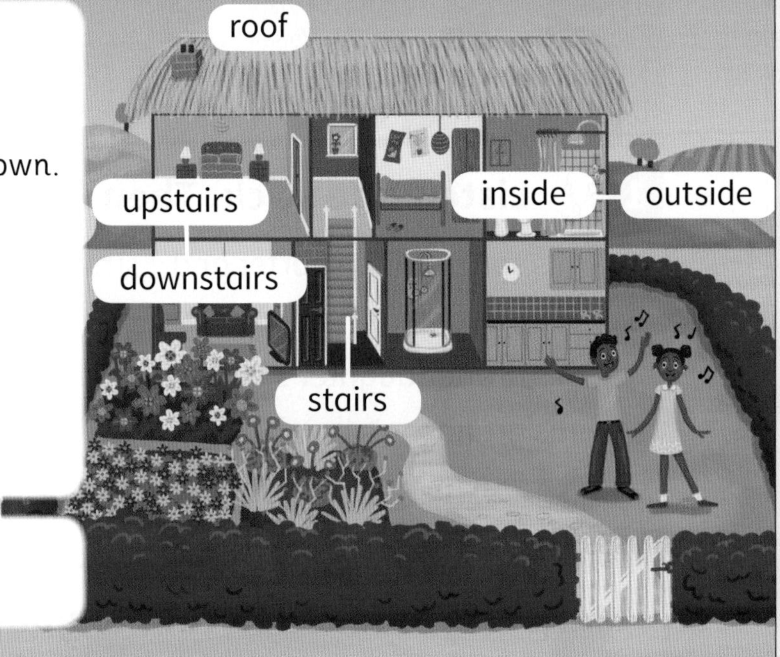

Town centre, in the town centre.
Small village, in the small village.

2 Describe the picture to your friend.

There are stairs inside.

It's the house.

There are cars in the basement.

It's the flat.

I live in a barn on a farm. Where do you live?

Learning outcomes By the end of the lesson, learners will have practised the language through song.

New language *balcony, basement, downstairs, (first/second/third) floor, inside, lift* (n), *outside, roof, stairs, upstairs, town centre, village*

Recycled language extended family, rooms and objects in a house, *barn, car, flat, flower, garden, guitar, house, in, live, on, plant, shower, small, up/down, have got, There is/are … , Where do you live?*

Materials Friendly Farm animal character flashcards, In and around the home flashcards, picture from Digital photo bank of a block of flats (optional), audio, video

Warm-up

- Show the animal character flashcards and revise names.
- Choose a card and hold it so learners can't see. Make comparisons, e.g. *She's smaller than a horse. She's bigger than a cat. She's got curlier hair than Harry.* Learners guess, e.g. *Shelly*. Repeat with different characters.
- Display all the cards. Learners play the game in pairs (taking turns to choose a card without saying who it is).

  Stronger learners Review the spelling rules for comparative adjectives. Say an adjective, then begin to spell it, e.g. *happier. H-A-*Point to a learner to say the next letter (*P*) and so on, around the class. The learner who finishes the word chooses another comparative adjective and begins to spell it. This can be played as a team game.

Presentation

- Show a picture of a block of flats. Count the floors and say *There are … floors. What about your home?* Ask a learner *How many floors are there where you live?* Then ask another *Is your home taller? How many floors? Which floor do you live on? Has anyone in your family got a taller home? What about your uncle and aunt / grandparents?*
- Teach the rest of the words using the flashcards.
- Ask *Are there any stairs in your house? Is there a lift? Have you got a balcony? Can you go onto the roof of your home? Is there a basement? Is your bedroom upstairs/downstairs? Where are we now? Are we inside or outside? Are we on the first floor?*
- Revise rooms in a house and features such as *window, door* and *wall.*
- **SA** Use self-assessment to check how well learners think they understand the vocabulary. See Introduction.

Pupil's Book, page 48

1 2.06 Listen and complete. Then sing the song.

- Say *Open your Pupil's Books at page 48.* Ask *What can you see?* Learners say, e.g. *bedroom, roof, garden.* Ask *Is the flat in the countryside?* (*No, the town*) Teach *town centre*. Ask *Where's the house?* (*In the countryside*) Teach *village*. Ask learners *Do you live in the town centre or in a village?*
- Ask *Where are the stairs? Where's the first floor / basement?* etc. Learners point.
- Say *Listen and complete.* Point to the spaces and the example. Play the audio or video.

Track 2.06

Rocky: I'm Rocky-Doodle-Doo and here's our song for today: *Town centre, small village*

See song on Pupil's Book page 48

Key: 2 room 3 flowers 4 white

- Learners stand up. Practise the song in sections.
- Play the audio or video again. Make two groups. One group sings about the flat, one about the house. They can also do actions for *third floor, door, car, guitar*, etc.

2.07 **Extension** Once learners are confidently singing along, try singing the karaoke version as a class.

2 Describe the picture to your friend.

- Demonstrate the activity. Make a sentence about the flat or the house with *There is/are …* or *It's got …*, e.g. *There are lots of flowers in the garden.* Learners say, e.g. *It's the house.*
- Put the class into pairs. They take turns to make a sentence. Monitor and support.
- Show the picture of Rocky in the bottom right-hand corner. Read out the question. Tell learners where you live. They talk about their own homes in pairs.

  Extra support Write useful phrases on the board, e.g. *I live in a flat/house in … I live on the (second) floor. There's a … There are two …*

  Stronger learners Ask and answer questions, e.g. *Is there a balcony? / Are there stairs inside your house?*

Activity Book, page 48

See pages TB120–132

Ending the lesson

- **SA** Repeat the self-assessment used after the Presentation to see how well learners think they understand the vocabulary. Is there any change?
- Play the song again. Learners join in.

Learning outcomes By the end of the lesson, learners will be able to use possessive pronouns.

New language *mine, yours, hers, his, ours, theirs*

Recycled language classroom objects, extended family, home, comparative adjectives, possessive *'s* and possessive adjectives, *Whose is this?*

Materials pictures from Digital photo bank of two flats, audio, worksheets/drawings from Mission Stage 1 lesson, paper, coloured pens or pencils, digital Mission poster

Warm-up

- Write *homes* on the board as the heading of a Venn diagram. Draw two overlapping circles headed *inside* and *outside*. Learners copy and add as many words as they can (e.g. *inside – kitchen, outside – balcony, both – door*).
- Call learners to the front to add words. Check spelling.

  Extra support Make the diagram as a class, with learners calling out words and spelling aloud.

Presentation

- Show pictures of a home. Say, e.g. *This is my flat. It's mine. It's got two bedrooms. It's new.* Show pictures of a different home and say, e.g. *This is my sister's flat. It's hers. My sister's flat is older than mine.*
- Show the first picture again and write *This is my flat. It's mine.* on the board. Show learners that *mine* means the same as *my flat*.
- Show the second picture and write *This is my sister's flat. It's hers*. Ask *What does 'hers' mean?* (*My sister's*)

Pupil's Book, page 49

1 2.08 Which is Aunt Jane's kitchen? Listen and tick ✓.

- Say *Open your Pupil's Books at page 49. Point to the small, old kitchen. Point to the small, new kitchen. Point to the big, old kitchen.*
- Ask *Which is Aunt Jane's kitchen?* Play the audio.

Track 2.08

Daisy:	Hi, Peter. My aunt Jane's got a new flat in the town centre.
Peter:	Oh! That's interesting, Daisy.
Daisy:	Yeah, our house is older than her flat, but some of our things are better.
Peter:	Really? Tell me about the flat.
Daisy:	Well, my cousin's bedroom is nice, but mine's bigger than his.
Peter:	Have they got a big bathroom in their new flat?
Daisy:	Yes, and it's beautiful. Our bathroom's smaller than theirs.
Peter:	What about their kitchen? Is it bigger than yours?
Daisy:	No, it isn't. It's smaller than ours. It's got white cupboards.
Peter:	Yours has got white cupboards too.
Daisy:	Yes, but hers are newer.

Key: Picture 1

2.09 Gracie's Grammar

- Write the sentences on the board.
- Play the audio. Pause for learners to repeat.

  Track 2.09

  See Pupil's Book page 49

  Extra support Write the phrases with the possessive pronouns next to them in columns, e.g. *my ruler – mine, your ruler – yours, my brother's hair – his,* and so on.

2 Talk to your friends. Describe things in your classroom.

- Read the examples and ask learners for more, e.g. *My pencil case is longer than yours.* They work in small groups and make as many sentences as they can.

  Extra support Learners make sentences about possession, not comparisons, e.g. *This rubber is mine.*

mission Stage 2

- Show learners the second stage of the Mission poster: *Draw your family's home and talk to your cousin.*
- Learners complete the second worksheet task in the Teacher's Resource Book (page 44). See teaching notes on TRB page 37.
- Alternatively, if you do not have the Teacher's Resource Book, learners draw their imaginary home on a piece of paper. Groups work together on a floorplan but each learner draws the plan and labels the rooms.
- Learners compare homes with their cousin from another 'family'. Encourage them to use possessive pronouns.

Activity Book, page 49

See pages TB120–132

Activity Book, page 44

- Review *My unit goals*. Ask *How is your Mission?* Learners reflect and choose a smiley face for *My mission diary 2*.

Ending the lesson

- **SA** Go back to Stage 2 on the digital Mission poster. Add a tick to the 'Draw your family's home ... ' stage. Use self-assessment (see Introduction).
- Give out a completion sticker.

1 2.08 Which is Aunt Jane's kitchen? Listen and tick ✓.

1

2

3

2.09 Gracie's Grammar

My **brother's hair** is shorter than my **sister's hair**, but **hers** is curlier than **his**.

Our car is smaller than my **aunt and uncle's car**, but **ours** is newer than **theirs**.

My ruler is older than **your ruler**, but **mine** is longer than **yours**.

2 Talk to your friends. Describe things in your classroom.

My rubber's older than Mary's, but hers is smaller than mine.

The teacher's table's bigger than ours.

mission STAGE 2

Draw your family's home and talk to your cousin.

- In your group, decide where you live: a house or flat.
- Draw the rooms.
- Talk to the same cousin as before.

Our house is smaller than yours, but my bedroom is bigger than your brother's.

STAGE 2

My mission diary
Activity Book page 44

Machines in our homes

1 Watch the video.

2 Which machines do we use at home? Which do you use at school? Write *H* (Home), *S* (School) or *B* (Both).

1  ☐
2  ☐
3  ☐
4  ☐
5 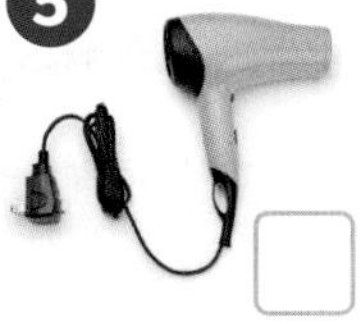 ☐
6  ☐

3 2.10 Listen and read. Answer the questions.

Machines make our lives easier. They can be simple machines with only a few parts or they can be complex machines with lots of parts. Simple machines always need our energy to make them work. We have to pull or push them. A **swing** in a park is a simple machine.

Some complex machines need our energy too, like a bike. A **bike** is a complex machine with many different parts. Many complex machines need electricity to work, like a **computer**. Machines help us at home and at school or at work. We use machines every day.

1 What machines do you have at home? Make a list with a partner.

2 Which machines do you use at school? What do they do?

Learning outcomes By the end of the lesson, learners will have learnt about machines around the home and how they work.

New language *a few, complex, different, easier, electricity, energy, machine, make (something) work* (= function), *part* (of a machine), *pull, push, simple, swing* (n)

Recycled language *bike, computer, help* (v), *home, lots of, need, park, school, use, work* (n)

Materials paper, coloured pens or pencils, pictures from Digital photo bank of simple and complex machines (optional), video, scissors, audio, dictionaries (optional)

Warm-up

- Draw a simple picture of a house. Ask *Is it a flat or a house? How many floors/windows/doors has my house got?*
- Ask learners to draw a picture of the outside of a home. Explain that it can be a flat or a house, with as many floors, windows, doors, etc. as they like. Set a time limit.
- Learners stand in a circle, holding their pictures. Choose a feature from your drawing and compare it to someone else's, e.g. *His house has got three windows. Mine has got four.* Learners do the same, around the circle.

Presentation

- Show pictures of machines or point to the door handle, CD player, etc. Say *These are machines.* Write *machines* on the board. Ask *Can you see any more machines?* Learners point. Encourage them to look for simple machines too, e.g. wheels on furniture.

Pupil's Book, page 50

1 Watch the video.

- Say *Let's watch the video.* Learners watch the video about machines and answer the questions at the end.

2 Which machines do we use at home? Which do you use at school? Write *H* (Home), *S* (School) or *B* (Both).

- Say *Open your Pupil's Books at page 50.* Read the instructions and check comprehension of *both*. Learners write *H*, *S* or *B*. Check answers. Encourage learners to make a sentence, e.g. *We use it at home.*

  Stronger learners Teach *food mixer, pencil sharpener, stapler, dishwasher, hairdryer*. Point out that many names of machines in English are compound nouns ending in *-er*.

Key: (possible answers) 1 H 2 B 3 B 4 H 5 H 6 H

3 2.10 Listen and read. Answer the questions.

- Show a pair of scissors and say *Machines have parts. This is a simple machine. It hasn't got lots of parts.* Point to a complex machine, e.g. a CD player, and say *This is a complex machine. It's got lots of parts inside.*
- Point to each photo and ask *Is this a simple machine or a complex machine?* Teach *swing*. Say *Listen and read.* Play the audio.

  Track 2.10
  See Pupil's Book page 50
- Mime sitting on a swing that isn't moving. Ask *How do you make a swing work?* Mime pushing. Say *We need to push a swing*. Practise *push* with the class. Point to a handle and ask *What about this?* Pull and say *We need to pull.* Practise *pull*. Say *Some simple machines need our energy.*
- Ask *Do simple machines use electricity?* (No) *Which machines use electricity?* Learners point to examples (e.g. lamps, heaters, air conditioning units).
- Read the questions. Divide the class into pairs. They could use dictionaries to help them. Monitor and help.
- Learners share their lists with the class. Write them on the board. Pairs who have found a word no-one else found explain what it means.
- Help learners make sentences about the uses of machines, e.g. *Scissors cut things. A pencil sharpener sharpens pencils.*

  Extra support Write the names of machines on the board. Learners put them into two lists – *home* and *school*.

Key: (possible answers) Home: lift, vacuum cleaner, washing machine, fridge, microwave, mobile phone, dishwasher, DVD/CD player, TV, computer/tablet, tap, shower, light School: pencil sharpener, scissors, projector, DVD/CD player, TV, computer, lamp, playground equipment (see-saws, swings)

Activity Book, page 50

See pages TB120–132

Ending the lesson

- Ask learners to write a letter *S* on one piece of paper and *C* on the other. Say the name of a machine. Learners hold up *S* for *simple* or *C* for *complex*.
- **SA** Use self-assessment to see how well learners think they understand any new vocabulary from the lesson. See Introduction.

Learning outcomes By the end of the lesson, learners will be able to talk about machines at home.

New language *dishwasher, invent, lay the table, vacuum* (v), *vacuum cleaner, washing machine*

Recycled language homes, *camera, clean* (v), *clothes, floor, help, lift* (n), *machine, photo, take, up/down, use, wash, work* (n), adverbs of frequency, *How often do you (lay the table)?*

Materials audio, worksheets/drawings from Mission Stages 1 and 2 lessons, coloured pens or pencils, digital Mission poster

Warm-up

- Say *Think about your day. How many machines do you use? You wake up and what do you do? Have you got an alarm clock? Do you use the shower? Do you have a hot drink in the morning?* Write a list of machines learners / learners' parents used before they came to class, helping with new vocabulary.

  Stronger learners For each machine ask *How does it help you? What does it do? Does it use electricity?* Help learners to make simple sentences, e.g. *An alarm clock wakes me up. I push a button. It's got a battery inside.*
- Say *Let's think more about machines we use at home.*

Pupil's Book, page 51

4 2.11 Listen and number the photos.

- Say *Open your Pupil's Books at page 51.* Teach *vacuum cleaner* and *washing machine* using the photos and revise *camera* and *lift*.
- Learners listen and number, then compare in pairs. Check answers.

  Track 2.11

  1 [sound of vacuum cleaner] This machine cleans floors.
  2 [sound of washing machine] This machine washes clothes.
  3 [sound of lift] This machine takes people up and down.
  4 [sound of camera] This machine takes photos. Smile!

  Stronger learners Play the audio again. Pause after each description and ask *What does this machine do?*

Key: a 4 (b 1) c 3 d 2

5 Machines help us with work at home. Do you help? What do you do? Do you use a machine?

- Point to each picture and ask *What's he/she doing?* Teach *laying the table, helping with the dishwasher* and *vacuuming*. Say *They're all helping at home. Do you help at home? What do you do?* Read the example speech bubbles and write typical chores on the board, e.g. *tidy my room, make my bed, feed the pets*. Ask different learners *How often do you (tidy your room)?*
- Ask *Who's using a machine in the pictures? Which machines do you use to help with work at home? Do you use the (washing machine)?*
- Put learners into pairs to talk about what they do and the machines they use. Monitor and help with new vocabulary.

  Fast finishers Write some sentences about how they help (and how often).

  Extension Put learners into different pairs. One learner mimes something he/she does to help at home. The other learner guesses, e.g. *You feed the fish.* Then they swap over. Alternatively, learners could take turns to mime for the class to guess.

mission Stage 3

- Show the class the third stage of the Mission poster: *Invent a machine for your home.* Read the instructions and the example.
- Put learners into their Mission groups. They work together to design the machine and each draw a picture of it. They think of a name for their invention and a way to explain what it does. Monitor and support.
- Learners show and describe their invention to their cousin from the other family group.

  Extra support Write questions on the board for learners to ask and answer: *What's your machine called? What does it do? Does it use electricity?*

Activity Book, page 51

See pages TB120–132

Activity Book, page 44

- Review *My unit goals*. Ask *How is your Mission?* Learners reflect and choose a smiley face for *My mission diary 3*.

Ending the lesson

- **SA** Go back to Stage 3 on the digital Mission poster. Add a tick to the 'Invent a machine for your home' stage. Use self-assessment (see Introduction).
- Give out a completion sticker.

4 2.11 Listen and number the photos.

a

b
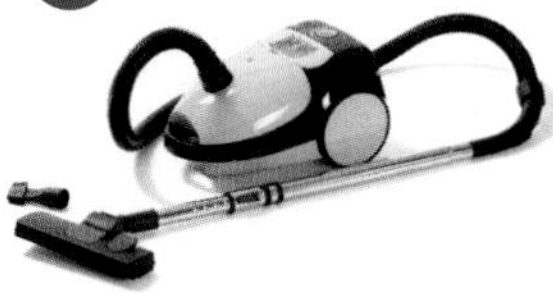
1

c
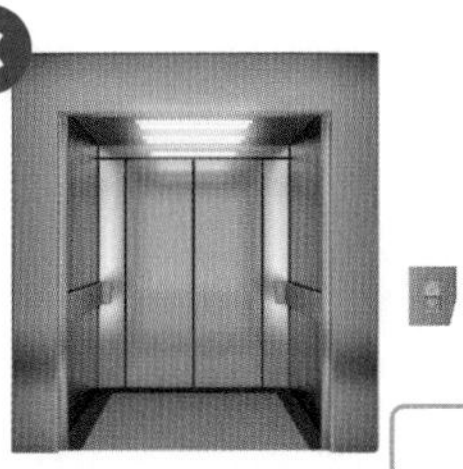

d

5 Machines help us with work at home. Do you help? What do you do? Do you use a machine?

I lay the table.

I help with the dishwasher.

I vacuum the floor.

mission STAGE 3

Invent a machine for your home.

- In your group, invent a machine.
- Draw the machine.
- Talk to the same cousin as before.

This is our machine. It makes burgers in fun shapes.

STAGE 3

My mission diary
Activity Book page 44

1 Talk about the robots in the pictures.

I think they're cousins.

They're having a party.

2.12

Surprise!

Today is my mum's birthday and we're having a surprise party for her. There are lots of sandwiches and a chocolate cake. All the family are here. Well, not everyone. Where's Mum? She works in the town centre, but she's usually home at five o'clock.

Dad's calling her and he's texting her, but she isn't answering. My cousins are talking about their party hats. 'My party hat's bigger than yours,' Mary says. 'Well, mine's nicer than yours,' Joe says.

'Oh dear, no-one's having fun,' I think. The music's playing, but people aren't dancing. It isn't a good party.

Now Uncle Paul and Grandma are standing on the balcony upstairs. They can see the street from there.

Learning outcomes By the end of the lesson, learners will have read a story about a surprise party.

New language *ring* (v), *speaker phone, text* (v), usually

Recycled language extended family, homes, *birthday, call, chocolate cake, dance, everyone, hat, have fun, late, party, robot, sandwich(es), sing, surprise, town centre, work,* comparative adjectives, possessive pronouns, present continuous, present simple

Materials sentences about parties on A4 pieces of paper, e.g. *My birthday party's on Thursday. She's wearing a pirate costume. Have we got music for the party?,* audio

Warm-up

- Pick ten learners to stand in a line at the front of the class. Choose a sentence from the ones you have prepared, e.g. *My birthday party's on Thursday.*
- Whisper it to the first learner in the line. The learner whispers it to the next learner, and so on. The last learner says the sentence out loud.
- See if it is the same as the original sentence. Show the learners the sentence and say it aloud so they can hear if it is correct. Say *Well done!* or *Let's try again.*

Presentation

- Write *surprise party* on the board and ask *What happens at a surprise party?* Say *You don't tell the person about the party. It's a secret. When the person arrives, everyone says 'Surprise!' Let's all shout 'Surprise!'* Learners practise.
- Ask *Do you sometimes have surprise parties for your family?* Learners share experiences.
- Say *We're going to read a story about a surprise party.*

Pupil's Book, pages 52 and 53

1 Talk about the robots in the pictures.

- Say *Open your Pupil's Books at pages 52 and 53. What can you see? What's happening?* Learners talk in pairs.
- Ask for ideas about the characters and story, but don't confirm or correct.

2.12 Surprise!

- Look at each picture and ask questions, e.g. Picture 1: *Why is everyone looking at the door?* (*They're waiting.*) Picture 2: *Who's Dad calling?* (*The person who has a birthday*) Picture 3: *Where are they?* (*On the balcony*) *Why?* (*They're looking for the person.*) Picture 4: *What are they all doing?* (*Listening to the phone*) Teach *speaker phone.* Picture 5: *Who's the purple robot? Do you think it's her birthday?* (Learners guess.)
- Say *The main character in the story is Max. Let's read and listen to the first part.* Play the audio. Learners listen and read. Pause the audio after *five o'clock.* Ask *Whose birthday is it?* (*Max's mum*) *What type of cake is it?* (*Chocolate*) *Where does Mum work?* (*In the town centre*) *What time does she usually get home?* (*five o'clock*)

  Track 2.12
  See story on Pupil's Book pages 52–53
- Say *Read and listen to the next part.* Play the audio. Pause after *good party.* Ask *Is Mum answering her phone?* (*No, she isn't.*) *What are Max's cousins talking about?* (*Their party hats*) *Is it a good party?* (*No*) *Why not?* (*People aren't having fun. / They aren't dancing.*) Check comprehension of *have fun.*
- Play the next part. Pause after *from there.* Ask *Who's on the balcony?* (*Uncle Paul and Grandma*) *What can they see?* (*The street*)
- Play the next part of the story. Pause after *big party.* Ask *Why is Mum late?* (*Because her friends at work are giving her a surprise party*) *What happens?* (*Mum invites her friends home – they can have a big party at their house.*)
- Play the rest of the story. Ask *What's Mum doing in the street?* (*She's dancing/singing.*) *Is the party a surprise now?* (*No*) *Is it a good party?* (*Yes, it's great.*)

  Extra support Instead of asking questions, make sentences, pausing for learners to say key words, e.g. *Today is Max's mum's (birthday).*

  Extension Play the whole story again, without pauses, for learners to listen and read.

Activity Book, page 52

See pages TB120–132

Ending the lesson

- Write lines of speech from the story on the board in a column, with the names of the speakers on the right, in random order (*Uncle Paul, Max, Joe, Uncle Paul and Grandma, Mum, Mary*):

  1 *My party hat's bigger than yours.*
  2 *Mine's nicer than yours.*
  3 *We can see the street from here.*
  4 *Sorry I'm late.*
  5 *We can all have one big party.*
  6 *They're dancing in the street.*
- Learners match the lines with the speakers. Check answers. Encourage them to say the lines with the appropriate emotions. Answers: 1 Mary, 2 Joe, 3 Uncle Paul and Grandma, 4 Mum, 5 Max, 6 Uncle Paul.

Learning outcomes By the end of the lesson, learners will have thought about initiative and managing their own emotions.

New language *excited, feel, worried*

Recycled language language from the story, *angry, happy, sad*

Materials card for each learner, coloured pens or pencils, audio

Social and Emotional Skill: Initiative and managing one's own emotions

- After reading the story, ask learners *Who's the surprise party for? (Mum) Where's Mum? (At a surprise party with her friends at work) Is the party at home good in the end? (Yes) Why? (Mum's friends come to the party and everyone is happy.) Whose idea is it? (Max's)*
- Ask learners *What makes you happy? What makes you sad?* Learners answer.
- Divide the class into four or six groups, depending on the number of learners. Allocate an emotion to each group. Each member of the 'happy' group must mime something that makes them happy. The other groups guess what it is. Repeat with all the groups and their different emotions.
- Hand out card. Learners divide the card into four sections. Draw faces showing four emotions on the board for the learners to copy: happy, sad, excited and angry.
- In the top left, learners draw a smiley face and something that makes them happy. In the top right, they draw a sad face and something that makes them sad.
- In the bottom left, they draw an excited face and something that makes them excited. In the bottom right, they draw an angry face and something that makes them angry.
- In pairs, learners look at their pictures of things that make them angry and sad and help each other to think of ways to make the situation better.

Warm-up

- Ask learners *What do you remember about the story?* Tell the story with mistakes. Learners interrupt and correct, e.g. *Today's Grandma's birthday.* (*No, it's Mum's birthday.*) *The family are having a costume party.* (*No, they're having a surprise party.*) and so on.

Pupil's Book, pages 52 and 53

- Say *Open your Pupil's Books at pages 52 and 53.* Play the audio. Learners read and listen to the story again.

  Track 2.12
  See story on Pupil's Book pages 52–53

2 Read and circle the correct picture.

- Ask *How do you usually feel at a party? Happy* (make a happy face) *or sad* (make a sad face)*?* Learners say *Happy*. Encourage them to make a happy face.
- Read the instructions. Point to the first two emojis and ask learners to make the same face. Read the beginning of the short text and ask learners to make the right face. They circle the 'excited' emoji.
- Learners read and circle. Check answers. Learners make the correct face for each one (they can say *happy* for number 3).

  Stronger learners Copy the emojis on the board. Revise *angry* and teach *excited* and *worried.* Learners say the words as they make the faces when you check answers.

Key: 1 excited 2 worried 3 happy

Extra support Say *Act out the story*. Summarise the story, sentence by sentence, and mime, e.g. *It's Mum's birthday. Max and his family are having a surprise party.* Mime jumping out as if surprising someone. *There's party food* … Mime putting food on a table. … *and party hats.* Mime putting on a party hat. *But where's Mum? She usually gets home at five o'clock*. Point to your watch. *Dad calls and texts her.* Mime pressing buttons on a phone. *She doesn't answer*. Look disappointed and shake your head. *Uncle Paul and Grandma stand on the balcony looking for Mum*. Mime looking out into the street. *Then Mum calls Dad*. Mime answering a phone, looking happy. *She's late because her friends are giving her a surprise party*. Mime jumping out as if surprising someone. *Max says 'We can have one big party!'* Gesture with your arms open to show 'big'. *Mum comes home with all her friends.* Mime shaking hands with people. *They sing and dance. It's a great party*. Mime dancing happily.

- Repeat and encourage learners to act the story with you.

Activity Book, page 53

See pages TB120–132

Ending the lesson

- **SA** Use self-assessment to see how well learners think they understand the story. See Introduction.

4

Then Dad's phone rings.

'Hello?' Dad says.

'Is that Mum?' I ask.

'Yes!' Dad answers.

'Put her on speaker phone! Let's all listen!'

Now we can hear Mum. 'Sorry I'm late, but my friends at work are giving me a surprise party.'

'But Mum,' I say, 'we're having a party for you here!'

'Really?'

'Yes, but it isn't a surprise now!'

'What can we do?' Joe and Mary ask.

'I know!' I say. 'Mum! Invite your friends home! We can all have one big party.'

Uncle Paul sees them first. 'There they are!' he calls. We all go upstairs to the balcony. 'Look! Here they come! They're dancing in the street. And I think your mum's singing, Max!'

'Wow, now everyone's happy and we're all having fun! It isn't a surprise, but it's a great party.'

2 Read and circle the correct picture.

We're all 1  /  about the surprise party. There's chocolate cake for everyone! But where's Mum? She isn't at home. We all feel 2  /  . Oh, here she is! When Mum comes home, everyone feels 3  /  .

1 2.13 Paul is talking to Mr Field. Listen. Who are they talking about?

His …

his grandpa ☐

his aunt ☐

his daughter ☐

2 2.13 Listen again. Circle the answer.

Mr Field is talking about his family and his **holiday** / **new home** / **dog**.

3 What can you see in these pictures of Mr Field's home?

A

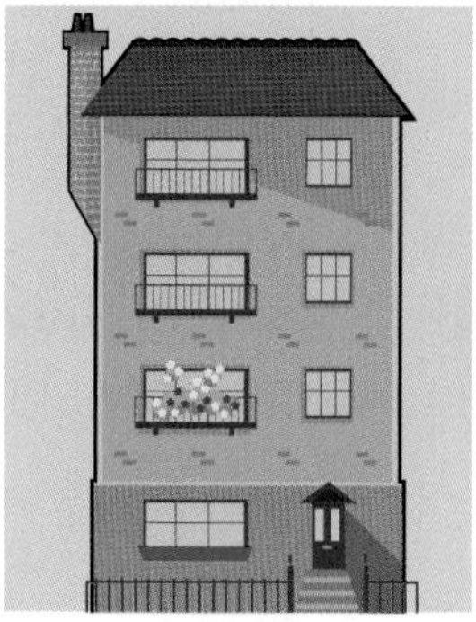

B

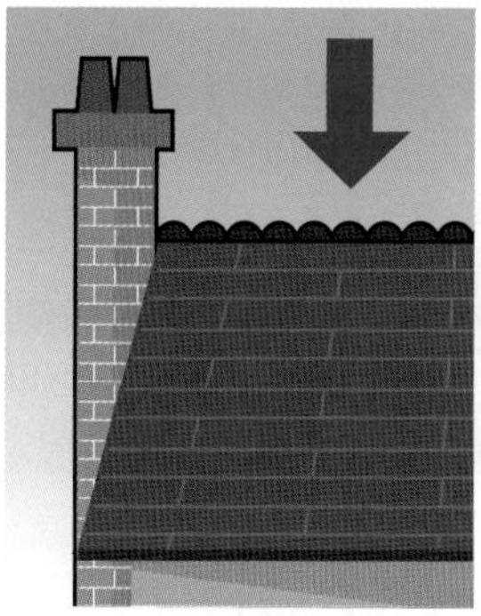

C

D

4 2.14 Look at Activity 1. Which is their favourite place in Mr Field's home? Listen and write a letter in each box.

In the exam, there are eight pictures to match with six people. There are two extra pictures.

Learning outcomes By the end of the lesson, learners will have practised listening for gist and specific details (A1 Movers Listening Part 3).

Test skills Listening for words, names and detailed information

New language *weak*

Recycled language extended family, homes, comparative adjectives, present simple questions, *There is/are …*

Materials In and around the home flashcards, practice paper for Movers Listening Part 3 (optional), audio

Warm-up

- Review In and around the home vocabulary using the flashcards.

Presentation

- Say *Let's practise for a listening exam.* If possible, show the Movers Listening Part 3 paper. Say *In Part 3 of the exam you hear a conversation. You need to match the people they talk about with pictures on the next page. Let's practise.*

Pupil's Book, page 54

1 2.13 Paul is talking to Mr Field. Listen. Who are they talking about?

- Say *Open your Pupil's Books at page 54.* Point to each picture and ask *Who's this? How old is he/she?*
- Tell learners not to write in the boxes at this stage. Play the audio. Pause after each section for the answer (*His …*).

Track 2.13

1 Paul: Do you live near an aunt or an uncle?
Mr Field: Yes, my Aunt Jill lives in these flats too.
2 Paul: Your daughter's a grown-up now. Does she live here?
Mr Field: No, but she often comes here. She works at a garden shop in the town centre.
3 Paul: Are there stairs?
Mr Field: Yes, and my grandpa doesn't like those!

Key: 1 his aunt 2 his daughter 3 his grandpa

2 2.13 Listen again. Circle the answer.

- Read the sentence/options. Play the audio.
- Explain that in the exam there is an introduction to the conversation with a question. This helps them to understand the topic and the task.

Key: new home

3 What can you see in these pictures of Mr Field's home?

- Learners name the things.

Key: A lift B balcony C roof D stairs

4 2.14 Look at Activity 1. Which is their favourite place in Mr Field's home? Listen and write a letter in each box.

- Explain that learners listen and write a letter in the boxes in Activity 1 for each person. There is one picture in Activity 3 they won't use.
- Play the audio twice for learners to listen and match. Pause after each section.
- Check answers. Ask which picture they didn't use (D).
- Ask *Why doesn't Mr Field's grandpa like stairs?* (*Because he's 92/old*) Say *His legs are getting weak.* Write *weak* on the board and practise.

Track 2.14

Paul: Hello, Mr Field. Are those photos of your new flat?
Mr Field: Yes. It's in the town centre.
Paul: Your daughter's a grown-up now. Does she live here?
Mr Field: No, but she often comes here. She works at a garden shop in the town centre.
Paul: Does she like your flat?
Mr Field: Oh, yes! She likes the windows in the living room because they're bigger than hers, but her favourite thing is the balcony. It's got pink and yellow flowers.
Paul: Are there stairs?
Mr Field: Yes, and my grandpa doesn't like those! So his favourite thing about my new home is …
Paul: The lift! How old is he?
Mr Field: He's 92 now and his legs are getting weak.
Paul: Have you got an uncle or an aunt?
Mr Field: Yes, my Aunt Jill lives in these flats too. And she really loves the roof!
Paul: Why's that?
Mr Field: Because it's new – and better than the old one! Aunt Jill lives on the third floor and now she doesn't get water in her flat on a bad day!

Key: his grandpa – A his aunt – C his daughter – B

Point to the monkey at the bottom of the page and read. Remind learners not to repeat the letter which is used in the example. They hear the conversation twice in the exam.

Activity Book, page 54

See pages TB120–132

Ending the lesson

- **SA** Use self-assessment to see how well learners think they understand the vocabulary. See Introduction.

Learning outcomes By the end of the lesson, learners will have revised the language in the unit and acted out visiting extended family.

Recycled language unit language, *best*

Materials Extended family flashcards, In and around the home flashcards, word cards, worksheets/drawings from Mission Stages 2 and 3 lessons, dice and counters (for Activity Book game), coloured pens or pencils, digital Mission poster

Warm-up

- Stick the Unit 4 flashcards on the board in random order, at a height learners can reach. Hand the word cards out around the class. Call learners to come and stick their word card under the correct flashcard.
- Practise the words with the class. Leave the flashcards on the board but remove the word cards.
- Put learners into two or more groups. They line up facing the board, with one learner at the front.
- Define one of the words on the board, e.g. *This is something you find inside or outside a house. You use them to go up and down. They don't use electricity.* The learners at the front of their teams race to be the first to take the correct flashcard from the board (*stairs*). The learner who takes the card first and says the word correctly gets a point for his/her team. These learners go to the back of the line. Define the other words, with learners taking turns at the front of the lines. The team with the most cards/points wins.

  Stronger learners Learners keep the flashcards and at the end of the game get extra points if they can say a definition for each one.

Pupil's Book, page 55

mission in action!

Act out a visit to your other cousins' new home.

- Say *Open your Pupil's Books at page 55.* Point to the Mission box or show learners the last stage of the digital Mission poster. Say *Let's put our Mission in action!* Say *Act out a visit to your other cousins' new home.*
- Read the instructions. Put pairs of learners from each group together with pairs from another group (not learners they have worked with in previous stages) to act out visiting each other's new homes and describing the homes/machines. They use their pictures from Mission Stages 2 and 3. Give them time to practise in their Mission groups first.

Extension Each group makes a poster/display with a picture of their machine and a short written description of what it is called and what it does. Learners walk around the classroom and look at all the inventions, noting down their favourites. The class vote to find the top three inventions.

Self-assessment

- **SA** Say *Did you like our 'Act out a visit to your other cousins' new home' Mission? Think and draw a face.* Learners draw a happy face, neutral face or sad face and then hold it up in the air.
- Ask *Did you do better in this Mission than in the last one? Or worse?* Learners show thumbs up or thumbs down. Praise or say *That's OK. We can try again.*
- Say *Our next Mission is 'Plan an animal documentary.'* Explain the meaning of *documentary.* Ask *Do you sometimes watch animal documentaries? Do you like them? What's your favourite animal?*

Activity Book, page 55

See pages TB120–132

Activity Book, page 44

- Review *My unit goals.* Ask *How is your Mission?* Learners reflect and choose a smiley face for *My mission diary* the final stage.
- Point to the sunflower. Learners read the 'can do' statements and tick them if they agree they have achieved them. They colour each leaf green if they are very confident or orange if they think they need more practice.
- Point to the word stack sign. Ask learners to look back at the unit and find at least five new words they have learnt. They write them in their word stack.

Ending the lesson

- **SA** Go back to the completion stage on the digital Mission poster. Add a tick or invite a learner to do it. Use self-assessment (see Introduction).
- Give out a completion sticker.
- Tell learners *You have finished your Mission! Well done!*

mission in action!

4

Act out a visit to your other cousins' new home.

My mission diary
Activity Book page 44

★ **Your cousins show you their home.**

This is the balcony.

★ **Talk about your homes.**

Our house is smaller than yours, but my bedroom is bigger than your brother's.

★ **Your cousins show you their special machine.**

Look at this machine. It makes burgers in fun shapes.

Wow! That's cool.

5 Animal world

1 Watch the video. Write a name for the documentary.

mission Plan an animal documentary

In this unit I will:

1. Choose animals for a documentary.
2. Write about what animals can do.
3. Write about what animals eat.

★ Act out an animal documentary.

Unit 5 learning outcomes

In Unit 5, learners learn to:

- talk about wild and domestic animals and what animals do
- use superlative adjectives
- describe location with prepositions of place
- learn about animals and their food
- read an Australian dreamtime story and think about helping others

Materials Farm animals and Zoo animals flashcards from level 1, video, digital Mission poster, a short video clip from a wildlife documentary (optional), a copy of the Mission worksheet (Teacher's Resource Book page 54)

Self-assessment

- **SA** Say *Open your Pupil's Books at page 56. Look at the picture. What's happening? (They're filming / making a programme about a lion.)*
- Ask *Do you sometimes watch TV programmes about animals? Which animals? Do you like going to zoos and wildlife parks? Which are your favourite animals?* Use self-assessment (see Introduction). Say *OK. Let's learn.*

Warm-up

- Show flashcards of animals learners already know. Learners say the name. Hold up different flashcards and ask *What can it do? Where does it live?*
- Hide the flashcards. Give two minutes. In pairs, learners write down as many of the names as they can remember.
- Check how many each pair could write. Show the flashcards again one by one. Learners check to see if they remembered.

Pupil's Book, page 56

1 Watch the video. Write a name for the documentary.

- Say *In this unit we're talking about animals.* Say *Let's watch the video.* To introduce the topic of the unit, play the video.
- Say *Look at page 56. A programme about real life is called a documentary.* Say *documentary.* Repeat and clap your hands on the stressed syllable: *documentary*. Learners repeat.
- Ask *What's this documentary about? Can you think of a name?* Point to the space on page 56.
- Put learners into pairs to think of a title for the programme. Monitor and help with new vocabulary. They write the name.

Extra support Learners can be given different names to choose from.

Fast finishers Learners work in groups. They each think of one or two names and then vote on the best name.

mission Plan an animal documentary

- Point to the Mission box or the digital Mission poster and say *This is our Mission.*
- Say *Plan an animal documentary.* Remind learners of the meaning of *documentary.* If possible, show a clip from a wildlife documentary. Ask *What does a documentary tell us about an animal? (Where it lives, what it eats, what it does / its habits)*
- Say *Point to number 1. Choose animals for a documentary.* Tell learners that they are going to work in groups. They choose the animals and decide who will be the narrator.
- Say *Point to number 2. Write about what animals can do.* Say *You need to prepare the documentary. First you write about what animals can do. What can a polar bear do? Can it walk? Can it run? Can it swim? Can it fly? What can a duck do?*
- Say *Point to number 3. Write about what animals eat.* Ask *What do animals eat?* Prompt with names of animals, e.g. *What about lions? (Meat)* Check comprehension of *meat.* Say *In Stage 3 you write about what the animals in your documentary eat.*
- Say *The last stage is 'Act out an animal documentary.'* Say *You put the information about your animals together. One of you talks about an animal and someone else in the group acts the animal. You show your documentary to the class.*
- Say *This is our Mission.* Go through the stages of the Mission again.
- For ideas on monitoring and assessment, see Introduction.

Activity Book, page 56

My unit goals

- Help learners to complete the unit goals. See notes on page TB6.
- You can go back to these unit goals at the end of each Mission stage during the unit and review them.

Ending the lesson

- Hold one of the animal flashcards from the Warm-up so learners can't see it. They ask yes/no questions to guess your animal.

  Extra support Write example questions on the board, e.g. *Is it a pet? Does it eat plants? Has it got four legs?*
- Learners can play the same game in pairs, choosing from pictures or names of animals on the board.

Learning outcomes By the end of the lesson, learners will be able to talk about wild and domestic animals.

New language *bat, bear, cage, dolphin, kangaroo, lion, panda, parrot, penguin, rabbit, whale, wildlife park, fly* (v)

Recycled language animals, *asleep, awake, eat, jump, live, meat, move, outside, sleep, teacher, wall*

Materials Farm animals and Zoo animals flashcards from level 1, Wild and domestic animals flashcards, audio, video

Warm-up

- Show flashcards of animals learners already know. Learners say the names. Ask *Is this a farm animal / a wild animal / a pet?* Check comprehension of *wild*.

Presentation

- Present the new animals using the flashcards.

Pupil's Book, page 57

1 (2.15 2.16) Listen and point. Then listen and number.

- Say *Open your Pupil's Books at page 57. Who can you see? Where are they?* Read the caption. Check understanding of *wildlife park*.
- Ask *Where's the small tractor? Can you find it?*
- Say *Listen and point*. Play Track 2.15. Learners point to the animals and cage.

Tracks 2.15 and 2.16

(1) This morning the children are in a wildlife park with their teacher.

Tom:	Ooh, look at that big brown kangaroo next to the tree.
(2) Eva:	Ooh, yes, and the little brown rabbit's jumping.
(3) Jenny:	Miss Field, that bat in the tree isn't moving. Is it asleep?
Teacher:	Yes, it is. Bats often sleep in the day and they're awake at night.
(4) Jim:	Ooh! There's a parrot flying in front of us. It's prettier than the bats.
(5) Tom:	Miss Field, why's that black bear over there, look, under that tree?
Teacher:	It isn't with the kangaroos and rabbits because it sometimes eats meat.
(6) Eva:	And where are the lions?
(7) Eva:	Are they in a cage?
Teacher:	No, there aren't any cages here, but there are some very big walls. All the animals live outside.
Jim:	Lions eat meat … and they aren't in cages.
Jenny:	It's OK, Jim. We're staying inside the bus.
Jim:	OK, ...
(8)Jim:	... now let's go and look at the pandas. They don't eat meat!

(9) In the afternoon.

Jim:	Look!
Jenny:	Hey!
Eva:	Look at that whale!
(10) Eva:	It's bigger than the dolphins!
(11) Jenny:	Oh, penguins are sea birds. Are there any here?
Teacher:	That's right, they're birds, but they can't fly. There aren't any here, sorry.
Tom:	Look! Dolphins! They're cleverer than a lot of animals.
Jim:	Yes, I like them because they don't want to eat us.

- Say *Now listen and number*. Play Track 2.16. Learners number the animals and the cage 2–11.

Key: 2 rabbit 3 bat 4 parrot 5 bear 6 lion 7 cage 8 panda 9 whale 10 dolphin 11 penguin

2 (2.17) Say the chant.

- Play the audio or video. Learners point and chant.

Track 2.17

Panda, whale, bat and bear,
Parrot, lion, penguin,
Panda, whale, bat and bear,
Kangaroo, rabbit, dolphin. [x2]

3 (2.18) Listen and say the animal.

- Play the audio. Pause for learners to say the animal.

Track 2.18

1 This big cat likes eating meat.
2 These small black animals sleep in the day and they're awake at night.
3 This animal lives in the sea. It's bigger than a dolphin.
4 This beautiful bird's got a lot of colours.
5 These little animals live under the ground, but they like jumping on the grass.
6 These black and white sea birds can't fly.
7 This big black or brown animal eats plants, fruit, fish and meat.
8 These sea animals are cleverer than a lot of other animals.
9 This big animal's got a long tail and it can jump.
10 This big black and white bear doesn't eat meat.

Key: 1 lion 2 bat(s) 3 whale 4 parrot 5 rabbit(s) 6 penguin(s) 7 bear 8 dolphin(s) 9 kangaroo 10 panda

Activity Book, page 57

See pages TB120–132

Ending the lesson

- **SA** Show the animal flashcards. Ask *Do you know the words?* Use self-assessment (see Introduction).

1 2.15 2.16 **Listen and point. Then listen and number.**

2 2.17 **Say the chant.**

3 2.18 **Listen and say the animal.**

The Friendly Farm

2.19

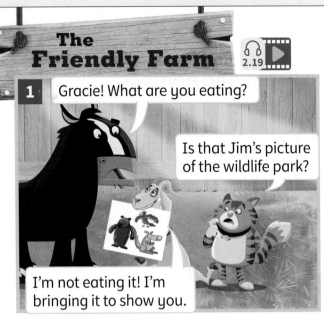

1
Gracie! What are you eating?
Is that Jim's picture of the wildlife park?
I'm not eating it! I'm bringing it to show you.
2
What's that?
Look! It's Jim's picture of a bear and a kangaroo … oh, and a parrot!
The bear's the biggest, but the kangaroo's got the longest tail.
3
What? Is its tail longer than mine?
Yes, I think so, Harry.
Hmm, so, which is the best animal?
4
Well, I don't know which one's the best, but the parrot's the prettiest.
In this barn, Shelly, you're the prettiest.
And you're the biggest and the oldest, Harry.
5
And Gracie's the angriest!
And you're the worst singer! … And Rocky's the naughtiest animal in this barn!
And you think you're the cleverest, but … you … aren't!
6
What? Not again! Stop it! Be quiet, everyone!
Mum's the angriest animal in the barn!
Sorry, Henrietta!

1 2.20 **Who says it? Listen and say the name.**

Learning outcomes By the end of the lesson, learners will be able to understand when they hear superlative adjectives.

New language *bring,* superlative adjectives

Recycled language adjectives, animals, *barn, tail, wildlife park, Be quiet, Sorry,* possessive pronouns

Materials three or more items to present superlatives (e.g. three balls of different sizes, one the newest; three books of different sizes/widths, one the prettiest) (optional), audio, video

Warm-up

- Ask *What's the opposite of big?* (*Small*) Write the adjectives on the board. Repeat with *tall – short, long – short, old – new/young, good – bad/naughty, beautiful/pretty – ugly, fat – thin, happy – sad* and *clean – dirty*.

  Alternative Write all the adjectives on the board or give them out on slips of paper and ask learners to find pairs.
- **SA** Use self-assessment to check how well learners think they understand the vocabulary. See Introduction.

Presentation

- Use real items to present superlatives, e.g. say *This ball is bigger than this ball. But this ball is the biggest. This one is the smallest. Which ball is the newest? Which is the oldest? / This book is thinner than this one. But this is the thinnest book. Which is the prettiest?*

  Alternative Draw three different-sized cats on the board, with tails of different length and ears of different size. Make sure one cat is the fattest, one the thinnest and one the prettiest. Name the cats, e.g. Alex, Ben and Clare. Say, e.g. *Alex is smaller than Ben and Clare. He's the smallest cat. Clare's bigger than Alex and Ben. She's the biggest cat. Alex's tail is shorter than Ben's and Clare's. Alex has got the shortest tail. Ben's tail is longer than Alex's and Clare's. His is the longest tail.* Ask *Which is the fattest cat? Which is the thinnest? Which is the prettiest? Which has got the biggest ears?* etc.
- Teach *best* and *worst*, e.g. using books (*This book is good. This one is better. But I love this book. It's the best book.*).

  Stronger learners Say the name of a cat or hold up an item. Learners make a sentence with a superlative.

Pupil's Book, page 58

2.19 The Friendly Farm song

- Play the introductory song at the beginning of the cartoon story. Learners listen and sing.

  Track 2.19
  See The Friendly Farm song on page TB5

2.19 The Friendly Farm

- Say *Open your Pupil's Books at page 58.* Ask *What has Gracie got?* (*A picture of animals from the wildlife park*) Ask *What animals are there?*
- Ask *Who's the angriest animal in the barn?* Write the question on the board. Check comprehension of *the angriest.* Use mime/actions to help. Play the audio or video. Learners listen and read. Check answers. (*Henrietta / Rocky's mum is the angriest.*) Check that learners remember the meaning of *best* and *worst.*

  Track 2.19
  The Friendly Farm song + see cartoon on Pupil's Book page 58
- Play the audio or video again. Pause after each picture and ask questions: 1: *Whose picture is it?* (*Jim's*) *Is Gracie eating the photo?* (*No, she isn't.*) Explain the meaning of *bring*. Practise by asking learners to bring you different items. 2: *Which is the biggest animal?* (*The bear*) *Which animal has got the longest tail?* (*The kangaroo*) 3: *Is the kangaroo's tail longer than Harry's?* (*Yes, it is.*) 4: *Who's the prettiest animal in the barn?* (*Shelly*) *Who's the biggest and oldest animal in the barn?* (*Harry*) 5: *Who's the worst singer?* (*Shelly*) *Who's the naughtiest?* (*Rocky*) 6: *Why do the animals say 'sorry' again?* (*Because they aren't being nice*)

1 2.20 Who says it? Listen and say the name.

- Play the audio and pause for learners to say the name.

Track 2.20

1	Rocky:	And you're the biggest and the oldest, Harry.
2	Shelly:	Well, I don't know which one's the best, but the parrot's the prettiest.
3	Harry:	And you think you're the cleverest, but … you … aren't!
4	Gracie:	And Rocky's the naughtiest animal in this barn!
5	Harry:	Is its tail longer than mine?
6	Gracie:	I'm not eating it! I'm bringing it to show you.
7	Rocky:	Mum's the angriest animal in the barn!
8	Gracie:	And you're the worst singer!

Key: See names in audioscript

Activity Book, page 58

See pages TB120–132

Ending the lesson

- **SA** Repeat the self-assessment to see how well learners think they understand the vocabulary. Is there any change?

Learning outcomes By the end of the lesson, learners will be able to use superlative adjectives to describe people, animals and things.

New language *My baby sister's the youngest in our family. This kitten's the prettiest. That puppy's the fattest. These ice skates are the best. ice skates, road*

Recycled language adjectives, animals, *asleep, baby, car, face, first, jump, lake, second, sister, sticker, tail, tree, wildlife park,* prepositions of place, present continuous

Materials Wild and domestic animals flashcards, audio, Mission worksheets (Teacher's Resource Book page 54) or paper, digital Mission poster

Warm-up

- Show each animal flashcard. Say the word and pretend to be the animal / make the noise. Learners copy. Say *Be a (parrot)!* Learners do the action / make the noise.
- Learners play in pairs – one mimes, the other guesses.

Presentation

- Talk about your family, e.g. *My grandmother is the oldest person. She's 87. My son is the youngest. He's three.* Write the regular superlatives on the board. Point out that the superlative is formed by adding *-est*.
- Write *the funniest* on the board. Point out that the spelling for superlative adjectives ending in *-y* is similar to the comparative (*y* changes to *i*), e.g. *happiest, dirtiest, prettiest.*
- Write *the biggest* and point out the spelling for superlative adjectives ending in some consonants (similar to the comparative form), e.g. *saddest, fattest, thinnest.*

Pupil's Book, page 59

2.21 Gracie's Grammar

- Say *Open your Pupil's Books at page 59.* Point to Gracie's Grammar box. Write the sentences on the board. Revise *worst.*
- Play the audio. Pause for learners to repeat.

Track 2.21
See Pupil's Book page 59

1 2.22 Listen and stick. Then look, read and write.

- Ask *What can you see? (A lake, a tree, a road, a car)*
- Learners name the animals on the stickers. Play the audio. Learners point to the correct sticker.
- Play the audio again. Learners stick the animals in the spaces. Check and ask *Where's the (lion)? What's it doing?*

Track 2.22

1 Girl: Look, Mum! I'm putting stickers in my sticker book. This is my wildlife park.
Mum: I see. Which animal are you putting in first?
Girl: I'm putting the oldest animal on the ground, between the road and that small lake. It's the lion.
Mum: Good!
2 Mum: What's your second animal?
Girl: Well, I think it's the tallest animal when it's standing … and I'm putting it under the tree. Look! It's a bear.
Mum: Oh, yes. And it's got the dirtiest face!
3 Girl: My third animal's got the longest tail, and it's jumping behind the car.
Mum: Oh, yes. That's the kangaroo.
4 Mum: What now? Which is your last animal?
Girl: It's my favourite because it's the prettiest animal in my park.
Mum: And where are you putting it?
Girl: Here. Look! The parrot's on the car.
Mum: Oh, yes. That's a nice picture.

- Say *Now look, read and write.* Check answers.

Key: 2 dirtiest 3 longest 4 prettiest

mission Stage 1

- Point to the Mission box or show learners the first stage of the digital Mission poster: *Choose animals for your documentary.*
- Put learners into groups of six. Learners complete the worksheet task in the Teacher's Resource Book (page 54). See teaching notes on TRB page 47.
- Alternatively, if you do not have the Teacher's Resource Book, learners work together to choose animals for their documentary. They choose who will be the narrator and who will play each animal. They write the narrator's name and the animals/performers at the top of a piece of paper.

Activity Book, page 59

See pages TB120–132

Activity Book, page 56

- Review *My unit goals.* Ask *How is your Mission?* Learners reflect and choose a smiley face for *My mission diary 1.*

Ending the lesson

- **SA** Go back to Stage 1 on the digital Mission poster. Say *We chose animals for our documentary.* Add a tick to the 'Choose animals … ' stage. Use self-assessment (see Introduction).
- Give out a completion sticker.

2.21 Gracie's Grammar

young: My baby sister's the **youngest** in our family.
pretty: This kitten's the **prettiest**.
fat: That puppy's the **fattest**.
good: These ice skates are the **best**.

1 2.22 Listen and stick. Then look, read and write.

1 The lion's asleep. It's the oldest animal.

2 The bear is the biggest and it's got the ________ face.

3 The kangaroo's got the ________ tail.

4 The parrot's the ________ animal in her park.

mission STAGE 1

Choose animals for your documentary.

- In groups, choose five animals.
- Decide who is the narrator and who is each animal.

Let's talk about bats.

OK. And how about pandas?

Can I be the penguin? They're the funniest animals!

STAGE 1

My mission diary
Activity Book page 56

1 2.23 Listen and number. Then sing the song.

This is our wildlife park. We've got our masks.
And we're all moving like wild animals!

He's [1]**running**, running, running like a lion.
She's [2]**climbing**, climbing, climbing like a bear.
He's [3]**jumping**, jumping, jumping like a kangaroo.
She's [4]**hiding**, hiding, hiding. Can you see the kitten there?

The parrot's getting food.
It likes to fly.
It's [5]**losing** its banana!
It's [6]**falling** in the sky!

He's jumping, jumping, jumping like a rabbit.
She's [7]**flying**, flying, flying like a bat.
She's very slow. She's [8]**moving** like a snail.
He's [9]**walking** like a penguin. Can you do that?

2 Play the game. Correct your friend.

The bear's sleeping.

No, it isn't. It's climbing a tree!

The parrot's eating its banana.

No, it isn't. It's losing its banana!

Move like an animal. Can your friend guess?

Learning outcomes By the end of the lesson, learners will have practised the language through song.

New language *climb, fall, fly, hide, jump, lose, move, run, walk, mask, sky, slow, snail, like (a) …*

Recycled language animals, *banana, food, wild, wildlife park, Can you … ?*, present continuous

Materials Farm animals and Zoo animals flashcards from level 1, Wild and domestic animals flashcards, Action verbs flashcards, audio, video

Warm-up

- Put animal flashcards on the board (include animals from level 1). Ask *Which is the smallest animal? Which is the biggest? Which is the prettiest? Which is the cleverest?*
- Make three or four teams. Teams line up with one learner at the front facing the board. Make a sentence, e.g. *It's got the longest ears*. The learners race to the board to take or touch the correct flashcard. The learners at the front go to the back of the line. Repeat with different sentences, e.g. *It's the best flyer.* (*Parrot*) *It's the biggest bird.* (*Penguin*) *It's the quickest animal.* (*Lion*) *It's the slowest animal.* (*Panda*) *It's got the longest tail.* (*Kangaroo*) *It's got the best ears. / It's the best listener.* (*Bat*) *It's the best jumper.* (*Kangaroo*)

Presentation

- Do actions for the verbs learners already know: *fly, jump, move, run, walk*. Learners say the words. Show the flashcards and say the words to confirm.
- Teach the rest of the verbs using the flashcards and actions. For *lose,* mime looking for some keys and say *I always lose my keys in the morning. Where are they? What do you lose?*
- Show an animal flashcard, e.g. the penguin, and ask *Can it (fly)?* (*Yes, it can. / No, it can't.*) Repeat with different animals.
- Show a flashcard and invite learners to make as many sentences with *It can/can't* as possible.
- Draw a snail on the board and teach the word. Ask *Is it slow or quick? Can it walk? Can it move?*
- **SA** Use self-assessment to check how well learners think they understand the vocabulary. See Introduction.

Pupil's Book, page 60

1 (2.23) Listen and number. Then sing the song.

- Say *Open your Pupil's Books at page 60.* Ask *Where are they?* (*At a wildlife park*) *What are they wearing?* (Teach *mask.*) Say *Point to the (lion).* Learners point to the child who is wearing the mask.
- Say *Look at number 1*. Point and show learners that number 1 is written next to the picture of the boy with the lion mask. Say *Let's listen and write the numbers.*
- Play the audio or video. Learners listen and write numbers in the boxes. Check answers.

Track 2.23

Rocky: I'm Rocky-Doodle-Doo and here's our song for today: *Moving like wild animals!*

See song on Pupil's Book page 60

Key: a 5 b 6 c 7 d 8 e 2 f 4 g 9 h 3 (i 1)

- Learners stand up. Practise the song in sections, doing the different actions for learners to copy.
- Play the audio or video again. Learners sing and do the actions.

Extra support Learners stand up. Give instructions with *like a …* for learners to mime, e.g. *Walk like a penguin. Swim like a dolphin. Jump like a kangaroo. Sleep like a bat/bear. Hide like a rabbit.*

(2.24) **Extension** Once learners are confidently singing along, try singing the karaoke version as a class.

2 Play the game. Correct your friend.

- Demonstrate the activity. Make an incorrect sentence about one of the 'animals', e.g. *The kitten's running*. Learners say *No, it isn't*. Encourage them to say the correct sentence. (*It's hiding.*) Give more examples, if necessary.
- Put the class into pairs. They take turns to make a sentence. Monitor and support.
- Show the picture of Rocky in the bottom right-hand corner. Read out the instructions. Demonstrate by moving like one of the animals. Learners guess. Encourage them to make a sentence in the present continuous (e.g. *You're climbing like a bear.*). Learners play the same game in pairs. Write more animals on the board as prompts (e.g. *monkey, duck, snake, crocodile*).

Activity Book, page 60

See pages TB120–132

Ending the lesson

- **SA** Repeat the self-assessment used after the Presentation to see how well learners think they understand the vocabulary. Is there any change?
- Play the song again. Learners join in and do the actions.

Learning outcomes By the end of the lesson, learners will be able to use prepositions *above, below, near* and *opposite.*

New language *The bat's above the tree. The snail's below the flower. The parrot's near the cage. The bus stop's opposite the zoo. bus stop*

Recycled language action verbs, animals, family, *feed, flower, tree, zoo, can*, prepositions, present continuous, superlative adjectives

Materials audio, coloured pens or pencils, paper, worksheets/notes from Mission Stage 1 lesson, digital Mission poster

Warm-up

- Play 'Simon says' with animals and actions (*Simon says 'Walk like a penguin / jump like a kangaroo'*, etc.). Then give instructions with prepositions learners already know, e.g. *Simon says 'Put your book under your chair.'*

Presentation

- Teach *above, below, near* and *opposite* using classroom items. Teach a hand movement for each preposition, e.g. *opposite* – hold your palms in front of your body facing each other. Practise the movements, then say the prepositions while learners move their hands.
- Give instructions for the class to follow, e.g. *Daniel, stand opposite Carla, please. Hold your books above your heads.*

Pupil's Book, page 61

1 2.25 Which kind of animal is in Vicky's picture? Listen and tick ✓.

- Say *Open your Pupil's Books at page 61.* Point to each animal and ask *What's this?* (*A panda*)
- Ask *Which kind of animal is in Vicky's picture?* Play the audio. Learners listen and tick. Check answers.

Track 2.25

Boy:	That's a nice picture, Vicky.
Vicky:	Thank you. It's a family of my favourite animals. Look, the daddy's here, above this tree.
Boy:	Oh, yes. He's the biggest of the four.
Vicky:	Yes, but the mummy's the prettiest. She's on the ground below the tree.
Boy:	Oh, yes. She's beautiful. What's she doing?
Vicky:	She's feeding her daughter. Her daughter's opposite her.
Boy:	Oh. And what about that little parrot near the cage?
Vicky:	That's their son. He's going there because he wants to sleep.
Boy:	I like your parrot family, Vicky.
Vicky:	So do I.

Key: Picture 3

Extension Ask *Where are all the parrots?* Play the audio again for learners to answer.

2.26 Gracie's Grammar

- Write the sentences on the board.
- Play the audio. Learners repeat the sentences.

  Track 2.26
  See Pupil's Book page 61
- Ask questions about the classroom, e.g. *Where's the clock?*

2 In pairs, draw your favourite animal family. Describe it to two friends.

- Draw an animal family on the board, e.g. penguins on some ice, with water below the ice. Draw them in different places, e.g. one below the ice, one near a rock, one next to its mum or dad. Point and say, e.g. *This is the mummy penguin. She's below the ice. The daddy penguin is near the baby.*
- Show learners the example speech bubbles.
- Put learners into pairs to draw their picture. Monitor and support. Encourage them to position their animals in order to practise the new prepositions.
- Put pairs into groups of four to describe their pictures.

mission Stage 2

- Show learners the second stage of the Mission poster: *Write about what animals can do.*
- Put learners into their Mission groups. They complete the second worksheet task in the Teacher's Resource Book (page 54). See teaching notes on TRB page 47.
- Alternatively, if you do not have the Teacher's Resource Book, ask learners to write about what the animals they have chosen can do. They also need to think about where each animal will be in the classroom when they act out their documentary. If time, they can rehearse this section of the documentary.

Activity Book, page 61

See pages TB120–132

Activity Book, page 56

- Review *My unit goals*. Ask *How is your Mission?* Learners reflect and choose a smiley face for *My mission diary 2*.

Ending the lesson

- **SA** Go back to Stage 2 on the digital Mission poster. Add a tick to the 'Write about what animals can do' stage. Use self-assessment (see Introduction).
- Give out a completion sticker.

1 2.25 Which kind of animal is in Vicky's picture? Listen and tick ✓.

1 
2 
3 

2.26 Gracie's Grammar

The bat's **above** the tree.

The snail's **below** the flower.

The parrot's **near** the cage.

The bus stop's **opposite** the zoo.

2 In pairs, draw your favourite animal family. Describe it to two friends.

Our sister rabbit's opposite the brother rabbit. They're playing. Our mummy rabbit's above the ground. She's watching her children.

Here, our baby rabbit's asleep below the ground … and this is our daddy rabbit. He's jumping near the flowers.

mission STAGE 2

Write about what animals can do.

- Write what each animal can do.
- Choose places in the classroom for your actions.

Dolphins can swim. The sea is near the board!

Bats can fly above trees! The tree's behind the door!

My mission diary

Activity Book page 56

The animal kingdom

1 **Watch the video.**

2 2.27 **What do you think these animals eat? Listen and check.**

dolphin

bear

lion

penguin

panda

parrot

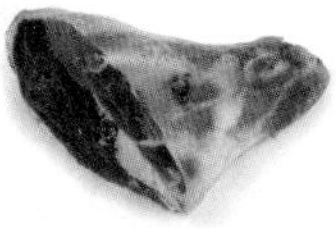
meat

leaves

fruit

fish

seeds

3 2.28 **Listen and read. Then complete the table with the animals from Activity 2.**

We can classify, or put animals into groups, when we know what they eat. There are three groups: carnivores, herbivores and omnivores.

- Carnivores only eat meat and fish. Tigers and sharks are carnivores.
- Herbivores only eat plants. Kangaroos and rabbits are herbivores.
- Omnivores eat meat and plants. People and chickens are omnivores.

Carnivore		Herbivore		Omnivore
tiger	dolphin	kangaroo	______	people
shark	______	rabbit	______	chicken
	______			______

Learning outcomes By the end of the lesson, learners will have learnt about animals and their food.

New language *carnivore, classify, herbivore, kingdom, omnivore, seed*

Recycled language animals, *fish, fruit, leaf (leaves), meat, people, plant* (n), prepositions

Materials Wild and domestic animals flashcards, Countryside flashcards, flashcard of meat from level 1, video, audio

Warm-up

- Before class, move items around so they are not in their usual places (put things above, below, in, under, near and opposite other items). Ask *What's different in the classroom today?* Learners say, e.g. *The clock is under your chair.* Ask *Where is it usually?* (e.g. *Above the board*) Put items back when learners tell you correctly where they usually are.

Presentation

- Put flashcards of a rabbit and a lion on the board. Show the flashcard for grass and ask *Which animal eats grass?* (*The rabbit*) Stick the grass flashcard next to the rabbit. Ask *What does the lion eat?* (*Meat*) Stick the meat flashcard next to the lion. Say *Animals eat different things. What other things do they eat?* Encourage learners to say, e.g. *fruit, leaves, fish.*

Pupil's Book, page 62

1 Watch the video.

- Say *Let's watch the video.* Learners watch the video about what animals eat and answer the questions at the end.

2 2.27 What do you think these animals eat? Listen and check.

- Say *Open your Pupil's Books at page 62.* Teach *kingdom.* Check comprehension of *seeds.* Learners talk in pairs, then share ideas. Don't confirm answers.
- Play the audio.

Track 2.27

Park ranger: Welcome to Old Town Safari Park. Now, who can tell me the name of these animals?
Boy: They're dolphins.
Girl: Dolphins live in the sea. They eat fish.
Park ranger: And what's the name of this animal?
Girl: I've got a teddy like that! It's a bear.
Park ranger: That's right. And what do bears eat?
Boy: Meat!
Girl: Fruit!
Park ranger: Yes, you're both right. Bears eat meat, fish, leaves and fruit. Now, what about these animals?
Boy: They're lions and they live in Africa.
Park ranger: Correct! What do lions eat?
Girl: They eat meat.
Park ranger: Yes, they do. Now, here in the water, you can see some birds. They can't fly, but they can swim.
Girl: Penguins!
Boy: And they eat fish!
Park ranger: And these big black and white animals? What are they?
Girl: Pandas!
Park ranger: And … what do they eat?
Girl: They eat leaves.
Park ranger: And here we are at the parrot house.
Boy: Gosh! They're very noisy!
Girl: What do parrots eat?
Park ranger: They eat fruit and seeds.

Key: dolphins – fish bears – meat, fish, leaves and fruit lions – meat penguins – fish pandas – leaves parrots – fruit and seeds

3 2.28 Listen and read. Then complete the table with the animals from Activity 2.

- Learners stand up. Ask *Who's wearing black shoes? Stand in a group, please. Who's wearing brown shoes? Stand in a group*, and so on, until all the learners are in different groups. Say *We can put things, animals or people in groups. We classify them.* Write *classify* on the board. Say *Let's learn about classifying animals.*
- Learners listen and read. Check comprehension by asking *What do (herbivores) eat? Are (chickens) carnivores?*

Track 2.28
See Pupil's Book page 62

- Learners complete the table individually or in pairs.

Key: Carnivore: lion, penguin Herbivore: panda, parrot Omnivore: bear

Activity Book, page 62

See pages TB120–132

Ending the lesson

- Assign an animal to each learner. Say, e.g. *Animals who can fly, stand over here. Animals who can swim, stand over here. Animals who can't fly or swim, over here.* Then change the groups, e.g. carnivores, herbivores and omnivores; animals who live in the sea / on the ground; wild/domestic animals.

Learning outcomes By the end of the lesson, learners will be able to talk and write about animals and their food.

New language *beak, feather, grassland, mammal, quickly, stripe, wing*

Recycled language action verbs, animals, colours, parts of the body, *carnivore, herbivore, omnivore, can*, comparative adjectives, *have got*

Materials animal flashcards from levels 1 and 2, worksheets/notes from Mission Stages 1 and 2 lessons, dictionaries (optional), coloured pens or pencils, digital Mission poster

Warm-up

- Hide animal flashcards around the room before the learners come in.
- Choose learners to come up to the front in pairs. Describe one of the animals, sentence by sentence, e.g. *It's a carnivore. It's got a long tail. It lives in Africa. It can run, climb and jump. It's near the window.* They run to get the correct flashcard.

  Alternative Split learners into two groups and ask them to stand in two lines in front of you. Show an animal flashcard. The learners at the front of each line play. The first learner who names the animal correctly gets a flashcard. At the end of the game, the team with the most flashcards wins.

Pupil's Book, page 63

4 Read about zebras and penguins.

- Say *Open your Pupil's Books at page 63.* Talk briefly about cards with information (some learners may collect or play games with cards like this). Ask *Which is a bird?* Learners point to the penguin. Point to the zebra and teach *mammal*. Ask for more examples of mammals. (*People, lions, cats, dogs, horses*) Ask *Which is a herbivore?* Learners point to the zebra.
- Say *Let's read about zebras and penguins.* Learners read the information silently.
- Check comprehension of the new words by asking, e.g. *Do zebras run slowly?* (*No. They run quickly.*) Check comprehension of *quickly*. Say *Point to the stripes on the zebra. What colour are they? Point to the penguin's beak. Where are its wings?*

5 Read and write *Z* (zebras) or *P* (penguins).

- Read the first sentence and point out the example answer. Ask learners to show you where the information is in Activity 4 .(*Food: Carnivore (fish)*)
- Learners read and write *Z* or *P* individually, then compare answers in pairs.
- Check and ask where they found the information.

  Fast finishers Write prompts on the board for learners to complete: *Zebras are … They live … They eat …* Then they complete the sentences about Adélie penguins.

Key: 2 Z 3 Z 4 P 5 Z 6 P

mission Stage 3

- Show the class the third stage of the Mission poster: *Write about what animals eat.* Read the instructions.
- Put learners into their Mission groups. They write about what their animals eat. They can do this as a group or each learner can write about one animal. Monitor and help with vocabulary.
- Ask learners to practise acting how their animals eat. Demonstrate with a confident learner. Ask him/her to listen and act out as you play the part of the narrator, e.g. *Look. This penguin is swimming very quickly. It's got a fish. It's eating the fish.*

  Extra support Write prompts on the board: *… are carnivores. They eat meat. … are herbivores. They eat leaves from plants. … are omnivores. They eat meat, fruit, eggs and seeds.*

  Fast finishers Write extra information about what the animals look like, e.g. *It's got soft fur. / It's got a long beak.* They can use dictionaries to find new words.

Activity Book, page 63

See pages TB120–132

Activity Book, page 56

- Review *My unit goals.* Ask *How is your Mission?* Learners reflect and choose a smiley face for *My mission diary 3.*

Ending the lesson

- **SA** Go back to Stage 3 on the digital Mission poster. Add a tick to the 'Write about what animals eat' stage. Use self-assessment (see Introduction).
- Give out a completion sticker.

4 Read about zebras and penguins.

NAME: Zebra
GROUP: Mammal
COLOUR: Black and white stripes
LIVES: In African grasslands
FOOD: Herbivore (grass)

Zebras have got four legs and a long tail. Their ears are bigger than a horse's ears. They can run quickly. They live in big groups.

NAME: Adélie Penguin
GROUP: Bird
COLOUR: Black and white
LIVES: In Antarctica
FOOD: Carnivore (fish)

Penguins have got two short legs, wings and a beak. They have feathers. They can swim very quickly, but they can't fly. They live in big groups.

5 Read and write *Z* (zebras) or *P* (penguins).

1 They are carnivores. P
2 They live in Africa. ☐
3 They can run very quickly. ☐
4 They like moving in water. ☐
5 They have stripes. ☐
6 They don't eat grass. ☐

mission STAGE 3

Write about what animals eat.

- Write what each animal eats.
- Practise actions to show how each animal eats.

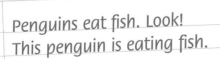

Penguins eat fish. Look!
This penguin is eating fish.

My mission diary
Activity Book page 56

Literature

1 **What do you know about kangaroos?**

They're … | They've got … | They can … | They live …

2.29

Why the kangaroo has a pouch

One morning a mummy kangaroo's near the river. She's playing with her joey. A joey's a baby kangaroo.

But what's that noise? The kangaroo looks and sees a very old wombat. The wombat's crying.

'What's the matter?' the kind kangaroo asks.

'I can't see and I need to eat and drink. I haven't got any friends to help me!' the wombat answers.

'I'm your friend,' the kangaroo says. 'Hold my tail.'

The wombat holds the kangaroo's tail and she takes him to the river. 'Here! Now you can drink,' she says. Then she takes the wombat to the greenest grass and says, 'Here! Now you can eat.'

Text type: An Australian dreamtime story

Learning outcomes By the end of the lesson, learners will have read an Australian dreamtime story.

New language *brilliant, carry, cry, joey, kind, look for, noise, pouch, shout, take, wombat, What's the matter?*

Recycled language *asleep, baby, drink, eat, find, friend, grass, help, hold, late, present, river, tail, wake up, can/can't, have got,* prepositions of place, present continuous, present simple, superlative adjectives

Materials animal flashcards from levels 1 and 2, globe/world map (optional), pictures from Digital photo bank of Australian landscapes, landmarks and animals (optional), audio

Warm-up

- Mix up the animal flashcards. Take out the kangaroo flashcard and put it to one side.
- Learners stand in a circle. Show an animal flashcard, e.g. penguin, and make a positive sentence, e.g. *They can swim.* Give the first flashcard to a learner and ask him/her to make a sentence with *can't*, e.g. *They can't fly.* This learner passes the flashcard to the next person in the circle. He/She makes a positive sentence, e.g. *They've got two legs.* The next learner makes a negative sentence, e.g. *They haven't got stripes.* Continue in this way until the flashcard comes back to you (or learners can't find anything more to say). Start again with a different flashcard.

  Extra support Write useful language on the board:
  They're / They aren't (*big/small/brown/tall/thin/fat*)
  They can / They can't (*swim/climb/fly/jump/walk/run*)
  They've got / They haven't got (*tails/wings/feathers/legs*)
  They eat / They don't eat (*meat/fruit/seeds/fish/plants/grass*)

  Stronger learners Play the game in several smaller circles.

Presentation

- Show photos of Australian landscapes and landmarks. Ask *Where's this?* Write *Australia* on the board and ask/show learners where it is, using a globe or world map.
- Tell learners they are going to read and listen to a 'dreamtime story' from Australia. This is a kind of legend originally told by the Aboriginal people.
- Ask *Which animals live in Australia?* Learners suggest animals (e.g. *kangaroos, wild dogs, sharks, spiders, snakes*). Show photos.

Pupil's Book, pages 64 and 65

1 What do you know about kangaroos?

- Say *Open your Pupil's Books at page 64. What do you know about kangaroos?* Learners talk in pairs then share ideas, e.g. *They live in Australia. They can jump. They've got long tails. They're fast. They eat plants.*
- Read the title of the story and teach *pouch*.

2.29 Why the kangaroo has a pouch

- Look at each picture and ask questions, e.g. Picture 1: *What can you see?* (*A river, plants, a mummy kangaroo and her baby*) Teach *wombat. Is the wombat happy?* (*No, he's sad.*) Picture 2: *What's the wombat doing?* (*Holding the kangaroo's tail*) *Where are they going?* (*To the river*) Picture 3: *What's the mummy kangaroo doing?* (*Looking for her baby*) *Where's the baby?* (*Under/Below the tree*) Picture 4: *Where's the baby now?* (*In the mummy kangaroo's pouch*)
- Say *Let's read and listen to the first part of the story.* Play the audio. Pause the audio after *crying*. Ask *What are the kangaroos doing?* (*Playing*) *What's a joey?* (*A baby kangaroo*) *What's the wombat doing?* (*Crying*)

  Track 2.29
  See story on Pupil's Book pages 64–65
- Say *Read and listen to the next part.* Pause after *Hold my tail.* Ask *Can the wombat see?* (*No, he can't.*) Check comprehension of *What's the matter?* Ask *What does the wombat need to do?* (*Eat and drink*) *What does the kangaroo do?* (*She helps the wombat.*)
- Play the next part. Pause after *Now you can eat.* Ask *Where does the kangaroo take the wombat to drink?* (*The river*) *Where does she take him to eat?* (*The grass*)
- Play the next part of the story. Pause after *sleep, too.* Ask *What does the kangaroo shout?* (*Where are you?*) *Does she find her joey?* (*Yes, she does.*)
- Play the rest of the story. Ask *What does the kangaroo put in the pouch?* (*Her baby/joey*) *Where does the pouch come from?* (*The wombat – it's a present*)

  Extension Play the whole story again, without pauses, for learners to listen and read.

Activity Book, page 64

See pages TB120–132

Ending the lesson

- Say *When the answer is 'kangaroo', jump in the air. When the answer is 'wombat', walk on the spot.* Demonstrate the actions. Learners practise.
- Say sentences. Learners do the correct action.

It needs food and water. (W)	*It gives someone a present.* (W)
It's got a baby. (K)	*It's got a long tail.* (K)
It's very kind. (K)	*It can't see.* (W)
It hasn't got any friends. (W)	*It looks for its baby.* (K)

Learning outcomes By the end of the lesson, learners will have thought about helping others.

New language *How does (the wombat) feel when … ?*

Recycled language language from the story, *be kind to (someone)*

Materials A4 paper, coloured pens or pencils, scissors, stapler, audio

Social and Emotional Skill: Helping others

- After reading the story, ask learners *How is the kangaroo kind to the wombat?* (*The wombat can't see. The kangaroo takes him to the river to drink and to the grass to eat.*) *How does the wombat feel?* (*Happy*) *How is the wombat kind to the kangaroo?* (*He makes a pouch for her.*) *How does the kangaroo feel?* (*Happy*)
- Say *Yes, when someone is kind to us and helps us, we feel happy. When we are kind to someone else, we feel happy too.*
- Give learners two or three situations and they work in pairs and think of ways to be kind and to help, e.g. *a new boy or girl comes to the school.* (*Play with him or her in the playground, take him or her to the dining room at lunchtime, share a snack*) Or *a teacher is carrying a lot of books to the classroom.* (*Help him/her carry the books, open the door for him/her*)
- Tell learners they are going to make a booklet about being kind and helping others. Hand out A4 paper. They fold it in four and cut along the folds. Staple the pages together. On the front cover, they write *Ways to be kind by …* and their name.
- Then inside, tell them to draw three ways to be kind, e.g. *sharing my new crayons, playing with my little sister, talking to my grandparents, helping Mum with the shopping.* They use the right-hand side of each double page.
- Optional: encourage the learners to do one kind act today and tell the class tomorrow.

Warm-up

- Write these words on the board: *wombat, see, pouch, old, babies, river, kangaroo.*
- Tell the story and pause for learners to say the word: *A mummy kangaroo and her joey are playing near the …* (*river*). *A joey is a baby …* (*kangaroo*). *They meet a wombat. He's very …* (*old*) *and he can't …* (*see*). *The mummy kangaroo helps the …* (*wombat*). *The wombat gives the kangaroo a …* (*pouch*). *From that day, mummy kangaroos have pouches to carry their …* (*babies*).

Pupil's Book, pages 64 and 65

- Say *Open your Pupil's Books at pages 64 and 65.* Play the audio. Learners read and listen to the story again.

Track 2.29

See story on Pupil's Book pages 64–65

2 Talk about the questions.

- Read the questions with the class and check comprehension.
- Talk about each question as a class. Prompt learners to explain their answers, e.g. *Why does the wombat feel sad?* (*Because he hasn't got any friends / he needs help / he's scared*) *Why does the kangaroo need a pouch?* (*Because she can't find her joey*) *How do we know that the kangaroo likes the pouch?* (*She says it's 'brilliant'.*)

Key: 1 sad / hungry and thirsty 2 happy 3 to say 'thank you' / because she's the kindest kangaroo he knows 4 happy/surprised

Extension Learners act out the story in pairs. Write a simple script on the board. Encourage them to show emotions and act, e.g. the kangaroo jumps and the wombat follows behind to the 'river' and then the 'grass', the kangaroo acts looking for the joey, going to sleep, waking up, etc.

Kangaroo:	*Hello. What's the matter?*
Wombat:	*I'm sad. I can't see and I haven't got any friends.*
Kangaroo:	*Hold my tail. I can take you to the river.*
Wombat:	*Thank you!*
Kangaroo:	*Now I can take you to the grass.*
Wombat:	*Goodbye! Thank you again.*
Kangaroo:	*Where's my joey? … There you are! Let's sleep. What's this? It's brilliant!*
Wombat:	*It's a present. You're the kindest kangaroo I know!*

3 Who's kind to you? Are you kind to people? What do you do?

- Read the first question. Give learners a minute to make a list of all the people who are kind to them. They share ideas.
- Read the second and third questions. Learners talk in pairs about ways they are kind. Monitor and support. Write their suggestions on the board, e.g. *I'm kind to my grandparents. I call them every day.*

Activity Book, page 65

See pages TB120–132

Ending the lesson

- **SA** Use self-assessment to see how well learners think they understand the story. See Introduction.

The kangaroo's kind to the old wombat all day. When it's late, she says goodbye to him and she looks for her baby. Where is he? She can't find him! 'Joey! Joey! Where are you?' the kangaroo shouts.

It's OK. He's asleep below the biggest tree. The kind kangaroo finds him and goes to sleep, too.

The next day she wakes up and sees a pouch. She puts her joey in the pouch. Then she sees the old wombat. 'Look! This pouch is brilliant, but where does it come from?'

'It's my present to you. You're the kindest kangaroo that I know,' the wombat says.

And from that day, all mummy kangaroos have pouches to carry their babies.

2 Talk about the questions.

1 How does the wombat feel at the start of the story?
2 How does the wombat feel when the kangaroo helps him?
3 Why does the wombat give her the pouch?
4 How does the kangaroo feel when the wombat gives her the pouch?

3 Who's kind to you? Are you kind to people? What do you do?

1 Where are Mary and Jack? What are they doing?

2 Match the questions with the answers.

1 What do you want to see after this?
2 Are the bears near the lions?
3 Can you see the penguins?

a No, I can't see them.
b Let's go and see the bats.
c Yes, they are.

3 Read what Mary says and Jack's three answers. Which two are wrong?

Mary: Bats are funny! I like them.

Jack:
a I think there are ten.
b Do you like bats?
c So do I.

Why are the two answers wrong? Write a letter in each box.

1 We know Mary likes them. ☐

2 Mary doesn't say 'How many'. ☐

4 Read and think. Choose the best answer.

1 **Mary:** Why don't we get a drink?
Jack:
a Because we haven't got a drink.
b That's a good idea.
c We mustn't give drinks to the animals.

2 **Mary:** There's Mum! She's waving at us!
Jack:
a Yes, she wants to go.
b Yes, let's tell Mum.
c Yes, that's Mum's.

Read all the answers before you choose. Then check your answers.

Learning outcomes By the end of the lesson, learners will have practised completing a multiple-choice task (A1 Movers Reading and Writing Part 2).

Test skills Reading a dialogue; Choosing the correct responses

New language *wrong, Why don't we … ?*

Recycled language animals, *drink* (n), *wave* (v), *Let's …*

Materials practice paper for Movers Reading and Writing Part 2 (optional)

Warm-up

- Put learners into pairs. Write *Do you like going to the zoo? Which wild animals do you like?* on the board. Learners talk in pairs.

Presentation

- Say *Let's practise for a reading and writing exam.* Show the Movers Reading and Writing Part 2 paper (the picture and dialogue with multiple-choice answers). Say *In Part 2 of the exam you read a conversation. You need to choose the correct answers from three choices. Let's practise.*

Pupil's Book, page 66

1 Where are Mary and Jack? What are they doing?

- Say *Open your Pupil's Books at page 66. In the exam there's a picture of the people talking in the dialogue.* Read the questions. Learners share their ideas. Ask *What do you think they're talking about?* Point out that the picture in the exam can help them to understand what they read.

Key: They're at the zoo. They're looking at the pandas.

2 Match the questions with the answers.

- Explain that in the exam learners sometimes need to match a question with an answer. Learners read and match individually, then compare answers in pairs.

  Extra support For each question, ask if a yes/no answer is needed (2 and 3) or if the question is more open (1). Ask which words in the answers helped them to match.

Key: 1 b 2 c 3 a

3 Read what Mary says and Jack's three answers. Which two are wrong?

- Explain that in the exam some lines in the conversation are sentences, not questions. Learners need to choose an appropriate response / continuation of the conversation. Read the instructions. Check comprehension of *wrong*.
- Learners work individually or in pairs to identify the two incorrect choices.

Key: a and b are wrong

Why are the two answers wrong? Write a letter in each box.

- Learners look back at Jack's incorrect responses (a and b). Talk about each option with the class. Learners write the letters in the correct boxes.

Key: 1 b 2 a

4 Read and think. Choose the best answer.

- Tell learners that the two questions are the same format as the exam (show the practice paper again). Read the questions and options. Check comprehension of *Why don't we … ?* (explain that it means the same as *Let's …*) and *wave.*
- Learners read and choose their answers individually. Remind them to look again and check that their answers make sense after they have chosen.
- Check answers. Ask learners to explain why the options they didn't choose are wrong.

Key: 1 b 2 a

Extra support Learners practise the complete conversation in pairs (Activities 2 to 4). Pairs can read it / act it out for the class.

- Point to the monkey at the bottom of the page and read. Remind learners to consider all the options before they choose an answer. Going back and reading the whole conversation is the best way to check it makes sense.

Activity Book, page 66

See pages TB120–132

Ending the lesson

- Write phrases on the board: *So do I. / No, I don't. / Yes, I do. / Yes, of course I can. / You're welcome. / Great idea. / Yes, there is. / No, thank you.* Say a sentence or ask a question. Learners say a response from the board, e.g. *Can you help me? (Yes, of course I can.) Thank you very much. (You're welcome.) Do you like snakes? (No, I don't.)*

Learning outcomes By the end of the lesson, learners will have revised the language in the unit and acted out an animal documentary.

Recycled language unit language

Materials three large pieces of paper or card with *carnivore*, *herbivore* and *omnivore* written on them, worksheets/notes from Mission Stages 1–3 lessons, animal masks/costumes (optional), video equipment (optional), dice and counters (for Activity Book game), coloured pens or pencils, digital Mission poster

Warm-up

- Put the pieces of paper/card with *carnivore, herbivore* and *omnivore* in three corners of the room. Ask *What does a carnivore eat?* (*Meat, fish*) *What about a herbivore?* (*Plants, leaves*) *Which animals are omnivores?* (*Bears, people*)
- Say and clap the stress with the learners: *carnivore, herbivore, omnivore.*
- Demonstrate the game. Stand in the middle of the room and close your eyes. Say *Go!* Learners run to one of the three corners with signs. Say the name of an animal, e.g. *Lion*. All the learners standing by the *carnivore* sign stay in the game. The rest sit down.
- Repeat with new animals until only one learner is left as the winner.
- Play several times.

  Alternative The learners standing in the correct place get a point each time. If you want, choose learners who are out of the game to come to the middle and call out the animal names (make sure they keep their eyes shut). At the end, check how many points each learner has.

Pupil's Book, page 67

mission in action!

Act out an animal documentary.

- Say *Open your Pupil's Books at page 67.* Point to the Mission box or show learners the last stage of the digital Mission poster. Say *Let's put our Mission in action!* Say *Act out an animal documentary.*
- Read the instructions. Give learners time to rehearse their documentary, using their scripts from Stages 2 and 3. Monitor and help.
- If possible, groups video each other's documentaries.

  Extension Learners make animal masks or costumes for their documentary.
- Groups take turns to present their documentary or show their video. Have a class vote on the best performance.

Self-assessment

- **SA** Say *Did you like our 'Act out an animal documentary' Mission? Think and draw a face.* Learners draw a happy face, neutral face or sad face and then hold it up in the air.
- Ask *What did you do better in this Mission? Working together? Writing a script? Presenting to the class?* Learners each say one thing, or, if you have a large class, they can tell partners.
- Say *Our next Mission is 'Create a holiday island.'* Explain that learners will create an imaginary island and talk about things to see there and the weather. Check understanding of *weather.*

Activity Book, page 67

See pages TB120–132

Activity Book, page 56

- Review *My unit goals*. Ask *How is your Mission?* Learners reflect and choose a smiley face for *My mission diary* the final stage.
- Point to the sunflower. Learners read the 'can do' statements and tick them if they agree they have achieved them. They colour each leaf green if they are very confident or orange if they think they need more practice.
- Point to the word stack sign. Ask learners to look back at the unit and find at least five new words they have learnt. They write them in their word stack.

Ending the lesson

- **SA** Go back to the completion stage on the digital Mission poster. Add a tick or invite a learner to do it. Use self-assessment (see Introduction).
- Give out a completion sticker.
- Tell learners *You have finished your Mission! Well done!*

mission in action!

Act out an animal documentary.

My mission diary
Activity Book page 56

★ **Present your animals.**

This is the bat. It's the smallest animal in our documentary.

★ **Say and show what each animal can do.**

Dolphins can swim.

★ **Say what each animal eats and show how it eats.**

Penguins eat fish. Look! This penguin is eating a fish.

★ **Vote for the best documentary.**

This group's actions are the funniest!

6 Our weather

1 Watch the video. Draw a picture of yourself in this weather.

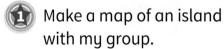

mission Create a holiday island

In this unit I will:

1. Make a map of an island with my group.
2. Add things to see on our island.
3. Create weather symbols for our map.

★ Present our island to the class.

Unit 6 learning outcomes

In Unit 6, learners learn to:

- talk about the weather and clothes
- use *was/were* and *There was / There were* to talk about the past
- learn about instruments to measure the weather and weather symbols
- read a poem and learn about thinking positively

Materials sun and snow symbols on pieces of paper, video, coloured pens or pencils, digital Mission poster, a copy of the Mission worksheet (Teacher's Resource Book page 64), Clothes flashcards from level 1 or real clothing

Self-assessment

- SA Say *Open your Pupil's Books at page 68. Look at the picture. Is it a hot day or a cold day? What can you see? What are the children doing? What are they wearing?* Read the title and check understanding of *weather.* Use self-assessment (see Introduction). Say *OK. Let's learn.*

Warm-up

- Ask learners *Do you like hot or cold weather?* Show a symbol/picture to represent *hot* (e.g. a sun) and say *It's hot.* Show a picture for *cold* (e.g. a snowflake) and say *It's cold.* Stick the pictures on different walls in the classroom.
- Mime an activity or say, e.g. *playing tennis.* Learners point to the correct symbol. Say, e.g. *Yes, that's right. We can play tennis when it's hot.* Repeat with different activities.

  Stronger learners Take turns to lead by saying an activity.

Pupil's Book, page 68

1 Watch the video. Draw a picture of yourself in this weather.

- Say *In this unit we're talking about weather.* Say *Let's watch the video.* To introduce the topic of the unit, play the video.
- Say *Look at page 68.* Point to the empty space for drawing. On the board, draw yourself as a simple outline and add clothes for a winter's day (jacket, hat, boots, etc.). Say *This is me in the photo.* Say *Draw you. It's cold. What are you wearing?*
- Learners draw pictures of themselves.
- Put learners into pairs. They show their drawing to their partner.

mission Create a holiday island

- Point to the Mission box or the digital Mission poster and say *This is our Mission.*
- Say *Our mission is: Create a holiday island.* Show learners a picture of an island. Say *This is an island.* Ask learners to name islands they know. Say *Our mission is to create an island for a holiday.*
- Say *Point to number 1. Make a map of an island with my group.* Show the Mission worksheet, if available. Say *You make a map. You write the names of the different places.*
- Say *Point to number 2. Add things to see on our island.* Ask *What things can we see on the island?* Draw simple pictures on the board to give learners ideas (e.g. *a river, trees, animals).*
- Say *Point to number 3. Create weather symbols for our map.* Show a weather map from the internet or a newspaper. Say *A weather map shows the weather in different places.* Point to the symbols and say *These are symbols. They show us the weather.* Point to the sun symbol and ask *What does this symbol show? (Sun)*
- Say *The last stage is 'Present our island to the class.'* Say *You complete your map and then you show it to the class. You talk about the places on your island, the things you can see and the weather.*
- Say *This is our Mission.* Go through the stages of the Mission again.
- For ideas on monitoring and assessment, see Introduction.

Activity Book, page 68

My unit goals

- Help learners to complete the unit goals. See notes on page TB6.
- You can go back to these unit goals at the end of each Mission stage during the unit and review them.

Ending the lesson

- Show flashcards from level 1 of clothes/accessories learners already know (boots, cap, dress, glasses, hat, jacket, jeans, shirt, shoes, shorts, skirt, sunglasses trousers, T-shirt,) or real clothing. Learners say the name.
- Learners stand up. Give an instruction, e.g. *Sit down if you're wearing white shoes.* Repeat with different items until only one or two learners are left standing (they are the winners).

Learning outcomes By the end of the lesson, learners will be able to talk about the weather.

New language *cloud, cloudy, cold, hot, make a video call, rain* (n, v), *rainbow, snow* (n, v), *sunny, wind, windy, terrible, weather, put on, What's the weather like? It's …*

Recycled language *asleep, board game, jacket, leaves, mountain, noise, outside, pick up, sun, tablet, can/can't, have got, Let's …*, present continuous, present simple

Materials The weather flashcards, audio, video, coloured pens or pencils

Warm-up

- Say *Where am I?* Mime relaxing on the beach. Say *The sun's in the sky. It's hot. I'm wearing my sunglasses and my sun hat. What's that noise? The sea …* Learners say *The beach!* Repeat, this time with learners joining in with the actions/ words. Then mime walking in the mountains, e.g. *It's cold. I'm wearing boots and a big jacket. I'm walking up. What's that noise? The wind …* Learners guess (*The mountains*) and then copy and join in, as before.

Presentation

- Teach the new weather words using the flashcards and mime.
- Draw the sun and ask *What's this?* Write *sun* in the centre. Draw a cloud. Ask *What's this?* and write *cloud* in the centre. Say *I can see the sun. It's sunny.* Write *It's sunny* below the sun. Draw more clouds and say *I can see lots of clouds … It's cloudy.* Write *It's cloudy*. Mime trying to walk on a windy day and say *I can feel the wind today. It's windy.* Write *It's windy*.
- Draw and teach *It's raining* and *It's snowing*.
- Ask *What's the weather like today? Is it sunny/cloudy/cold?*

Pupil's Book, page 69

1 (2.30, 2.31) Listen and point. Then listen and number.

- Say *Open your Pupil's Books at page 69. What are Jim and Jenny doing?* (*Talking to Grandma and Grandpa on a tablet*) *Where are Grandma and Grandpa?* (*In the mountains*)
- Ask *Where's the small tractor? Can you find it?*
- Read the caption and check comprehension of *make a video call*. Play Track 2.30. Learners listen and point.

Tracks 2.30 and 2.31

(1) This afternoon the children are making a video call to their grandparents.

Jim:	Hello, Grandpa. Hi, Grandma. How's your holiday? Is it snowing?
Grandpa:	It isn't snowing now, but there's a lot of snow.
(2) Jenny:	Is it cold?
Grandma:	It's cold on the mountains, but it's OK here.
(3) Grandma:	It's very sunny.
(4) Grandpa:	What's the weather like there on the farm?
Jenny:	Ah, it's terrible, Grandpa! There are a lot of grey clouds …
(5) Jenny:	… and a lot of wind.
Grandma:	Oh, dear. I'm sorry it's cloudy and windy.
(6) Grandma:	What's that noise? Is there a problem with the call?
Jim:	No, Grandma. It's Cameron. He's asleep. He's nice and hot.
(7) Jenny:	It's Saturday, but we can't play outside!
Grandpa:	You can play outside! Put on your big jackets and go and pick up the leaves in the garden. That's fun!
Jim:	It's raining. We can't pick up leaves in the rain, Grandpa.
Grandma:	You can play a board game.
Jim:	Yes! That's a good idea. Come on, Jenny!
(8) Jenny:	Oh! Look, Jim – there's a rainbow. Let's show Grandma and Grandpa.
Grandpa:	You need sun and rain to have a rainbow.
Jim and Jenny:	That's right, Grandpa.

- Say *Now listen and number.* Play Track 2.31.
- Ask *What's the weather like on the farm?* Teach *terrible*.

Key: 2 cold 3 sunny 4 cloud 5 wind 6 hot 7 rain 8 rainbow

2 (2.32) Say the chant.

- Play the audio or video. Learners point and chant.

Track 2.32

Weather, weather,
What's the weather like?
Hot, cold,
Sun, sunny,
Wind, windy,
Cloud, cloudy.

Weather, weather,
What's the weather like?
Snow, it's snowing.
Rain, it's raining.
I can see a rainbow.
What's the weather like?

3 (2.33) Listen and write the words.

- Play the audio. Pause for learners to write each word.

Track 2.33

1 w-i-n-d-y
2 w-e-a-t-h-e-r
3 r-a-i-n-b-o-w
4 c-l-o-u-d-y
5 h-o-t
6 s-n-o-w
7 s-u-n-n-y
8 r-a-i-n
9 c-o-l-d
10 w-i-n-d

Activity Book, page 69

See pages TB120–132

Ending the lesson

- **SA** Show The weather flashcards. Ask *Do you know the words?* Use self-assessment (see Introduction).

1 2.30 2.31 **Listen and point. Then listen and number.**

2 2.32 **Say the chant.**

3 2.33 **Listen and write the words.**

The Friendly Farm

2.34

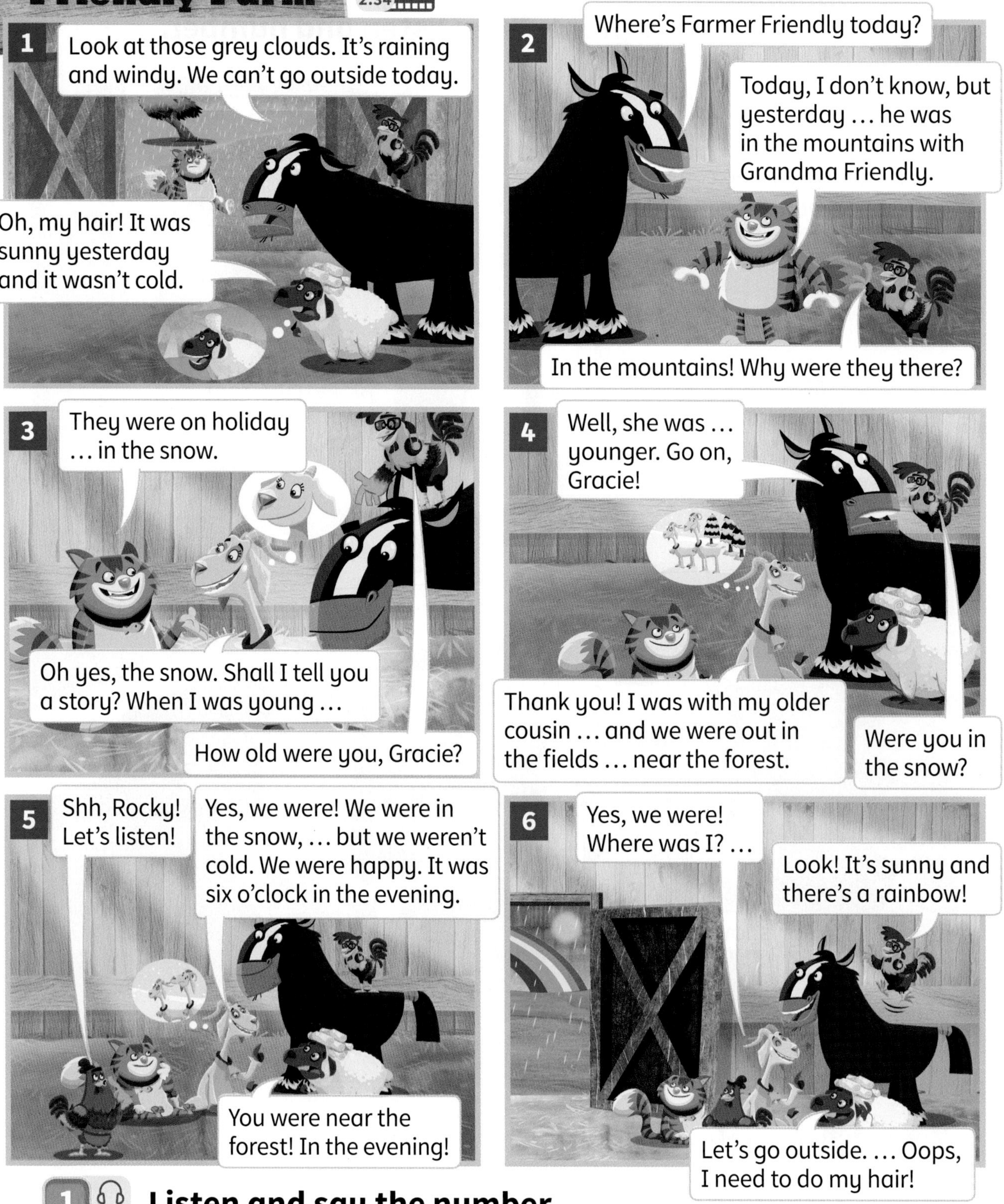

1
Look at those grey clouds. It's raining and windy. We can't go outside today.
Oh, my hair! It was sunny yesterday and it wasn't cold.
2
Where's Farmer Friendly today?
Today, I don't know, but yesterday … he was in the mountains with Grandma Friendly.
In the mountains! Why were they there?
3
They were on holiday … in the snow.
Oh yes, the snow. Shall I tell you a story? When I was young …
How old were you, Gracie?
4
Well, she was … younger. Go on, Gracie!
Thank you! I was with my older cousin … and we were out in the fields … near the forest.
Were you in the snow?
5
Shh, Rocky! Let's listen!
Yes, we were! We were in the snow, … but we weren't cold. We were happy. It was six o'clock in the evening.
You were near the forest! In the evening!
6
Yes, we were! Where was I? …
Look! It's sunny and there's a rainbow!
Let's go outside. … Oops, I need to do my hair!

1 2.35 **Listen and say the number.**

Learning outcomes By the end of the lesson, learners will be able to understand *was* and *were*.

New language *do your hair, yesterday, Shall I … ?, was, were*

Recycled language adjectives, countryside, days of the week, weather, *near, outside, today, What's the weather like?, can/can't,* comparatives

Materials The weather flashcards, audio, video

Warm-up

- Review the weather words with the flashcards. Ask *What's the weather like today?* Learners say, e.g. *It's cloudy. It's cold. It isn't raining.*
- Teach a mime for each type of weather, e.g. putting up an umbrella for *It's raining*, putting on sunglasses for *It's sunny.* Practise the mimes with the learners, saying the sentences at the same time.
- **SA** Use self-assessment to check how well learners think they understand the vocabulary. See Introduction.

Presentation

- Ask *What day is it today?* Learners say *Today is (Friday).* Gesture behind you and say *Yesterday was (Thursday).* Learners repeat the sentence and the gesture.
- Say *Yesterday the weather wasn't (cold). It was (hot and sunny). It wasn't (rainy).* Ask *Was it sunny/windy/cold?* Help learners to reply with short answers *Yes, it was. / No, it wasn't.* Then ask *Were you in the town centre last weekend?* Focus on a negative answer and present *weren't*, e.g. *You weren't in the town centre. Where were you?*
- Ask a strong learner *How old are you?* (*I'm seven.*) Gesture behind you and ask *How old were you last year?* (*Six*) Help the learner reply *I was (six).* Ask different learners the same two questions. Then ask other learners *How old was (Antonio) last year? He was (six).*

Pupil's Book, page 70

2.34 The Friendly Farm song

- Play the introductory song at the beginning of the cartoon story. Learners listen and sing.

Track 2.34
See The Friendly Farm song on page TB5

2.34 The Friendly Farm

- Say *Open your Pupil's Books at page 70.* Point to the first picture and ask *What's the weather like?* (*It's cloudy/windy. It's raining.*) Point to the rainbow at the end and ask *What's this? What's the weather like now?*
- Say *Gracie is telling the animals a story. Where were Gracie and her cousin in the story?* Write the question on the board. Play the audio or video. Learners listen and read. Check answers. (*They were in the fields near the forest.*) Check comprehension of *Shall I tell you a story?* and *do my hair.*

Track 2.34
The Friendly Farm song + see cartoon on Pupil's Book page 70

- Play the audio or video again. Pause after each picture and ask questions: 1: *What was the weather like yesterday?* (*It was sunny and it wasn't cold.*) 2: *Where's Grandpa Friendly today?* (*The animals don't know.*) *Where was he yesterday?* (*He was in the mountains with Grandma Friendly.*)
3: *Why were they in the mountains?* (*They were on holiday.*)
4: *Is Gracie's cousin older or younger than her?* (*Older*)
5: *Were they in the snow?* (*Yes, they were.*) *Were they cold?* (*No, they weren't.*) *Were they sad?* (*No, they were happy.*) *What time was it?* (*Six o'clock*) 6: *What do the animals do at the end?* (*They go outside.*)

1 2.35 Listen and say the number.

- Read the instructions. Play the first sentence as an example. Learners find the correct picture, point and say the number. Play the rest of the audio. Pause after each sentence for learners to answer.

Track 2.35

a	Gracie:	Where was I? [6]
b	Cameron:	They were on holiday … in the snow. [3]
c	Shelly:	It was sunny yesterday and it wasn't cold. [1]
d	Gracie:	It was six o'clock in the evening. [5]
e	Rocky:	How old were you, Gracie? [3]
f	Rocky:	Why were they there? [2]
g	Harry:	Well, she was … younger. [4]
h	Gracie:	We were in the snow, … but we weren't cold. [5]

Key: See numbers in audioscript

Activity Book, page 70

See pages TB120–132

Ending the lesson

- **SA** Repeat the self-assessment to see how well learners think they understand the vocabulary. Is there any change?

Learning outcomes By the end of the lesson, learners will be able to use *was* and *were*.

New language *Were your grandparents here last weekend? Yes, they were. / No, they weren't. Were you at school on Tuesday? Yes, I was. / No, I wasn't.*

Recycled language days of the week, family, places, weather, *island, town*

Materials The weather flashcards, audio, Mission worksheets (Teacher's Resource Book page 64), coloured pens or pencils, paper, digital Mission poster

Warm-up

- Stick The weather flashcards on the board and number them. Say *Look and remember*. Then turn them over. Ask *What was number (3)?* Show the card to confirm. Repeat, asking about all the cards. Prompt with questions, e.g. *Was 'rain' next to 'rainbow'?*

Presentation

- Say *Last weekend I was in the countryside. I was with my grandparents. We were at their house in the village.* Write *Where were you at the weekend? Who were you with?* on the board. Ask different learners. Ask extra questions, e.g. *Were you happy? Was the weather nice?*

Pupil's Book, page 71

2.36 Gracie's Grammar

- Say *Open your Pupil's Books at page 71.* Point to Gracie's Grammar box. Write the questions and answers on the board.
- Play the audio. Pause for learners to repeat.

Track 2.36

See Pupil's Book page 71

1 2.37 Listen and stick. Then look, read and write.

- Say *A girl is talking to her grandma about last week.* Point to each sticker and ask *What was the weather like? Was she inside or outside? Was she (walking)?*
- Play the audio. Learners point to the correct sticker.
- Play the audio again. Learners stick the stickers under the heading for the correct day. Check and ask, e.g. *Where was she on (Thursday)? What was the weather like?*

Track 2.37

1 Grandma: I was on holiday last week. The weather was hot and sunny. What was it like here?
Girl: Well, Grandma, it was different every day.
Grandma: Really? What was it like on Wednesday?
Girl: It wasn't bad on Wednesday: sunny, but windy too. I was in the park in the afternoon.
Grandma: That's nice!
2 Grandma: Was the weather better last weekend?
Girl: Yes, it was. On Saturday it was sunny, but it wasn't hot. I was with Dad.
Grandma: Where were you?
Girl: We were in the forest.
3 Grandma: OK, tell me about Thursday.
Girl: On Thursday, it was cold and rainy, so I was inside with my older cousin.
Grandma: Your older cousin? Why?
Girl: Because Mum and Dad weren't at home. They were in the town centre.
4 Girl: And on Friday it was terrible again. It was cold and windy. And I was outside when it was rainy too.
Grandma: Why were you outside?
Girl: Because I was on my way to school.

- Point to the example. Say *Now look, read and write.*

Key: 2 were 3 weren't 4 was

mission Stage 1

- Point to the Mission box or show learners the first stage of the digital Mission poster: *Make a map of an island.*
- In groups, learners complete the worksheet task in the Teacher's Resource Book (page 64). See teaching notes on TRB page 57.
- Alternatively, if you do not have the Teacher's Resource Book, give each group paper to draw a map of an imaginary island. They choose a name for their island and mark/name five towns. Then they imagine they were on holiday on the island last week. They talk about what the weather was like in each town and make notes.

Activity Book, page 71

See pages TB120–132

Activity Book, page 68

- Review *My unit goals*. Ask *How is your Mission?* Learners reflect and choose a smiley face for *My mission diary 1*. Monitor.

Ending the lesson

- SA Go back to Stage 1 on the digital Mission poster. Say *We made a map of an island.* Add a tick to the 'Make a map of an island' stage. Use self-assessment (see Introduction).
- Give out a completion sticker.

Gracie's Grammar

2.36

Were your grandparents here last weekend? — Yes, they **were**. / No, they **weren't**.

Were you at school on Tuesday? — Yes, I **was**. / No, I **wasn't**.

1 Listen and stick. Then look, read and write.

2.37

Wednesday	Thursday
Friday	**Saturday**

1 The weather wasn't bad on Wednesday.

2 We ________ in the forest on Saturday.

3 Mum and Dad ________ at home on Thursday.

4 What ________ the weather like on Friday?

mission STAGE 1

Make a map of an island.

- In groups, imagine you were on holiday last week.
- Draw five places on your map. Talk about the weather.

What was the weather like in ...?

It was cold and sunny.

My mission diary
Activity Book page 68

1 2.38 Listen and complete. Then sing the song.

It's hot and sunny, sunny today.
Put on your T-shirt and shorts and go out to play.
I'm wearing my T-shirt and shorts.
I'm wearing my 1 T-shirt and 2 ________.

It's cold and windy, windy today.
Put on your sweater and scarf and go out to play.
I'm wearing my sweater and scarf.
I'm wearing my 3 ________ and 4 ________.

There's snow, it's snowing, snowing today.
Put on your coat and boots and go out to play.
I'm wearing my coat and boots.
I'm wearing my 5 ________ and 6 ________.

Come inside, near the fire. It's nice and hot there.
Take off your coat and boots and sit on that chair.
Now I'm not wearing my coat.
Now I'm not wearing my boots. (x2)

2 Imagine the weather. Talk to your partner.

It's cold and raining. What are you wearing?

I'm wearing my big coat and my black boots.

Have you got a favourite scarf or sweater? What colour is it?

Learning outcomes By the end of the lesson, learners will have practised the new language through song.

New language *boots, coat, put on, scarf, shorts, sweater, T-shirt, take off, fire*

Recycled language clothes, colours, weather, *go out, inside, near, today, I'm wearing …*, imperatives, present continuous

Materials Clothes flashcards from levels 1 and 2, real items of clothing that learners can put on, e.g. boots, coat, scarf, shorts, sweater and T-shirt, plus others they know, e.g. skirt, shirt, hat, baseball cap, sunglasses, two dice, audio, video, your favourite scarf or sweater (optional)

Warm-up

- Say *Today I'm wearing (a red shirt and black trousers).* Ask a learner *What are you wearing today?* He/She says, e.g. *I'm wearing black trousers, a green T-shirt and black shoes.* Ask, e.g. *Are you wearing socks? What colour are they?*
- In pairs, learners take turns to say what they're wearing. Then they stand back to back and say as much as they can about their partner's clothes (*You're wearing …*).

Presentation

- Teach *coat, scarf* and *sweater* and revise *boots, shorts* and *T-shirt* with the flashcards or real items of clothing.
- Stick the flashcards for boots, coat, scarf, shorts, sweater and T-shirt on the board and number them 2 to 7. Add flashcards for three more items learners know (or draw pictures), e.g. sunglasses, shirt, hat. Number these 8 to 10.
- Demonstrate the game. Show a real item of clothing corresponding to each flashcard on the board. Put the clothes on a table at the front. Ask a learner to throw the two dice. Say *I put on the item which has the same number.* If the learner throws a four, point to flashcard 4 and say *Put on the (scarf).* Put on the scarf from the table or mime putting it on (if you don't have real clothes). Ask the learner to throw another number. Put on the corresponding item of clothing, until the class get the idea. Explain that if a number 11 or 12 is thrown, the learner at the front takes off the item of clothing. The learner who threw 11 or 12 throws the dice again, then comes to the front and puts on the corresponding item of clothing.
- Play the game, with learners passing the dice around and taking turns to throw. When they throw a number they say, e.g. *Number two. Put on the boots.*
- **SA** Use self-assessment to check how well learners think they understand the vocabulary. See Introduction.

Pupil's Book, page 72

1 2.38 Listen and complete. Then sing the song.

- Say *Open your Pupil's Books at page 72.* Ask *What's the boy doing?* (e.g. *Watching TV*) *What has his dad got?* (e.g. *A T-shirt and shorts*) *What's the weather like?* (e.g. *It's hot and sunny.*) Teach *fire.*
- Say *Listen and complete.* Point to the spaces and the example. Play the audio or video. Check answers.

  Extra support Point out that they can copy the missing words from line 3 in each verse.

  Track 2.38

  Rocky: I'm Rocky-Doodle-Doo and here's our song for today: *All weather clothes*

  See song on Pupil's Book page 72

Key: 2 shorts 3 sweater 4 scarf 5 coat 6 boots

- Learners stand up. Practise the song in sections.
- Play the audio or video again. Learners sing and do actions (for the weather and putting on the clothes).

2.39 **Extension** Once learners are confidently singing along, try singing the karaoke version as a class.

2 Imagine the weather. Talk to your partner.

- Read the instructions and example speech bubbles.
- Put the class into pairs. One learner imagines the weather and asks the question, the other responds with his/her own ideas of what to wear.

  Extension The learner who is describing his/her outfit draws a picture of it and labels the items of clothing.
- Show the picture of Rocky in the bottom right-hand corner. Read Rocky's questions. Tell the class about your favourite scarf or sweater (show them if possible), e.g. *My favourite sweater's blue and purple. It's got stripes. It was a birthday present from my sister. I wear it on very cold days.* Learners talk in pairs. Monitor and support.

Activity Book, page 72

See pages TB120–132

Ending the lesson

- **SA** Repeat the self-assessment used after the Presentation to see how well learners think they understand the vocabulary. Is there any change?
- Play the song again. Learners join in and do actions.

Learning outcomes By the end of the lesson, learners will be able to use *There was* and *There were*.

New language *Was there a scarf in the bedroom? Yes, there was. / No, there wasn't. Were there any boots in the bedroom? Yes, there were. / No, there weren't.*

Recycled language clothes, countryside, homes, prepositions of place

Materials Clothes flashcards from levels 1 and 2, audio, timer(s), worksheets/maps and notes from Mission Stage 1 lesson, coloured pens or pencils, digital Mission poster

Warm-up

- Learners stand or sit in a circle. Demonstrate the activity: stand in the centre of the circle and mime putting on or taking off an item of clothing. Learners say, e.g. *You're putting on your boots.*
- Choose a learner to stand in the middle and mime. The others guess. Continue until as many learners as possible have had a go.

Presentation

- Put the flashcards for boots, shorts, scarf, coat, sweater, T-shirt on the board. Let learners look for 20 seconds. Take the flashcards down, take one away and substitute it with another. Mix the flashcards and put them back on the board in a different order.
- Ask *What's different?* Learners say, e.g. *No coat / There isn't a coat*. Say *Yes. There was a coat, but now there's a (shirt).*
- Remove boots and put in jeans to present the plural, e.g. *There were some boots, but now there are some jeans.*
- Write the model sentences (singular and plural) on the board. Learners copy in their notebooks.
- Practise a few more times, substituting a singular noun for a singular noun, or a plural noun for a plural noun.

Pupil's Book, page 73

1 2.40 Which room are they talking about? Listen and tick ✓.

- Say *Open your Pupil's Books at page 73.* Point to each room and ask, e.g. *Where's the coat?* (*On the bed*)
- Ask *Which room are they talking about?* Play the audio. Learners listen and tick. Check answers.

Track 2.40

Teacher: OK. I want you to look at this picture for one minute. … OK. Stop. Now, close your books, please. Was there a coat in the picture?
Zoe: Yes, there was.
Teacher: Good, Zoe. Where was it?
Zoe: It was in the cupboard.
Teacher: Were there any shorts in the picture, Jane?
Jane: Er … No, there weren't.
Teacher: That's right, there weren't any shorts … and was there a scarf, Jack?
Jack: No, there wasn't.
Teacher: Well, Jack, there was a scarf. It was with the coat.
Jack: Oh, yes, that's right. There was a red-and-white scarf.
Teacher: Excellent. Were there any boots in the bedroom?
Paul: Yes, there were. They were behind the door.
Teacher: Very good, Paul. Now …

Key: Picture 2

2.41 Gracie's Grammar

- Write the questions and answers on the board.
- Play the audio. Pause for learners to repeat.

Track 2.41
See Pupil's Book page 73

2 Choose a page. Look at a picture. Ask your partner.

- Show learners the example speech bubbles. Demonstrate the game. You look at page 57 for one minute, then close your book and learners ask you questions.
- Put learners into pairs. Give each pair a timer, or time the minute yourself. Monitor and support. Make sure pairs choose a picture with plenty of things to talk about.

mission Stage 2

- Show learners the second stage of the Mission poster: *Add things to see on your island.*
- Read the instructions and the speech bubbles. Learners work in their Mission groups. They talk about what there was to see in or near each town on their island and draw small pictures on their map.

Activity Book, page 73

See pages TB120–132

Activity Book, page 68

- Review *My unit goals*. Ask *How is your Mission?* Learners reflect and choose a smiley face for *My mission diary 2.*

Ending the lesson

- **SA** Go back to Stage 2 on the digital Mission poster. Add a tick to the 'Add things to see on your island' stage. Use self-assessment (see Introduction).
- Give out a completion sticker.

1 2.40 Which room are they talking about? Listen and tick ✓.

1 

2 

3 

2.41 Gracie's Grammar

Was there a scarf in the bedroom?
Yes, **there was**. / No, **there wasn't**.

Were there any boots in the bedroom?
Yes, **there were**. / No, **there weren't**.

2 Choose a page. Look at a picture. Ask your partner.

Look at page 57, please. OK. Stop. Close your book, please. Was there a bear?

Yes, there was.

Were there any crocodiles?

No, there weren't.

Excellent! Well done!

mission STAGE 2

Add things to see on your island.

- Think about your holiday from Stage 1. What was there to see in each place?
- Talk in your group and draw on your map.

There were lots of boats in River Town.

There was a forest at White Rock.

My mission diary
Activity Book page 68

What's the weather like today?

1 **Watch the video.**

2 **Look at the photos. What's the weather like?** It's …

cloudy sunny windy snowing raining

1 

2 

3 

4 

5 

3 2.42 **Listen and read. Match the weather instruments with the photos.**

When we want to know about the weather, we can listen to a weather report on the radio or watch the report on television. Scientists study the weather in weather stations and send the information around the world. They have special instruments that help them.

They use a [1]**thermometer** to measure how hot or how cold it is.

They use a [2]**rain gauge** to measure how much rain falls.

They use a [3]**weather vane** to show the direction of the wind.

Scientists can use this information to make weather maps and reports.

a 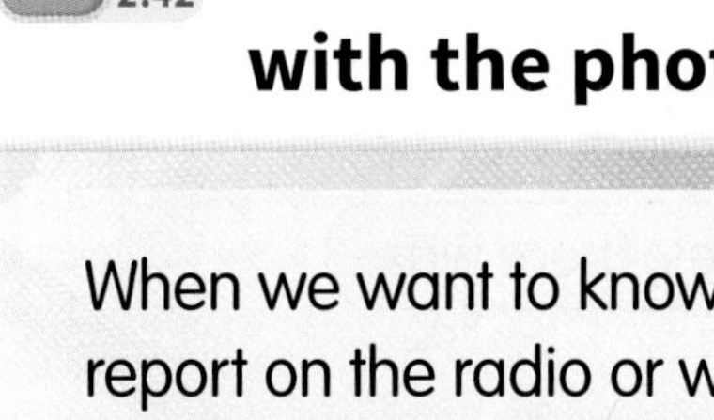

b 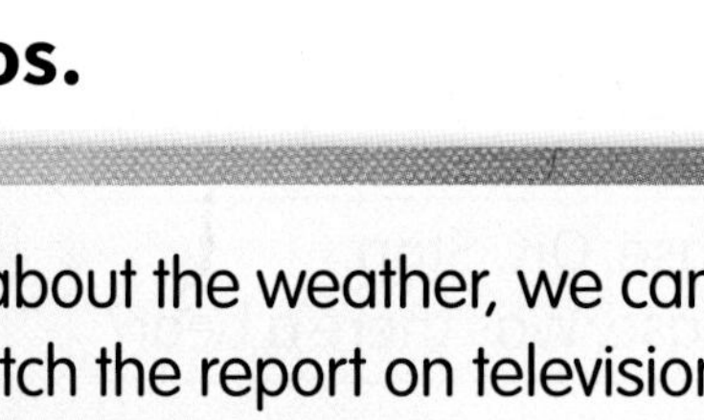

c 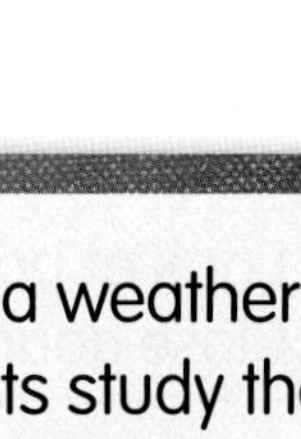

Learning outcomes By the end of the lesson, learners will have learnt about instruments to measure the weather.

New language *around the world, direction, how* (+ adj), *how much, instrument, measure, rain gauge, scientist, send, thermometer, weather report, weather station, weather vane*

Recycled language clothes, weather, *fall, listen to, map, radio, television, watch, What's the weather like today? What was the weather like yesterday?*

Materials real (small) items of clothing (e.g. hat, scarf, sunglasses), toy animals (e.g. rabbit, bear), a tray and a cloth to cover it (optional), Clothes and The weather flashcards, a real thermometer (optional), video, audio, pictures of local weather vanes (optional), materials for each learner for making a weather vane (Activity Book): card, a straw, a pin, a pencil with an attached rubber, scissors, coloured pens or pencils

Warm-up

- Put seven or eight items on a tray or on a table everyone can see. Include some real clothes, soft toy animals and some plural items, e.g. scissors or pencils. Ask *What is there on my tray/table?* Hold each item up. Learners say, e.g. *There's a hat. There are some pencils.* Say *Look for one minute and remember.* Time one minute as learners memorise the items. Then cover the tray/table with a cloth.
- Ask different learners to say what was on the tray/table, e.g. *There was a hat. There were some pencils.* You can also play this as a team game, with teams writing sentences.

Alternative Play with flashcards instead of real items – stick them on the board and give learners a minute to look and remember, then remove them or turn them over.

Presentation

- Revise weather with the flashcards. Ask *What kind of weather do you like best?*
- Ask *What's the weather like today?* Encourage learners to make sentences, e.g. *It's cloudy. It's raining. It isn't hot.*
- Say *Today the temperature is (21).* Write *temperature* on the board. Ask *How do we know what the temperature is?* Say *We can measure the temperature.* Teach *measure* by demonstrating – you can measure the temperature of some water with a real thermometer or measure the length of something with a ruler / tape measure.
- Say *Let's find out more about how we measure the weather.*

Pupil's Book, page 74

1 Watch the video.

- Say *Let's watch the video.* Learners watch the video about weather instruments and answer the questions at the end.

2 Look at the photos. What's the weather like?

- Say *Open your Pupil's Books at page 74.* Read the instructions. Learners match each picture with a type of weather. Check answers.

Key: 1 It's sunny. 2 It's raining. 3 It's cloudy. 4 It's snowing. 5 It's windy.

3 2.42 Listen and read. Match the weather instruments with the photos.

- Point to each photo and ask *What does this measure?* (a *wind*, b *temperature / hot and cold*, c *rain*) or ask *Does this measure (rain)?*
- Play the audio. Learners listen and read. They match each weather instrument in bold with a photo.

Track 2.42
See text on Pupil's Book page 74

- Check answers. Check comprehension of *scientist, weather report* and *direction.*

Key: thermometer – b rain gauge – c weather vane – a

Extension Ask *Which of these instruments can we see in our town? Are there any thermometers in the street? Where? What about weather vanes?* Show photos of any weather vanes in the learners' town, if appropriate, and ask learners where they are.

Activity Book, page 74

See pages TB120–132

Ending the lesson

- Write on the board: *thermometer, rain gauge, weather vane, ruler, clock.* Draw a simple picture of each thing or stick photos on the board. Say *I want to know how much rain there was yesterday. What do I need?* Learners say the instrument. (*Rain gauge*) Repeat with the different instruments. Example sentences: *I want to know the direction of the wind so I can fly my kite.* (*Weather vane*) *I want to know if I'm late for school.* (*Clock*) *I want to know how long my pencil is.* (*Ruler*) *I want to know if I need to wear a coat today.* (*Thermometer*)

Extra support Number the instruments, so learners reply, e.g. *Number 3,* instead of saying the name.

Learning outcomes By the end of the lesson, learners will be able to talk about weather symbols.

New language *symbol*

Recycled language clothes, countryside, weather, *island, map, What's the weather like in … ?*, present continuous

Materials The weather and Countryside flashcards, two plastic fly swatters (optional), audio, worksheets/maps and notes from Mission Stages 1 and 2 lessons, paper, coloured pens or pencils, scissors, glue, digital Mission poster

Warm-up

- Put the flashcards for different types of weather on the board, including *rainbow*. Make sure they are at a height learners can reach. Practise the words (point and ask *What's the weather like?*).
- Divide the class into two teams. Teams line up facing the board. Give the two learners at the front a plastic fly swatter each. Say a sentence with one of the weather words, e.g. *It's raining*. The two learners race to be the first to hit the correct flashcard. The learner who is first gets a point for his/her team.
- Two new learners come to the front of the team. Make a different sentence. Continue until one team reaches five points. If you don't have fly swatters, learners can touch the flashcard with their hands.
- Play the game again, moving the flashcards around and adding flashcards for *mountain, forest, lake* and *river* (example sentences: *I'm walking in the mountains. / We're swimming in the lake.*).

Pupil's Book, page 75

4 Look at the weather map. Ask and answer.

- Say *Open your Pupil's Books at page 75.* Ask *What's this?* (*A map of an island*) Ask *What's the name of the island?* (*Bear Island*) *What's the name of the village in the centre?* (*Farmfield*) *What's the name of the forest?* (*The Green Forest*) *Where's Shell Beach?* Learners point.
- Point to the weather symbols and ask *What do the symbols show us?* (*The weather*) Say *The weather is different in different places on Bear Island.*
- Show learners the example speech bubbles. Put learners into pairs to ask and answer about the different places.

  Extra support Ask more questions before the pair work, e.g. *Is it raining in Farmfield?* (*No, it isn't.*)

5 2.43 Where are the children? Listen and point. Then listen again and match.

- Say *There are four children on Bear Island. They're talking on a video call. They're all in different places. Where are they? Listen and point.*
- Play the audio. Pause where indicated (*) and ask, e.g. *Where's Vicky?* Learners hold up their books and point.

Track 2.43

Vicky: Hi. It's Vicky. Is everyone there?
Paul/Clare/Fred: Yes./Yeah.
Vicky: Well, Bear Island has lots of different weather. Where I am, it's a hot sunny day today. I'm wearing a dress! * What's the weather like for you, Paul?
Paul: It's cold and raining here. I can't go outside today! * What about you, Clare?
Clare: Well, I can fly my kite today because it's very windy. * Is it windy where you are, Fred?
Fred: Windy? No, it isn't! It's snowing here. Hooray!

- Say *Listen again and match.* Play the audio again. Learners draw lines to match. Check answers.

Key: Paul is in the Green Forest. Clare is in Whitewater. Fred is in the Black Mountains.

mission Stage 3

- Show the class the third stage of the Mission poster: *Create weather symbols for your map.* Read the instructions.
- Put learners into their Mission groups. They look at their notes about the weather from Stage 1. They draw and cut out weather symbols and stick them on their map.

Activity Book, page 75

See pages TB120–132

Activity Book, page 68

- Review *My unit goals.* Ask *How is your Mission?* Learners reflect and choose a smiley face for *My mission diary 3*.

Ending the lesson

- **SA** Go back to Stage 3 on the digital Mission poster. Add a tick to the 'Create weather symbols for your map' stage. Use self-assessment (see Introduction).
- Give out a completion sticker.

4 Look at the weather map. Ask and answer.

What's the weather like in Whitewater?

It's windy.

Is it raining in the Black Mountains?

No, it isn't.

5 2.43 Where are the children? Listen and point. Then listen again and match.

1	Vicky is in	Whitewater.
2	Paul is in	Farmfield.
3	Clare is in	the Black Mountains.
4	Fred is in	the Green Forest.

mission STAGE 3

Create weather symbols for your map.

- Look at your notes from Stage 1 and create weather symbols.
- Put them on your map.

In River Town there was a rainbow.

OK, let's make a rainbow symbol.

My mission diary
Activity Book page 68

1 Look at the pictures. What different kinds of weather can you see?

2.44

Fun in all types of weather!

It's raining, raining all around.
It's raining on you and me.

I put on my boots and my coat
And I imagine that I'm at sea.

I'm jumping in the puddles.
I'm splashing a lot too.

I'm having lots of fun.
How about you?

The wind is blowing all around.
It's blowing on you and me.

The trees are dancing from side to side,
But the wind can't catch me!

I'm jumping in the leaves.
I'm kicking them too.
I'm having lots of fun. How about you?

It's cloudy, cloudy all around.
Clouds are flying over me.

On my back here on the grass,
I imagine the things I see.

There are elephants and rabbits
And running horses too.
I'm having lots of fun. How about you?

Learning outcomes By the end of the lesson, learners will have read a poem about different kinds of weather.

New language *back* (n), *blow, from side to side, ice, pool, puddle, shine, slide* (v), *snowman, splash, How about you?*

Recycled language clothes, weather, *catch, elephant, fly* (v), *friendly, grass, ground, have fun, horse, jump, kick, leaves, put on, rabbit,* present continuous

Materials beanbag (optional), The weather and Clothes flashcards, audio, coloured pens or pencils

Warm-up

- Put The weather and Clothes flashcards on the floor. Learners stand around them in a circle. They take it in turns to throw a beanbag and say the flashcard it lands on.
  Stronger learners Make a true sentence with the word the beanbag lands on, e.g. *I'm not wearing boots today. / It was sunny yesterday.*
  Alternative Put the flashcards for *hot* and *cold* on opposite walls. Say an item of clothing or a sentence, e.g. *I'm wearing a coat, hat and scarf.* Learners point to the correct flashcard.

Presentation

- Draw the sun on the board or show the sunny flashcard. Ask *What things can you do when it's a sunny day? Where can you go?* Learners suggest places and activities, e.g. *Go to the beach. Go to the park. Have a picnic. Play tennis.*
- Say *Let's read a poem about different kinds of weather.*

Pupil's Book, pages 76 and 77

1 Look at the pictures. What different kinds of weather can you see?

- Say *Open your Pupil's Books at pages 76 and 77. What different kinds of weather can you see?* Learners talk in pairs. Check answers.
- Say *In picture 3 the wind's blowing.* Mime blowing out a candle or blowing up a balloon. Practise the word. Say *In picture 6 the sun's shining.* Check comprehension of *shine* and practise the word.

Key: In pictures 1 and 2 it's raining. In picture 3 it's windy. In picture 4 it's cloudy. In picture 5 it's snowing and cold. In picture 6 it's hot and sunny.

2.44 Fun in all types of weather!

- Look at the first picture and ask *Where's the girl? (In her garden / In the park) What's she playing? (She's playing sailing / being in a boat.)* Teach *puddle.*
- Say *Let's read and listen to the first part of the poem.* Play the audio. Learners listen and read. Pause the audio after the first *How about you?*
- Ask *What's the girl wearing?* (*Boots and a coat*) *Where does she imagine that she is?* (*At sea*) *Is she happy?* (*Yes – she's having fun.*)

  Track 2.44
  See poem on Pupil's Book pages 76–77
- Say *Read and listen to the next verse.* Play the audio. Learners listen and read. Pause at the end of the verse. Ask *What are the trees doing?* (*They're dancing.*) Check comprehension of *from side to side.* Ask *What's the girl doing?* (*She's jumping in the leaves and kicking them.*)
- Play the next verse. Ask *What's the girl doing?* (*She's looking up at the sky.*) *What can she see in the clouds?* (*Elephants, rabbits and horses*)
- Play the next verse. Ask *What's the girl wearing now?* (*Boots, a coat and a scarf*) *What's she doing?* (*She's sliding on the ice.*) Teach *slide* using mime and check comprehension of *ice.* Ask *What's she making?* (*A snowman*)
- Play the last verse. Ask *Why does the snowman go away?* (*Because the sun is shining / it's hot*) *Is the girl sad?* (*No, she isn't.*) *What does she like doing?* (*Splashing at the pool*)
  Extension Play the whole poem again, without pauses, for learners to listen and read.

Activity Book, page 76

See pages TB120–132

Ending the lesson

- Say sentences and do an action to match. Learners copy.
  I imagine that I'm at sea. (Mime looking through a telescope.)
  I'm jumping in the puddles.
  I'm kicking the leaves.
  I'm looking at the clouds.
  I'm sliding on the ice.
  I'm making a snowman.
  I'm splashing at the pool.
- Say the sentences in a different order. Learners do the correct actions.
- Write the sentences on the board. Put learners in pairs. One learner says a sentence, the other does the action. Then they swap.

Learning outcomes By the end of the lesson, learners will have learnt about thinking positively.

Recycled language language from the poem, free time activities, *can, What's your favourite ... ? My favourite ... is ...*

Materials a large piece of coloured paper for a collage and paper for each learner, pictures from Digital photo bank of clouds (optional), audio

Social and Emotional Skill: Thinking positively

- After reading the story, ask learners *How does the girl think positively? How does the girl have fun?* Say the beginning of the sentence and the learners complete it: *On rainy days she ... (jumps in the puddles), on windy days, she ... (kicks the leaves), on cloudy days, she ... (watches the clouds) and on snowy days, she ... (makes a snowman).*
- Point out that sometimes the weather isn't good but she has fun. She thinks of fun things to do in all situations. That's being positive. A lot of situations can be fun if you think positively.
- Play the 'Glad' game. Ask the learners to think of things that they like. Go round the class and the learners say *When I feel sad, this makes me glad ...* and something that makes them happy.
- Set up a colourful background for a collage. Hand out white paper and the learners draw something that helps them to have fun, e.g. singing when you tidy your room or counting the cars on a long journey or wearing funny clothes when you do your homework.
- Display the collage in the class.

Warm-up

- Ask *What does the girl in the poem do on cloudy days?* (*She looks at the sky and sees different shapes.*) *Do you find shapes in the clouds? What do you see?* If possible, show photos of clouds and ask *What can you see?*
- Ask learners if they can remember the different things the girl in the poem does – on rainy days (e.g. playing in a 'boat', splashing in puddles), on windy days (jumping in leaves / kicking leaves), on snowy days (sliding on ice / making a snowman) and on sunny days (going to the pool).

Pupil's Book, pages 76 and 77

- Say *Open your Pupil's Books at pages 76 and 77.* Play the audio. Learners read and listen to the poem again.

Track 2.44
See poem on Pupil's Book pages 76–77

2 What's your favourite weather? Does the girl in the poem do the same things as you?

- Read the questions with the class and check comprehension.
- Put learners into pairs to talk about their favourite weather and the things they do. Share ideas. Ask *Who does the same things as the girl in the poem?* Say *Put up your hand if you ... jump in puddles in the rain / kick leaves when it's windy / watch the clouds on a cloudy day / slide on ice when it's snowing / make a snowman / go to the pool when it's hot.*

  Extension Learners act out the poem. Play the audio and encourage them to do all the actions (putting on the items of clothing, blowing like the wind, moving their arms like trees in the wind, etc.).

3 Is there a type of weather you don't like? What fun things can you do?

- Read the first question. Ask different learners about weather they don't like. Provide new vocabulary as necessary (e.g. *fog*, *storm*). Encourage the rest of the class to suggest fun activities for that type of weather.

Activity Book, page 77

See pages TB120–132

Ending the lesson

- Learners choose a type of weather and write two sentences about what happens (e.g. *The trees dance from side to side.*) and what they do (e.g. *I fly my kite.*).
- Put learners into small groups. They read their sentences. The other learners guess what the weather is.

  Extra support Learners can be given gapped sentences on strips of paper with the type of weather. They complete the sentences.
- **SA** Use self-assessment to see how well learners think they understand the poem. See Introduction.

It's snowing, snowing all around.
Everything is white!

I'm wearing my boots, my coat and scarf
And I'm sliding on the ice.

Look at my friendly snowman!
He's wearing a long scarf too!
I'm having lots of fun. How about you?

Then the sun starts shining
On the ground and on me.

There was a snowman on the grass,
But tell me, where is he?

When it's nice and sunny
And it's very hot too,

I love splashing at the pool!
How about you?

2 What's your favourite weather? Does the girl in the poem do the same things as you?

My favourite is sunny weather, but she goes to the pool and I like the beach.

3 Is there a type of weather you don't like? What fun things can you do?

I don't like windy weather, but I can fly my kite.

1 2.45 **Listen to the names. Are they for a boy, a girl or both?**

2 2.46 **Listen and tick ✓ the things you hear about the boy.**

1	red sweater	☐	2	pointing	☐
3	dirty clothes	☐	4	green boots	☐

3 **Work with a friend. Describe people in the picture. Find and point.**

4 2.47 **Look. Do you need a word or a number? Listen and write.**

Going to Zoe's house:	..........34..........	Dream Street
1 Going by:	....	
2 Party time:	....	o'clock
3 Name of cousin:	....	
4 Must take:	a	

In the exam, there are names around the picture in Part 1 and you draw lines. Practise numbers and the alphabet for Part 2.

Learning outcomes By the end of the lesson, learners will have practised listening to identify people in a picture and listening for and writing names and numbers (A1 Movers Listening Parts 1 and 2).

Test skills Listening for names and descriptions; Listening for names, spellings and other information

Recycled language adjectives, clothes, colours, numbers, physical descriptions, telling the time

Materials practice paper for Movers Listening Part 1 and Part 2 (optional), audio

Warm-up

- Describe a learner, e.g. *She's got long, brown hair. She's wearing a grey skirt.* Learners say the name. Repeat several times, then learners practise in pairs.

Presentation

- Say *Let's practise for two parts of the listening exam.* Show the Movers Listening Part 1 paper. Say *In Part 1 of the exam you listen to match names with people in a picture.* Show Part 2 and say *In Part 2, you complete some notes.*

Pupil's Book, page 78

1 (2.45) Listen to the names. Are they for a boy, a girl or both?

- Say *Open your Pupil's Books at page 78.* Play the audio. Pause after each name for learners to answer. Write the names on the board – ask learners to spell them.

Track 2.45

That's Pat. I can see Lily! Is that Jim? Where's Jack? Which one is Alex? Do you know Charlie? Can you see Zoe?

Key: Pat – both Lily – girl Jim – boy Jack – boy Alex – both Charlie – boy Zoe – girl

2 (2.46) Listen and tick ✓ the things you hear about the boy.

- Play the audio twice if necessary. Ask *What's the boy's name?* (*Charlie*) Say *Point to Charlie in the picture*. Check answers.

Track 2.46

Man: Look at that naughty boy! His clothes are getting dirty!
Girl: Charlie? The boy who's wearing a red sweater?
Man: Yes, he's having fun.
Girl: Yes, he is! Oh dear!

Key: 1 red sweater 3 dirty clothes

3 Work with a friend. Describe people in the picture. Find and point.

- Demonstrate the activity. Learners practise in pairs. They talk about clothes, appearance, where the person is or what they are doing.

4 (2.47) Look. Do you need a word or a number? Listen and write.

- Before playing the audio, read through the notes and ask *Word or number?* for each space.
- Play the audio twice. Pause after each section. Check answers.

Track 2.47

Mum: Come on, Peter. We're going to my friend Zoe's house now.
Peter: What's her address, Mum?
Mum: She lives at number 34 Dream Street.
Peter: Really? My friend Alex lives at 30 Dream Street.
Mum: That's very near Zoe's house!

Can you see the answer? Now you listen and write.

1 Peter: Oh, no! It's raining. Are we going by car?
Mum: No, we're getting the bus. But look, the rain's stopping.
Peter: And there's a rainbow! That's because it's sunny too.
Mum: That's right, Peter.

2 Peter: Why are we going to Zoe's house today?
Mum: It's her birthday.
Peter: Brilliant! Is there a party?
Mum: Yes, it's four o'clock now and the party's at five o'clock.

3 Peter: Has Zoe got any children?
Mum: No, but Zoe's cousin Lucas is there today. He's at school, but he's older than you.
Peter: What's his name?
Mum: Lucas. L-U-C-A-S.
Peter: That's a cool name!

4 Peter: I've got my coat. Can we go now?
Mum: Yes, but you must take a scarf too.
Peter: Oh, Mum!
Mum: Yes, you must. It's cold in the evening. Look, I'm wearing mine.
Peter: Oh, all right then!

Key: 1 bus 2 5/five 3 Lucas 4 scarf

- Point to the monkey and read.

Activity Book, page 78

See pages TB120–132

Ending the lesson

- In pairs or teams, learners test each other on spelling words from the lesson (e.g. clothes, names).

Learning outcomes By the end of the lesson, learners will have revised the language in the unit and presented their island to the class.

Recycled language unit language

Materials The weather flashcards, island map and notes from Mission Stages 1–3 lessons, a recipe book (optional), dice and counters (for Activity Book game), coloured pens or pencils, digital Mission poster

Warm-up

- Put the flashcards for sunny and hot on one wall of the classroom and for snowy and cold on the opposite wall. Clear a space in the middle of the classroom.
- Point to the sunny/hot flashcards and ask *What's the weather like?* (*It's hot and sunny.*) Do the same for the other cards. (*It's cold and it's snowing*.)
- Demonstrate the game. Stand in the middle of the room and close your eyes. Say *Go!* Learners run to one of the walls with flashcards. Say *I'm wearing sunglasses*. All the learners standing by the wall with the 'hot and sunny' flashcards stay in the game. The rest sit down.
- Repeat with different items of clothing (always for hot and sunny or cold and snowy weather, e.g. *shorts, T-shirt, swimsuit, sunhat, baseball cap, scarf, boots, coat, sweater*) until only one learner is left as the winner.

  Alternative The learners standing in the correct place get a point each time. If you want, choose learners who are out of the game to come to the middle and call out the items of clothing, showing them the appropriate flashcard first (make sure they keep their eyes shut). At the end, check how many points each learner has.

Pupil's Book, page 79

mission in action!

Present your island to the class.

- Say *Open your Pupil's Books at page 79.* Point to the Mission box or show learners the last stage of the digital Mission poster. Say *Let's put our Mission in action!* Say *Present your island to the class.*
- Read the instructions and speech bubbles. Put learners into their Mission groups. Give them time to practise their presentation, using their island maps and notes from the Mission stages. Monitor and check that each member of the group gets the chance to speak. Encourage learners to use the past tense, as in the example speech bubbles.
- Groups take turns to present their islands.

Self-assessment

- **SA** Say *Did you like our 'Create a holiday island' Mission? Think and draw a face.* Learners draw a happy face, neutral face or sad face and then hold it up in the air.
- Say *Tell me things you can do now*. Learners suggest ideas. (*We can talk about places on the island. We can talk about the weather.*)
- Say *Our next Mission is 'Make a class recipe book.'* Explain the meaning of *recipe.* If possible, show a real recipe book. Say *How can we do better? Tell me one thing the class will do better* (e.g. *We can work better in groups.*).

Activity Book, page 79

See pages TB120–132

Activity Book, page 68

- Review *My unit goals*. Ask *How was your Mission?* Learners reflect and choose a smiley face for *My mission diary* the final stage.
- Point to the sunflower. Learners read the 'can do' statements and tick them if they agree they have achieved them. They colour each leaf green if they are very confident or orange if they think they need more practice.
- Point to the word stack sign. Ask learners to look back at the unit and find at least five new words they have learnt. They write them in their word stack.

Ending the lesson

- **SA** Go back to the completion stage on the digital Mission poster. Add a tick or invite a learner to do it. Use self-assessment (see Introduction).
- Give out a completion sticker.
- Tell learners *You have finished your Mission! Well done!*

mission in action!

Present your island to the class.

My mission diary
Activity Book page 68

★ **Show your map and say the name of the island.**

This is our weather map of Friendly Island.

★ **Say what there was to see in each place.**

There were lots of boats in River Town.

★ **Say what the weather was like in each place.**

In River Town, there was sun and rain, so there was a rainbow!

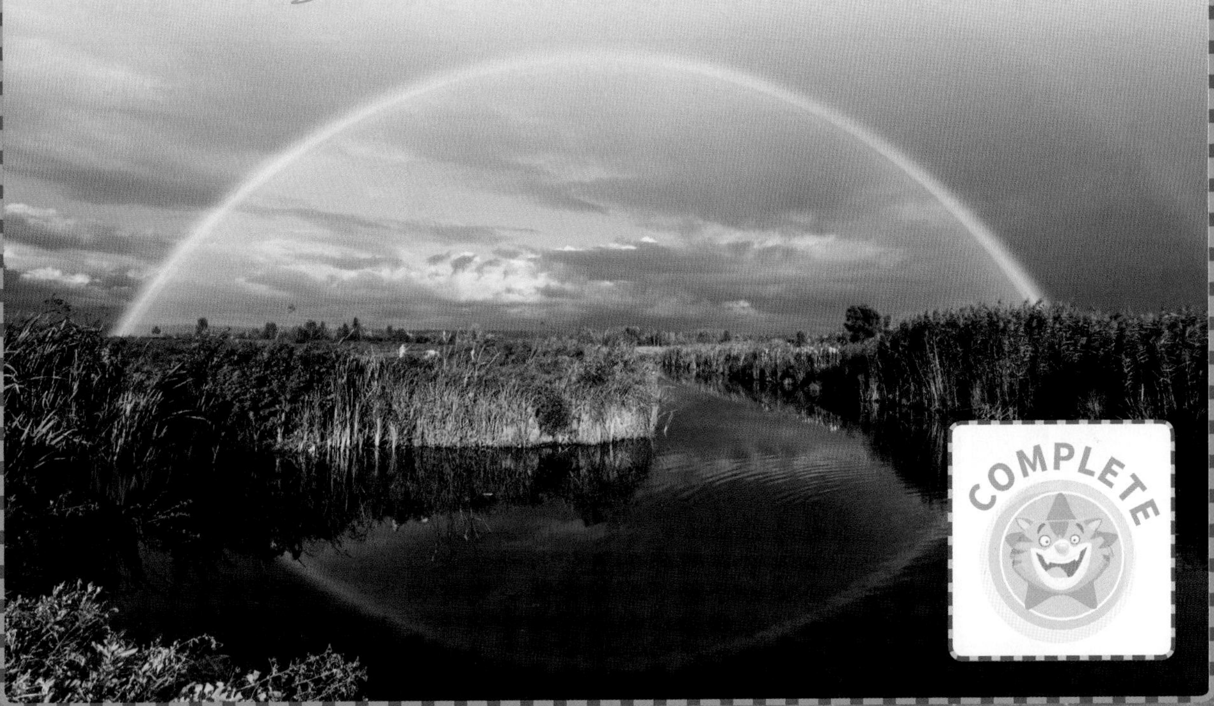

COMPLETE

Review ••• Units 4–6

1 Watch the video and do the quiz.

2 2.48 Listen and tick ✓.

3 Play the game. In pairs, choose, give clues and guess.

climb fly jump swim big small above below near opposite

It can jump. It's smaller than the kangaroo. It's near the bear.

Is it the rabbit?

Learning outcomes By the end of the lesson, learners will have consolidated language from Units 4–6.

Recycled language action verbs, animals, clothes, countryside, family, weather, *I'm wearing ...*, *can/can't*, comparative and superlative adjectives, prepositions of place, *(There) was/were*

Materials Action verbs and Wild and domestic animals flashcards from Unit 5, video, audio, Friendly Family flashcards, Extended family flashcards from Unit 4

Warm-up

- Say *Stand up.* Give instructions with action verbs from Unit 5, e.g. *Climb a tree. Swim. Jump up and down. Fly.* Learners do the actions. Show the flashcards as prompts the first time, then repeat with just the instructions.
- Show some flashcards of animals. Ask learners *What is it? What colour is it? Has it got long ears? What can it do? Tell me about it.* Learners describe them.
- Tell learners to choose one of the animals. Put them into groups of four. Each learner describes their chosen flashcard. Other learners try to guess which it is.

  Extra support You can give learners sentences describing one of the animals with the name written underneath. They can read the clues.

  Fast finishers Learners can remember and describe more than one flashcard.

Pupil's Book, page 80

1 Watch the video and do the quiz.

- Show the video to learners.
- Ask learners to do the quiz. Check their answers to see how much learners can remember.
- Repeat this at the end of the Review unit and compare the results to measure progress.

2 2.48 Listen and tick ✓.

- Say *Open your Pupil's Books at page 80.* Describe one of the pictures, e.g. *It's swimming. It's black and white.* Learners point to the correct picture and say, e.g. *It's a penguin.* Learners do the same in pairs.
- Read the instructions and go through the example. Play the audio twice. Learners listen and tick the correct picture in each pair. Check answers.

Track 2.48

1 I was in the countryside at the weekend with my cousin.
2 My sweater was green and yellow.
3 The weather was hot, but cloudy.
4 There were rabbits in a field!
5 And in the evening, there were bats too. They were cool!
6 My cousin's got straight, blonde hair. Mine's darker and curlier than hers. In this photo, we're jumping on the grass.
7 My cousin jumps like a kangaroo!
8 But when we swim, I'm quicker than she is. My dad says I swim like a dolphin!

Key: 2 A 3 A 4 A 5 B 6 A 7 B 8 A

3 Play the game. In pairs, choose, give clues and guess.

- Focus on the picture. Revise prepositions *above, below, near* and *opposite* by asking *Which animal is (above) the (tree)? Where is the (lion)?*
- Read the instructions and the speech bubbles. Model the activity with another example, e.g. *It can swim. It's bigger than a rabbit. It's next to the bear.* (Penguin)
- Put the class into pairs. Learners take it in turns to give clues.

  Extension Say *Let's play 'True or false'.* Make a line down the centre of the room and tell learners that one side of the line is 'true' and the other 'false'. Hold up a flashcard of an animal and make a sentence about it, e.g. say its name, describe it, make a comparison or talk about its diet. If learners think your sentence is true, they jump on the true side of the line; if not, they jump on the false side, e.g. *It's a herbivore* (showing a lion – false). Example sentences: *It's bigger than a rabbit. It swims better than a bear. It's got stripes. It eats fruit. It's the biggest mammal in the world.*

  Alternative Put signs with *true* and *false* on opposite walls. Learners point to the correct sign instead of jumping.

  Stronger learners Volunteer to lead the activity.

Activity Book, page 80

See pages TB120–132

Ending the lesson

- Use the Friendly family flashcards to make a family tree on the board. Add names to the tree and ask questions to revise the words, e.g. *Who's Jim's cousin? Who's Grandpa Friendly's son?* Learners say the names. They can repeat the activity in pairs.
- Ask questions with superlative adjectives, e.g. *Who's got the longest hair? Who's the youngest in the family? Who's the oldest?*

  Stronger learners Choose one person from the family and write as many sentences as they can about him/her, using comparatives, superlatives and family words.

Learning outcomes By the end of the lesson, learners will have consolidated language from Units 4–6.

Recycled language clothes, family, homes, weather, *hide, What's the weather like today? What was the weather like yesterday?* comparative and superlative adjectives, prepositions of place, *(There) was/were*

Materials In and around the home flashcards from Unit 4, picture from Digital photo bank of a room in a house (optional), a photo of you in your favourite outfit (optional), coloured pens or pencils, video

Warm-up

- Revise home words and *first, second, third* with the flashcards.
- Learners stand up. Say *Sit down if your home has got a basement.* (Learners whose homes have basements sit down and the rest of the class remain standing.) Repeat with more sentences about homes until only one or two learners are still standing (they are the 'winners'). Possible sentences: *Sit down if … you live on the second floor / your building hasn't got a lift / you live with your grandparents / you live in a house / your home has got a balcony / you live in a village / people live upstairs from you / you can walk on the roof of your home.*

Pupil's Book, page 81

4 Where are Aunt Laura's things? Find and circle.

- Say *Open your Pupil's Books at page 81.* Focus on the picture and ask questions about where things are, e.g. *Is the bedroom upstairs or downstairs? (Upstairs) What's under the chair in the hall? (A sweater) Where's the boy? (On the stairs)*
- Read the instructions and show learners the example answer.
- Learners work in pairs to read and circle. Monitor and support. Check answers.

Key: Learners circle the green and orange scarves on the wall downstairs, the long boots on the floor in the bedroom and the sweater on the chair in the bedroom.

Extension Show learners a large picture of a room, e.g. a living room or bedroom. Say *Look and remember.* Time one minute, then turn the picture over. Learners work in groups of three and write as many sentences as they can about the picture in the past tense, e.g. *There was a lamp on the table. There were some posters on the wall.* The group with the most correct sentences are the winners. You can set a time limit for the writing stage.

Alternative Groups play as teams. Ask teams yes/no questions about the picture in turn, e.g. *Was there a lamp on the table? Were there any pictures above the desk?* Team members confer to try to remember the answer. The team with the most correct answers wins. If two teams have an equal score, ask a 'decider' question, e.g. *How many posters were there on the wall?*

5 Write about you.

- Read the questions and check comprehension. Ask two or three learners to give answers to the first two questions.
- Learners write their answers individually. Monitor and help.

  Extra support Write model answers / prompts on the board.
- Put learners into pairs with someone they don't know very well. They ask and answer the questions. Ask different learners to tell the class the best answer their partner gave.

  Fast finishers Write two more questions for their partner beginning *Are you wearing … ?*

Activity Book, page 81

See pages TB120–132

Ending the lesson

- Tell learners about your favourite outfit and show a photo of it, if possible, e.g. *My favourite clothes are my green trousers, black boots and blue coat. I wear them when the weather's cold.*
- Check learners have coloured pens or pencils. Tell them to draw their favourite clothes.

  Fast finishers Learners write sentences describing the outfit, e.g. *My favourite clothes are my shorts, a blue-and-red T-shirt and sunglasses. I wear them when it's hot and sunny.*
- Collect up all the pictures and give them out randomly. Learners need to find the owner of the outfit. They find the learner they think it belongs to and ask questions: *Are you wearing a T-shirt in the picture? Do you like shorts? Are your clothes for hot weather?*
- Once they have found the person who owns the drawing, they give it back.
- Repeat the video and quiz.

4 Where are Aunt Laura's things? Find and circle .

Aunt Laura's coat is the longest one. She's got two scarves. The second one on the wall downstairs is hers, and the shortest one is hers too. Her boots are on the floor upstairs. They're bigger than the boots downstairs. Her sweater is on the chair below the clock. And where's her son? Oh look, he's hiding on the stairs!

5 Write about you.

What's the weather like today?

____

What was the weather like yesterday?

____

What clothes do you wear to school?

____

What's the biggest animal you know?

____

What's your oldest cousin's name?

____

Where were you yesterday?

____

Who's the youngest person in your family?

____

7 Let's cook!

1 **Watch the video. Draw some food which you'd like to cook.**

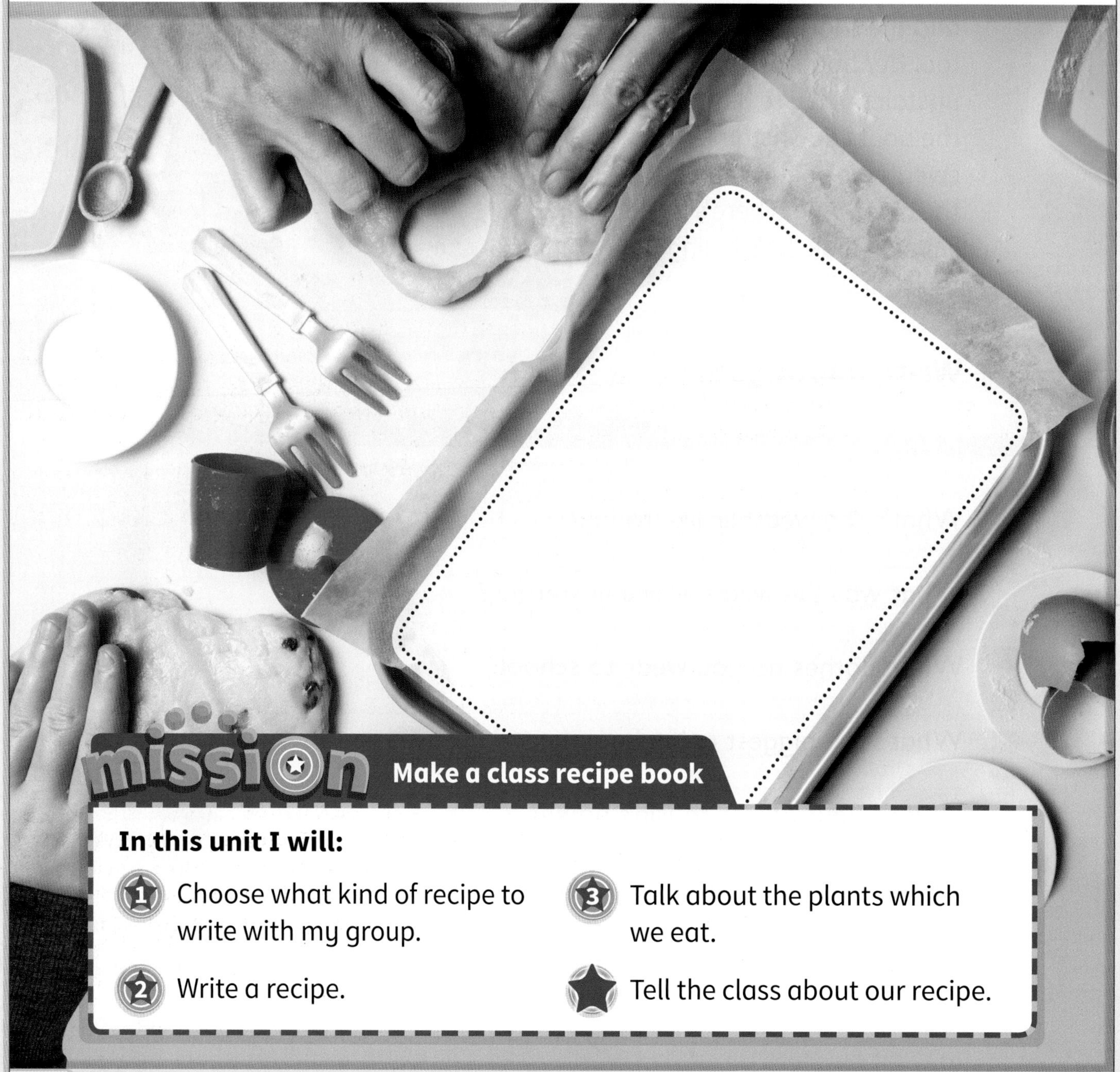

mission **Make a class recipe book**

In this unit I will:

1. Choose what kind of recipe to write with my group.
2. Write a recipe.
3. Talk about the plants which we eat.

★ Tell the class about our recipe.

Unit 7 learning outcomes

In Unit 7, learners learn to:

- talk about food and cooking
- use the past simple with regular and irregular verbs
- learn about how we use plants in food and other products
- read a fantasy story and think about perseverance

Materials large pieces of paper with the words *breakfast* and *lunch*, video, coloured pens or pencils, digital Mission poster, a recipe book (optional), a copy of the Mission worksheet (Teacher's Resource Book page 74), Food flashcards from level 1 or real food items (bread, fruit, cake, chocolate, lemonade, salad, water, cheese, pasta, eggs, beans, juice, sandwiches, etc.)

Self-assessment

- **SA** Say *Open your Pupil's Books at page 82. Look at the picture. What are they doing?* (*Cooking*) *What can you see?* Learners name things they already know. Ask *What do you think they're making?* Use self-assessment (see Introduction). Say *OK. Let's learn.*

Warm-up

- Mime waking up and eating breakfast. Ask *Am I having lunch?* (*No*) *What am I doing?* (*Having breakfast*) Say *We have breakfast in the morning. We have lunch at (two) o'clock in the afternoon.*
- Show pieces of paper with *breakfast* and *lunch* and put them on opposite walls. Say a food that learners know, e.g. *meatballs.* They point to the correct sign or move to the correct wall.

  Alternative Instead of pointing, learners do a mime for breakfast (e.g. drinking) and a different mime for lunch (e.g. eating with a knife and fork).

Pupil's Book, page 82

1 Watch the video. Draw some food which you'd like to cook.

- Say *In this unit we're talking about food.* Say *Let's watch the video.* To introduce the topic of the unit, play the video.
- Say *Look at page 82.* Point to the empty tray. Ask *What food would you like to cook? Draw it here.* Learners draw. Monitor. Tell each learner the name of the food/dish they have drawn.

  Fast finishers Learners draw a plate in their notebook and draw some of their favourite foods, labelling them in English, if they can.

mission Make a class recipe book

- Point to the Mission box or the digital Mission poster and say *This is our Mission.*
- Say *Make a class recipe book.* Check learners remember the meaning of *recipe* and practise pronunciation, clapping the stress (*recipe*). If possible, show a real recipe book and ask *What are the different parts of a recipe? First there's a list of the food you need. The ingredients. Then there's a list of instructions – how to make the dish. There are also usually some pictures of the food.*
- Say *Point to number 1. Choose what kind of recipe to write with my group.* Ask *What type of food do you like? Do you have any favourite dishes?* Learners share their ideas.
- Say *Point to number 2. Write a recipe.* Say *You need to think carefully about your recipe and write it step by step. People need to read and understand the instructions.* Show the numbered instructions in a recipe book, if possible, or write an example list on the board.
- Say *Point to number 3. Talk about the plants which we eat.* Say *We're going to read about plants in Unit 7. Then you can think about how to use more plants in your recipe. We eat different parts of plants – which foods are fruit?* (*Banana, mango, apple, orange, grapes*)
- Say *The last stage is 'Tell the class about our recipe.'* Say *You're going to show your recipe to the class and talk about it. Then we're going to put all the recipes together in a book.*
- Say *This is our Mission.* Go through the stages of the Mission again.
- For ideas on monitoring and assessment, see Introduction.

Activity Book, page 82

My unit goals

- Help learners to complete the unit goals. See notes on page TB6.
- You can go back to these unit goals at the end of each Mission stage during the unit and review them.

Ending the lesson

- Show flashcards of food learners already know or real food. Learners say the names. Ask different learners *Do you like (bananas)?* They talk in pairs about which foods they like/dislike.
- Offer a flashcard or a real piece of food to a learner and ask, e.g. *Would you like (some grapes)?* The learner replies *Yes, please* or *No, thank you.* If he/she says 'yes', hand him/her the flashcard or food. Continue until you have handed out all the flashcards/food.
- Then ask different learners *What has (Amelia) got?* (*She's got (an apple).*)

Learning outcomes By the end of the lesson, learners will be able to talk about food and things we use to serve food.

New language *bottle, bowl, cheese, cooking, cup, glass, pasta, plate, salad, sandwich, soup, vegetables, a (cup) of (hot chocolate), kind (What kind of … ?)*

Recycled language food, *class, cold, drink* (n), *hot, hot chocolate, lunch, outside, Can you … ?, Do you like … ?, have got, There were some / lots of … Would you like … ? Yes, please. / No, thank you.*

Materials Food flashcards from levels 1 and 2, real new food items, a bottle, bowl, glass, cup and plate (optional), audio, video

Warm-up

- Say *Stand up. Jump to the right if you like beans*. Point and demonstrate. *Jump to the left if you don't like beans.* Repeat with different known food and drink items. Use food flashcards from level 1 as prompts.

Presentation

- Teach the new words using the flashcards or real items. Ask *Do you like (vegetables)?*
- Hold up a bottle (or flashcard) and say *A bottle of …* Learners say, e.g. *water, milk, juice, lemonade*. Repeat with *A plate of … (salad, sandwiches), A bowl of … (soup, salad), A cup of … (tea, coffee)* and *A glass of … (water, juice, milk).*
- Explain *What kind of … ?* Ask different learners *What kind of ice cream do you like?*

Pupil's Book, page 83

1 3.02 Listen and point. Then listen again and colour.

- Say *Open your Pupil's Books at page 83. Who can you see? (The children, Mr Friendly and a woman) Point to the (bread). Who's got a bottle? (Eva) Who's got some cups? (The woman)*
- Ask *Where's the small tractor? Can you find it?*
- Read the caption. Check comprehension of *cooking class.*
- Say *Listen and point to the words.* Play the audio.

Track 3.02

Today Mr Friendly's giving the children a cooking class at their school.

Mr Friendly: Good afternoon, everyone. Today we're making some different things to eat. First, the vegetables.
Mr Friendly: OK. Jenny, what kind of sandwich have you got?
Jenny: Well, there was some bread and cheese, so I've got a fantastic cheese sandwich.
Mr Friendly: OK, can you put it on that green plate, please? Now, Jim, what kind of soup have you got in that blue bowl?
Jim: There were lots of vegetables. There were some potatoes, carrots and onions, so I've got a nice bowl of hot soup.
Mr Friendly: Mmm! Hot vegetable soup and a cheese sandwich make a great lunch! It's cold outside, but it's very hot in here. Now, Tom, what's in the red bowl?
Tom: There were some beans and tomatoes and there was some pasta, so we've got some pasta in the red bowl, and we've got a salad in this purple one.
Mr Friendly: Mmm, lovely! And what's in that yellow bottle?
Eva: It's lemonade. Would you like a glass of nice, cold lemonade?
Mr Friendly: Oh, yes, please. Thank you!
Teacher: Hello. It's cold today, so here are some cups of hot chocolate.
Mr Friendly: Not for me, thank you. I've got a nice, cold glass of lemonade.

- Point to the plate, bowl and bottle. Say *Listen and colour.*

Key: plate – green bowl – red bottle – yellow

2 3.03 Say the chant.

- Play the audio or video. Learners point and chant.

Track 3.03

Cheese, pasta, sandwich,
Salad, vegetables, soup
Bowl, bottle, plate,
Cup and glass. [x2]

3 3.04 Listen and answer.

- Play the audio. Pause for learners to answer.

Track 3.04

1 What colour's the plate?
2 Who's got some soup?
3 What kind of soup has Jim got?
4 What have Tom and Eva got in their purple bowl?
5 What kind of drink is in the bottle?
6 Who's holding the bottle?
7 What kind of drink is in the cups?

Key: 1 green 2 Jim 3 vegetable soup 4 a salad 5 lemonade 6 Eva 7 hot chocolate

Activity Book, page 83

See pages TB120–132

Ending the lesson

- **SA** Show the flashcards. Ask *Do you know the words?* Use self-assessment (see Introduction). Learners show how they feel.

1 3.02 **Listen and point. Then listen again and colour.**

Today Mr Friendly's giving the children a cooking class at their school.

2 3.03 **Say the chant.**

3 3.04 **Listen and answer.**

The Friendly Farm

3.05

1
Mr Friendly went to Jim and Jenny's classroom. They had a cooking class!
Did they bring the food home?
2
No, they didn't. They ate it all at school: soup, sandwiches, pasta, salad … and they drank hot chocolate!
3
The children love cooking now.
Yes, I saw them in the kitchen yesterday, but I didn't see the food.
I did. They made a pasta salad.
4
In the afternoon I saw them in the car with their dad.
Did they go shopping?
Yes, they did, but they only got vegetables.
5
Oh, they got vegetables for us!
Soup … ?
Yes. I can make some nice soup.
6 *Lunch time the next day*
Look at Gracie's soup.
But we ate the nice, cold vegetables this morning. What did you put in the soup, Gracie?
Socks! My favourite kind of soup is sock soup!

1 3.06 **Who says it? Listen and say the name.**

Learning outcomes By the end of the lesson, learners will be able to understand the past simple (irregular verbs).

New language *ate, drank, got, had, made, put, saw, went, Did they (eat)? Yes, they did. / No, they didn't. I didn't (see). What did you (put in the soup)?*

Recycled language daily routines, food and things for serving food, *afternoon, at school, bring, car, classroom, cold, cooking, favourite, go shopping, home, kind* (n), *kitchen, nice, only, sock, yesterday, can,* telling the time

Materials Food flashcards, audio, video

Warm-up

- Review the words for food and things we use to serve food using the flashcards.
- Say *I went to a party yesterday. At the party there was a plate of sandwiches.* Point to a learner, who repeats your sentence and adds a new item, e.g. *At the party there was a plate of sandwiches and a bottle of orange juice.* Continue around the class, with learners adding an item each time.
- **SA** Use self-assessment to check how well learners think they understand the vocabulary. See Introduction.

Presentation

- Say *I get up at seven o'clock every day, so yesterday I got up at seven o'clock.* Ask different learners *What time did you get up yesterday?* and encourage them to answer *I got up at …* Repeat with *I have breakfast at eight o'clock every day, so yesterday I had breakfast at eight o'clock. What time did you have breakfast yesterday? (I had breakfast at …)* and *I go home by bus every day, so yesterday I went home by bus. How did you go home yesterday? (I went home …)*
- Write verbs in a column on one side of the board: *eat, drink, get, go, have, make, put, see* and the past tense forms in a column on the right: *ate, drank, got, went, had, made, put, saw.*
- Practise saying the infinitive and past forms together. Then say the infinitive for learners to say the past form.
- Ask *Did you get up at six o'clock yesterday?* and encourage learners to reply *Yes, I did. / No, I didn't.* Repeat with *Did you have lunch at school yesterday? Did you eat (soup) yesterday?*

Pupil's Book, page 84

3.05 The Friendly Farm song

- Play the introductory song at the beginning of the cartoon story. Learners listen and sing.

Track 3.05
See The Friendly Farm song on page TB5

3.05 The Friendly Farm

- Say *Open your Pupil's Books at page 84.* Point to the thought bubbles at the beginning of the story and ask *What are the animals talking about? (The cooking class / food)*
- Say *Gracie made some soup.* Ask *What did Gracie put in the soup?* Write the question on the board. Play the audio or video. Learners listen and read. Check answers. (*Socks*)

Track 3.05
The Friendly Farm song + see cartoon on Pupil's Book page 84

- Play the audio or video again. Pause after each picture and ask questions. Don't insist on learners answering with correct past forms. 1: *Who went to Jim and Jenny's classroom? (Mr Friendly)* 2: *Did the children eat the food at home? (No, (they ate it) at school) What did they drink? (Hot chocolate)* 3: *Did Rocky see the food? (No, he didn't.) Did Cameron see the food? (Yes, he did.)* 4: *Where did Harry see them in the afternoon? (In the car) Did they go shopping? (Yes, they did.) What did they get? (Vegetables)* 5: *What can Gracie make? (Soup)* 6: *Why didn't Gracie put the vegetables in the soup? (Because the animals ate them)*

1 3.06 Who says it? Listen and say the name.

- Say *Listen and say the name.* Play the audio and pause for learners to say the name.

Track 3.06

1	Shelly:	Did they go shopping?
2	Gracie:	Did they bring the food home?
3	Cameron:	No, they didn't. They ate it all at school.
4	Rocky:	I saw them in the kitchen yesterday, but I didn't see the food.
5	Shelly:	Oh, they got vegetables for us!
6	Gracie:	Socks! My favourite kind of soup is sock soup!
7	Cameron:	Yes, they did, but they only got vegetables.
8	Harry:	What did you put in the soup, Gracie?

Key: See names in audioscript

Activity Book, page 84

See pages TB120–132

Ending the lesson

- **SA** Repeat the self-assessment to see how well learners think they understand the vocabulary. Is there any change?

Learning outcomes By the end of the lesson, learners will be able to use the past simple (irregular verbs).

New language *I went swimming last Saturday. I didn't go shopping yesterday. Did you go to the park? Yes, I did. / No, I didn't. (the) same*

Recycled language animals, daily routines, family, food, places, *drink* (n), *hot, last, (have) lunch, picnic, weekend, What about … ?*, irregular past simple forms

Materials three pictures (see Warm-up), audio, digital Mission poster

Warm-up

- Before class, draw some mountains, some apples and a bear on a piece of paper.
- Hide the picture and say *Yesterday I went on a picnic. Guess three things. Where did I go? What did I eat? What animal did I see?* Tell learners they have 20 questions.
- Write *Did you go to the park? Did you eat burgers?* and *Did you see a rabbit?* on the board. Practise pronunciation.
- Learners ask *Did you … ?* Answer *Yes, I did. / No, I didn't.* Count the questions. Show your pictures at the end and say *I went to the mountains. I ate some apples. I saw a bear.*
- Learners can play in pairs.

Presentation

- Say *I don't have salad for breakfast, so yesterday I didn't have salad for breakfast.* Write the sentence on the board. Underline *yesterday* and *didn't have* and explain that *didn't* shows the verb is in the past and negative.
- Say *I don't go to bed at six o'clock in the evening, so yesterday I (didn't go to bed at six o'clock). I don't have a shower at 12 o'clock at night, so yesterday (I didn't …). We don't go to school on Sundays, so last Sunday (we didn't …). She doesn't get dressed in the kitchen, so yesterday (she didn't …).*

Pupil's Book, page 85

3.07 Gracie's Grammar

- Say *Open your Pupil's Books at page 85.* Point to Gracie's Grammar box. Write the sentences on the board.
- Play the audio. Pause for learners to repeat.

Track 3.07
See Pupil's Book page 85

1 3.08 Listen and stick. Then look, read and write.

- Say *A girl is talking about what she ate for lunch last weekend.* Point to each sticker and ask *What's this?*
- Play the audio. Learners point to the correct sticker.
- Play the audio again. Learners stick in the stickers. Check and ask, e.g. *What did the girl eat? What did her aunt make?*

Track 3.08

1 Girl: I went to my aunt and uncle's house for lunch last weekend.
Boy: Ah, what did you eat?
Girl: I ate a bowl of hot tomato soup and a big piece of bread!
Boy: Mmm, that's nice!
2 Girl: My cousin had a big plate of pasta and meatballs.
Boy: Oh, yum. But why did he have pasta?
Girl: Because he doesn't like tomatoes and we all ate different things because my uncle likes cooking.
3 Boy: What about your uncle? What did he have?
Girl: He had soup too, but he didn't have the same drink.
Boy: What did he drink?
Girl: He drank a big glass of orange juice.
4 Boy: What about your aunt? Did she have lunch with you?
Girl: Yes, of course! And she made a fantastic chocolate cake. She put strawberries on top.
Boy: Oh, brilliant! I think I need some food now!

- Read the sentences. Check understanding of *the same*. Say *Now look, read and write*. Check answers.

Key: 2 had 3 didn't 4 put

mission Stage 1

- Point to the Mission box or show learners the first stage of the digital Mission poster: *Choose what kind of recipe to write.*
- Put learners into groups to talk about the food they ate last week and find a dish they all want to write about.

Activity Book, page 85

See pages TB120–132

Activity Book, page 82

- Review *My unit goals*. Ask *How is your Mission?* Learners reflect and choose a smiley face for *My mission diary 1*.

Ending the lesson

- **SA** Go back to Stage 1 on the digital Mission poster. Say *We chose what kind of recipe to write.* Add a tick to the 'Choose what kind of recipe … ' stage. Use self-assessment (see Introduction).
- Give out a completion sticker.

Gracie's Grammar

3.07

I **went** swimming last Saturday.

I **didn't go** shopping yesterday.

Did you **go** to the park? Yes, I **did**. / No, I **didn't**.

1 3.08 Listen and stick. Then look, read and write.

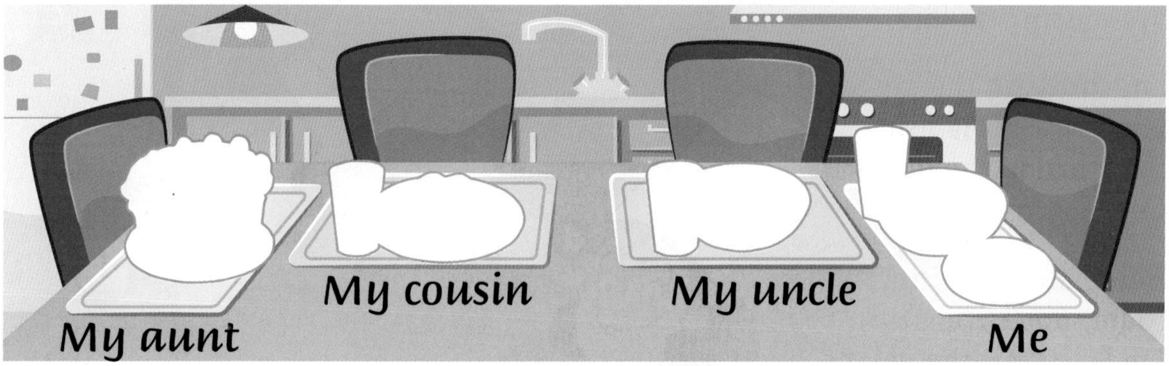

1. I ___ate___ a bowl of hot tomato soup.
2. My cousin __________ a big plate of pasta and meatballs.
3. My uncle __________ have the same drink.
4. My aunt __________ strawberries on top of the chocolate cake.

mission STAGE 1

Choose what kind of recipe to write.

- In groups, discuss the food which you ate last week.
- Choose a kind of recipe.

We ate pasta for dinner last Friday.

We had chicken on Sunday.

OK. Let's make a recipe for chicken pasta!

My mission diary

Activity Book page 82

1 3.09 Listen and number. Then sing the song.

We're in the kitchen.
We're helping our dad.
We're [1]cooking the dinner.
We're all wearing hats.

[2]**Wash** the glasses.
[3]**Carry** the plates.
Don't [4]**drop** the bowl!
We mustn't be late.

I'm [5]**boiling** the pasta.
I'm [6]**frying** the fish.
I'm starting the dinner.
Can you try this?

Mum, stop [7]**crying**.
Mum, don't cry.
I'm [8]**cutting** the onions.
It's all right.

We're in the kitchen. …

2 3.11 Listen and colour. Then close your books. Play the game.

He's wearing a yellow hat.

He's Mr Friendly. He's cooking. He's …

Do you help in the kitchen?

Learning outcomes By the end of the lesson, learners will have practised the language through song.

New language *boil, carry, cook, cry, cut, drop, fry, wash*

Recycled language food and things for serving food, *all right, dinner, hat, help, kitchen, late, start, stop, wear, Can you (try this)?* imperatives, *mustn't,* present continuous

Materials two large pieces of paper, one with a tick and one with a cross (optional), Actions in the kitchen flashcards, audio, video, coloured pens or pencils

Warm-up

- Put a piece of paper with a large tick on it on one wall of the classroom and a large cross on the opposite wall. Clear a space in the middle of the classroom.
- Point to the tick and say *I ate a sandwich yesterday.* Point to the cross and say *I didn't eat chicken yesterday.*
- Demonstrate the game. Stand in the middle of the room and close your eyes. Say *Go!* Learners run to the wall with the tick or the wall with the cross. Say *I didn't eat an orange yesterday*. All the learners standing by the wall with the cross stay in the game. The rest sit down.
- Repeat with different food and drink, e.g. *I drank water yesterday. / I didn't drink lemonade. / I ate some pasta. / I didn't eat potatoes.* until only one learner is left as the winner.
- If you don't have space for learners to move around, they can point to the tick or cross instead.

Presentation

- Teach the new verbs using flashcards and mime.
- Give instructions for learners to mime, e.g. *Cut some onions. Cry! Fry some fish. Wash a plate. Carry lots of glasses. Drop a glass. Oh no!* Learners can do the same activity in pairs.
- **SA** Use self-assessment to check how well learners think they understand the vocabulary. See Introduction.

Pupil's Book, page 86

1 3.09 Listen and number. Then sing the song.

- Say *Open your Pupil's Books at page 86.* Ask *Who's in the kitchen? (Jenny, Jim, Grandma Friendly, Mr Friendly) Who's cooking? (Mr Friendly) Who's helping? (The others) What's (Jenny) doing? (Carrying plates and bowls)*
- Say *Listen and write the numbers.* Show the example.
- Play the audio or video. Check answers. Point out the spelling of *cutting* (double *t*).

Track 3.09

Rocky: I'm Rocky-Doodle-Doo and here's our song for today: *We're in the kitchen.*

See song on Pupil's Book page 86

Key: a 3 b 4 c 2 d 7 (e 1) f 6 g 5 h 8

- Learners stand up. Practise the song in sections.
- Play the audio or video again. Learners sing and do actions (washing glasses, carrying plates, etc.).

3.10 **Extension** Once learners are confidently singing along, try singing the karaoke version as a class.

2 3.11 Listen and colour. Then close your books. Play the game.

- Point to the hats for colouring and say *Listen and colour.*
- Play the audio. Pause for learners to colour.

Track 3.11

1 He's helping his dad. He's wearing a green hat.
2 He's boiling the pasta. He's wearing a yellow hat.
3 She's crying, but she's smiling. She's wearing a blue hat.
4 She's carrying the plates. She's wearing an orange hat.

Key: Jim's hat – green Mr Friendly's hat – yellow Grandma's hat – blue Jenny's hat – orange

Extension Ask *What's Grandma Friendly doing? (She's cutting onions. / She's crying.)* Ask about the other characters. Encourage learners to use as many verbs as they can to describe the scene.

- Read the speech bubbles for the game. Learners play in pairs. Give them a minute to look at the picture carefully. One learner closes his/her book. The other says *He's/She's wearing a (yellow) hat.* The first learner says which person it is and makes as many sentences as they can about what that person is doing/wearing.
- Show the picture of Rocky in the bottom right-hand corner. Read the question. Learners talk in pairs. They explain how they help, e.g. *I wash the dishes.* Monitor and help with new vocabulary. Have a vote to see which jobs learners help with most in the kitchen.

Activity Book, page 86

See pages TB120–132

Ending the lesson

- **SA** Repeat the self-assessment used after the Presentation to see how well learners think they understand the vocabulary. Is there any change?
- Play the song again. Learners join in and do actions.

Learning outcomes By the end of the lesson, learners will be able to use the past simple (regular verbs).

New language *like: I liked cooking them! fry: I fried the onions. stop/start: I stopped because you started asking me questions.*

Recycled language actions in the kitchen, food, past simple questions

Materials Actions in the kitchen flashcards, audio, Mission worksheets (Teacher's Resource Book page 74) or paper, coloured pens or pencils, digital Mission poster

Warm-up

- Review the kitchen action verbs. Learners take turns to choose a flashcard and mime for the class to guess.

Presentation

- Say *On Saturday I played basketball. I jumped a lot!* Write the sentences on the board and underline the *-ed* endings. Ask *Did you play any sport at the weekend? What did you play?* Encourage learners to answer *I played …*
- Point out the different pronunciation of *-ed* in *played* /d/ and *jumped* /t/. Practise the words. Write *started* on the board and practise pronunciation (/ɪd/). Explain that these are the three different pronunciations of *-ed*.
- Write numbered lists on the board: *1 'id' counted, painted, pointed, started, wanted; 2 't' liked, dropped, cooked, talked, washed; 3 'd' cleaned, listened, lived, boiled, cried.* Read the lists, emphasising the different pronunciation of *-ed*. Learners repeat. They copy the lists in their notebooks.
- Say more verbs. Learners tell you which group they go in, e.g. *looked* (2), *fried* (3), *snowed* (3), *danced* (2), *needed* (1), *planted* (1), *kicked* (2), *skated* (1).

Pupil's Book, page 87

1 3.12 What did Paul boil? Listen and tick ✓.

- Say *Open your Pupil's Books at page 87.* Point to each picture and ask *What are these?*
- Ask *What did Paul boil?* Play the audio.

Track 3.12

Cook: This is your first day at work, Paul. You can help to make lunch this morning.
Paul: Great! OK …
Cook: OK, good. Did you cook the meat?
Paul: No, I didn't cook the meat, but I cooked the vegetables.
Cook: Did you wash all the vegetables?
Paul: Yes, I did. Of course I washed the vegetables!
Cook: Ah, good. Did you boil the carrots?
Paul: No, I didn't boil the carrots, but I boiled the beans.
Cook: Did you fry the potatoes?
Paul: No, I didn't fry the potatoes, but I fried the onions.
Cook: Why did you stop?
Paul: I stopped because you started asking me questions.
Cook: Oh!

- Ask *What did Paul cook?* (*The vegetables*) *What did he fry?* (*The onions*) *Why did he stop?* (*Because the cook started asking him questions*)

Key: Picture 1 – the beans

3.13 Gracie's Grammar

- Write the verbs and sentences.
- Play the audio. Pause for learners to repeat. Ask which pronunciation of *-ed* each example shows.

Track 3.13
See Pupil's Book page 87

- Focus on the spelling patterns for *-ed* endings.

2 Ask and answer with the words.

- Show learners the example speech bubbles and make sure they understand the colours (blue for a question, red for a negative answer, green for positive). Learners ask and answer around the class, with your help, then in pairs.

mission Stage 2

- Show learners the second stage of the Mission poster: *Write a recipe.* Put learners into groups. Learners complete the worksheet task in the Teacher's Resource Book (page 74). See teaching notes on TRB page 67.
- Alternatively, if you don't have the Teacher's Resource Book, give each group a piece of A4 paper. Learners imagine they cooked their dish. They start with a heading *How we made* (*name of dish*) and draw a picture of the dish. They write a list of ingredients (they can draw these, if space) and then write what they did, step by step.

Activity Book, page 87

See pages TB120–132

Activity Book, page 82

- Review *My unit goals.* Ask *How is your Mission?* Learners reflect and choose a smiley face for *My mission diary 2.*

Ending the lesson

- **SA** Go back to Stage 2 on the digital Mission poster. Add a tick to the 'Write a recipe' stage. Use self-assessment (see Introduction).
- Give out a completion sticker.

1 3.12 What did Paul boil? Listen and tick ✓.

1  ☐

2  ☐

3  ☐

3.13 Gracie's Grammar

like: I lik**ed** cooking them!

fry: I fr**ied** the onions.

stop/start: I stop**ped** because you start**ed** asking me questions.

2 Ask and answer with the words.

Did you cook the meat?

No, I didn't cook the meat, but I cooked the vegetables.

1 cook/meat? cook/meat ✗ cook/vegetables ✓

2 fry/eggs? fry/eggs ✗ fry/tomatoes ✓

3 boil/potatoes? boil/potatoes ✗ boil/vegetables ✓

4 help/Mum? help/Mum ✗ help/Dad ✓

5 need/onions? need/onions ✗ need/eggs ✓

6 wash/beans? wash/beans ✗ wash/carrots ✓

mission STAGE 2

Write a recipe.

- In groups, imagine you cooked your recipe yesterday. What did you put in it?
- Write how you made it.

In this recipe, we put …

We washed the tomatoes. We …

STAGE 2

My mission diary
Activity Book page 82

Plants are delicious!

1 **Watch the video.**

2 3.14 **Listen and read about the bean plant. Then look at photos 1–4. Which part of the plant are they?**

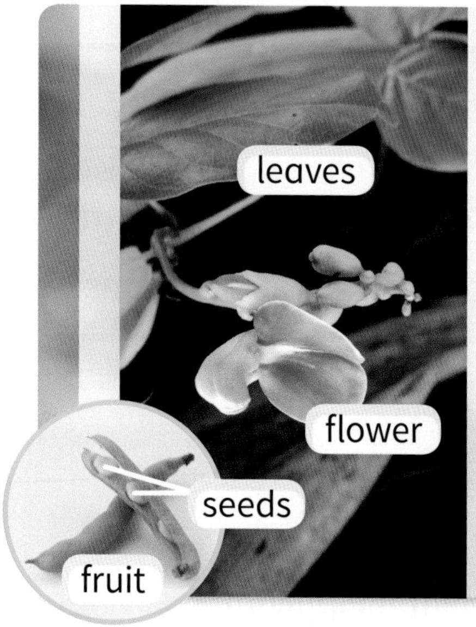

Look at the bean plant. The beans which we eat are the **seeds** of the bean plant. They grow in the pod, which is the **fruit** of the plant. We don't eat the **leaves** or the **flower** of the bean plant.

1

kiwi

2

cauliflower

3

peas

4

lettuce

3 **Read and check.**

We eat different parts of different plants. We eat the **leaves** of the lettuce plant and kiwis are the **fruit** of the kiwi plant. Do we eat any flowers and seeds? Yes, the white part of a cauliflower is the **flower** and peas are the **seeds** of the pea plant.

4 3.15 **Which part of the plant are these? Listen and check.**

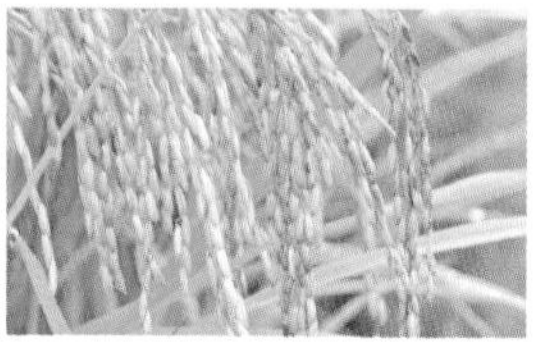
rice

spinach

pepper

broccoli

Learning outcomes By the end of the lesson, learners will have learnt about how we use plants in food.

New language *broccoli, cauliflower, delicious, grow, lettuce, pepper, pod, spinach*

Recycled language food, *cold, cook* (v), *eat, flower, fruit, grass, kind* (n), *leaves, part, plant* (n), *seed, vegetables*

Materials real vegetables and fruits which come from different parts of plants (optional), food flashcards for fruit from level 1 (banana, mango, apple, grapes, orange) and pictures from Digital photo bank of vegetables learners know (potato, carrot, onion) (optional), video, dried or fresh beans (optional), audio

Warm-up

- Say *Think about yesterday. What did you do? Put your hand up if you talked to your grandparents.* Ask *Did you talk on the phone? What did you talk about?* Repeat with different *-ed* verbs, e.g. *Put your hand up if you listened to music / watched TV / painted a picture.* Follow up each time, e.g. *What kind of music did you listen to? What did you watch on TV?*

Presentation

- Put flashcards and pictures of fruit and vegetables on the board (or show real fruit and vegetables). Ask *Which are fruit? Which are vegetables?* Learners come to the front and put them into groups.
- Ask *Where do fruits and vegetables come from?* (*Plants*)

Pupil's Book, page 88

1 Watch the video.

- Say *Let's watch the video.* Learners watch the video about how we use plants in food and answer the questions at the end.

2 3.14 Listen and read about the bean plant. Then look at photos 1–4. Which part of the plant are they?

- Show learners some dried or fresh beans or draw a picture. Ask *What are these?* (*Beans*) Say *Open your Pupil's Books at page 88.* Read the title and teach/review *delicious.* Read the instructions. Learners look at the photo of the bean plant first. Say *Point to the leaves. Point to the flowers.* Play the audio for learners to listen and read.

  Track 3.14
  See text on Pupil's Book page 88
- Check comprehension of *seeds, grow* and *pod.*
- Say *Look at photos 1–4. Which part of the plant are they?* Learners discuss in pairs. Don't confirm answers.

3 Read and check.

- Learners read the next text to check their answers.
- Check by asking *Which part of the plant is a (kiwi)?*

Key: kiwi – fruit cauliflower – flower peas – seeds lettuce – leaves

Extension Show a picture of a carrot. Ask *Which part of the plant is a carrot?* Draw a diagram and teach *root.*

4 3.15 Which part of the plant are these? Listen and check.

- Practise pronunciation of *rice, spinach, pepper* and *broccoli.* Learners look and guess in pairs. Learners can share their ideas, but don't confirm.
- Play the audio for learners to listen and check.

Track 3.15

Teacher: OK, everyone. Let's check. Rice is a kind of grass. What part do we eat?
Boy: The seeds?
Teacher: That's right. Now, spinach. What part do we eat?
Girl: Is it … the leaves?
Teacher: Yes, we eat spinach leaves. We can cook them or eat them cold in a salad. And what about peppers? What are they?
Boy: Are peppers … the fruit?
Teacher: Well done! Yes, some vegetables that we eat are the fruit of their plant. And is broccoli the fruit?
Girl: No, it's the flower, like cauliflower!
Teacher: Yes, you're right. Now, can you draw …

Stronger learners Write questions on the board and play the audio again, e.g. *What kind of plant does rice come from? (Grass) Can you cook spinach? (Yes, or eat it cold)*

Key: rice – seeds spinach – leaves pepper – fruit broccoli – flower

Activity Book, page 88

See pages TB120–132

Ending the lesson

- Books closed. Write on the board: *banana, cauliflower, mango, beans, apple, lettuce, grapes, broccoli, tomato, rice, pepper, kiwi, spinach, peas.* Add questions: *Which part of the plant is it? Do you like it? Do we usually cook it?* Learners talk about each food in pairs or small groups.

Learning outcomes By the end of the lesson, learners will be able to talk about how we use plants.

New language *aloe vera, coffee, cotton, flour, medicine, sauce, tea, wheat*

Recycled language food, *beautiful, chair, clothes, eat, give, important, make, need, oxygen, paper, plant, protect, sun cream, table, tree, use,* present simple

Materials word cards for food from levels 1 and 2 and homemade word cards for *broccoli, pepper, spinach, cauliflower, peas, lettuce, rice,* timer (optional), real products made from plants (e.g. cotton T-shirt, tea leaves, coffee beans, paper, cork, rubber gloves, a wooden spoon), audio, worksheets/recipes from Mission Stage 2 lesson, coloured pens or pencils, digital Mission poster

Warm-up

- Review parts of a plant by drawing a diagram on the board – learners help you label *fruit, flower, seeds* and *leaves.*
- Show learners word cards for food items and a timer, if you have one. Explain that you are going to describe as many of the words as you can to the class in two minutes. You need to do this without saying the word. Ask a learner to come to the board and keep score.
- Set the timer for two minutes. Take a word card without showing the class, e.g. *rice*. Explain what it is, e.g. *This is a food from the seeds of a plant. It's a vegetable. It can be white or brown. We boil it. We must cook it. We usually eat it with something – with meat or beans. The parts are very small.* When learners guess, you pick up another card and describe it. Continue until the time runs out, then check your score.

  Stronger learners Play the same game in two teams. Each team has a four-minute turn, with a different learner from the team defining each word. Allow time for learners to prepare their descriptions. Monitor and help.

Presentation

- Show different products made from plants (or pictures). Ask learners what they all have in common. Say *They all come from plants.* Ask *Which things come from trees?*
- Say *Let's find out more about how we use plants.*

Pupil's Book, page 89

5 3.16 Listen and read. Answer the questions.

- Say *Open your Pupil's Books at page 89.* Read the questions first and check comprehension of *protect.* Teach *flour* using the photo. Say *Listen and read.*
- Play the audio for learners to listen and read. They answer the questions in pairs. Check answers.

  Track 3.16
  See text on Pupil's Book page 89

Key: 1 It comes from trees. 2 We use cotton.
3 Aloe vera can help protect us from the sun.
4 We can make bread, pasta and cakes.

Extension Ask further questions about the topic: *Which part of the plant does coffee come from? (The seeds – they're beans) Which part of the cotton plant do we use to make cloth? (The flowers) Which part of the plant does tea come from? (The leaves) What about chocolate? (The seeds – we make it from cocoa beans)*

mission Stage 3

- Show the class the third stage of the Mission poster: *Talk about the plants which we eat.* Read the instructions. Check comprehension of *new idea!*
- Put learners into their Mission groups. They look at their recipe from Stage 2. Together they think about which of their ingredients come from plants and come up with ways to add more plant products.
- Each group then adds a 'new idea' to their recipe. Monitor and help with new vocabulary.

  Fast finishers Write about where the plant-based ingredients in their recipe come from and which part of the plant they are.

Activity Book, page 89

See pages TB120–132

Activity Book, page 82

- Review *My unit goals.* Ask *How is your Mission?* Learners reflect and choose a smiley face for *My mission diary 3.*

Ending the lesson

- **SA** Go back to Stage 3 on the digital Mission poster. Add a tick to the 'Talk about the plants which we eat' stage. Use self-assessment (see Introduction).
- Give out a completion sticker.

5 3.16 Listen and read. Answer the questions.

Plants are beautiful and important for us too. We need oxygen and plants give us oxygen when they make their food. We can also use plants for many different things.

- We use trees to make paper, chairs and tables.
- We use cotton to make clothes.
- We use many plants for medicines.
- We can use aloe vera to make sun creams.

We eat plants, but we also make a lot of food with them. We make flour from the wheat plant and we use flour to make bread, pasta and cakes. Chocolate, tea and coffee also come from plants.

1 Where does paper come from?

2 Which plant do we use to make T-shirts?

3 Which plant can help protect us from the sun?

4 What can we make with flour?

mission STAGE 3

Talk about the plants which we eat.

STAGE 3

- Talk about how to use more food from plants.
- Write a new idea for your recipe.

NEW IDEA! *Put peppers in the sauce too!*

My mission diary
Activity Book page 82

1 **Look at the pictures. What do you think the story is about?**

3.17

Sonny's dream job

Sonny was a big, brown bear. He loved food and he loved cooking. Every Saturday, he helped in the kitchen of his uncle's café, but he wasn't a cook. He washed plates, bowls, cups and glasses. The cooks were always angry and the waiters shouted, 'More vegetables for table 3!' Sonny didn't like the job, but he worked there because he wanted to be a cook one day. He also helped in the kitchen at home because he wanted to practise.

One Saturday, everything changed. Sonny got to the café and said, 'Good morning, Uncle Raymond.'

'It isn't a good morning,' his uncle said. 'I haven't got any cooks today because they aren't well. They're ill. And Selina Redman is coming for lunch today. Selina Redman!'

Selina Redman was a famous cook. Everyone watched her TV show *In my kitchen*.

'Can *I* cook, Uncle Raymond?'

'You can't cook, Sonny! Your job is to wash the dishes.'

'But I cook every day at home,' Sonny said.

Uncle Raymond said yes … and Sonny started making his favourite pasta.

Learning outcomes By the end of the lesson, learners will have read a fantasy story about a dream job.

New language *café, dream, ill, lovely, waiter, wash the dishes*

Recycled language actions in the kitchen, food and things for serving food, *bear, beautiful, cook* (n, v), *famous, job, kitchen, lunch, practise, shout, TV show, wash, well, How about … ?*, past simple

Materials a video clip from a TV cookery programme (optional), pictures of famous TV chefs (optional), audio

Warm-up

- Say *Look and remember.* Show a clip from a TV cookery programme in which the cook is using ingredients learners recognise and doing actions they can describe, e.g. *cut, mix, boil, fry, wash.* Ask learners questions about what they saw, e.g. *Which ingredients did you see? Were there any (onions)? What did the cook do? What did he/she cut? How many plates did you see?*
- Play the clip again and pause for learners to check their answers.

  Alternative Review actions, food and things for serving food by playing 'Simon says', e.g. *Simon says 'Cut some onions', Simon says 'Cry'*, etc.

Presentation

- Ask learners for names of famous TV chefs or show pictures. Ask *What does a TV chef do? (Shows people how to cook, makes new recipes, writes books)*
- Say *Let's read a story.*

Pupil's Book, pages 90 and 91

1 Look at the pictures. What do you think the story is about?

- Say *Open your Pupil's Books at page 90. Look at the pictures. What's the story about?* In pairs, learners write as many words as they can to describe the pictures. List ideas on the board. Use the pictures to teach *café* and *waiter.*

Key: Learners' own answers, but they should predict that the story takes place in a kitchen, then a café, and is about a young cook.

3.17 Sonny's dream job

- Read the title and explain the meaning of *dream job* (*A job you really want to do / Your perfect job*). Ask learners *What's your dream job?*
- Look at the first picture and explain that Sonny is the younger bear. Ask *Who do you think the bear near the door is?* Learners guess. Ask *Is he happy?* (*No, angry*) Learners guess why.
- Say *Let's read and listen to the first part of the story.* Play the audio. Pause after *he wanted to practise.* Ask *What did Sonny love? (Food and cooking) Where did he work on Saturdays? (At his uncle's café) What did he do at the café? (He washed the plates, cups, etc.)* Teach *wash the dishes.* Ask *Did Sonny like the job at the café? (No, he didn't.) Why did he work there? (Because he wanted to be a cook one day)*

  Track 3.17

  See story on Pupil's Book pages 90–91
- Say *Read and listen to the next part of the story.* Pause after *In my kitchen.* Ask *Why was Uncle Raymond angry? (Because all his cooks weren't well)* Teach *ill.* Ask *Who was Selina Redman? (A famous cook) What was the name of her TV show? ('In my kitchen')*
- Play the next part of the story. Pause after *his favourite pasta.* Ask *What did Sonny ask his uncle? ('Can I cook?') Did his uncle say 'yes'? (Yes, he did.) What did Sonny start cooking? (His favourite pasta)*
- Play the rest of the story. Ask *Why did Selina need a new pasta cook? (Because her cook went to Paris) When did she want Sonny to help? (On Saturday afternoons) What did she ask Sonny at the end of the story? ('How did you cook it / the pasta?')*

  Extension Play the whole story again, without pauses, for learners to listen and read.

Activity Book, page 90

See pages TB120–132

Ending the lesson

- Write these sentences on the board and the missing verbs in random order (*want, like* (x2), *ask, talk, go, have, work*). In pairs, learners complete the sentences with the correct verb in the past simple (positive or negative).

  1 *Sonny … in his uncle's café.*
  2 *Sonny … his job.*
  3 *He … to be a cook one day.*
  4 *On Saturday Uncle Raymond … any cooks in the café.*
  5 *Sonny … 'Can I cook?'*
  6 *After lunch, Selina Redman … to Sonny.*
  7 *Selina … Sonny's pasta very much.*
  8 *Sonny … to work for Selina.*
- Check answers: *1 worked, 2 didn't like, 3 wanted, 4 didn't have, 5 asked, 6 talked, 7 liked, 8 went.*

  Extra support Write the correct verb in the infinitive at the end of each sentence – learners change it to the past tense. Add a cross to show the negative sentences to make the task simpler.

Learning outcomes By the end of the lesson, learners will have thought about perseverance.

New language *give up*

Recycled language language from the story, *like* (*Are you like Sonny?*)

Materials audio

Social and Emotional Skill: Perseverance

- After reading the story, ask learners *Where did Sonny work? (His uncle's café) What did he do? (He washed the dishes.) What did he want to do? (He wanted to be a cook.) What happened in the end? (He got a job as a cook in Selina Redman's restaurant.)*
- Say *Yes, he got his dream job. He didn't give up.* Write on the board as a flow diagram:
  goal: to be a cook
  work in uncle's café → *help in the kitchen* → *learn from cooks there* → *practise cooking at home* → *take an opportunity*
- Explain that they are the steps Sonny took to get to his dream job. Say *Imagine you want to be a famous singer, what do you do?* Learners give their ideas. Write them on the board in the flow diagram in order.
- Remind the learners that they may have things they have to or want to do and it's important to work hard to achieve them and not to give up.
- Write a list of things that learners at this age have to or want to do (e.g. *do a difficult exam, learn a new instrument, play in the football team, sing in the school choir*).
- Also write some steps (e.g. *buy an instrument, practise playing my instrument every day, have music classes, listen in class, ask questions, study, do my homework, go to football practice after school, practise at home*).
- The learners work in pairs. They match the steps on the board to the goals and write their own ideas.
- They share their ideas with the class.

Warm-up

- Write *Sonny, Uncle Raymond, Selina Redman* on the board. Ask *Who's the youngest character in the story? (Sonny) Who's got a café? (Uncle Raymond) Who works on TV? (Selina Redman) Who wants to be a cook? (Sonny) Who's famous? (Selina Redman) Who gets angry in the story? (Uncle Raymond) Who gets a new job? (Sonny)*

Pupil's Book, pages 90 and 91

- Say *Open your Pupil's Books at pages 90 and 91.* Play the audio. Learners read and listen to the story again.

  Track 3.17
  See story on Pupil's Book pages 90–91

2 What happens next? What do the characters say? Talk with a friend and then tell the class.

- Read the instructions. Ask *What happens next in the story?* Write some of the learners' ideas on the board, e.g. *Sonny talks to Uncle Raymond about his new job. Uncle Raymond is angry.*
- Say *Imagine Sonny is telling Uncle Raymond about his new job. What does he say? How does he feel? Do you think Uncle Raymond is happy?* Read the speech bubbles with the class. Learners then read them in pairs, swapping roles.
- They work in pairs to continue the conversation and practise it.
- Pairs perform their conversation for the class, starting with the speech bubbles in the Pupil's Book and continuing with their own ideas.

  Extra support Ask for ideas about how to continue the conversation. Write them on the board, with learners helping you with the wording, e.g.

Uncle Raymond:	*What's your new job?*
Sonny:	*Selina Redman wants me to work in her restaurant!*
Uncle Raymond:	*I can't believe it! Why?*
Sonny:	*Because she really liked my pasta.*

3 Read about Sonny. What does *give up* mean? Are you like Sonny?

- Read the first question and the short text with the class. Ask learners to explain *give up* (= stop doing something) and translate it. Say *Sonny didn't give up and in the end he got a new job. What about you?* Ask learners for examples of times when they didn't give up.

Activity Book, page 91

See pages TB120–132

Ending the lesson

- **SA** Use self-assessment to see how well learners think they understand the story. See Introduction.
- Tell learners to each choose a food and make it into an anagram, e.g. *asatp – pasta*. Monitor and check. Put learners into pairs. Ask them to give their anagram to their partner. Their partner tells them the word. Repeat, giving each learner a new partner.

  Alternative Play 'Hangman' with the food words (see page TB41 for instructions).

7

That day, after lunch, Selina Redman asked Sonny to come to her table. 'Did you really boil that beautiful pasta?' she asked.

'Yes, I did,' Sonny answered.

'And do you like cooking?'

'Yes, I do,' Sonny said. 'I want to be a famous cook like you one day.'

'Well,' Selina said, 'I have an idea. I'm looking for a new pasta cook. My pasta cook is going to Paris. How about helping me on Saturday afternoons in Restaurant Redman?'

'Me?' Sonny asked. 'But what about the other cooks here?'

'They didn't cook that lovely pasta! That was you! Now, tell me, how did you cook it?'

2 What happens next? What do the characters say? Talk with a friend and then tell the class.

I'm very happy, Uncle Raymond.

Why's that, Sonny?

I've got a new job!

3 Read about Sonny. What does *give up* mean? Are you like Sonny?

Sonny wanted to be a cook. He worked at his uncle's café and practised at home. His job was sometimes difficult, but he didn't give up.

1 **Find three word families:**
Circle the food blue.
Circle the actions red.
Circle the things for drinking green.

2 3.18 **Which picture is different? Why? Listen and check.**

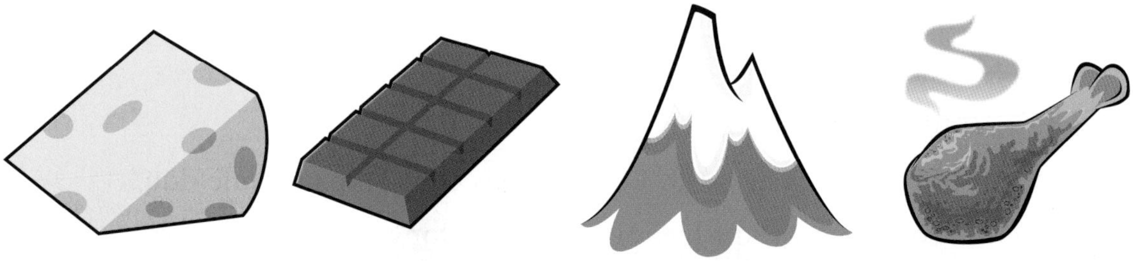

3 3.19 **Look at the pictures. Listen to the boy's ideas. Correct any mistakes.**

You don't need to say a lot: only which picture is different and why.

Learning outcomes By the end of the lesson, learners will have practised talking about the 'odd one out' in a set of pictures (A1 Movers Speaking Part 3).

Test skills Suggesting a picture which is different and explaining why

Recycled language actions, clothes, food and things we use to serve food, weather, present continuous

Materials Food flashcards, Actions in the kitchen flashcards, practice paper for Movers Speaking Part 3 (optional), coloured pens or pencils, audio

Warm-up

- Learners stand in two or three lines in front of you. Show a flashcard. The learners at the front of each line play. The first learner who names the item or action correctly gets the flashcard. At the end of the game, the team with the most flashcards wins.

Presentation

- Say *Let's practise for a speaking exam.* Show the Movers Speaking Part 3 paper. Say *In Part 3 of the exam you see groups of four pictures. You need to find one picture which is different. You have to explain why. The examiner does the first as the example, then there are three more groups of pictures.*

Pupil's Book, page 92

1 Find three word families: Circle the food blue. Circle the actions red. Circle the things for drinking green.

- Say *Open your Pupil's Books at page 92.* Make sure learners have coloured pens or pencils. Read the instructions and check understanding. Point to the first picture (bottle) and ask *What colour must you use?* (*Green*) Learners circle individually, then check in pairs.
- Check answers. Ask learners to say what is in each picture / what is happening. Ask for other reasons why the words can be put in a group, e.g. *Soup, pasta and sandwich are all hot.* Explain that it doesn't matter if they give a reason the examiner is not expecting, as long as it is a valid grouping.

Key: blue – soup, pasta, sandwich red – washing dishes, washing a bicycle, washing a tractor
green – bottle, glass, cup

2 3.18 Which picture is different? Why? Listen and check.

- Learners look at the pictures in pairs and find the different one. Check answers before playing the audio, and ask pairs to give their reasons.
- Play the audio. Ask what reason the child gives. Point out that other ways to say the difference are fine, e.g. *These are food and this isn't.*

Track 3.18

Examiner:	Now, you look at these pictures. Which one is different?
Candidate:	Um … These three pictures are … they are … all things you can … um … eat.
Examiner:	And this?
Candidate:	It's … um … This is … er ... not food. It's a mountain.
Examiner:	Good!

Key: The mountain, because it isn't food / you can't eat it.

3 3.19 Look at the pictures. Listen to the boy's ideas. Correct any mistakes.

- Ask learners to name each thing/action before they listen.
- Play the audio twice. Pause after each section for learners to say if it is right or correct any mistakes.

Track 3.19

Mmm … I think … yes … this woman is crying and these people are dropping things.
The carrot and the potato are small, and the onion is small, but the ... the watermelon is shorter.
The sun, the rainbow and the cloud are on … in the sky. The T-shirt … er … isn't.

Key: First group: no mistakes
Second group: the watermelon isn't shorter, it's bigger
Third group: it isn't a cloud, it's snow

Extension Ask learners for different reasons, e.g. *The watermelon is a fruit, the others are vegetables.*

- Point to the monkey at the bottom of the page and read. Learners should say what the difference is, as well as finding the three things that are the same.

Activity Book, page 92

See pages TB120–132

Ending the lesson

- Display sets of four flashcards on the board for learners to find and explain the odd one out. You can play this as a team game.

  Extension Learners work in groups to make sets of four flashcards with an odd one out. The class find the odd one out.

Learning outcomes By the end of the lesson, learners will have revised the language in the unit, presented their recipes and made a class recipe book.

Recycled language unit language

Materials recipes from Mission Stages 2 and 3 lessons, a recipe book (optional), card (to make a class recipe book) or a large notebook, scissors and glue, examples of online trip reviews (optional), dice and counters (for Activity Book game), coloured pens or pencils, digital Mission poster

Warm-up

- Write on the board: *What did you do yesterday after school?* Below the title, write:

  Did you … watch TV?
  make some food?
  go out?
  play a game or sport?
  help someone?
- Ask learners to copy the title and questions. They should leave space after each question to write the name of a learner. Practise the questions and check comprehension.
- Learners stand up and walk around the classroom. When you say 'stop' they ask the learner nearest to them the five questions. If a learner says *Yes, I did.* they write their name next to the question.

  Stronger learners Ask another question and write down more information about the learner who said 'yes', e.g. *What did you watch? What did you make? Where did you go? What did you play? Who did you help?*

  Fast finishers Write past simple sentences about their classmates.
- Set a time limit for the mingling stage. Then ask learners to report back about what they found out, e.g. *Marina watched TV. She watched a programme about animals.*

Pupil's Book, page 93

mission in action!

Make a class recipe book.

- Say *Open your Pupil's Books at page 93.* Point to the Mission box or show learners the last stage of the digital Mission poster. Say *Let's put our Mission in action!* Say *Make a class recipe book.* Show a real recipe book to remind learners what they are making.
- Read the instructions and speech bubbles. Put learners into their Mission groups. Give them time to practise presenting their recipe to the class, using their worksheets/notes from the Mission stages. Monitor and check that each member of the group gets the chance to speak.
- Groups take turns to present their recipe. The class can vote on the recipe they would most like to try.
- Learners put the recipes together in a class book. They should decide how to organise the recipes (e.g. alphabetically or by type of dish, e.g. soup, meat, dessert) and make a cover. Let learners pass it round the class so that they can look at their classmates' work.

  Extension Learners swap recipes and try making them at home.

Self-assessment

- **SA** Say *Did you like our 'Make a class recipe book' Mission? Think and draw a face.* Learners draw a happy face, neutral face or sad face and then hold it up in the air.
- Say *Tell me things you can do now*. Learners suggest ideas. (*We can talk about food. We can say what we did yesterday or last weekend.*)
- Say *Our next Mission is 'Write a trip review.'* Explain the meaning of *trip review.* If possible, show an example of an online trip review. Ask *What wasn't so good this time? How can we do better in the next Mission?* Learners suggest ideas, e.g. *We can practise spelling more.*

Activity Book, page 93

See pages TB120–132

Activity Book, page 82

- Review *My unit goals*. Ask *How was your Mission?* Learners reflect and choose a smiley face for *My mission diary* the final stage.
- Point to the sunflower. Learners read the 'can do' statements and tick them if they agree they have achieved them. They colour each leaf green if they are very confident or orange if they think they need more practice.
- Point to the word stack sign. Ask learners to look back at the unit and find at least five new words they have learnt. They write them in their word stack.

Ending the lesson

- **SA** Go back to the completion stage on the digital Mission poster. Add a tick or invite a learner to do it. Use self-assessment (see Introduction).
- Give out a completion sticker.
- Tell learners *You have finished your Mission! Well done!*

mission in action!

Make a class recipe book.

My mission diary
Activity Book page 82

Say what kind of recipe you chose.

We chose a recipe for chicken pasta.

Say how you made it.

In our recipe, we put …

We washed the tomatoes. We …

Give your idea for using more plants.

Put peppers in the sauce too.

Put your recipe in the class book.

8 Around town

1 **Watch the video. Draw and write the name of a place in town.**

mission Write a trip review

In this unit I will:

1. Write about a trip. Draw a picture.
2. Help people who want to do the same trip.
3. Write how to be safe on the trip.
4. ★ Show my review to the class.

Unit 8 learning outcomes

In Unit 8, learners learn to:

- talk about a day trip and places in town
- use more irregular verbs in the past simple
- use *have to* and *don't have to*
- learn about road safety
- read a fantasy story and think about being optimistic

Materials video, coloured pens or pencils, digital Mission poster, flashcards or pictures of four different places (e.g. beach, park, forest, town centre) (optional)

Self-assessment

- SA Say *Open your Pupil's Books at page 94. Look at the picture. What can you see?* (e.g. *A town, a street, shops, a door, windows, people with bags, plants*) Use self-assessment (see Introduction). Say *OK. Let's learn.*

Warm-up

- Say *Look at the picture and remember.* Time one minute, then say *Close your books!* Ask, e.g. *Did you see any (children)? Did you see a (white) bag? Were all the windows/ doors closed? What colour were the shops?*
- You can play this as a team game, asking each team a question in turn and scoring a point for each correct answer.

Pupil's Book, page 94

1 Watch the video. Draw and write the name of a place in town.

- Say *In this unit we're talking about places in town.* Say *Let's watch the video.* To introduce the topic of the unit, play the video.
- Say *Look at page 94.* Point to the blank shop front. Say *Which place is this? You choose and draw. It can be a kind of shop or a different place. Write the name.* Monitor and help with names of places.

mission Write a trip review

- Point to the Mission box or the digital Mission poster and say *This is our Mission.*
- Say *Write a trip review.* Check comprehension of *trip.* Ask *When did you last go on a trip? Was it a day trip or a longer trip? Where did you go? Who went with you?* Learners tell a partner.
  Stronger learners Tell the class about their partner's trip.
- Say *Sometimes people write about their trip when they get back. They say what they did, and what was good and bad. They write a review of their trip.*
- Say *Point to number 1. Write about a trip. Draw a picture.* Ask *What kind of things do you tell your friends when you come back from a trip?* Learners share their ideas. Write them on the board. Ask *Do you take photos? Do you use a camera or a phone?*
- Say *Point to number 2. Help people who want to do the same trip.* Say *To help someone who wants to go on a trip you can give them lots of information. What do they want to know? Maybe how did you get there? What clothes did you take? Which are good places to visit and eat? What was the weather like?*
- Say *Point to number 3. Write how to be safe on the trip.* Check comprehension of *safe.* Explain that in this stage learners will give other people advice on what they must and mustn't do to stay safe.
- Say *The last stage is 'Show my review to the class.'* Say *You're going to talk about your trip and show your review to the class.*
- Say *This is our Mission.* Go through the stages of the Mission again.
- For ideas on monitoring and assessment, see Introduction.

Activity Book, page 94

My unit goals

- Help learners to complete the unit goals. See notes on page TB6.
- You can go back to these unit goals at the end of each Mission stage during the unit and review them.

Ending the lesson

- Ask learners to stand up. Put the pictures or flashcards of four places people could visit on a day trip on the walls in different parts of the classroom, e.g. beach, park, forest, town centre.
- Describe a place but don't say which one it is, e.g. *There's lots of sand here. You can go swimming. You can look for shells.* Learners run to the correct picture. (If you prefer, learners can just point to the correct picture.)
- Practise counting aloud from 1 to 20.
- Learners stand in a circle. Count aloud but clap every time you get to a multiple of three, e.g. *One, two,* [clap], *four, five,* [clap], *seven, eight,* [clap], etc. Learners join in.
- Say *Don't say the 'threes'!* Then say *One* and point to the learner next to you. He/She says *Two.* The next learner claps his/her hands. The next says *Four*, and so on.
  Extension Make this competitive – a learner who says a number when he/she should clap hands is 'out'.

Learning outcomes By the end of the lesson, learners will be able to talk about a day trip.

New language *car park, city centre, funfair, map, plan* (v), *ride* (n), *road, station, ticket, trip,* numbers 21–30, *adventure, buy,catch (a bus/train), drive* (n, v), *get off, get on, website*

Recycled language numbers 1–20, places, vehicles, *bus stop, countryside, have a picnic, near, outside, Can we … ?,* comparative adjectives, *must*

Materials A day trip flashcards, audio, video, coloured pens or pencils

Warm-up

- Practise counting from 1 to 20 using the procedure at the end of the previous lesson. This time, clap multiples of four.

Presentation

- Draw a bus with 21 on the front. See if any learners can say the number. Teach/practise numbers 21 to 30.

  Note: there is a full presentation of numbers 21 to 100 in Unit 9 and on page 120 of the Pupil's Book.
- Teach the day trip words with the flashcards. Then ask, e.g. *Do you like going to the funfair? Which rides are your favourites? Is there a car park / station near the school?*
- Teach *go for a drive* and *get on / get off* (*a bus*) using mime. Ask *What do you need to buy before you get on a bus or train? (A ticket) Where do you get on the bus? Is there a bus stop near your house?*

Pupil's Book, page 95

1 3.20 3.21 Listen and point. Then listen and number.

- Say *Open your Pupil's Books at page 95. Who can you see? What are they looking at? (A map/website)*
- Ask *Where's the small tractor? Can you find it?*
- Read the caption. Check comprehension of *planning a trip*.
- Play Track 3.20. Learners listen and point.

Tracks 3.20 and 3.21

(1) Mrs Friendly and Grandma are planning a trip.
Jim: What's that map, Mum?
(2) Mrs Friendly: I'm looking at the website for a new funfair.
(3) Mrs Friendly: It's called Funland and it's outside the city centre.
(4) Jenny: Ooh, can we go there, please?
Mrs Friendly: We can buy a ticket for the day for 20 pounds.
(5) Mrs Friendly: We can go on all the rides.
Jim: Oh, must we go on all the rides?
Jenny: No, Jim. We can choose our rides.
Jim: Oh, phew!
(6) Mrs Friendly: There's a big car park so we can drive there.
Jim: Great! We can go for a drive in the countryside.
(7) Grandma: We can go by bus and train. There's a small station near Funland.
Jenny: Yes, we can get on the number 23 bus at the bus stop outside the farm.
Mrs Friendly: That's right. Then we can catch the train at the big station and get off at Funland.
(8) Jim: But it's a good road, Mum. It's easier and quicker by car.
Mrs Friendly: But it's sometimes fun to travel by bus and train, …
Grandma: … and we can have a picnic.
Jim: That's a good idea! I like picnics.
Jenny: Yes! What a great adventure!

- Say *Listen and number*. Play Track 3.21.

Key: 2 funfair 3 city centre 4 ticket 5 ride 6 car park 7 station 8 road

2 3.22 Say the chant.

- Play the audio or video. Learners point and chant.

Track 3.22

Road trip, road trip,
Get on, get off,
Catch a bus,
Trip, map, station, ticket,
City centre, car park, funfair, ride. [x2]

3 3.23 Listen and say *yes* or *no*.

- Play the audio. Pause for learners to answer.

Track 3.23

1 Mrs Friendly and Grandma are planning a trip to the funfair.
2 The funfair is called Sadland.
3 They can buy a ticket for the day for 12 pounds.
4 There's a big car park at the funfair.
5 They can go by car, or they can go by bus and train.
6 There's a small train station in the city centre.
7 They can get on the train outside the farm.
8 They can have a picnic.

Key: 1 yes 2 no 3 no 4 yes 5 yes 6 no 7 no 8 yes

Activity Book, page 95

See pages TB120–132

Ending the lesson

- **SA** Show The day trip flashcards. Ask *Do you know the words?* Use self-assessment (see Introduction). Learners show how they feel.

1 3.20 3.21 **Listen and point. Then listen and number.**

2 3.22 **Say the chant.**

3 3.23 **Listen and say *yes* or *no*.**

The Friendly Farm

3.24

1
Look! I found my old hat this morning.
Farmer Friendly's old hat! He bought it last year and he wore it on holiday.
He chose it because green's his favourite colour.
2
The family drove to the beach. We were there for a week.
What an adventure!
Adventure, hmm … we came to the farm last year. That was the longest trip of our lives.
3
Yes, we rode in Farmer Friendly's lorry. I sat in the back and slept.
I didn't sleep. It was fantastic. I stood and watched the beautiful countryside.
4
Shall I tell you about my adventure? I lost my cousin in the forest.
You didn't lose her! She hid behind a tree …
Farmer Friendly brought you home. I saw you!
5
Gracie! You told us a different story!
Ours was a very long trip. Farmer Friendly stopped and fed us nice vegetables when we were hungry.
6
Farmer Friendly's a good man. He gave me his favourite green hat.
He didn't give you the hat. You took it from the garden!

1 3.25 **Listen and complete. Use two words.**

Learning outcomes By the end of the lesson, learners will be able to understand when they hear more irregular past simple forms.

New language *bought, brought, came, chose, drove, fed, found, gave, hid, lost, rode, sat, slept, stood, told, took, wore, hungry, Shall I … ?*

Recycled language *adventure, beach, behind, countryside, cousin, different, farm, favourite colour, forest, hat, last (year), lorry, on holiday, this (morning), vegetables*, past simple, *was, were*

Materials pairs of word cards (*drink – drank, eat – ate, get – got, go – went, have – had, make – made, put – put, see – saw*) (optional), audio, video

Warm-up

- Show word cards for infinitives from Unit 7. For each verb make a sentence in the present, e.g. *I usually drink apple juice*. Then show the past form and ask a learner to make a sentence about yesterday, e.g. *But yesterday I drank orange juice*.
- Stick the word cards on the board in two columns – infinitive and past simple. If you don't have word cards, write the words. Practise the infinitives and past forms. Gradually remove/erase the past forms until learners are saying them from memory.
- **SA** Use self-assessment to check how well learners think they understand the past forms. See Introduction.

Presentation

- Say *I drive to school every morning, so this morning I drove to school*. Ask different learners *Did your parents drive this morning?* and encourage them to answer, e.g. *My mum drove to work*. Repeat with *I see my grandparents every weekend, so last weekend I saw my grandparents. When did you last see your grandparents? (I saw them …)*
- Write verbs in a column on the board: *buy, bring, come, choose, drive, feed, find, give, hide, lose, ride, sit, see, sleep, stand, tell, take, wear* and past tense forms on the right: *bought, brought, came, chose, drove, fed, found, gave, hid, lost, rode, sat, saw, slept, stood, told, took, wore*.

Pupil's Book, page 96

3.24 The Friendly Farm song

- Play the introductory song at the beginning of the cartoon story. Learners listen and sing.

Track 3.24
See The Friendly Farm song on page TB5

3.24 The Friendly Farm

- Say *Open your Pupil's Books at page 96*. Point to Cameron in picture 1 and ask *Who's Cameron talking about? (Farmer Friendly / Grandpa)*
- Ask *What happened to Farmer Friendly's hat?* Write the question on the board. Play the audio or video. Learners listen and read. Check answers. (*Harry took it.*) Say the past tense forms from the story, and learners say the infinitives.

Track 3.24
The Friendly Farm song + see cartoon on Pupil's Book page 96

- Play the audio or video again. Pause after each picture and ask questions. Accept short answers and model the new past forms. 1: *When did Farmer Friendly buy the hat? (He bought it last year.) Why did he choose it? (He chose it because green is his favourite colour.)* 2: *When did Rocky and Henrietta come to the farm? (They came last year.)* 3: *What did Henrietta do in the lorry? (She slept.) What did Rocky do? (He watched the countryside.)* 4: *What did Gracie's cousin do? (She hid behind a tree.) Who brought Gracie and her cousin home? (Farmer Friendly brought them home.)* 5: *What did Farmer Friendly feed Henrietta and Rocky? (He fed them vegetables.)* 6: *Did Farmer Friendly give Harry his hat? (No, Harry took it.)*

1 3.25 Listen and complete. Use two words.

- Play the first sentence and pause for learners to say the next two words. Play the rest of the audio. Check answers.

Track 3.25
1 He bought it last year and he wore it …
2 He chose it because green's his …
3 The family drove to the beach. We were there for …
4 I stood and watched the …
5 Shall I tell you about my adventure? I lost my cousin in …
6 You didn't lose her! She hid behind …
7 Gracie! You told us a …
8 He didn't give you the hat. You took it from …

Key: 1 on holiday. 2 favourite colour. 3 a week. 4 beautiful countryside. 5 the forest. 6 a tree. 7 different story! 8 the garden!

Activity Book, page 96

See pages TB120–132

Ending the lesson

- **SA** Use self-assessment to see how well learners think they understand the new past forms.

Learning outcomes By the end of the lesson, learners will be able to use more irregular past simple forms.

New language *find: I found my old hat. lose: I lost my cousin in the forest. buy: He bought it last year. come: We came to the farm last year. huge*

Recycled language day trips, *chocolate cake, draw a picture, scariest, take a photo,* irregular past simple forms

Materials pairs of infinitive / past simple word cards for verbs from the previous lesson (optional), audio, Mission worksheets (Teacher's Resource Book page 84), coloured pens or pencils, digital Mission poster

Warm-up

- Write *Town* and *Countryside* on the board. Say a word, e.g. *field*, and ask *Town or countryside?* Continue with other words, e.g. *bus stop*, *forest*, *shop*, *houses*, *grass*. Learners can make a sound effect (e.g. a car horn / sheep) instead of saying the category.

Presentation

- Show a past simple word card (or write on the board). Learners say the infinitive. Stick both cards on the board. Repeat with the other new forms.
- Give each learner an infinitive or a past simple word card. Learners walk around saying their word until they find their partner.
- Pairs sit together and write a sentence with their verb in the past (e.g. *sleep – We both slept for nine hours last night.*).

Pupil's Book, page 97

3.26 Gracie's Grammar

- Say *Open your Pupil's Books at page 97.* Point to Gracie's Grammar box. Write the verbs and sentences on the board.
- Play the audio. Pause for learners to repeat.

  Track 3.26
  See Pupil's Book page 97
- Ask learners to make the sentences negative.

1 3.27 Listen and stick. Then look, read and write.

- Say *A boy is talking to his grandma about a trip to the funfair.* Point to each sticker and ask *What's this?*
- Play the audio. Learners point to the correct sticker.

Track 3.27

1 Boy: Last Saturday we went to the new funfair outside town. Look! I drew these pictures for you, Grandma.
Grandma: Oh, thank you. Is that you there?
Boy: Yes, it is.
Grandma: What have you got in your hand?
Boy: That's our all-day ticket. Dad bought it online.
2 Boy: Dad doesn't like funfairs, so he didn't go on many rides.
Grandma: Oh. What did he do there?
Boy: He took a lot of photos.
Grandma: Ah, yes. I can see. He had his camera with him.
Boy: Yes, he did.
3 Boy: We had a great time. Mum loved the biggest ride.
Grandma: Oh, I don't like big rides. What was it called?
Boy: It was called the 'Crazy Train'.
Grandma: Oh, yes. She rode on the scariest rides when she was a child too.
4 Grandma: Did you have lunch there?
Boy: Yes, we took a picnic. My uncle made some lovely cheese sandwiches.
Grandma: Oh, that's nice. Did you have anything else?
Boy: Oh, yes. He brought a huge chocolate cake.
Grandma: Mmm. Yes, it is big!

- Play the audio again. Learners stick in the stickers. Check and ask, e.g. *Where did Dad buy the ticket? What did Dad do at the funfair? What did Mum do? What did the boy's uncle bring to eat?*
- Say *Now look, read and write*. Check answers.

Key: 2 took 3 rode/went 4 brought

mission Stage 1

- Point to the Mission box or show learners the first stage of the digital Mission poster: *Write about a trip. Draw a picture.*
- Learners complete the worksheet task in the Teacher's Resource Book (page 84) individually. See teaching notes on TRB page 77.
- Alternatively, if you do not have the Teacher's Resource Book, learners write about a trip, answering the questions, and draw a picture of their favourite part. Monitor and help.
- Put learners into pairs to talk about their trips.

Activity Book, page 97

See pages TB120–132

Activity Book, page 94

- Review *My unit goals*. Ask *How is your Mission?* Learners reflect and choose a smiley face for *My mission diary 1*.

Ending the lesson

- **SA** Go back to Stage 1 on the digital Mission poster. Say *We wrote about a trip and we drew a picture.* Add a tick to the 'Write about a trip ... ' stage. Use self-assessment (see Introduction).
- Give out a completion sticker.

Gracie's Grammar

3.26

find: I **found** my old hat.
lose: I **lost** my cousin in the forest.
buy: He **bought** it last year.
come: We **came** to the farm last year.

1 3.27 **Listen and stick. Then look, read and write.**

1 I ___drew___ these pictures for you, Grandma.
2 My dad __________ a lot of photos.
3 My mum __________ on the scariest rides when she was a child.
4 My uncle __________ a big chocolate cake.

mission STAGE 1

Write about a trip. Draw a picture.

- Write answers to these questions:
  Where did you go? How did you get there?
- Draw your favourite part and tell a friend.

This ride was my favourite part. I came down very fast!

STAGE 1

My mission diary
Activity Book page 94

1 3.28 Listen and write. Then sing the song.

Last week, in town, in town,
Dad and I did a lot of things.
Last week, in town, in town,
We did a lot of things.

We sat in the **café** in the pretty **square**.
We saw a film at the **cinema**.

We got a book from the **library**.
We gave it to Jane in the **hospital**.
Last week ...

We chose some clothes at the **shopping centre**.
We bought some food at the **supermarket**.

We played tennis at the **sports centre**.
We went for a swim at the **swimming pool**.
Last week ...

We bought some vegetables at the **market**.
We caught a bus home from the **bus station**.
Last week ...

1

2

3

4

5

2 Ask and answer. Use the places in the song and your own ideas.

What did they do in the square?

They sat in the café.

What did they do in the café?

They drank lemonade.

Where did you go on your last trip into town?

Learning outcomes By the end of the lesson, learners will have practised the language through song.

New language *bus station, café, cinema, hospital, library, market, shopping centre, sports centre, square, supermarket, swimming pool,* numbers 31–100

Recycled language day trips, numbers 1–30, *book, bus, clothes, film, food, go for a swim, home, park, play tennis, pretty, shop, vegetables,* irregular past simple forms

Materials Places in town flashcards, a map of a city centre (optional), audio, video

Warm-up

- Say *Look at the story on page 96.* Give learners two minutes to look and remember what happened. Ask questions with *Who ... ?* e.g. *Who found the hat? Who bought the hat? Who rode in Farmer Friendly's lorry?*

  Extra support Learners work in pairs and score a point for each correct answer.

Presentation

- Ask *What can you see in the city centre?* Prompt learners to say words they already know, e.g. *Where do you go to buy things?* (*Shops*) *Where do you go to ride a bike?* (*Park*) Write more places they know on the board.
- Teach the new places using the flashcards. Practise pronunciation and clap the stress. Ask *Do you buy books in a library?* (*No*) to check learners understand the difference between *library* and *bookshop*.
- If possible, show a map of a city centre with key places such as squares, hospitals and shopping centres marked. Ask *Where's the (hospital)? Is there a (sports centre)? Where is it?* Ask learners about their hometown / home city: *What's the name of the biggest square in our town/city? Do you sometimes go to the* (name) *sports centre? Is it near here? How many swimming pools are there in our town/city? Which swimming pool do you go to? What's the name of your favourite café?*

  Extension Learners ask and answer in pairs.
- **SA** Use self-assessment to check how well learners think they understand the vocabulary. See Introduction.

Pupil's Book, page 98

1 3.28 Listen and write. Then sing the song.

- Say *Open your Pupil's Books at page 98. Listen and point.* Say *They're swimming / playing tennis / shopping / visiting someone / catching a bus.* Learners point to the picture.
- Say *Listen and write.* Point to the numbered pictures and the example answer, *café.* Point out that *café* has an accent because it comes from French.
- Play the audio or video. Learners listen and write the names of the places in the spaces in pictures 1, 2, 3 and 5.

Track 3.28

Rocky: I'm Rocky-Doodle-Doo and here's our song for today: *Last week in town*

See song on Pupil's Book page 98

Key: 1 library 2 market 3 cinema (4 café) 5 hospital

- Learners stand up. Practise the song in sections.
- Play the audio or video again. Learners sing and do actions (sitting in a café, eating popcorn at the cinema, etc.).

3.29 **Extension** Once learners are confidently singing along, try singing the karaoke version as a class.

Extra support Ask learners *What number bus did they catch?* (*25*) Practise numbers 1 to 30, counting around the class. Use the activities on Pupil's Book page 120 to present and practise numbers from 21 to 100. There is an audioscript and answer key for the second activity on page TB132.

2 Ask and answer. Use the places in the song and your own ideas.

- Read the example speech bubbles and ask one or two more questions, e.g. *What did they do at the library?* (*They got a book.*)
- Learners ask and answer in pairs.
- Show the picture of Rocky in the bottom right-hand corner. Read the question. Learners talk in pairs. Encourage them to ask more questions, e.g. *What did you do/buy/ eat there? Who did you go with?* Monitor and help with new vocabulary. Ask learners to tell the class about their partner, e.g. *George went to the market. He bought a toy.*

Activity Book, page 98

See pages TB120–132

Ending the lesson

- **SA** Repeat the self-assessment used after the Presentation to see how well learners think they understand the vocabulary. Is there any change?
- Play the song again. Learners join in and do actions.

Learning outcomes By the end of the lesson, learners will be able to use *have to* and *don't have to*.

New language *I have to see the eye doctor at the hospital. My brother has to wear glasses. Do you have to wear glasses? Yes, I do. / No, I don't.*

Recycled language places in town, *clean your bedroom, do your homework, help at home, make your bed, make your breakfast, plate, ride* (n), *wash, wear (glasses)*

Materials Places in town flashcards, audio, worksheets / descriptions of trips from Mission Stage 1 lesson, digital Mission poster

Warm-up

- Review places in town with the flashcards.
- Learners take turns to choose a flashcard and mime for the class to guess.

Presentation

- Say *I live outside town. I can't walk to school. I have to catch the bus*. Ask different learners *Do you have to catch the bus to school?* Encourage them to reply *Yes, I do. / No, I don't*. Say, e.g. *Hugo has to / doesn't have to catch the bus to school.*
- Write *Do you have to … ?* on the board. Ask different learners *Do you have to make your bed in the morning?* Learners practise asking the person next to them.
- Practise more questions with *have to* around the class, e.g. *listen to the teacher in class / go to football practice today.*
- Explain that *have to* describes an obligation (it is similar to *must*).

Pupil's Book, page 99

1 3.30 Which are Zoe's mum's glasses? Listen and tick ✓.

- Ask *Who has to wear glasses in your family? Does your (mum) have to wear glasses?*
- Say *Open your Pupil's Books at page 99.* Point to each pair of glasses and ask *What colour are they?*
- Ask *Which are Zoe's mum's glasses?* Play the audio.

Track 3.30

Girl: Zoe, your mum's here to get you.
Zoe: Yes, I have to go now.
Girl: Really? Why?
Zoe: Because I have to see the eye doctor at the hospital.
Girl: Oh! Why? What's wrong? Do you have to wear glasses?
Zoe: No, I don't. Well, not now … but in the classroom I have to sit near the board because I can't read the words well.
Girl: Hmm … there are some brilliant glasses, you know. My brother has to wear glasses and his are great.
Zoe: Yes, I know. My mum has to wear glasses too. Hers are fantastic and they're blue and black. She never wants to take them off!
Girl: Haha. Well, good luck at the hospital.
Zoe: Thanks. We all really have to look after our eyes.
Girl: Yes, we do.

- Ask *Why does Zoe have to sit near the board at school? Who has to wear glasses in Zoe's friend's family?*

Key: Picture 3

3.31 Gracie's Grammar

- Write the sentences on the board.
- Play the audio. Pause for learners to repeat.

Track 3.31
See Pupil's Book page 99

- Write negative sentences on the board: *I don't have to wear glasses. My sister doesn't have to wear glasses.*

2 Ask and answer. What do you have to do? Write three sentences for you.

- Check comprehension of the phrases in the box.
- Learners ask and answer in small groups first using their own ideas as well as the phrases in the box.
- Learners then write three sentences about themselves.

mission Stage 2

- Show learners the second stage of the Mission poster: *Help people who want to do the same trip.*
- Learners complete the next worksheet task in the Teacher's Resource Book (page 84). See teaching notes on TRB page 77.
- Alternatively, if you don't have the Teacher's Resource Book, learners work individually to write some advice for people who want to do the trip they wrote about in Stage 1.
- Put learners into pairs to exchange advice.

Activity Book, page 99

See pages TB120–132

Activity Book, page 94

- Review *My unit goals*. Ask *How is your Mission?* Learners reflect and choose a smiley face for *My mission diary 2*.

Ending the lesson

- **SA** Go back to Stage 2 on the digital Mission poster. Add a tick to the 'Help people who want to do the same trip' stage. Use self-assessment (see Introduction).
- Give out a completion sticker.

1 3.30 Which are Zoe's mum's glasses? Listen and tick ✓.

1

2

3

3.31 Gracie's Grammar

I **have to** see the eye doctor at the hospital.

My brother **has to** wear glasses.

Do you **have to** wear glasses? Yes, I **do**. / No, I **don't**.

2 Ask and answer. What do you have to do? Write three sentences for you.

clean your bedroom help at home do your homework
wash the plates after dinner make your breakfast make your bed

Do you have to clean your bedroom?

Yes, I do.

No, I don't. I have to …

mission STAGE 2

Help people who want to do the same trip.

- Write what you have to do, and don't have to do, on this trip.
- Tell a friend.

You have to wear a swimsuit on the rides.
You don't have to go on the scariest rides!

My mission diary
Activity Book page 94

Road safety

1 Watch the video.

2 Tick ✓ the things in the street that help to keep us safe.

1

street lamp ☐

2

litter bin ☐

3

pedestrian crossing ☐

4

traffic lights ☐

5

pavement ☐

6

road ☐

7

road sign ☐

8

bench ☐

3 Complete the poster.

Always walk on the [1] pavement .

Use a safe place to cross. Don't run across the [2]__________. Stop, look and listen.

Wait for the [3]__________ light at a [4]__________ __________.

Hold a grown-up's [5]__________ when you cross the road.

Carry a ball in the street. [6]__________ play with it.

Learning outcomes By the end of the lesson, learners will have learnt about how to be safe in town.

New language *across, bench, cross (the road), hold (someone's) hand, litter bin, pavement, pedestrian crossing, road sign, safety, street lamp, traffic lights*

Recycled language places in town, vehicles, *always, ball, carry, grown-up* (n), *listen, look, play, road, safe, stop, wait, walk,* imperatives

Materials Places in town flashcards, video, a picture of a city street with street lamps, traffic lights, road signs, etc. (optional), two circles of paper or card per learner, coloured pens or pencils (optional)

Warm-up

- Review places in town with the flashcards. Stick the flashcards on the board as if they were part of a city centre map and ask, e.g. *Is the car park next to the hospital? What's near the cinema?*
- Tell learners to imagine it's the weekend. Say *You're going to the town centre. Make a list of six places you need to go to and things you have to do there.*
- Write some examples on the board, e.g. *The library – to get a book. The shopping centre – to buy a T-shirt.* Monitor and help as learners write their lists.
- Put learners in pairs with someone they weren't sitting next to. Tell them they have to find out if they have written the same place or reason on their lists. They don't look at their partner's list (they can sit back to back). They need to ask questions, e.g. *Do you have to go to the library? Do you have to get a book?* Demonstrate the task with a learner first.
- Ask pairs to tell you the things they both have to do, e.g. *We have to go to the shopping centre.*

  Extra support Learners write the list of places in pairs, then join with another pair to compare their lists in a group.

  Stronger learners After the speaking activity, learners write sentences about the things they have to do.

Presentation

- Stand at one side of the classroom and say *Imagine I'm in a street.* Make sound effects of traffic (motors, horns, etc.). Ask *What can I see?* Learners suggest, e.g. *cars, motorbikes, people, bikes.* Point to the other side of the classroom and say *I want to cross to the other side of the street.* Mime stepping straight out in front of traffic and ask *Is that OK? Why not?*
- Say *It isn't safe.* Write *Road safety* on the board and ask learners what they think it means.
- Say *Let's find out more about being safe in the street.*

Pupil's Book, page 100

1 Watch the video.

- Say *Let's watch the video.* Learners watch the video about road safety and answer the questions at the end.

2 Tick ✓ the things in the street that help to keep us safe.

- Say *Open your Pupil's Books at page 100.* Present the things in the photos and practise pronunciation. Ask *What colour is the litter bin?* (Orange) *What number is on the road sign?* (30)
- Say *Tick the things that help to keep us safe.* Check comprehension of *keep (someone) safe.* Learners discuss in pairs and choose which pictures to tick. Check answers. For each answer ask *Why does it keep us safe?* Learners say, e.g. *Because the cars have to stop when we use a pedestrian crossing.*

Key: Pictures 1, 3, 4, 5, 7

Extension Show a photo of a city street. Say *Look and remember. You have one minute.* Turn the photo over and ask learners questions, e.g. *Was there a bench in the photo? How many street lights were there?* You can make this a team game by asking groups a question each and keeping score.

3 Complete the poster.

- Ask learners if there are any information/safety posters in the school. Read through the poster with the class and check comprehension of *grown-up* and *carry.*
- Learners complete the poster individually, then compare answers in pairs.

  Fast finishers Write another tip for keeping safe in town using the imperative.

Key: 2 road/street 3 green 4 pedestrian crossing 5 hand 6 Don't

Activity Book, page 100

See pages TB120–132

Ending the lesson

- Give each learner two circles of paper or card. Ask them to design two signs – one with the word *YES* and one with the word *NO* on it. Give instructions, some correct, some incorrect, e.g. *Don't run across the road. Hold hands with a child when you cross the road.* Learners show their *YES* sign if the sentence is correct and the *NO* sign if it is wrong.

Learning outcomes By the end of the lesson, learners will be able to talk about being safe in town.

Recycled language *bench, cross (the road), hold (someone's) hand, litter bin, pavement, pedestrian crossing, road sign, safe, street lamp, traffic lights,* imperatives, *must/mustn't,* prepositions of place

Materials pieces of paper with instructions for a mime game (some safe actions and some not safe), e.g. *Run across the road. Hold hands when you cross the road. Look before you cross. Use your phone when you cross the road. Stop, look and listen. Kick a ball across the street,* worksheets / trip descriptions and advice from Mission Stages 1 and 2 lessons, digital Mission poster

Warm-up

- Draw a horizontal line on the board and say *This is a street. What shall I draw in the street?* Learners say the features they remember from the previous lesson. Ask questions as prompts, e.g. *Where do people put their litter? What if people want to sit down? Shall I draw lights? What kind of lights?* Draw the items learners suggest and ask *Where shall I draw the (bench)? Under a street lamp?*

  Stronger learners Give out paper and dictate a picture for learners to draw, e.g. *Draw a street. Draw four street lamps. Draw a bench under the second street lamp.* Learners compare pictures in pairs.

Presentation

- Ask learners to stand up. Ask *What do you have to do before you cross the road? There are three things.* Write the first letter of each verb on the board, if necessary (*S…, L…, L…*). Learners say *Stop, Look, Listen.* Mime walking on the spot, stopping, looking and listening before crossing the road. Learners copy.

  Extension Take learners outside, e.g. to the playground, to practise crossing the road safely.
- Say *Let's find out more about being safe.*

Pupil's Book, page 101

4 Are they being safe? Tick ✓ or cross ✗ the photos. Say why or why not.

- Say *Open your Pupil's Books at page 101.* Read the instructions. Learners look at the photos and talk about them in pairs.
- Check answers. Make sure learners explain why / why not. Encourage them to use *have to* and *must* or rephrase to include language from the unit.

Key: (possible answers) 1 (✗) You mustn't run across the road. 2 (✗) You mustn't play with balls in the street. 3 (✓) You have to hold a grown-up's hand when you cross the road. 4 (✓) You must use a pedestrian crossing. 5 (✓) You must walk on the pavement, not the road. 6 (✗) You mustn't use your mobile phone in the street.

- Point to picture 1. Ask *Why mustn't we run across the road?* Discuss as a class. Learners should understand that running is dangerous, even on a pedestrian crossing. You can fall and a car may not see you.

5 Make sentences about the photos in Activity 2 for a friend to guess.

- Read the instructions and the example. Make some more definitions for the class to guess, e.g. *We must put our litter in this.* (*Litter bin*) *These tell drivers what they must and mustn't do.* (*Road signs*)
- Learners make definitions in pairs.

  Extension Call a learner to the front and give him/her a piece of paper with an instruction for a mime (some of the actions should be safe and some not safe), e.g. *Run across the road.* The class call out *Safe* or *Not safe.* Ask a learner (or the learner who mimed) to make a sentence, e.g. *You mustn't run across the road.* Repeat with different sentences.

mission Stage 3

- Show the class the third stage of the Mission poster: *Write how to be safe on this trip.* Read the instructions and the example.
- Learners complete the next worksheet task in the Teacher's Resource Book (page 84). See teaching notes on TRB page 77.
- Alternatively, if you don't have the Teacher's Resource Book, learners write safety tips individually.
- Put learners into pairs to tell each other their safety tips.

Activity Book, page 101

See pages TB120–132

Activity Book, page 94

- Review *My unit goals.* Ask *How is your Mission?* Learners reflect and choose a smiley face for *My mission diary 3.*

Ending the lesson

- **SA** Go back to Stage 3 on the digital Mission poster. Add a tick to the 'Write how to be safe on this trip' stage. Use self-assessment (see Introduction).
- Give out a completion sticker.

4 Are they being safe? Tick ✓ or cross ✗ the photos. Say why or why not.

You mustn't run across the road.

1

2

3

4

5

6

5 Make sentences about the photos in Activity 2 for a friend to guess.

These help us at night.

Street lamps.

mission STAGE 3

Write how to be safe on this trip.

- Think about your trip and what you did there. How can people be safe on the same trip? Write ideas.
- Tell a friend.

You can wait on the pavement for the bus or use the pedestrian crossing to the car park. You mustn't run near the swimming pool.

My mission diary
Activity Book page 94

1 **Look at the pictures. How do you think the boy feels about going on the school bus? Why?**

3.32 Tom's first day on the school bus

Tom and his mum stood at the school bus stop.

A small red bus stopped in front of them. The doors opened.

'Go on,' Tom's mum said.

'I don't want to,' Tom said.

'But you have to!' she said kindly and gave him a little push.

The big doors closed.

Tom didn't believe what he saw.

The bus was very big inside and it had blue walls with flowers on them. There were lots of happy children sitting on the purple seats.

The friendly driver smiled.

'Good morning, Tom. Welcome. I'm Brenda and this is your bus buddy, Bruno!'

'Hi, Tom. This is your seat, next to mine,' Bruno said.

When Tom sat down, Brenda called, 'Put on your seatbelts everyone, please!'

Learning outcomes By the end of the lesson, learners will have read a fantasy story about taking the school bus for the first time.

New language *believe, buddy, driver, heard, (higher) and (higher), kindly, seat, seatbelt, thought*

Recycled language adjectives, colours, places in town, *catch (the bus), close, dream, first, funfair, get ready, late, open, push, put on, ride, smile, Don't worry, have to*, past simple, prepositions

Materials Places in town flashcards, audio

Warm-up

- Play 'Noughts and crosses'. Put a grid on the board, three columns by three rows (nine squares). Divide learners into two groups (noughts or crosses). Put a Places in town flashcard in each square. To win their square, learners make a sentence with the word in the square, e.g. *I have to go to the market to get some fruit.* When they make a correct sentence, replace the flashcard with their symbol.
- The first group to make a row, horizontally, vertically or diagonally, wins.

  Alternative Write infinitives of verbs with irregular past forms in the grid, instead of flashcards. Include verbs from the story (*stand, give, see, sit, go, come*). Learners make sentences in the past simple to win their square.

Presentation

- Ask learners *How did you get to school today? Who walked to school? Who came by car? Who caught the bus?* Ask learners who caught the bus *Where did you catch the bus? Is the bus stop near your house? Did you have to buy a ticket? Did you sit with your friends?*
- Write *school bus* on the board and explain that in some countries there are buses especially for taking children to school.
- Say *Let's read a story about a school bus.*

Pupil's Book, pages 102 and 103

1 Look at the pictures. How do you think the boy feels about going on the school bus? Why?

- Say *Open your Pupil's Books at page 102. Look at the pictures.* Use picture 1 to teach *driver* and picture 2 to teach *seat* and *seatbelt.* Ask *How do you think the boy feels about going on the school bus?* Learners guess. (*Excited, worried, happy*) Don't confirm answers at this stage, but ask learners for their reasons.

3.32 Tom's first day on the school bus

- Read the title and check comprehension of *first day*.
- Look at the first picture and ask *Who is the woman waiting with the boy?* Learners guess. (*His mum*)
- Say *Let's read and listen to the first part of the story.* Play the audio. Pause after *what he saw.*
- Ask *Why did Tom's mum give him a little push?* (*Because he didn't want to get on the bus*) Ask *Why didn't he want to get on?* Learners share ideas, e.g. *Because it was his first day / He didn't know the other children.*

  Track 3.32
  See story on Pupil's Book pages 102–103
- Say *Read and listen to the next part of the story.* Play the audio. Pause after *everyone, please!* Explain the meaning of *believe* and ask *Why didn't Tom believe what he saw?* (*Because the bus was big and the colours were different*) *What did the driver do?* (*She smiled.*) *Who was Bruno?* (*He was Tom's 'bus buddy'.*) Explain that *buddy* means *friend.* Ask *What do you think a 'bus buddy' does?* (*Makes friends with people who are new*) *Where was Tom's seat?* (*Next to Bruno*) *What did the children have to do when they sat down?* (*Put on their seatbelts*)
- Play the next part of the story. Pause after *catch the bus.* Ask *What did Tom see from the bus?* (*His town – the sports centre and the market*) *What did Tom hear?* (*His mother say 'You have to get up.'*) Check that learners realise that *heard* is the past of *hear.*
- Play the rest of the story. Ask *What did Tom think when he woke up?* (*It was a dream.*) Explain that *thought* is the past of *think.* Ask *Who did he see on the bus?* (*Brenda and Bruno*)

  Extension Play the whole story again, without pauses, for learners to listen and read.

Activity Book, page 102

See pages TB120–132

Ending the lesson

- Write sentence halves on the board. Learners match in pairs.

1 Tom stood	*a) his town below.*
2 Tom sat	*b) it was a dream.*
3 Brenda said	*c) at the bus stop.*
4 Tom saw	*d) on the bus the next day.*
5 Tom thought	*e) 'Put on your seatbelts.'*
6 Brenda and Bruno were	*f) next to Bruno.*

- Check answers: 1 c, 2 f, 3 e, 4 a, 5 b, 6 d.

Learning outcomes By the end of the lesson, learners will have thought about being optimistic.

New language *optimistic*

Recycled language language from the story

Materials a bright, happy picture and a grey, sad picture, paper, coloured pens or pencils, audio

Social and Emotional Skill: Being optimistic

- After reading the story, ask learners *What was Tom's dream about? (His first day on the school bus) Was it a happy dream? (Yes) Why? (The walls on the bus had flowers on them, the children were happy, the driver was friendly and Tom had a bus buddy.) Did Tom's dream help him? What do you think?*
- Say *Yes, the bus was a happy bus and the people were friendly. Tom was happy to see Bruno and Brenda.*
- Ask *How do you feel when you do something for the first time?* Draw faces on the board or write the words (e.g. *happy, sad, excited, anxious, worried, shy, surprised, angry*). Invite learners to choose one or more and to say why they feel that way.
- Show two illustrations or photos – one is a happy, optimistic-looking one with bright colours and the other looks sad and grey. Ask learners how the pictures make them feel.
- Explain that it's important to be optimistic about things. Being optimistic means you feel excited and happy and you think about all the good things that can happen. Being pessimistic means you feel worried and scared and you think about all the bad things that can happen.
- Say *Let's think about the good things*. Hand out paper and the learners draw a happy, optimistic picture of something they do. Point out that they need to use bright, happy colours.

Warm-up

- Ask learners to stand up. Give instructions for learners to mime, e.g. *Stand at the bus stop. Look at your watch. Look for the bus. Here it is! The bus doors are opening. Get on the bus. Show your ticket. Sit down in your seat. Put on your seatbelt. Wait for the bus to stop. The doors are opening. Get off the bus.*

Pupil's Book, pages 102 and 103

- Say *Open your Pupil's Books at pages 102 and 103.* Play the audio. Learners read and listen to the story again.

  Track 3.32

  See story on Pupil's Book pages 102–103

2 How does Tom feel when he gets on the bus at the end of the story? Why?

- Read the question and then the last section of the story from *'Do I have to catch the bus, Mum?'* Ask *How does Tom feel after he wakes up? (Worried) Why does he feel better when the bus comes? (Because he sees Brenda and Bruno and he thinks that he knows them)*
- Say *Let's act out the story.* Summarise the story and mime. Encourage learners to copy. Say *Tom and his mum waited for the school bus.* Mime waiting at a bus stop. Say *Tom didn't want to go. His mum gave him a little push.* Mime gently pushing someone. Say *Tom didn't believe what he saw on the bus.* Act being surprised/amazed. Say *Brenda the bus driver was friendly. She said 'Welcome Tom!'* Mime waving and smile. Say *Bruno was Tom's bus buddy. He said 'This is your seat.'* Mime showing someone to their seat. Say *Tom put on his seatbelt.* Mime putting on a seatbelt. Say *The bus went higher and higher. Tom looked at the town below.* Mime looking down, amazed. Say *Then Tom woke up.* Mime waking up. Say *He thought it was a dream.* Look sad/shocked. Say *He didn't want to catch the bus.* Shake your head and look worried. Say *When the bus came, he saw Brenda and Bruno from his dream. He wasn't worried any more.* Mime waving and getting on a bus, happily.

  Extension In groups of four (Tom, Mum, Brenda, Bruno), learners act the last part of the story (from when Tom's mum wakes him up).

3 Talk with a friend.

- Learners talk about their first day at school. Read the speech bubbles. Ask the class *How did you feel?* Write key words on the board, e.g. *excited, worried, anxious, shy.* Monitor and support.

Activity Book, page 103

See pages TB120–132

Ending the lesson

- **SA** Use self-assessment to see how well learners think they understand the story. See Introduction.

The bus went higher and higher. Tom saw his town below. It got smaller and smaller.

'Oh look! There's the sports centre! And there's the market!' he said.

The bus went up and down like a ride at the funfair.

After a few minutes, Brenda said, 'OK, get ready. We're coming down to the bus stop.'

At that moment, Tom heard his mum say, 'Tom! Tom! You have to get up. We don't want to be late. You have to catch the bus.'

'Oh no!', Tom thought. 'It was all a dream.'

'Do I have to catch the bus, Mum?' Tom asked.

'Yes, you do. But don't worry!' his mum answered.

Finally, the school bus came. It was small and red. The doors opened.

Tom looked up and saw Brenda from his dream.

'Good morning, Tom. Welcome. I'm Brenda and this is your bus buddy, Bruno!'

'Brenda! Bruno!' Tom said and he got on the bus.

2 How does Tom feel when he gets on the bus at the end of the story? Why?

3 Talk with a friend.

Tell me about the first day you went to school.

It was fun. Everyone was very nice.

1 3.33 **Listen. Who's talking? Circle the correct picture.**

1 
2 
3 

2 3.34 **Listen and point as you hear each place. Listen again. Where's Pat's dad now? Tick ✓ the box.**

A ☐

B ☐

C ☐

3 3.35 **Listen and look at Maya's tick. Why is her answer wrong? What was her mistake?**

1 Who is Grace?

A ☑

B ☐

C ☐

4 3.36 **Listen and tick ✓ the box.**

2 What clothes does Mary need today?

A ☐

B ☐

C ☐

3 What does Nick do at the weekend?

A ☐

B ☐

C ☐

Wait and think before you tick a box. Listen again and check.

Learning outcomes By the end of the lesson, learners will have listened and found the correct picture by listening for detail (A1 Movers Listening Part 4).

Test skills Listening for specific information of various kinds

Recycled language clothes, colours, countryside, food and drink, places in town, *bookshop*, present continuous

Materials practice paper for Movers Listening Part 4 (optional), audio

Warm-up

- Each learner chooses a word from the unit and spells it out to their partner. Their partner writes it down, says the word and explains what it means.

Presentation

- Say *Let's practise for a listening exam.* Show the Movers Listening Part 4 paper. Say *In Part 4 there are groups of three pictures. Each group has a question above it. You need to read and listen and then choose the correct picture.*

Pupil's Book, page 104

1 3.33 Listen. Who's talking? Circle the correct picture.

- Say *Open your Pupil's Books at page 104.* Read the instructions and play the audio. Explain that thinking about who is speaking can help them understand.

Track 3.33

Pat: Mum, where's Dad? Is he at the market?
Mum: No, he isn't.

Key: Picture 2

2 3.34 Listen and point as you hear each place. Listen again. Where's Pat's dad now? Tick ✓ the box.

- Point to each picture and ask *Where's this?* (*A road, a market, a shop*) Say *Listen and point as you hear each place.* Play the audio. Check comprehension of *bookshop*.

Track 3.34

Pat: Mum, where's Dad? Is he at the market?
Mum: No, he isn't. He's buying a map.
Pat: In the bookshop?
Mum: That's right.
Pat: Good – because then we can drive to that village in the mountains!

- Ask *Where's Pat's dad now?* Play the audio again. Explain that all three places are mentioned, but only one is correct.

Key: Picture C

3 3.35 Listen and look at Maya's tick. Why is her answer wrong? What was her mistake?

- Read the instructions. Play the audio.

Track 3.35

1 Who is Grace?
Girl: Look, Uncle Bill! There's my friend Grace.
Uncle: Is she the girl with the glass of milk?
Girl: No, she's got a glass of orange juice. She's putting on her coat, look.
Uncle: Oh, yes. I can see her now. Let's go and say hello.
Girl: OK!

- Ask *Which is the correct answer?* Play the audio again.
- Say *Don't tick the first thing you hear. Wait until the end.*

Key: Maya heard the word milk and ticked picture A. The correct answer is B.

4 3.36 Listen and tick ✓ the box.

- Give learners time to read the questions and look at the pictures. Play the audio twice. Make sure learners have put a tick in one box only in each row. Explain that if they tick two answers it is marked wrong in the exam.

Track 3.36

2 What clothes does Mary need today?
Woman: Can you help Mary get dressed, please?
Girl: Yes. How about this red sweater?
Woman: No, it's hot today. A dress is better.
Girl: How about this purple one?
Woman: That's a good idea. And … a pair of white socks too, please.

3 What does Nick do at the weekend?
Boy: Do you have to work in the café at weekends, Nick?
Nick: No, but I make a lot of soup at the weekend!
Boy: Why? Have you got a big family?
Nick: No! But I go and help in the town centre. We give soup to people who haven't got a home. Why don't you help me next weekend?

Key: 2 Picture C 3 Picture A

- Point to the monkey at the bottom of the page and read. Learners must use a tick in the box, not a cross.

Activity Book, page 104

See pages TB120–132

Ending the lesson

- Ask *Which names did you hear in today's lesson? Can you remember?* Divide the class into teams to suggest names.

Learning outcomes By the end of the lesson, learners will have revised the language in the unit and presented their review to the class.

Recycled language unit language

Materials word cards with infinitives of verbs from the unit (*bring, buy, choose, come, draw, drive, feed, find, give, hear, hide, lose, ride, see, sit, sleep, stand, take, tell, think, wear*), a bag or box (optional), worksheets/reviews from Mission Stages 1–3 lessons, a globe / world map (optional), coloured pens or pencils, dice and counters (for Activity Book game), digital Mission poster

Warm-up

- Learners sit in a circle. Put word cards with irregular verb infinitives from the unit into a bag or box. Take out a card, show it to the class and make a sentence with the verb in the past simple to start a story, e.g. *Last week I lost something very important.* Stick the card on the board.
- The next learner in the circle takes a card and makes another sentence with the new verb, trying to continue the story, e.g. *It came from England.* Stick the verb card on the board next to the first card. Continue in this way, making a story as a class. Repeat previous sentences, point to the cards on the board as prompts and help with new vocabulary, as necessary.

  Alternative Use word cards with the past tense forms, rather than the infinitives.

  Extra support Learners choose the word cards but you make the story. They repeat the sentences after you / add ideas and act out the story, if appropriate.

  Extension Practise counting around the class from 1 to 100 (e.g. in twos, threes, fives, tens). Dictate a list of eight numbers between 1 and 100. Learners write them and then compare in pairs. Write the numbers on the board for learners to check. Ask volunteers to read the numbers back. Learners can do the same dictation activity in pairs.

Pupil's Book, page 105

mission in action!

Show your review to the class.

- Point to the Mission box or show learners the last stage of the digital Mission poster. Say *Let's put our Mission in action!* Say *Show your review to the class.*
- Read the instructions and speech bubbles. Give learners time to practise talking about their review using their worksheets/reviews from the Mission stages. If there is time, learners could draw more pictures to illustrate their trip.
- Learners take turns to present their review to the class or to a group.
- Display the reviews around the classroom. Learners walk around and read the reviews. They choose which place they would like to visit.
- Learners sit down again. Ask different learners to say which place they want to visit and what they liked about the review / what helped them to decide.

Self-assessment

- **SA** Say *Did you like our 'Write a trip review' Mission? Think and draw a face.* Learners draw a happy face, neutral face or sad face and then hold it up in the air.
- Say *Tell me two things you learnt during this Mission.* Learners talk in pairs and then tell you examples.
- Say *Our next Mission is 'Plan a holiday world tour.'* Explain the meaning of *world tour.* If possible, show a globe or world map and say *A world tour is a trip around the world.* Ask *What countries would you like to visit on a world tour?*
- Ask *How can we do better in the next Mission?* Learners suggest ideas, e.g. *We can speak more English when we work in groups.*

Activity Book, page 105

See pages TB120–132

Activity Book, page 94

- Review *My unit goals.* Ask *How was your Mission?* Learners reflect and choose a smiley face for *My mission diary* the final stage.
- Point to the sunflower. Learners read the 'can do' statements and tick them if they agree they have achieved them. They colour each leaf green if they are very confident or orange if they think they need more practice.
- Point to the word stack sign. Ask learners to look back at the unit and find at least five new words they have learnt. They write them in their word stack.

Ending the lesson

- **SA** Go back to the completion stage on the digital Mission poster. Add a tick or invite a learner to do it. Use self-assessment (see Introduction).
- Give out a completion sticker.
- Tell learners *You have finished your Mission! Well done!*

mission in action!

Show your review to the class.

My mission diary
Activity Book page 94

★ Tell the class about your trip.

I went to a water park with my mum, dad, uncle and cousins. We went by bus.

★ Show your picture and talk about it.

This ride was my favourite part. I came down very fast!

★ Tell people how to be safe on this trip.

Wait on the pavement for the bus or use the pedestrian crossing to the car park.

You mustn't run near the swimming pool.

★ Look at the reviews. Find a new place to go.

9 A big change

1 Watch the video. Draw how you feel about these activities. Add one more.

mission Plan a holiday world tour

In this unit I will:

1. Talk about different kinds of holidays.
2. Choose a kind of holiday for a class tour.
3. Write our group's idea for the class tour.
4. Put our group's idea on the holiday world tour map.

Unit 9 learning outcomes

In Unit 9, learners learn to:

- use adjectives to talk about opinions and feelings
- use comparative adjectives with *more*
- talk about a new adventure
- use superlative adjectives with *most*
- learn about natural and manmade wonders of the world
- read a counting poem and think about taking pride in their work

Materials video, coloured pens or pencils, digital Mission poster, a globe / world map (optional), a copy of the Mission worksheet (Teacher's Resource Book page 94), Friendly family flashcards

Self-assessment

- **SA** Say *Open your Pupil's Books at page 106. Look at the pictures.* Indicate people and items in the pictures and ask questions using language from the unit or the level, e.g. *What's he/she doing? What's he/she wearing? Who's under the water? Which is more interesting?* Use self-assessment (see Introduction). Say *OK. Let's learn.*

Warm-up

- Read the title and check comprehension of *change*. Give examples of a big change, e.g. moving to a new house or school, a new baby brother/sister arriving.
- Ask learners to think about one big change in their life. They say what happened in pairs. Monitor and help with new language. Learners share ideas with the class. Ask questions, e.g. *When did you move house? Where did you move from? How old were you? How did you feel?*

Pupil's Book, page 106

1 Watch the video. Draw how you feel about these activities. Add one more.

- Say *In this unit we're talking about Adventures.* Say *Let's watch the video.* To introduce the topic of the unit, play the video.
- Draw simple emojis for *happy, sad, scared* and *excited* on the board. Write the words below the pictures. Mime each one and say, e.g. *It's my birthday! I feel happy.* Learners copy the mime.
- Say *Show me (sad).* Learners mime.
- Point to the first activity and the 'scared' emoji. Ask *How do you feel about climbing?* Learners say/mime.
- Learners draw an emoji for each activity. They draw one more activity of their choice.
- Ask different learners *How do you feel about (birdwatching)? Show me.* Learners show their emoji and mime.

mission Plan a holiday world tour

- Point to the Mission box or the digital Mission poster and say *This is our Mission.*
- Say *Plan a holiday world tour.* Check learners remember the meaning of *world tour.* If possible, show a globe or map and gesture around the world, saying *Nowadays we can travel around the world. Some people go on a world tour for a holiday. Pop stars also go on world tours.*
- Say *Point to number 1. Talk about different kinds of holidays.* Ask learners for examples of places to go on holiday, e.g. the beach, the mountains. Ask *Where did you last go on holiday? What did you like best about it?*
- Say *Point to number 2. Choose a kind of holiday for a class tour.* Explain that learners are going to work in groups to talk about their ideas, and then vote for the best holiday. If you have the Teacher's Resource Book, show the worksheet they will use for recording and scoring the ideas.
- Say *Point to number 3. Write our group's idea for the class tour.* Tell learners they are going to do research and work on their group's idea for the class tour.
- Say *The last stage is 'Put our group's idea on the holiday world tour map.'* Explain that learners are going to make a large map with all the ideas on.
- Say *This is our Mission.* Go through the stages of the Mission again.
- For ideas on monitoring and assessment, see Introduction.

Activity Book, page 106

My unit goals

- Help learners to complete the unit goals. See notes on page TB6.
- You can go back to these unit goals at the end of each Mission stage during the unit and review them.

Ending the lesson

- Choose a Friendly family flashcard and hold it so learners can't see. Talk about the character with comparatives and superlatives, e.g. *He's got smaller glasses than Jim. He's the oldest person in the Friendly Family.* Learners guess. Repeat with different characters.
- Display the cards. Learners play the game in pairs.

Learning outcomes By the end of the lesson, learners will be able to use adjectives to describe opinions and feelings.

New language *afraid, boring, dangerous, difficult, easy, exciting, frightened, hungry, surprised, thirsty, tired, circus, net*

Recycled language adjectives, *asleep, catch, enjoy, have a picnic, lemonade, lunch, sun, ticket, trip, Would you like to go?*

Materials Adjectives for opinions and feelings flashcards, audio, video

Warm-up

- Say *Show me a happy face!* Learners act being happy. Repeat with *sad*, *angry* and *surprised*.
- Act one of the emotions and learners guess, e.g. *You're sad.* In pairs, learners take turns to act and guess.

Presentation

- Teach the new adjectives for opinions and feelings using mime, actions and the flashcards. Explain that *afraid* and *frightened* mean the same thing.
- Say an adjective. Learners do the mime/action.
- Ask, e.g. *Is riding a bike easy or difficult? When do you feel hungry/thirsty/tired?*

Pupil's Book, page 107

1 3.37 3.38 Listen and point. Then listen and number.

- Say *Open your Pupil's Books at page 107. Who can you see? What are they doing?* (*Having a picnic*) *What's Jim looking at?* (*A poster*) *Can you see the circus on the poster? People are watching the acrobats.* Write *circus* on the board.
- Ask *Where's the small tractor? Can you find it?*
- Read the caption. Ask if any learners know Cambridge.
- Say *Listen and point.* Play Track 3.37. Learners point to the labelled parts of the picture.

Tracks 3.37 and 3.38

(1) The Friendly family are on a day trip to Cambridge. It's hot and sunny and they're having a picnic.

Mrs Friendly:	Look, children! There's a circus in town. Would you like to go?
Jenny:	Yes, please! Look at that girl's face. She's really surprised!
(2) Mr Friendly:	Well, we've got tickets for this afternoon.
Mrs Friendly:	Now you're surprised!
Jim:	But look at that boy there. He's frightened.
(3) Mr Friendly:	Hmm, yes. I think that's because it's dangerous.
(4) Jim:	Well, I'm afraid … and it's only a photo.
(5) Jenny:	It's a dangerous jump, but there's a net to catch them.
Jim:	They need it! It's difficult to catch someone. It isn't easy!
(6) Mrs Friendly:	But look, those people are enjoying it.
Mr Friendly:	And Grandpa isn't frightened. He thinks it's boring. He's asleep!
Grandpa:	I'm not asleep. I'm tired.
(7) Grandpa:	And I don't think the circus is boring.
Grandma:	No! The circus is exciting! It isn't boring!
(8) Jim:	Oh, all right. Let's go.
Mr Friendly:	Mmm. I'm hungry. When's lunch?
Grandma:	Shall I get the picnic out?
(9) Mrs Friendly:	And shall I get some cold lemonade? Is everyone thirsty?
Jenny:	Yes! I think we all are! It's hot in the sun.

- Say *Now listen and number.* Play Track 3.38. Check answers.
- Ask *Who's afraid?* (*Jim*) *Why is he afraid?* (*He thinks the circus is dangerous.*) *Who's tired?* (*Grandpa*) *Who thinks the circus is exciting?* (*Grandma Friendly*)

Key: 2 frightened 3 dangerous 4 afraid 5 difficult, easy 6 tired 7 exciting, boring 8 hungry 9 thirsty

- Say *Look at the picture for one minute and remember.* Time a minute. Say *Close your books.* Learners work in groups of three to write as many sentences as they can about the picture, e.g. *Mr Friendly's hungry. Grandpa's sitting in a chair.*

2 3.39 Say the chant.

- Play the audio or video. Learners point and chant.

Track 3.39

Easy, difficult,
Exciting, boring,
Hungry, thirsty, tired.

Afraid, frightened,
Dangerous, surprised,
Hungry, thirsty, tired. [x2]

3 3.40 Listen and write the words.

- Play the audio. Pause for learners to write each word.

Track 3.40

1 t-h-i-r-s-t-y
2 b-o-r-i-n-g
3 a-f-r-a-i-d
4 t-i-r-e-d
5 e-x-c-i-t-i-n-g
6 h-u-n-g-r-y
7 s-u-r-p-r-i-s-e-d
8 d-i-f-f-i-c-u-l-t
9 d-a-n-g-e-r-o-u-s
10 f-r-i-g-h-t-e-n-e-d

Activity Book, page 107

See pages TB120–132

Ending the lesson

- **SA** Show the adjective flashcards. Ask *Do you know the words?* Use self-assessment (see Introduction). Learners show how they feel.

1 3.37 3.38 **Listen and point. Then listen and number.**

The Friendly family are on a day trip to Cambridge. It's hot and sunny and they're having a picnic.
DIVERSICUS
She's really **surprised**. 1
He's **frightened**.
It's **dangerous**.
It's **difficult** to catch someone. It isn't **easy**.
I'm **hungry**.
The circus is **exciting**. It isn't **boring**.
I'm **afraid**.
I'm **tired**.
Is everyone **thirsty**?

2 3.39 **Say the chant.**

3 3.40 **Listen and write the words.**

The Friendly Farm

3.41

1
We need to talk to you. We want to work for Diversicus.
Oh, the circus! Oh, I don't know …
I'm not surprised. I think your mother's more surprised than me.
2
Listen to this: the family want to be in Diversicus, the circus!
The circus is more exciting than the farm!
Farmer Friendly! Our Farmer Friendly … in the circus?!
3
No, only Mr and Mrs Friendly, and there's a circus school for the children.
Jumping and catching are dangerous!
But Mr Friendly's a cook and Mrs Friendly writes and plays music.
4
The beautiful costumes … circus clothes are more beautiful than these.
Yes, they are! I want to be in a circus, too! Shelly, get the best clothes. Harry, put on your hat. Let's make better costumes!
5
Welcome to the Friendly Circus. Today we've got …
Shall I sing for everyone?
We've got the brilliant, the brave Cameron Cat! He isn't afraid! Watch this!
6
And now, more difficult, more exciting and more dangerous than Diversicus, we've got Rocky and Harry!
Look at us, Mum! We're in the Friendly Circus! I'm riding Harry. I'm not frightened!
I am! I can't look!

1 3.42 **Who says it? Listen and say the name.**

Learning outcomes By the end of the lesson, learners will be able to understand comparative adjectives with *more.*

New language *brave*, comparatives with long adjectives: *more (surprised) than*

Recycled language adjectives, *better, the best, catch, children, circus, clothes, cook* (n), *costume, farm, jump, ride* (v), *school, sing, want to, work* (v), *write/play music, Shall I … ?*

Materials Adjectives for opinions and feelings flashcards, word cards, pictures for comparison (see Presentation) (optional), audio, video

Warm-up

- Review the new adjectives using mime and flashcards.
- Write the adjectives on the board or display word cards. Say *Some words describe the way people feel. Which are those? You can say 'I'm … '* (*afraid, frightened, hungry, surprised, thirsty, tired*). *Some words usually describe things, sports, activities. You can say 'It's … '* (*boring, dangerous, difficult, easy, exciting*). Write *I'm …* and *It's …* as column headings. Put the adjectives in the correct columns.
- Show the flashcards. Learners make sentences, e.g. *She's thirsty. It's dangerous.*
- **SA** Use self-assessment to check how well learners think they understand the vocabulary. See Introduction.

Presentation

- Show pictures or use items in the classroom to present comparisons with *more*, e.g. *This house is more beautiful than that one. Watching TV is more boring than going skating.*
- Then hold up the pictures and ask, e.g. *Which house is more beautiful?*
- Explain that we make comparisons using *more* for adjectives with two syllables which finish with a consonant sound (*afraid, frightened, surprised, boring*) and for all adjectives with three or more syllables (*beautiful, difficult, dangerous, exciting*). We also use *more* with *tired*.

  Extra support Write adjectives in groups – two syllables and three syllables. Practise pronunciation, encouraging learners to clap along with the syllables. Make sure they focus on the sound not spelling for *frightened* and *surprised*.

Pupil's Book, page 108

3.41 The Friendly Farm song

- Play the introductory song at the beginning of the cartoon story. Learners listen and sing.

  Track 3.41
  See The Friendly Farm song on page TB5

3.41 The Friendly Farm

- Say *Open your Pupil's Books at page 108.* Point to picture 1 and ask *How does Grandma feel?* Ask learners to guess what the Friendlys are talking about. Say *Look at the other pictures. What are the animals doing?* (*Dressing up / jumping*)
- Ask *Why does Henrietta say 'I can't look'?* Write the question on the board. Play the audio or video. Check answers. (*Because she's afraid/frightened. Because Rocky's doing something dangerous*) Say *Cameron is doing something dangerous but he isn't afraid. He's brave.*

  Track 3.41
  The Friendly Farm song + see cartoon on Pupil's Book page 108
- Play the audio or video again. Pause after each picture and ask questions: 1: *What do Mr and Mrs Friendly want to do?* (*Work for a circus*) Write *Diversicus* on the board and explain that it's the circus from the poster. Ask *Who is more surprised, Grandpa or Grandma?* (*Grandma*) 2: *Who thinks the circus is more exciting than the farm?* (*Rocky*) 3: *Are Grandpa and Grandma going to the circus too?* (*No, they aren't.*) *Why is Shelly surprised?* (*Because Mr Friendly is a cook and Mrs Friendly writes and plays music*) 4: *What does Rocky want to make?* (*Better costumes*) 5: *What does Shelly want to do?* (*Sing*) *Is Cameron afraid?* (*No, he's brave.*) 6: *Who's more difficult, more exciting and more dangerous than Diversicus?* (*Rocky and Harry*)

1 3.42 Who says it? Listen and say the name.

- Play the audio and pause for learners to say the name.

Track 3.42

1	Rocky:	We've got the brilliant, the brave Cameron Cat!
2	Grandpa:	I'm not surprised. I think your mother's more surprised than me.
3	Henrietta:	I can't look!
4	Shelly:	… circus clothes are more beautiful than these.
5	Rocky:	The circus is more exciting than the farm!
6	Gracie:	… more difficult, more exciting and more dangerous than Diversicus …
7	Mr Friendly:	We want to work for Diversicus.
8	Gracie:	Jumping and catching are dangerous!

Key: See names in audioscript

Activity Book, page 108

See pages TB120–132

Ending the lesson

- **SA** Repeat the self-assessment to see how well learners think they understand the vocabulary. Is there any change?

Learning outcomes By the end of the lesson, learners will be able to make comparisons with *more*.

New language *beautiful: Circus clothes are more beautiful than these. exciting: The circus is more exciting than the farm! dangerous: And now, more dangerous than Diversicus …*

Recycled language adjectives, days of the week, free time activities, holidays

Materials paper, coloured pens or pencils, Adjectives for opinions and feelings flashcards, audio, digital Mission poster

Warm-up

- Give out paper. Say *Draw a picture of a beautiful place.* Draw a picture yourself.
- Show your picture and say *This is* (*name*). *It's a beautiful place. Who has a more beautiful place?* Learners show their pictures and say *I think* (*name*) *is more beautiful than* (*name*).

Presentation

- Call two learners to the front. Show them both the same flashcard (afraid, frightened, hungry, surprised, thirsty or tired). They mime. Learners guess, e.g. *They're thirsty.*
- Ask the learners at the front to repeat the mime. Then ask *Who is more (surprised/afraid/frightened/tired)? Who is hungrier/thirstier?* Learners say, e.g. *Pablo's more surprised.*

Pupil's Book, page 109

3.43 Gracie's Grammar

- Say *Open your Pupil's Books at page 109.* Point to Gracie's Grammar box. Write the sentences on the board.
- Play the audio. Pause for learners to repeat.

Track 3.43

See Pupil's Book page 109

- Remind learners when we use *more* with adjectives.

1 3.44 Listen and stick. Then look, read and write.

- Say *Mary's talking to her friend.* Point to each sticker and ask *Where is she? Who is she with? What's she doing?*
- Play the audio. Learners point to the correct sticker.
- Play the audio again. Learners stick the stickers next to the correct day. Check and ask, e.g. *Where was Mary on (Thursday)? Was she (frightened)?*

Track 3.44

1 Boy: Hi, Mary. Did you have a good week, last week?
Mary: It wasn't bad. Saturday was the best day. I watched a DVD with my mum. It was called *Scary Monsters.*
Boy: Were you frightened?
Mary: I wasn't, but my mum was. She was more frightened than me!

2 Boy: What did you do on Thursday?
Mary: I had a really difficult test in the morning. It was terrible.
Boy: I think your school's more difficult than mine.
Mary: Erm, I don't know, but I was very tired in the evening. I was more tired than my younger sister, and she's only five!

3 Mary: Friday was better because I got the mark for my test.
Boy: Hmm. Were you afraid?
Mary: Yes, I was, but I was very surprised because I got a good mark.
Boy: Oh?
Mary: Yes, I was more surprised than my teacher. She was very happy.

4 Boy: What about Sunday? What did you do yesterday?
Mary: Dad and I went to the cinema.
Boy: Was the film good?
Mary: No, it was really boring. Dad was asleep after 20 minutes.
Boy: Was it more boring than doing your homework?
Mary: Yes, I think it was!

- Point to the example. Say *Now look, read and write.*

Key: 2 more tired 3 more frightened 4 more surprised

mission Stage 1

- Point to the Mission box or show learners the first stage of the digital Mission poster: *Talk about different kinds of holidays.*
- Learners work individually to think of a type of holiday they like and what they do there. Monitor and support.
- In pairs, learners talk about their ideas. Encourage them to make comparisons.

Activity Book, page 109

See pages TB120–132

Activity Book, page 106

- Review *My unit goals.* Ask *How is your Mission?* Learners reflect and choose a smiley face for *My mission diary 1.*

Ending the lesson

- **SA** Go back to Stage 1 on the digital Mission poster. Say *We talked about different kinds of holiday.* Add a tick to the 'We talked about … ' stage. Use self-assessment (see Introduction).
- Give out a completion sticker.

3.43 Gracie's Grammar

beautiful: Circus clothes are **more beautiful than** these.
exciting: The circus is **more exciting than** the farm!
dangerous: And now, **more dangerous than** Diversicus …

1 3.44 **Listen and stick. Then look, read and write.**

Thursday

Friday

Saturday

Sunday

1 The film on **Sunday** was more boring than doing my homework.
2 On **Thursday** evening I was ____ ____ than my little sister.
3 Mum was ____ ____ than me by **Saturday's** DVD!
4 At school on **Friday**, I was ____ ____ than my teacher.

mission STAGE 1

Talk about different kinds of holidays.

- Write what kind of holidays you like.
- Tell a friend.

I like going to the beach. I look for interesting shells and I love going for a swim.

I think holidays in the mountains are more exciting.

My mission diary
Activity Book page 106

1 3.45 Listen and circle. Then sing the song.

The 1 **email** / **DVD** came this morning.
We've got the jobs. We've got the jobs.
Let's all go on an 2 **apartment** / **adventure**!
A world tour! A world tour!

Let's get 3 **busy** / **hungry**. There's a lot to do.
4 **Call** / **Text** our family. Email our friends.
Let's get busy. There's a lot to do.
Let's get our 5 **books** / **blankets**
for the circus school.
On a world tour! On a world tour!
On a world tour round the world!

We can travel 6 **round** / **above** the world.
We've got the jobs. We've got the jobs.
Let's all look at this map.
An exciting trip!

On a world tour! ...

2 Ask and answer questions about the song.

Who What Where Why

Who's sending a text?

Grandma.

Why are the Friendly family happy?

Because Mr and Mrs Friendly have got the jobs.

Would you like to travel round the world?
Which countries would you like to visit?

Learning outcomes By the end of the lesson, learners will have practised the language through song.

New language *adventure, busy, email* (n, v), *round (the world), (send a) text, text* (v), *travel* (v), *world*

Recycled language adjectives, *apartment, blanket, book, call, circus, DVD, family, friend, job, map, school, tour, trip, have got, Let's …,* questions with *who, what, where* and *why*

Materials Animals and Free time activities flashcards (optional), A new adventure flashcards, globe / world map (optional), audio, video

Warm-up

- Write *beautiful, boring, dangerous, difficult* and *exciting* on the board. Tell learners to write as many sentences as they can with the comparative form of the adjectives. Give some examples, e.g. *Mountains are more beautiful than beaches.* Put them into pairs and time five minutes. Monitor and support.
- Ask a pair to read one of their sentences. Write it on the board. Ask other pairs in turn for their (different) sentences and write them up. Continue until you have ten sentences on the board.
- Ask pairs to put a cross next to their sentences if they are on the board. See which pair has the greatest number of original sentences. Ask *Did you use all the adjectives?*
  Extra support Stick flashcards of animals and free time activities on the board as prompts.

Presentation

- Show a globe or world map. Remind learners that their Mission is to plan a world tour. Write *world tour* on the board.
- Say *People travel round the world. How can you travel?* Learners give examples (*car, plane, train,* etc.). Check comprehension of *travel* and write it on the board. Say *Travelling round the world is an adventure.* Learners give more examples of adventures. Write *adventure* on the board.
- Say *When people are travelling round the world it's a long way. They don't see their friends and family for a long time. How can they send messages? How can they talk to their friends and family?* (*Call, email, text*) Write the ways of communicating on the board.
- Say *There's lots to do before you go on a trip. What do you have to do?* Learners give examples (e.g. *buy tickets, pack suitcases, find places to stay*). Say *When you have a lot to do, you're busy.* Mime being busy. Write *busy* on the board.
- Show the flashcards. Learners say the words.
- **SA** Use self-assessment to check how well learners think they understand the vocabulary. See Introduction.

Pupil's Book, page 110

1 3.45 Listen and circle. Then sing the song.

- Say *Open your Pupil's Books at page 110.* Say *The Friendly family are busy. Why do you think they're busy?* Ask for learners' ideas and talk about what they can see in the picture.
- Say *Listen and circle.* Point to the pairs of words in the song. Play the audio or video. Check answers. Teach/ Revise *blanket.*

Track 3.45

Rocky: I'm Rocky-Doodle-Doo and here's our song for today: *A world tour*

See song on Pupil's Book page 110

Key: 2 adventure 3 busy 4 Text 5 books 6 round

- Learners stand up. Practise the song in sections.
- Play the audio or video again. Learners sing and do actions (reading an email, a circling gesture for world tour, being busy / packing books / texting, etc.).

3.46 **Extension** Once learners are confidently singing along, try singing the karaoke version as a class.

2 Ask and answer questions about the song.

- Read the instructions and examples. Write a prompt on the board, e.g. *Where can / travel?* Choose a learner to make a question (e.g. *Where can the Friendly family travel?*) and ask a classmate. He/She answers (e.g. *Around the world*).
- Write more prompts on the board, e.g. *What / this morning?* (e.g. *What came this morning?*)
- Put the class into pairs to ask and answer.
  Extra support Learners work in pairs to make questions, then swap partners and ask and answer. Monitor and help.
- Show the picture of Rocky in the bottom right-hand corner. Read out the questions. Learners talk in pairs then share ideas with the class. Help with names of countries. Ask *Would you like to work in a circus? Why? / Why not?*

Activity Book, page 110

See pages TB120–132

Ending the lesson

- **SA** Repeat the self-assessment used after the Presentation to see how well learners think they understand the vocabulary. Is there any change?
- Play the song again. Learners join in and do actions.

Learning outcomes By the end of the lesson, learners will be able to use superlative adjectives with *most.*

New language *beautiful: This city is one of the most beautiful in the world. frightened: In my family, my brother is the most frightened of spiders.*

Recycled language animals, countryside, places, *buy, CD, circus, funfair, ride* (n), *ticket, in the morning/afternoon/evening*, comparatives, past simple

Materials audio, Mission worksheets (Teacher's Resource Book page 94) and notes from Stage 1 lesson, digital Mission poster

Warm-up

- Learners stand in a circle. Say *Stand in the centre if you're the tallest person in the class.* Say to the learner in the centre *Find the person with the longest hair and swap.*
- Repeat, making different 'swaps', e.g. *Find the person with the cleanest shoes / the curliest hair / the biggest feet.*

Presentation

- Write on the board *beautiful, boring, difficult, dangerous, exciting, afraid, frightened, surprised, tired*. Remind learners that we use *more* with these adjectives when we are comparing two things.
- Say and write on the board *I think tigers are more beautiful than elephants. I think tigers are the most beautiful animals in the world.* Ask *What do you think?* Help different learners to reply *The most beautiful animal is …*

Pupil's Book, page 111

1 3.47 What did Charlie's dad buy? Listen and tick ✓.

- Say *Open your Pupil's Books at page 111.* Point to each photo and ask *What's this? (A CD, tickets, a toy lion)*
- Say *Charlie's talking to his friend. He went to the circus.* Ask *What did Charlie's dad buy?* Play the audio.

Track 3.47

Girl: Hi, Charlie. Did you know the circus is in town?
Charlie: Yes, Mum got tickets and we went last week.
Girl: Did you? Did you enjoy it?
Charlie: Yes, I did! I think the circus is the most exciting place in the world.
Girl: Really? Do you think it's more exciting than a funfair?
Charlie: Oh, I don't like funfairs. I'm frightened on the rides.
Girl: Yes, but a circus is sometimes dangerous. Lions are one of the most dangerous animals in the world.
Charlie: Lions?! There weren't any animals. The best circuses never have animals. The most dangerous thing was when a woman jumped from a swing in the air, and a man caught her.
Girl: Wow! Were you frightened?
Charlie: We were all a little frightened, but my dad was the most frightened. He had to put his hands over his eyes and he only listened to the music. He thought it was the most beautiful music in the world, so he bought the CD.
Girl: Does he often play it?
Charlie: Yes, but when he listens to it, he goes to sleep!

Key: Picture 1

3.48 Gracie's Grammar

- Write the questions and answers on the board.
- Play the audio. Pause for learners to repeat.

Track 3.48
See Pupil's Book page 111

2 What do you think? Ask and answer.

- Read the instructions and the first question. Ask different learners to reply with a full sentence. Learners ask and answer with a partner. Encourage them to give reasons.

mission Stage 2

- Show learners the second stage of the Mission poster: *Choose a kind of holiday for a class tour.*
- Learners complete the worksheet task in the Teacher's Resource Book (page 94). See teaching notes on TRB page 87.
- Alternatively, if you do not have the Teacher's Resource Book, learners draw a two-column table with ten rows (one per group). Individual learners take turns to explain their ideas for holidays to the group and say why they like them (using comparatives and superlatives). Groups write ten ideas in the first column of the table. Then they award the ideas points from 1 to 10 (10 is the group's favourite idea).

Activity Book, page 111

See pages TB120–132

Activity Book, page 106

- Review *My unit goals*. Ask *How is your Mission?* Learners reflect and choose a smiley face for *My mission diary 2*.

Ending the lesson

- **SA** Go back to Stage 2 on the digital Mission poster. Add a tick to the 'Choose a kind of holiday' stage. Use self-assessment (see Introduction).
- Give out a completion sticker.

1 3.47 What did Charlie's dad buy? Listen and tick ✓.

1

☐

2

☐

3

☐

3.48 Gracie's Grammar

beautiful: This city is one of **the most beautiful** in the world.

frightened: In my family, my brother is **the most frightened** of spiders.

2 What do you think? Ask and answer.

1 Which are the most dangerous?

a tigers b puppies c sheep

2 Which is the most exciting?

a a sports centre b a funfair c a circus

3 Which is the most beautiful?

a the countryside b the mountains c the beach

mission STAGE 2

Choose a kind of holiday for a class tour.

- In groups, talk about your holiday ideas.

A holiday in the mountains is the most …

- Write your ideas. Find the group's favourite idea.

My mission diary
Activity Book page 106

The wonders of the world

1 Watch the video.

2 Find the continents on the map.

Our planet, Earth, has seven continents. Here they are in order, from the biggest to the smallest:

1 Asia
2 Africa
3 North America
4 South America
5 Antarctica
6 Europe
7 Australia

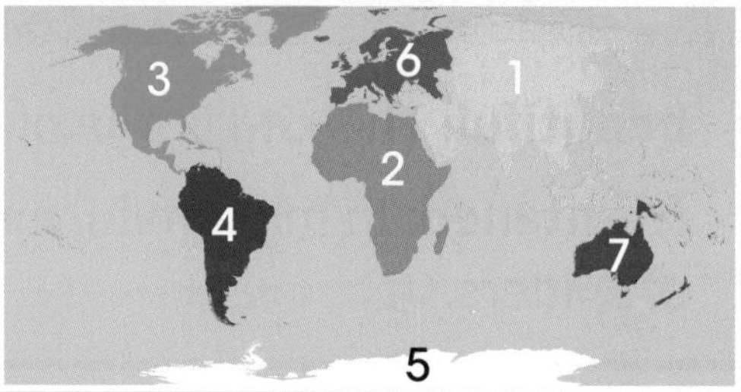

3 3.49 Match the places with the continents. Listen and check.

1

the Grand Canyon

2

the Taj Mahal

3

the Great Barrier Reef

4

Machu Picchu

5

the Victoria Falls

6

Stonehenge

a	Africa	
b	Europe	
c	South America	
d	North America	1
e	Asia	
f	Australia	

Learning outcomes By the end of the lesson, learners will have learnt about natural and manmade wonders of the world.

New language *Africa, Antarctica, Asia, Australia, Europe, North America, South America, bottom, build, canyon, continent, in order, wonder (n), (four thousand) years old*

Recycled language colours, natural features, *climb, different, Earth, famous, fish, huge, old, planet, river, rock, round the world, swimsuit, towel, water, have to*

Materials picture from Digital photo bank of Earth as seen from space (optional), video, audio, pieces of paper with names of continents on them (except Antarctica), coloured pens or pencils

Warm-up

- Write on the board the names of natural features your learners know in their country, but with parts of the name mixed up, e.g.

Ebro	*Mountains*
Canarias	*Beach*
Sierra Nevada	*River*
La Concha	*Islands*

- Learners work in pairs to match and make names. They say what they know about each place (using comparatives and superlatives where they can). Check answers.

Presentation

- Draw Earth on the board or show a picture. Say *This is our planet. What's it called?* Write *Earth* on the board.
- Point to one of the continents and say *This is a continent.* Ask *Do you know the names of the continents? How many are there? Which continent do we live on?* Don't confirm answers.
- Say *Let's find out more about the continents.*

Pupil's Book, page 112

1 Watch the video.

- Say *Let's watch the video.* Learners watch the video about continents and answer the questions at the end.

2 Find the continents on the map.

- Say *Open your Pupil's Books at page 112.* Read the introductory text and the names of the continents. Check understanding of *in order*. Ask *Which is the biggest continent? Which is the smallest?*
- Ask *Where's Asia?* Learners point and say the number.
- Ask *What's the (green) continent?* Practise pronunciation of the continent names.
- Learners practise asking and answering in pairs.

3 3.49 Match the places with the continents. Listen and check.

- Focus on the photos and say *Point to a green mountain. Point to a palace. Point to the sea.*
- In pairs, learners discuss which continent they think each place is in. Don't confirm answers at this stage.
- Play the audio. Learners listen and check.

Track 3.49

Come with me on a trip round the world. We can see a lot of exciting places.

1 This is the famous Grand Canyon in North America. The rocks are huge and they're different colours. There's a river at the bottom of the canyon.
2 This is called the Taj Mahal. It's in India. India's in Asia.
3 Have you got a swimsuit and a towel? Let's explore the Great Barrier Reef and see the fish that live there. The Great Barrier Reef's in the ocean in Australia.
4 You have to climb mountains to visit Machu Picchu. Machu Picchu's in Peru, in South America.
5 You have to travel to Africa to see the Victoria Falls. They're in Zambia and Zimbabwe. Look at all the water!
6 Stonehenge is in England, in Europe. It's very, very old – four or five thousand years old! How did they build it? We don't really know!

Key: a 5 b 6 c 4 (d 1) e 2 f 3

Extension Write on the board: *Which country is the Taj Mahal in? What can you see on the Great Barrier Reef? Where's Machu Picchu? Where are the Victoria Falls (two countries)?* Play the audio again. Check answers.

Activity Book, page 112

See pages TB120–132

Ending the lesson

- Put six pieces of paper with *Asia, Africa, North America, South America, Europe, Australia* around the walls of the classroom. Clear a space in the middle of the classroom.
- Demonstrate the game. Stand in the middle of the room and say *France.* Learners run to the correct continent sign. All the learners standing by the *Europe* sign stay in the game. The rest sit down.
- Repeat with different countries and cities, e.g. *Brazil, New York, Sydney, Japan, Italy, Argentina,* until only one learner is left as the winner.

Learning outcomes By the end of the lesson, learners will be able to talk about natural and manmade wonders of the world.

New language *coral, hard, living thing, manmade, natural, reef*

Recycled language continents, countryside, *animal, around, fish, home, house, make, rock, small, station, whale,* superlative adjectives

Materials a world map without continents labelled (optional), a selection of small natural things (e.g. a piece of chalk, a seed such as an acorn, a leaf, a shell) and manmade objects (e.g. a coin, a ring, a pencil sharpener, a plastic toy) (optional), pictures of manmade and natural wonders in learners' own country (optional), worksheets / tour ideas from Mission Stage 2 lesson, a slip of paper for each group, access to the internet for research (optional), digital Mission poster

Warm-up

- Show a world map without the continents labelled (or the map from Pupil's Book page 112, with the list of continents covered). Point and ask *Which continent is this?* (*It's Africa.*) *Which is the biggest continent?* (*Asia*) *Which is the smallest?* (*Australia*)
- Learners ask and answer *Which continent is this?* in pairs, using the map on page 112 (one learner covers the list of continents).

  Stronger learners Write more questions about the continents on the board. Learners guess the answers, e.g. *Which is the coldest continent? (Antarctica) Which continent has the most people? (Asia) Which continent has the most rain? (South America) Which continent has the most languages? (Asia) Which continent has the most countries? (Africa)*

Presentation

- Show a selection of natural and manmade items (or pictures) and start to sort them into two groups. Point to the natural things and ask *What's the same about all these things?* Learners guess. Ask *Did people make them?* (*No*) *They're natural things*. Write *natural* on the board. Let learners pass the items around the class.
- Show manmade things and ask *What about these things? Are they natural?* (*No*) Say *People made them. They're manmade.* Write *manmade* on the board.

Pupil's Book, page 113

4 Read and think. Are the places in Activity 3 *natural* or *manmade*?

- Say *Open your Pupil's Books at page 113.* Read the text with the class. Refer learners back to the pictures in Activity 3 and give them time to talk in pairs. Check answers.

Key: 1 natural 2 manmade 3 natural 4 manmade 5 natural 6 manmade

Extension Show pictures of natural and manmade wonders in the learners' own country (or write the names on the board). For each one, learners say *natural* or *manmade.* Follow up with additional questions, e.g. *Where's this? How old is it? Why is it famous?*

5 Read the text. Then circle the correct words.

- Point to the picture and ask *What's this?* Teach *reef.* Ask *Are reefs natural or manmade?* (*Natural*) *Are there any reefs in (learners' country)? Where are they?*
- Read the instructions and go through the example answer. Tell learners to read the whole text before they do the circling activity. They read individually and circle, then compare answers in pairs.
- Check answers. Check comprehension of *living thing, coral* and *hard.*

Key: 2 Australia 3 animal 4 are lots of

mission Stage 3

- Show the class the third stage of the Mission poster: *Write your group's idea for the class tour.* Read the instructions.
- Put learners into their Mission groups. They decide on the best country to travel to for the kind of trip they chose in Stage 2. If possible, they do research on the internet.
- Each group then writes a short description of the place and where it is on a slip of paper for the final Mission stage.

  Fast finishers Draw a picture of the destination or copy a map of the country and mark where it is.

Activity Book, page 113

See pages TB120–132

Activity Book, page 106

- Review *My unit goals.* Ask *How is your Mission?* Learners reflect and choose a smiley face for *My mission diary 3.*

Ending the lesson

- **SA** Go back to Stage 3 on the digital Mission poster. Add a tick to the 'Write your group's idea for the class tour' stage. Use self-assessment (see Introduction).
- Give out a completion sticker.

4 Read and think. Are the places in Activity 3 *natural* or *manmade*?

When we look at the things that are around us, we can see **natural** things and **manmade** things. A river and a forest are natural things. People didn't make them. A house and a station are manmade things. People made them.

5 Read the text. Then circle the correct words.

The Great Barrier Reef

What's the biggest living thing on Earth? Do you think it's a whale? No, it isn't. The biggest living thing on Earth is the Great Barrier Reef. The Great Barrier Reef is a coral reef near Australia. Coral looks like plants, but it's hard like rock. Did you know that it's lots of very, very small animals? A coral reef is home to many different kinds of fish and other animals like turtles.

1 A whale **is** / **isn't** the biggest living thing on Earth.

2 The Great Barrier Reef is near **Europe** / **Australia**.

3 Coral is a kind of **plant** / **animal**.

4 There **are lots of** / **aren't any** fish on the Great Barrier Reef.

mission STAGE 3

Write your group's idea for the class tour.

- Find places for your group's holiday.

Are there high mountains on every continent?

I don't know. Shall I look online?

- Write your holiday, the country and the continent.

On this part of our holiday tour we're in the mountains in India, in Asia.

My mission diary
Activity Book page 106

1 **Look at the pictures. What do you think the poem is about?**

4.02

The mystery picnic

Richard gave a picnic
For the children in Year 2.

He planned it very carefully
To make it fun to do.

Come to my picnic, everyone –
A picnic in the wood!

I'm hiding clues for you to find.
I think the clues are good!

Some of the clues were difficult,
But they were also fun!

More difficult than a TV quiz –
Exciting for everyone!

Richard walked into the sunny wood
And he hid the clues around:

Some were above, in the trees,
And some were on the ground.

When they looked for the clues,
The first was easy to find:

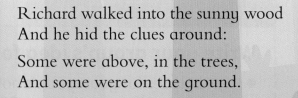

Walk past ten trees, please.
Then look on the grass behind!

Learning outcomes By the end of the lesson, learners will have read a poem about a mystery picnic.

New language *carefully, clue, good news, in the shape of, last, mystery, quiz, past* (prep), *reach, shiver, step* (n), *treat* (n), *wood*

Recycled language adjectives, countryside, food, numbers 1–100, *children, cross* (v), *find, first, giraffe, hide, laugh, picnic, plan* (v), *second, shoe, sunny, take off,* imperatives, past simple, prepositions of place

Materials audio, coloured pens or pencils

Warm-up

- Count with the class from 1 to 100. Practise counting in tens and in fives.
- Challenge learners to count backwards from 100 or from 20.

4.04 4.05 **Alternative** Learners perform the chant from Pupil's Book page 120 and do the listening activity. There is an audioscript and answer key for the second activity on page TB132.

Presentation

- Draw a picture of a picnic blanket with a basket and some plates on the board. Add trees, flowers, etc. Ask *What's this?* (*A picnic*) *Do you like picnics? What do you usually eat on a picnic?* Review food items.

  Extra support Write the food learners suggest on the board.
- Say *Draw your perfect picnic. Draw a blanket and some plates with food and glasses with drink. Is there any fruit in your picnic? Are there any vegetables? What about lemonade?* Set a time limit for the drawing.
- Put learners in pairs. They sit back to back. One learner guesses what is in his/her partner's picture by asking yes/no questions, e.g. *Is there any milk? Have you got sandwiches?* Then they swap roles.
- Say *Let's read a poem about a special kind of picnic.*

Pupil's Book, pages 114 and 115

1 Look at the pictures. What do you think the poem is about?

- Say *Open your Pupil's Books at page 114. Look at the pictures. What do you think the story is about?* Learners talk in pairs. Then they share ideas (e.g. *a picnic with friends, a day trip to the forest*).
- Point to picture 4 and ask *What are the children thinking about?* (*A giraffe*) Point to picture 5 and say *Look! It's a tree in the shape of a giraffe.* Write *in the shape of* on the board. Say *Put your hands in the shape of a bird / a rabbit / a triangle.* Learners practise. Point to picture 6 and ask *What are the children doing?* (*Crossing a river*)
- Point to the title and check comprehension of *mystery*. Ask *Why is it a mystery picnic?* Learners guess. Say *Let's find out.*

4.02 The mystery picnic

- Say *Let's read and listen to the first part of the poem.* Play the audio. Pause the audio after *I think the clues are good!*
- Ask *Who gave a picnic?* (*Richard*) *Who for?* (*The children in Year 2*) *What's he doing in picture 1?* (*Planning/writing*) Point to the first clue and say *This is one of Richard's clues.* Explain the meaning of *clue* and ask learners if they are good at solving clues. Ask *Did Richard give the clues to the children?* (*No, he hid them.*) *Where was the picnic?* (*In a wood*) Explain that a wood is a small forest. Say *Richard hid the clues in the wood carefully.* Use mime to show the meaning of *carefully.*

  Track 4.02

  See poem on Pupil's Book pages 114–115
- Say *Read and listen to the next part.* Pause after *grass behind!* Ask *Were all the clues easy?* (*No. Some were difficult.*) *Where did Richard hide the clues?* (*In the trees and on the ground*) *Was it difficult to find the first clue?* (*No, it was easy.*)
- Play the next part. Pause after *very near, you know!* Ask *What did they need to find for the second clue?* (*An amazing giraffe*) *Did the children walk to find the clues?* (*No, they ran.*) *How many steps was it from the last clue to the picnic?* (*A/One hundred*) Use mime to show the meaning of *steps.*
- Play the last part. Ask *What did the children take off when they crossed the river?* (*Their shoes*) *Was the water cold?* (*Yes, it was.*) Show the meaning of *shiver*. Ask *What did they find at the end of the quiz?* (*Richard and the picnic / lots of food*)

  Extension Play the whole poem again, without pauses, for learners to listen and read.

Activity Book, page 114

See pages TB120–132

Ending the lesson

- Play the last section of the story, from *Twenty, thirty …* Learners do the actions and join in with the counting.

Learning outcomes By the end of the lesson, learners will have thought about taking pride in their work.

New language *(be) proud (of)*

Recycled language language from the poem

Materials paper, coloured pens or pencils, audio

Social and Emotional Skill: Pride in your work

- After reading the poem, ask learners *What did Richard do?* (*He planned a picnic. He made a treasure hunt for Year 2 with clues.*) *Why was he proud of his work?* (*He wrote the clues carefully. It was fun for his friends. It was exciting. He did it himself.*) *Did the children in Year 2 have fun?* (*Yes*)
- Say some things that learners might be proud of. Abilities can vary, so say as many different options as possible: *Hands up if you …* e.g. *can sing, can dance, can play a team sport, can play an instrument, are good at drawing, are good at* (school subjects), *can run, can swim, can ride a bike.*
- Show two examples of pieces of work: one that is messy and another that's very neat.
- In groups, learners think of things that can make a piece of work look good and work well, e.g. presentation, planning, correct spelling, correct grammar, no crossing out or crossing out neatly.
- They share their ideas with the rest of the class.
- Hand out a piece of paper. Learners think, draw and write about something they are proud of. They write *I'm proud of …* They can decorate their work.
- Remind learners that they can be proud of school work or of something else, e.g. playing a sport, playing an instrument, making new friends, helping others, or getting a good mark in a test.
- Learners can present their work or you can display it around the classroom.

Warm-up

- Write adjectives and nouns from the story on the board in random order:

mystery	*giraffe*
difficult	*picnic*
sunny	*clues*
amazing	*water*
cold	*picnic*
fantastic	*wood*

- Draw a line from the last adjective *fantastic* to *picnic* and say *At the end of the poem there was a fantastic picnic. Richard planned it. Can you match the rest of the words from the poem?* Learners match the words in pairs.
- Check answers. (*mystery picnic, difficult clues, sunny wood, amazing giraffe, cold water*)

  Stronger learners Tell the story from the poem in pairs, using the pairs of adjectives and nouns to help them.

Pupil's Book, pages 114 and 115

- Say *Open your Pupil's Books at pages 114 and 115.* Play the audio. Learners read and listen to the poem again.

  Track 4.02

  See poem on Pupil's Book pages 114–115

2 Why is the poem called *The mystery picnic*? Why was Richard proud of his work?

- Read the questions with the class and explain the meaning of *proud*.
- Learners talk in pairs. Have a brief class discussion. Ask *Who planned the picnic? Who made all the clues and hid them?* (*Richard*) Say *Richard was proud of his work. He did it all himself.* Ask learners for examples of work they have been proud of (*I am/was proud of …*).

Key: (possible answers) It was a mystery picnic because the children had to find/follow clues. Richard was proud because he planned the picnic, he made all the clues and hid them, and it was fun.

Extension Learners act out the poem. Play the audio and encourage them to do all the actions (writing clues, hiding clues, looking in trees and on the ground, counting steps, etc.).

Activity Book, page 115

See pages TB120–132

Ending the lesson

- Write these sentences on the board in random order for learners to copy and reorder.

  Richard planned a picnic.
  He walked into the wood and hid clues.
  The children looked for the clues.
  They walked past ten trees.
  They saw an amazing giraffe.
  They counted 100 steps.
  They crossed a river.
  They found the picnic.
- Learners underline the verbs and tell you which are regular and which are irregular. They practise pronunciation of the *-ed* verbs.
- **SA** Use self-assessment to see how well learners think they understand the story. See Introduction.

9

‘One … two … three, four, five,
Six, seven, eight, nine, ten!
Now let’s look and find the clue.’
‘Hey! There it is!’ said Ben.

The children found the second clue
And everyone started to laugh
Because it said they needed to find
The most amazing giraffe!

Finally they saw it! ‘Hey! Look there! Can you see?
It’s in the shape of a giraffe, but really it’s a tree!’
The children ran from tree to tree finding all the clues.
When they reached the last one, it really was good news.

I hope you’re feeling hungry. One hundred steps to go
To the most fantastic picnic! You’re very near, you know!

Twenty, thirty, forty, fifty!
They had to cross a river,
So they all took off their shoes.
The cold water made them shiver.

Sixty, seventy, eighty, ninety,
A hundred! What a treat!
Richard with his picnic!
There was lots and lots to eat.

2 Why is the poem called *The mystery picnic*?
Why was Richard proud of his work?

1 Read the start of a story. Why are words a–c the correct answers?

Last weekend, Tom invited Sally to his house. He wanted to show her an old **go** / [a]**book** / **tired** about circuses. 'Look!' he said. 'There's a man who's [b]**riding** / **ticket** / **blue** on a horse's back.' 'Wow!' Sally said. 'That's **went** / **emails** / [c]**difficult!**'

2 Read the next part. Write *V* (Verb), *A* (Adjective) or *N* (Noun) next to 1–3.

'Yes, it is!' Tom said. 'And did they have **(1)** ☐ animals in those days too?' Sally asked. 'Yes, they did,' Tom answered. He was sad and he **(2)** ☐ to a picture of some **(3)** ☐ in the book.

3 Read again. Circle the correct answer.

1 parrots / dangerous   2 pointed / frightened   3 lions / jumped

4 Read the last part. Write the correct word from the box next to 4 and 5.

'But today the best circuses in the world don't have animals. That's because people **(4)** ____________ it's very sad for them,' Tom said. 'Yes, it is,' Sally answered, 'but a circus with **(5)** ____________ is funny. I'd like to go to that kind of circus one day.'

surprised

earache

clowns

think

Remember to check your spelling when you copy.
In the exam, you choose the name for the story too.

Learning outcomes By the end of the lesson, learners will have practised identifying word classes and choosing options in a cloze text (A1 Movers Reading and Writing Part 3).

Test skills Reading for specific information and gist; Copying words

New language *earache, in those days, one day*

Recycled language adjectives, animals, free time activities, *circus(es), clown, point, think, I'd like to …*

Materials pictures from Digital photo bank of a modern circus and an old-fashioned circus with elephants, lions, etc. (optional), practice paper for Movers Reading and Writing Part 3 (optional)

Warm-up

- Write *circus* on the board and ask *What can you see at a circus? What kind of animals did people see at circuses in the past?* Show pictures, if possible. Encourage learners to think about the living conditions of the animals and how circuses have changed.

Presentation

- Say *Let's practise for a reading and writing exam.* Show the Movers Reading and Writing Part 3 paper. Say *In Part 3 of the exam you read a story with five spaces. On the next page are nine pictures with words. You choose five words and copy them in the story. Then you choose the best title for the story.*

Pupil's Book, page 116

1 Read the start of a story. Why are words a–c the correct answers?

- Say *Open your Pupil's Books at page 116.* Read the instructions and the question.
- Learners read and talk about the answers in pairs. Check as a class, asking for reasons for each choice. Tell learners that looking at what comes before a space as well as reading the whole sentence helps in Part 3 of the exam.

Key: a: the word must be a noun (there is an adjective before the options) b: the word *is* before the options means the verb is in the present continuous c: the verb *is* is already there, so the answer must be an adjective

2 Read the next part. Write *V* (Verb), *A* (Adjective) or *N* (Noun) next to 1–3.

- Read the instructions. Make sure learners realise the boxes represent missing words. Remind them to look at the whole sentence and the words around the missing word. In the exam, the verbs can be in the present simple, present continuous or past simple.
- Learners think and write individually, then compare answers in pairs. Check answers and ask learners to explain what helped them choose.

Key: 1 A (the verb is already there before the missing word; the missing word must describe animals) 2 V (the subject pronoun *he* is before the missing word; the next word must be a verb) 3 N (there is a determiner before the missing word; it must be an uncountable or plural noun)

3 Read again. Circle the correct answer.

- Learners read again and choose the correct words for the text in Activity 2.
- Check answers. Learners explain how they chose (e.g. number 1 – *dangerous* is an adjective).

Key: 1 dangerous 2 pointed 3 lions

4 Read the last part. Write the correct word from the box next to 4 and 5.

- Read the instructions. Point out that the labelled pictures are similar to the ones in the exam. There are two extra words here, but there are four in the exam (they choose five from nine). Remind learners to copy the answers carefully.
- Learners read and choose individually, then compare answers in pairs.

Key: 4 think 5 clowns

- Point to the monkey at the bottom of the page and read. Learners lose marks if they copy the words incorrectly. Their handwriting needs to be clear too.
- Write these story titles on the board: *Sally's favourite animal / Sally and Tom's afternoon / A trip to the circus.* Ask learners to decide which title is best (*Sally and Tom's afternoon*) and explain why.

Activity Book, page 116

See pages TB120–132

Ending the lesson

- In pairs, learners test each other on spelling words from the unit. This can also be done as a team game.

Learning outcomes By the end of the lesson, learners will have revised the language in the unit and put their holiday ideas on a 'world tour' map.

Recycled language unit language

Materials Adjectives for opinions and feelings flashcards, audio, worksheets/notes and tour ideas from Mission Stages 1–3 lessons, a large piece of display paper with a world map drawn on it (continents only) or coloured paper/card for learners to make the seven continents (optional), dice and counters (for Activity Book game), coloured pens or pencils, digital Mission poster

3.45 Warm-up

- Review adjectives for opinions and feelings with the flashcards and mime. Revise the adventure words by playing the song from Pupil's Book page 110.
- Write a selection of 10–12 of the words from the unit on the board. Tell learners to study the words and remember the spelling.
- Divide the class into two teams. Choose a learner from each team and ask them to stand with their back to the board. Decide which learner is going first. Say a word from the board. The learner spells it aloud, letter by letter, without turning to look at the board. If he/she is correct he/she gets a point for the team. If not, the other learner can spell it for a bonus point. Then it is the second learner's turn to spell a word.
- The two learners at the front swap with different learners from their teams. The team with the most points wins.

Pupil's Book, page 117

mission in action!

Put your holiday ideas on the holiday world tour map.

- Point to the Mission box or show learners the last stage of the digital Mission poster. Say *Let's put our Mission in action!* Say *Put your holiday ideas on the world tour map.*
- Read the instructions and speech bubbles. Put learners into their Mission groups. Give them time to practise presenting their holiday idea, using their notes from the Mission stages. Monitor and check that each member of the group gets the chance to speak. Encourage learners to use the superlative to explain why they think their holiday idea is the best.
- Groups take turns to present their holiday ideas. Then they attach their slip of paper with the destination (from Stage 3) to the world map, together with a picture if they have drawn one.

  Alternative Instead of preparing the map yourself, divide the class into seven groups and get each group to draw, cut out and label one of the continents. They could use different-colour ed paper/card for each continent.

  Extension Learners discuss and mark the route of the world tour on the map.

Self-assessment

- **SA** Say *Did you like our 'Plan a holiday world tour' Mission? Think and draw a face.* Learners draw a happy face, neutral face or sad face and then hold it up in the air.
- Ask *Did you like all the Missions? Which did you like best?* Learners say their favourite Mission.
- Ask *How can you make your English better?* (e.g. *I can keep a vocabulary notebook. I can sing songs in English.*)

Activity Book, page 117

See pages TB120–132

Activity Book, page 106

- Review *My unit goals*. Ask *How was your Mission?* Learners reflect and choose a smiley face for *My mission diary* the final stage.
- Point to the sunflower. Learners read the 'can do' statements and tick them if they agree they have achieved them. They colour each leaf green if they are very confident or orange if they think they need more practice.
- Point to the word stack sign. Ask learners to look back at the unit and find at least five new words they have learnt. They write them in their word stack.

Ending the lesson

- **SA** Go back to the completion stage on the digital Mission poster. Add a tick or invite a learner to do it. Use self-assessment (see Introduction).
- Give out a completion sticker.
- Tell learners *You have finished your Mission! Well done!*

mission in action!

Put your holiday ideas on the holiday world tour map.

My mission diary
Activity Book page 106

★ Tell the class how you chose your idea.

We think a holiday in the mountains is the most exciting and the most dangerous.

★ Tell the class your idea for the tour.

For this part of our holiday tour, we go to the mountains in India, in Asia.

★ Put your group's idea on the class map.

Review ••• Units 7–9

1 **Watch the video and do the quiz.**

2 4.03 **Listen and match the children with the food.**

1 Zoe 2 Sam 3 Daisy 4 Lily 5 Jack

a 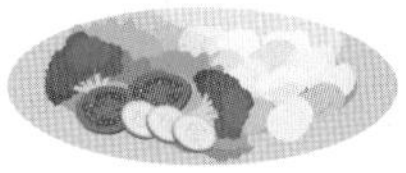

b 

c 

d 

e 

3 **Do the sums. Then find the places and complete the sentences.**

bus station café ~~sports centre~~ library supermarket

1 C twenty + thirteen
C __33__ : I scored a goal at the __sports centre__ !

2 B twenty + fifteen
B ______ : I went to the ____________ to buy a ticket.

3 E ten + twenty-two
E ______ : I bought some pasta and cheese at the ____________ .

4 D thirty-one + three
D ______ : I chose some great books at the ____________ .

5 A twelve + nineteen
A ______ : I drank a hot drink at the ____________ .

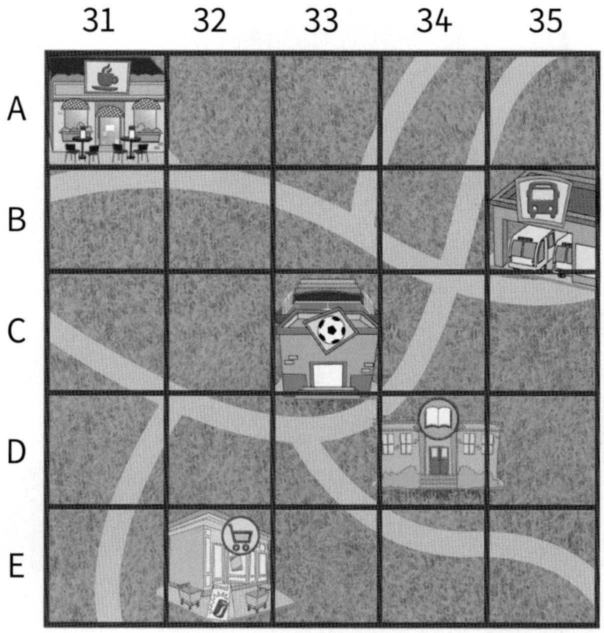

Learning outcomes By the end of the lesson, learners will have consolidated language from Units 7–9.

Recycled language adjectives for feelings, food and things we use to serve food, numbers 1–100, places in town, comparative and superlative adjectives, *have to,* infinitive of purpose (*I went there to watch a film*), past simple

Materials Adjectives for opinions and feelings and Places in town flashcards, video, audio

Warm-up

- Hand a learner an Adjectives for opinions and feelings flashcard or word card (afraid, frightened, tired, hungry, surprised or thirsty). Say *Guess the feeling!* The learner mimes for the class to guess (e.g. *You're tired.*).
- Repeat with the flashcards for places in town. The learner mimes being at the place on the flashcard and the rest of the class guess (e.g. *You're at the sports centre.*).

Pupil's Book, page 118

1 Watch the video and do the quiz.

- Show the video to learners.
- Ask learners to do the quiz. Check their answers to see how much learners can remember.
- Repeat this at the end of the Review unit and compare the results to measure progress.

2 4.03 Listen and match the children with the food.

- Say *Open your Pupil's Books at page 118.* Practise pronunciation of the names with the whole class. Then point to the food pictures in turn and ask *What's this?* Encourage learners to guess with a phrase, e.g. *I think it's a plate of sandwiches.*
- Play the example. Play the rest of the audio twice. Learners listen and match each name with a food item. Check answers.

Track 4.03

Jack: Hi! I'm Jack. My friends and I made lunch yesterday and we had it in the garden. Everyone helped to make the food and we were very hungry! Zoe made tomato soup and my mum put it in her biggest bottle for us. Sam made some cheese sandwiches. Daisy's food was the most delicious. She made potatoes and salad, but then she saw a rabbit in the garden. She was surprised and she dropped her plate! Lily helped me make some pasta. She said pasta was boring, so she ate hers with tomatoes and cheese. I think my pasta was more exciting. I cooked lots of vegetables with mine. We all sat under a tree and it was a nice sunny day.

Key: 2 b (cheese sandwiches) 3 a (potatoes and salad) 4 e (pasta with tomatoes and cheese) 5 d (pasta with lots of vegetables)

Extension Write questions on the board: *1 Where did they have lunch?* (*In the garden*) *2 Where did Zoe's mum put the tomato soup?* (*In her biggest bottle*) *3 What kind of sandwiches did Sam make?* (*Cheese*) *4 Whose food was the most delicious?* (*Daisy's*) *5 What did Daisy see in the garden?* (*A rabbit*) *6 Why did she drop her plate?* (*Because she was surprised*) *7 Where did they sit to eat their food?* (*Under a tree*) Play the audio again. Check answers.

3 Do the sums. Then find the places and complete the sentences.

- Focus on the map and ask *Where's the (library)?* Learners point to the correct building. Show learners how the grid references work and ask, e.g. *What's in square 33C?* (*The sports centre*)
- Read the example sum and show learners how the answer gives them the location of one of the places.
- Learners solve the sums first in pairs. Check answers before they do the second part of the activity.

Key: 2 35 3 32 4 34 5 31

- Learners then read the sentences and match the sum answers to the grid numbers to find out what each place is. Check answers.

Key: 2 bus station 3 supermarket 4 library 5 café

Stronger learners Ask *Why did he go to the bus station?* (*To buy a ticket*) Repeat with the different places. Learners practise asking and answering in pairs.

Activity Book, page 118

See pages TB120–132

Ending the lesson

- Learners stand in a circle. Practise counting from 1 to 100 around the circle.
- Say *Let's make up some rules! When someone says a number with a zero or a five, what do they have to do?* Learners suggest, e.g. *They have to turn around.* Count again from 1, applying the rule. Learners who don't do the correct action for a multiple of five are 'out' and have to sit down.
- Repeat, adding in a different rule, e.g. *When someone says a number with a two, they have to jump*, and starting from 1 again. Continue adding new rules until only a few learners are left. They are the winners.

Learning outcomes By the end of the lesson, learners will have consolidated language from Units 7–9.

Recycled language actions in the kitchen, adjectives for opinions, daily routines, food and drink, free time activities, places in town, *funfair, ride* (n), comparative and superlative adjectives, *have to*, past simple

Materials flashcards from Units 7 and 8, an example of a school yearbook (optional), a blank notebook to make a yearbook (optional), small pieces of paper for the yearbook entries (optional), coloured pens or pencils, video, audio

Warm-up

- Learners stand in two lines facing you. Mix up flashcards from Units 7 and 8 and divide them into two equal piles.
- Demonstrate how to play. Give a flashcard to the learner at the front of the line. This learner says the word/phrase and passes the flashcard over their head to the next learner. The second learner says the word and passes the flashcard under their legs to the next learner. The next learner passes the card over their head, the next under their legs, and so on, saying the word each time. When the flashcard reaches the last learner, he/she runs to the front and gives you the flashcard, saying the word. The first group to do this gets a point.

Pupil's Book, page 119

4 Choose two or three activities. Your partner compares them. Use the words in the box and your own ideas.

- Say *Open your Pupil's Books at page 119.* Read the instructions.
- Go through the activities in the first box and check comprehension – ask learners to mime.
- Revise the adjectives in the second box and ask *What's the opposite of difficult?* (*Easy*) *What's the opposite of exciting?* (*Boring*) *What's the opposite of dangerous?* (*Safe*)
- Learners read the example speech bubbles. Explain that if their partner chooses two activities, they use a comparative adjective, but if there are three, they use a superlative.
- Learners work in pairs. Monitor and support.

  Extension Encourage stronger learners to use adjectives which are not in the box.

  Extra support Choose activities yourself and ask pairs to come up with a comparative or superlative.

5 Write about you.

- Read the questions and check comprehension. Ask two or three learners to give answers to the first two.
- Learners write their answers. Monitor and help.

  Extra support Write model answers / prompts on the board.
- Put learners into pairs with someone they don't know well to ask and answer the questions. Ask different learners to tell the class the best answer their partner gave.

  Extension Say *Let's make a class yearbook.* Explain that a yearbook has pictures of everyone and what is special about them. Show an example, if possible.
- Give each learner a small piece of paper. Say *Draw a picture of the person next to you, head and shoulders, like a photo. Leave space to write below.* Show an example. Set a time limit.
- Tell learners to write a caption with a superlative below their picture. Write examples on the board, e.g. *The best at sports in the class. The person who does the most dangerous things. The friendliest in the class.* Monitor and help with new vocabulary.
- Stick the pictures in a book which learners can read.

Activity Book, page 119

See pages TB120–132

Ending the lesson

- Repeat the video and quiz.
- Say *We've finished the book. But let's sing one of the songs.* Ask *Which is your favourite?* If possible, play short snippets of the songs. Say *Let's listen again. Put your hand up for your favourite.*
- Play the song snippets again while learners vote. (If you can't play snippets, learners can call out the songs they remember.)
- Replay the song and sing it again using the actions, if appropriate. Encourage learners to give each other a round of applause.
- Ask learners to look at their Pupil's Books. Say *Find five things you can do in English really well.* Learners write sentences in their notebooks, e.g. *I can say the days of the week. I can talk about the weather.*
- Ask *What do you want to do more? What can you do better? Write two or three things.* Learners write sentences, e.g. *I need to practise irregular verbs.*
- Put learners into groups of four and ask them to share what they wrote.
- When they have finished, invite a few learners to share with the whole group. Ensure you choose a mix of learners (not just fast finishers).
- Say *Well done, everyone! You have learnt a lot!*
- Encourage learners to stand up, mingle and shake hands, saying *Well done!* to each other.

4 Choose two or three activities. Your partner compares them. Use the words in the box and your own ideas.

going on a funfair ride   going to the cinema   going to the library
going to the supermarket   reading a book   reading a comic
skating   watching a DVD

boring   dangerous   difficult   easy   exciting

Going on a funfair ride and going to the supermarket.

Going on a funfair ride is more exciting than going to the supermarket.

Reading a book, watching a DVD and skating.

Skating is the most dangerous.

5 Write about you.

What do you have to do to help at home?

____

Did you email a friend last month?

____

What did you eat and drink yesterday?

____

What do you think? Which unit had the best Friendly Farm adventure? What happened?

____

____

Which places do you go to in your town?

____

What's the most exciting thing to do at the weekend?

____

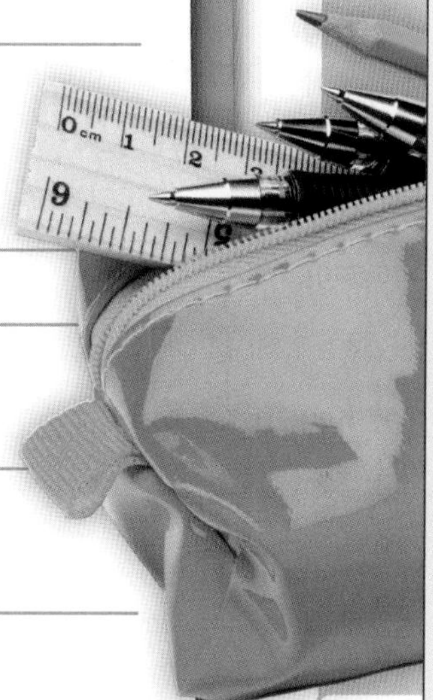

Activity Book answer key and audioscript

Meet the family

Page 4

1 **Key:** 1 eight 2 fine 3 name 4 live 5 meet 6 His

2 4.07

Woman:	Hello, what's your name?
Jack:	Hello. My name's Jack.
Woman:	J-A-C-K?
Jack:	Yes, that's right. Jack Brown.
Woman:	Ah, Brown is your family name. B-R-O-W-N? The same as the colour?
Jack:	Haha. Yes.
Woman:	And how old are you?
Jack:	I'm eight.
Woman:	Good, now, where do you live, Jack?
Jack:	My address is … er … number 7 …
Woman:	OK, 7 …
Jack:	Beach Street.
Woman:	B-E-A-C-H?
Jack:	Yes.
Woman:	Good. And do you live in the town of Bath?
Jack:	Bath, yes, B-A-T-H.
Woman:	Thank you very much. That's great.
Jack:	Thanks. Bye.
Woman:	Bye.

Key: Family name: Brown Age: eight/8
House number: seven/7 Street: Beach (Street)
Town: Bath

Page 5

1 4.08

1 C-a-m-e-r-o-n	4 S-h-e-l-l-y
2 R-o-c-k-y	5 H-a-r-r-y
3 H-e-n-r-i-e-t-t-a	6 G-r-a-c-i-e

Key: a 5 – Harry b 4 – Shelly c 6 – Gracie d 2 – Rocky (e 1 – Cameron) f 3 – Henrietta

2 **Key:** 2 (blue) g 3 (red) f 4 (orange) b 5 (pink) a 6 (purple) e 7 (green) d

Unit 1

Page 6

See page TB6

Page 7

1 **Key:** a 4 b 7 c 6 (d 1) e 8 f 5 g 3 h 2

2 4.09

	'r'	'r'
1	tractor	tractor
2	field	field
3	river	river
4	rock	rock
5	grass	grass
6	leaf	leaf

Key: Learners circle tractor, river, rock, grass
a 6 b 3 c 4 d 5 (e 1) f 2

Page 8

1 1.10

See Pupil's Book page 8

Key: 2 aren't 3 face 4 playing 5 face 6 eating

2 **Key:** (possible answers) Look at this puppy. It's looking at its face. Look at this puppy. It's playing with a ball. Look at the kittens. They're sleeping.

Page 9

1 **Key:** Learners colour borders: 2 blue 3 pink 4 orange

2 **Key:** 2 No, it isn't. 3 No, she isn't. 4 Yes, they are. 5 No, he isn't. 6 Yes, it is. 7 No, she isn't. 8 Yes, he is.

Page 10

1 **Key:** 2 shower 3 toothpaste 4 teeth 5 has 6 breakfast 7 dressed 8 lunch 9 wakes 10 washes
Secret word: toothbrush

2 4.10

1	Girl:	Mum, look at that beautiful kitten.
	Mum:	Which one? The grey one?
	Girl:	No, not the grey one, the black-and-white one.
	Mum:	Ah, yes. It's sleeping with its mother.
	Girl:	No, the other black-and-white one – it's drinking milk.
2	Dad:	Lunch is on the table. Is Peter washing his hands?
	Girl:	I don't know. I think he's in the hall.
	Dad:	Oh, that's good, he's taking off his shoes.
	Girl:	Hmm. He can't come in with dirty shoes.
3	Mum:	Charlie, is this your blue toothbrush?
	Charlie:	No, Mum. My toothbrush hasn't got toothpaste on it.
	Mum:	Ah. Is it the red one, then?
	Charlie:	No, that's Vicky's. My toothbrush is green.
4	Dad:	Good morning, Daisy. Would you like bread and milk for breakfast today?
	Daisy:	Hmm, not today, thank you. Can I have some chocolate, please?
	Dad:	Ah, how about some chocolate milk?
	Daisy:	Hmm, OK. Chocolate milk and a banana, please.

Key: 2 a 3 b 4 a

Page 11

1 **Key:** 2 Do the children have dinner with their family? 3 Jim doesn't have lunch at school. 4 Does Sally have breakfast with her mum? 5 Mary goes to school at nine o'clock. 6 Peter and Charlie clean their teeth in the bathroom.

2 **Key:** 2 gets 3 has 4 dressed 5 breakfast 6 cleans 7 walks 8 o'clock

Page 12

1 **Key:** Pictures (1), 4 and 5

2 **Key:** 2 yes 3 no 4 yes 5 yes

Page 13

3 **Key:** 2 a 3 b 4 b 5 b 6 b

Page 14

1 **Key:** 2 a 3 b 4 a 5 b

2 **Key:** 2 no (The poem says, 'Jess is their puppy.') 3 yes (The poem says, 'Every day Beth and Gwen run to see Jess.') 4 yes (The poem says, '… there's a rock in the leaves and she falls!') 5 no (The poem says, 'She helps her to stand.')

Page 15

4 4.11

Emma: Look, Dad. Everyone's here for Lucy's party.
Dad: Is that girl Sally?
Emma: Where?
Dad: She's sitting by the lake.
Emma: Yes, that's Sally. She likes birthday parties!
Emma: That's Peter, Dad.
Dad: Which one?
Emma: He's next to the tractor.
Dad: Is he the one wearing a hat?
Emma: That's right!
Dad: Look at that girl!
Emma: What's she doing?
Dad: She's taking a photo. Can you see her?
Emma: Oh, yes. She's standing in front of Lucy. That's Lily.
Emma: There's my friend John!
Dad: Where?
Emma: He's talking to Lucy.
Dad: Is he wearing sunglasses?
Emma: Yes, that's John!
Dad: Is that boy in Lucy's class?
Emma: Which boy?
Dad: He's standing in front of the big tree. He's next to Tom, the dog.
Emma: Oh, yes. His name's Nick.
Dad: I think he likes Tom.
Emma: Me too!
Emma: Can you see Mary?
Dad: Where is she, Emma?
Emma: Look! She's sitting in the tractor! She's next to her dad.
Dad: Oh, yes!

Key: Peter – boy in hat next to tractor Lily – girl taking photo John – boy wearing sunglasses Nick – boy next to dog Mary – girl in tractor

Page 16

1 4.12

Look at these pictures. They look the same, but some things are different. Here there's a mountain, but here there's a lake. What other different things can you see?

Key: (possible answers) In picture A there's a clock. In picture B there isn't a clock.

In picture A the baby's sleeping. In picture B it's awake / it isn't sleeping.

In picture A the kitten's playing with a toy helicopter. In picture B it's playing with a toy train.

In picture A there are oranges and bananas on the table / in the bowl. In picture B there are apples and bananas.

Page 17

1

Learners work in groups. They need a dice, and a counter each. Learners move around the board according to the number they roll on the dice. If they land on a picture square, they answer the question about it. If they answer correctly, they stay where they are. If not, they return to their last square. On a bonus/penalty square (green or red) they follow the instructions. The game finishes when one learner gets to the final square, or when all learners finish.

Unit 2

Page 18

See page TB18

Page 19

1 **Key:** 2 Thursday 3 Wednesday 4 Friday 5 Tuesday 6 weekend 7 Sunday 8 Saturday

2 4.13

'ay' 'ay'
On Monday and Tuesday, I don't play,
On Wednesday and Thursday, I do,
On Friday and Saturday, I play all day,
On Sunday, I play at the zoo!

Page 20

1 1.24

See Pupil's Book page 20

Key: 2 new pet 3 feed it 4 its face 5 think so 6 to cats

Page 21

1 **Key:** 2 before 3 evening 4 plays 5 sometimes 6 never 7 kitten

2 **Key:** 2 They always wash their hands before lunch. 3 How often does he play in the park? 4 She never eats burgers for breakfast. 5 We feed our puppy twice every day. 6 Do they always do their homework after school?

Page 22

1 **Key:** 2 write an email 3 go skating 4 read a comic 5 watch a DVD 6 go shopping 7 watch films 8 listen to music

2 **Key:** 2 watches 3 comics 4 go shopping 5 listen to 6 go skating 7 email 8 a DVD / DVDs

Page 23

1 **Key:** 2 bedroom 3 dad 4 shop 5 mangoes

2 **Key:** 2 f 3 b 4 g 5 a 6 e 7 c

Page 24

1 **Key:** Learners draw a helmet, elbow and knee pads and gloves

2 **Key:** 2 John 3 Nick 4 Jane 5 Sally 6 Charlie

Page 25

4 **Key:** Pictures (1), 4 and 8

5 **Key:** 2 water, drink 3 sun cream 4 clothes 5 helmet

Page 26

1 **Key:** Name: Alex
What's he like? always late, sleepy, slow
How do you know? he wants to stay in bed
At the beginning: at home, in bed, in the bedroom, eight o'clock on Monday morning
In the middle: in the kitchen, in the car
At the end: at school

2 **Key:** Learners tick answer b

Page 27

4 4.14

1 When are the football matches?
Lisa: Guess what, Dad! I'm on the school football team!
Dad: That's great, Lisa. How often do you play?
Lisa: Well, we practise on Wednesdays and Mondays after school.
Dad: And the football matches?
Lisa: On Saturdays.
Dad: Fantastic.

2 What does the boy want?
Mum: Here's your lunch.
Boy: But I don't like chicken or salad!
Mum: Well, what do you want?
Boy: Cheese and tomato sandwiches, please.
Mum: OK.
Boy: Thanks, Mum.

3 What does the boy want to do?
Girl: Do you want to go swimming after school?
Boy: No, thanks. I can't swim, but I've got a new bicycle.
Girl: Great, I've got one too.
Boy: Let's go to the park and ride our bikes.
Girl: OK.

4 Who is the girl's PE teacher?
Girl: Look, there's my PE teacher.
Man: The woman wearing the red T-shirt?
Girl: Yes. She's very tall.
Man: Yes. Is she nice?
Girl: She's really nice.

5 Where are the children?
Girl: Ah! The rabbits are really cute.
Boy: Yeah, but let's go and see the cows over there.
Girl: Why are the sheep running about?
Boy: Because the dog's moving them.
Girl: Oh, he's a farm dog. He's really intelligent.
Boy: Yes, he is!

6 What is the boy looking for?
Mum: Jack! Where are you?
Jack: I'm upstairs.
Mum: What are you doing? It's eight o'clock!
Jack: I'm looking for my notebook!
Mum: It's in your backpack with your books and pens.
Jack: No, it isn't.
Mum: OK, but hurry up!

Key: 2 b 3 c 4 c 5 a 6 c

Page 28

1 **Key:** 1 grass 2 an email 3 a forest 4 films 5 a lake

Page 29

1

Learners work in groups. They need a dice, and a counter each. First, each learner writes four sentences in their notebook. They choose three different squares from the board for each sentence: an activity, a day and an adverb of frequency. Example sentence: *I always read comics on Saturdays* (*always, read comics* and *Saturday* squares). Learners move around the board according to the number they roll on the dice. They need to 'collect' the twelve items they used to write their sentences. The game finishes when one learner collects all twelve items from the four sentences written in their notebook.

Unit 3

Page 30

See page TB30

Page 31

1 **Key:** 2 present 3 dentist 4 film star 5 pop star 6 nurse 7 doctor 8 farmer
Secret word: treasure

2 4.15

father costume party grandpa farmer nurse grandma pirate doctor film star

Key: yes: father, party, grandpa, farmer, grandma, film star
no: costume, nurse, pirate, doctor

3 4.16

father grandpa grandma party farmer film star

Key: f<u>a</u>ther, grandp<u>a</u>, grandm<u>a</u> p<u>ar</u>ty, f<u>ar</u>mer, film st<u>ar</u>

Page 32

1 1.38

See Pupil's Book page 32

Key: 2 (~~sheep~~) cows 3 (~~pop star~~) film star 4 (~~pirate~~) doctor 5 (~~clowns~~) people 6 (~~hat~~) eye

2 **Key:** 2 wear 3 helping 4 wants

Page 33

1 **Key:** 2 has 3 play 4 wears 5 's washing 6 skate 7 's getting 8 goes

2 **Key:** 1 Paul 2 Vicky 3 Lily

Page 34

1 4.17

1 This pirate's short and thin. He's got short, straight, blonde hair and a big, blonde moustache.
2 This pirate's got short, curly, fair hair and a long beard. He's tall and thin and he's got a small moustache.
3 This pirate is tall and fat. He's got long, fair hair and a small moustache. He hasn't got a beard.
4 This pirate's got a long, black beard and long, straight, black hair. He's short and fat and he's got a big moustache.
5 This pirate's short, fat and ugly. He's got short, curly, fair hair and a long beard. He hasn't got a moustache.
6 This pirate's tall and thin. He's got curly, black hair and a long, black beard. He hasn't got a moustache.

Key: a 3 b 6 (c 1) d 5 e 4 f 2

2 **Key:** 2 hair 3 He's a pop star. 4 They're dancing. 5 Learners' own answers

Page 35

1 **Key:** 2 I'm taking photos of her because she's a film star. 3 They can't play tennis because they haven't got a ball. 4 She's wearing a helmet because she's riding a horse. 5 Peter's very happy today because it's his birthday. 6 They're wearing costumes because they're at a party.

2 **Key:** 2 d 3 b 4 e 5 a

Page 36

1 **Key:** 2 police officer 3 doctor 4 nurse 5 firefighter 6 dentist

2 **Key:** 2 a 3 d 4 b 5 f 6 g 7 h 8 e

Page 37

3 **Key:** 2 firefighter 3 doctor/nurse 4 dentist

4 **Key:** 2 police officer 3 firefighter 4 teacher 5 dentist 6 farmer

Page 38

1 **Key:** 2 superhero 3 hat 4 superhero pirate clown

2 **Key:** 2 superhero 3 beard 4 pirate 5 pop 6 funny

Page 39

4 **Key:** 2 a hat 3 a party 4 a farmer 5 a sheep

Page 40

1 4.18

Look at these pictures. They show a story. It's called 'Mary and Zoe are pop stars'. Look at the pictures first.

Look at the first one. Mary and her sister Zoe are watching TV. The singer on the TV is dancing and singing. Mum is cooking in the kitchen.

Now you tell the story.

Key: (possible story) Mary and her sister Zoe are watching TV. The singer on the TV is dancing and singing. Mum is cooking in the kitchen. Now Mary is dancing and singing like the girl on the TV. Zoe is taking a banana in the kitchen. She's smiling. Mary and Zoe are singing and dancing now. Their mother is very happy.

Page 41

1

Learners work in groups. They need a dice, and a counter each. Learners move around the board according to the number they roll on the dice. If they can describe the person on the square, they stay where they are (they have to say what the person does and describe what he/she looks like). If not, they return to their last square. The game finishes when one learner gets to the final square, or when all learners finish.

Review Units 1–3

Page 42

1 4.19

Girl: Monday is my favourite day. I always roller skate in the countryside with my puppy! I love playing football. I never play on Wednesdays. I always play on Tuesdays. I usually go to the farm on Wednesday and I often sit on a tractor! Thursdays are quiet. I never do sport. Today is Thursday and I'm listening to music. Friday is party day! I have a clown costume for my party tomorrow.

Key: 1 Thursday 2 Tuesday (3 Monday) 4 Friday 5 Wednesday

2 **Key:** 2 clown (it isn't an activity) 3 bed (you don't find it in the bathroom) 4 farm (the others are water) 5 present (it isn't a job/costume) 6 fat (it doesn't describe hair) 7 go to bed (you don't do it in the morning)

Page 43

3 **Key:** 2 yes 3 no 4 no 5 yes 6 no 7 yes

4 **Key:** 2 mustn't wear 3 mustn't eat 4 mustn't eat 5 must have 6 mustn't walk 7 must wear

Unit 4

Page 44

See page TB44

Page 45

1 **Key:** 2 uncle 3 daughter 4 son 5 aunt 6 grandson 7 granddaughter 8 parents 9 grandparents

2 4.20

mother father brother son daughter mum dad uncle cousin

Key: yes: mother, brother, son, mum, uncle, cousin
no: father, daughter, dad

3 4.21

mother brother son mum uncle cousin

Key: mother, brother, son mum, uncle cousin

Page 46

1 2.02

See Pupil's Book page 46

1 **Key:** 2 ✗ 3 ✗ 4 ✗ 5 ✓ 6 ✓

2 **Key:** (possible answers) Harry's bigger than Shelly. Henrietta's older than Rocky. Shelly's prettier than Cameron. Rocky's smaller than Cameron. Gracie's thinner than Cameron. Rocky's younger than Harry.

Page 47

1 **Key:**

+er	y +ier	double letter +er	irregular
(longer)	(angrier)	(bigger)	(worse)
shorter	curlier	fatter	better
straighter	happier	sadder	
taller	naughtier	thinner	
younger	uglier		

2 **Key:** 2 The cat's tail's longer than the dog's tail.
3 The kittens are thinner than the puppies.
4 My dad's beard's shorter than my uncle's beard.
5 Our new house is better than our old one.

Page 48

1 **Key:** 2 first floor (it isn't a job/costume) 3 stairs (it isn't a place where people live) 4 doctor (it isn't a floor in a building) 5 basement (you don't find it in the countryside) 6 roof (it isn't an adjective / you can't use it to describe hair) 7 village (it isn't hair) 8 balcony (it isn't a person in a family) 9 basement (it isn't for parties) 10 downstairs (you can't watch it)

2 4.22

Jane: Hello, Jack. What are you doing today?
Jack: Hi, Jane. I'm helping my family. They're all doing different things. At the moment my aunt's outside in the garden picking up leaves.
Jane: Are you outside in the garden with her?
Jack: I'm outside, but I'm not in the garden.
Jane: What are you doing?
Jack: I'm watching my uncle. He's up on the roof. He's painting it.
Jane: Oh. Are you at your uncle's house?
Jack: No, I'm at my grandparents' house. We're all helping them.
Jane: Really? Where are they?
Jack: They're cleaning the balcony.
Jane: Are your parents with you?
Jack: Yes, they are, but they're inside. They're downstairs in the basement.
Jane: What are they doing?
Jack: They're putting some old things into boxes. I must go because I want to help them. I like helping my family. Bye!

Key: his uncle – d his grandparents – b his parents – a

Page 49

1 **Key:** 2 It's his. (orange) 3 It's hers. (yellow) 4 They're ours. (pink) 5 It's mine. (blue) 6 It's yours. (purple)

2 **Key:** 2 Mine, hers 3 theirs 4 his 5 yours

Page 50

1 **Key:** a 3 b 5 c 6 (d 1) e 2 f 4

2 **Key:** (possible answers) 2 in the street 3 in the house 4 in the classroom / in the house 5 in the street / in the park 6 in the park 7 in the classroom / in the house 8 in the classroom / in the house

Page 51

3 **Key:** a 5 (b 1) c 4 d 2 e 3 f 8 g 7 h 6

Page 52

1 **Key:** 2 Lots of sandwiches and a chocolate cake. 3 Because they want to see the street. 4 Her friends at work are giving her a surprise party. 5 To invite his mum's friends home. / To have one big party.

2 **Key:** 2 party 3 train 4 phone

Page 53

4 **Key:** 2 comics/magazines 3 orange juice 4 He's wearing a blue cap. 5 It's next to the table. 6 He's (roller) skating. 7 (possible sentences) There's a cake on the table. Marta and Juan are sitting under a tree.

Page 54

1 4.23

Teacher: Is that your brother? I remember he was in my class at school too.
Lily: Yes, that's John. He lives in the city centre now. In a flat with some friends.
Teacher: That looks nice.

Can you see the letter H? Now you listen and write a letter in each box.

1 Teacher: Does your uncle live in the city too?
Lily: He did, but now he lives in a much quieter place. He's got a small house in the mountains. You can see them from the window.
Teacher: What a beautiful place!
Lily: Yes, it's really lovely.

2 Teacher: What about your cousin? She isn't at our school now.
Lily: That's right. Her dad has a job in another country and they've got a big flat near the beach there.
Teacher: That looks lovely.
Lily: It is lovely, and my cousin likes her new school there too. We went to see them last month.

3 Teacher: Does your grandfather live near here?
Lily: Yes, that's right. If you cross the river and go out of town there are lots of fields with sheep and cows. It's difficult to see the house because it's in the fields.
Teacher: Is that the house in the picture there?
Lily: Yes, that's right, it's big and old.

4 Teacher: Does your aunt live in town now?
Lily: No, she doesn't. She had a boat on the river here, but it was very cold. She lives near water because she loves fishing, but she's got a house now.
Teacher: Is that near the sea?
Lily: No, it's next to a small lake. It's near here.

5 Teacher: Where would you like to live?
Lily: I love my grandmother's house. It's small but it's lovely. And she's got a garden with lots and lots of flowers and some trees.
Teacher: Is it here in town?
Lily: No, it's in a small village near here. There are only six other houses there and one small shop.

Key: her grandfather – B her cousin – C her uncle – A her aunt – F her grandmother – D

Page 55

1

Learners work in groups. They need a dice, and a counter each. Each learner chooses one of the four places in the corners to start from. They tick four things from the list in the centre – they must visit these places on the board. Learners move around the board according to the number they roll on the dice. If they land on a blue square with instructions, they follow the instructions. The game finishes when one learner has visited all four places they ticked on their list.

Unit 5

Page 56

See page TB56

Page 57

1 **Key:** 2 dolphin 3 rabbit 4 bat 5 lion 6 parrot 7 bear 8 kangaroo 9 panda 10 whale

2 4.24

/g/ /g/ goat goat
/dʒ/ /dʒ/ giraffe giraffe
1 cage cage
2 kangaroo kangaroo
3 penguin penguin
4 tiger tiger
5 orange orange

Key: 2 /g/ (goat) 3 /g/ (goat) 4 /g/ (goat) 5 /dʒ/ (giraffe)

Page 58

1 2.19

See Pupil's Book page 58

Key: 2 the biggest 3 tail 4 parrot 5 the worst 6 the angriest

Page 59

1 **Key:** Vicky – small girl with dark hair Sally – older girl with blonde hair Chu Lin – smallest panda Bao Bao – dirtiest panda Yang Yang – panda on the left eating Gu Gu – biggest/oldest panda on the right

2 **Key:** 2 biggest 3 best 4 cleverest 5 thinnest 6 curliest 7 worst 8 funniest

Page 60

1 **Key:** 2 jump 3 climb 4 fall 5 hide 6 lose 7 walk 8 run 9 fly

2 **Key:** 2 ✗ 3 ✓ 4 ✗ 5 ✗ 6 ✓

Page 61

1 **Key:** 2 no 3 no 4 no 5 no 6 yes

2 **Key:** (possible sentences) In picture A there's one bear near the rock, but in picture B there are two bears near the rock.
In picture A the snake is below a tree, but in picture B it's climbing/in a tree.
In picture A the brown bear is opposite the grey bear, but in picture B the brown bear is near the grey bear.
In picture A the snake is below the parrot, but in picture B it's opposite/near the parrot.
In picture A the parrot is above a tree, but in picture B it's below a tree.

Page 62

1 **Key:** 2 c 3 b 4 a

2 **Key:** 1 b 2 c 3 a

3 **Key:** 2 (This is) a kangaroo. (It eats) plants. (It is) a herbivore. 3 This is a rabbit. It eats plants. It is a herbivore. 4 This is a lion. It eats meat. It is a carnivore.

Page 63

4 **Key:** an elephant

Page 64

1 **Key:** a 4 b 3 c 6 d 2 e 5 (f 1)

(possible story) A mummy kangaroo and a baby kangaroo are playing near a river. A wombat is crying. He can't see. He needs to drink and eat. The mummy kangaroo helps the wombat. She takes him to the river and he drinks. Then she takes him to the grass and he eats. The mummy kangaroo can't find her baby. At the end, she finds her baby. She puts him in a pouch. It's a present from the wombat.

2 **Key:** (possible sentences) a A wombat is eating grass. b A wombat is drinking from the river. c The kangaroo is with her baby again. She's got a pouch now. d The wombat is crying. He can't see. e The kangaroo can't find her baby.

3 **Key:** (possible sentences) 2 The old lady can't cross the street. The man is helping her. 3 The cat can't get down from the tree. The boy is helping it.

Page 65

4 **Key:** (possible differences) In picture A there's a wombat. In picture B there's a rabbit.

In picture A there's a small flower near the rock. In picture B there's a big flower near the rock.

In picture A there are three trees. In picture B there are four trees.

In picture A it's sunny. In picture B it isn't sunny.

Page 66

1 **Key:** 1 B 2 A 3 A 4 C 5 A 6 B

Page 67

1

Learners work in groups. They need a dice, and a counter each. Learners move around the board according to the number they roll on the dice. If they can say what the animals pictured are doing, they stay where they are. If not, they return to their last square. If they land on a yellow, green or red square they follow the instructions. The game finishes when one learner gets to the final square, or when all learners finish.

Unit 6

Page 68

See page TB68

Page 69

1 **Key:** 2 snowing 3 windy 4 rainbow 5 sunny 6 clouds
a 2 b 3 (c 1) d 5 e 4 f 6

2 4.25

tree bee three windy sunny cloudy

3 4.26

tree bee three windy sunny cloudy

Key: (tree), bee, three windy, sunny, cloudy

Page 70

1 2.34

See Pupil's Book page 70

Key: 2 ~~forest~~ mountains 3 ~~rain~~ snow 4 ~~younger~~ older 5 ~~sad~~ happy 6 ~~cloudy~~ sunny

2 **Key:** 1 They were in the mountains. 2 It was cold. / There was snow. 3 They were out in the fields, near the forest. 4 It was cold. / There was snow. 5 Yes, they were.

Page 71

1 **Key:** 2 were 3 was 4 was 5 were 6 weren't 7 was 8 weren't, was

2 **Key:** 2 wasn't 3 weren't 4 were 5 was 6 were

2 It was windy, but it wasn't cold. 3 Because the weather was good for flying their (new) kite.
4 Because two silly birds were there. 5 They were above their heads.

Page 72

1 **Key:** clothes: coat, scarf, shorts, sweater
weather: cloud, rain, snow, sunny, wind
house: balcony, basement, floor, roof, stairs
animals: bat, bear, parrot, rabbit, whale

2 **Key:** 2 wear 3 take off 4 coat 5 put on 6 costume 7 shorts 8 boots
Secret word: sweaters

Page 73

1 **Key:** 2 Were there any leaves on the trees? 3 There was a rainbow above the field. 4 There wasn't a lake opposite the farm. 5 There were two clowns at the party, but only one pirate.

2 **Key:** 2 b 3 c 4 b

Page 74

1 **Key:** 1 c 2 a 3 b

Page 75

3 **Key:** (possible sentences, depending on where learners draw the symbols) It is sunny in Old Town. It is raining in Blue Lake. It is snowing in Foxton. It is cloudy in Riverside.

Page 76

1 **Key:** 1 (rain) / Jump, Splash
2 wind(y) / Jump, kick
3 cloud(y) / Imagine
4 snow / the ice, snowman

Page 77

4 **Key:** 2 All 3 when 4 snow 5 Sometimes 6 coming

Page 78

1 4.27

Dad: Daisy! We must go! Have you got your boots?
Daisy: Yes, Dad. Here they are! It's fun driving to see Grandma and Grandpa.
Dad: Yes. And Grandpa always knows what to do when the weather's bad. Come on, it's 12 o'clock. It's time to go!
Daisy: I know … and look, it's snowing!

Can you see the answer? Now you listen and write.

1 Daisy: Which road do we go on, Dad?
Dad: Today we're going on the G38.
Daisy: Not the G22, which goes near the forest?
Dad: No, not today! The G38 is the quickest road.

2 Daisy: Dad, I'd like to phone Grandma before we go.
Dad: OK. Look for her name on my phone.
Daisy: What's her name? 'Kitty' something?
Dad: That's right. Kitty Crumb. That's C-R-U-M-B.
Daisy: OK. Thanks. I've got it.

3 Daisy: What's in that green bag, Dad?
Dad: Grandpa's sweater. It was in my cupboard … by mistake! Don't put your scarf in the bag, Daisy.
Daisy: Oh … why not?
Dad: It's very big!
Daisy: Yeah, you're right!

4 Daisy: I can't wait to see their new pet!
Dad: Um, I don't know … It's very young!
Daisy: But I really want to play with the new rabbit!
Dad: OK, but be careful!

5 Daisy: I've got one more question, Dad. Will the weather be terrible all day today?
Dad: I don't know … let's listen to the radio in the car.
Daisy: Good idea!
Dad: And then, in the afternoon, Grandpa wants you to help him fix his skates.
Daisy: Oh, yeah. His skates! He loves those funny old things!

Key: 1 38 2 Crumb 3 Grandpa's sweater 4 The new pet (rabbit) 5 Grandpa's skates

2 4.28

Boy: Grandma, look at this photo of my friends at the lake.
Grandma: Oh, yes – it's really nice. Which friends were you with?
Boy: Well, that's Paul. Can you see him? He's wearing a coat.
Grandma: Is he fishing?
Boy: Yes, he is. He wants to catch something for lunch!

Can you see the line? This is an example. Now you listen and draw lines.

1 Grandma: That boy's wearing shorts! Isn't he cold?
Boy: You're right! He's Matt.
Grandma: And he's roller skating too!
Boy: Yes, he loves doing that.

2 Grandma: Is that your friend's mother?
Boy: Where?
Grandma: She's standing next to those rocks.
Boy: Do you mean the woman with straight hair?
Grandma: Yes.
Boy: That's Ann. She's Paul's big sister.

3 Grandma: That's Ben, isn't it? The man with the towel, I mean.
Boy: That's right.
Grandma: He's got a big moustache!
Boy: Yes, I know! He's walking towards the lake because he wants to go swimming.
Grandma: Really? But it looks very cold!

4 Boy: Do you know my friend's grandmother?
Grandma: No, I don't. Is she in the photo?
Boy: Yes. Look, she's putting a plate of burgers on the table.
Grandma: Now I can see her. What's she called?
Boy: Her name's Julia.
Grandma: There was lots of food. Were you hungry?
Boy: Yes, we were … and we ate it all!

5 Grandma: What about that woman?
Boy: Which one?
Grandma: She's putting on her scarf.
Boy: Her long, pink one? That's because she doesn't like windy weather. Her name's Kim.
Grandma: Well, it's a beautiful photo and a nice lake!

Key: Matt – boy wearing shorts and roller skating
Ann – woman with straight hair next to rocks
Ben – man with moustache walking towards lake
Julia – woman with plate of burgers
Kim – woman putting on scarf

Page 79

1

Learners work in groups. They need a dice, and a counter each. Learners move around the board according to the number they roll on the dice. If they land on a picture square, they say what they can see, using the past tense. If they say it correctly, they stay where they are. If not, they return to their last square. If they land on a square with a sentence on it, they find the matching picture square and move there. The game finishes when one learner gets to the final square, or when all learners finish.

Review Units 4–6

Page 80

1 4.29

1 Sally: Hi, I'm Sally. Look at this photo. It was sunny and hot yesterday. We were on my grandparents' balcony. They live on the second floor. In the photo I'm wearing a T-shirt and shorts.

2 Jane: Hello, I'm Jane. This is a picture of me yesterday. It was cloudy and windy. We were in my village. I'm wearing a scarf.
3 Tony: Hello, I'm Tony. This is a picture of me with my cousin Jack. He lives in the town centre and we're near his house. I'm wearing his sweater because it was cold that day!
4 Fred: Hi. I'm Fred. This is a photo of me and my aunt. In this photo there was a lot of snow! We're near the lake and I'm wearing my new boots.

Key: 1 Sally: (b,) a, b 2 Jane: b, a, b 3 Tony: b, b, b 4 Fred: a, a, a

Page 81

3 **Key:** Learners draw a dolphin above the whale. It's smaller than the whale but bigger than the penguin. They draw a bat near the penguin. It's smaller than the penguin. They draw a rabbit next to the bat.

Unit 7

Page 82

See page TB82

Page 83

1 **Key:** 2 sandwich 3 cheese 4 soup 5 pasta 6 (across) bowl 6 (down) bottle 7 salad 8 glass 9 cup 10 plate

2 4.30

/tʃ/ /tʃ/ armchair cheese chicken chocolate

Key: 1 chocolate 2 cheese 3 chicken

3 4.31

Richie likes eating chicken, cheese and chocolate in his armchair! [x2]

Page 84

1 3.05

See Pupil's Book page 84

Key: 2 salad 3 kitchen 4 shopping 5 us 6 put

2 **Key:** (possible questions) Did they drink hot chocolate? Yes, they did. Did they have a cooking class at home? No, they didn't. Did they make a salad? Yes, they did.

Page 85

1 **Key:** 2 didn't go 3 didn't have 4 didn't drink 5 didn't make

2 **Key:** Last Saturday Daisy made lunch for her parents. She went to the shops and got carrots and potatoes. She made carrot soup. Her parents were very happy. The soup was fantastic.

Page 86

1 **Key:** 2 wash (wash is a verb / something you do, the others are food) 3 sandwich (it's food, the others are verbs) 4 cut (it's a verb, the others are adjectives) 5 glass (it's a noun / something you drink from, the others are verbs) 6 carry (it's a verb, the others are people in a family) 7 drop (it's a verb, the others are things you use) 8 plate (it's a noun / something you use, the others are verbs)

2 4.32

Man: Look at this picture of a big kitchen. Can you colour it, please?
Girl: Hmm. There are a lot of busy cooks.
Man: Yes, there are. There's a man cooking pasta. He's boiling it. Colour his hat yellow, please.
Girl: Oh, yes, I like his yellow hat.
Man: Now I'd like you to colour the onions. Can you see them?
Girl: Oh, yes, they're on the table next to that woman.
Man: That's right. She's cutting them and crying.
Girl: But she isn't sad. What colour are they?
Man: Make them brown, please.
Man: Can you see the young man washing plates?
Girl: He hasn't got a hat on.
Man: That's right. Colour the plates blue, please.
Girl: OK. He's washing blue plates now.
Man: Great!
Girl: Can I colour one of the bowls now?
Man: That's a good idea. Which bowl do you want to colour?
Girl: Look at this young woman here. She's carrying some bowls and dropping one. Can I colour that one?
Man: OK, colour it purple, please.
Girl: Fantastic! I love purple!
Man: Can you see some bottles?
Girl: Yes, I can see two.
Man: Which bottle do you want to colour?
Girl: The bottle near the glasses. I can colour it red.
Man: Well done!
Girl: Look at that cook with a beard. He's frying sausages.
Man: Yes, he's very hot. Do you want to colour his boots?
Girl: All right. Can I colour them grey?
Man: Grey isn't my favourite colour. I'd like you to colour them green, please.
Girl: OK, he's got nice green boots on.

Key: onions – brown plates young man is washing – blue bowl woman is dropping – purple bottle near glasses – red boots of man who's frying sausages – green

Page 87

1 **Key:**

+ed	~~y~~ +ied	+d	consonant +ed
(boiled)	(carried)	(bounced)	(clapped)
cooked	copied	invited	dropped
laughed	cried	liked	hopped
started	fried	skated	skipped
washed	tried	smiled	stopped

2 **Key:** 2 invited 3 smiled 4 laughed 5 carried 6 dropped 7 cried 8 stopped

Page 88

1 **Key:** 2 fruit 3 leaf 4 seeds

2 **Key:** 2 fruit 3 seeds 4 flowers

Page 89

3 **Key:** 2 red 3 green 4 red 5 green 6 red 7 red 8 green

4 **Key:** 2 e 3 d 4 a 5 c

Page 90

1 **Key:** 2 yes They were at home because they weren't well. 3 yes He says 'You can't cook, Sonny!' / He thinks Sonny's job is to wash the dishes. 4 no She asks Sonny to cook in her restaurant.

2 **Key:** b

Page 91

4 **Key:** 2 happy 3 birthday 4 television 5 washed 6 cooking

Page 92

1 4.33

Look at these four pictures. One is different. The comic is different. A kiwi, a banana and a pear are fruit. You eat them. You don't eat a comic. You read it.

Key: (possible answers) 2 The second picture is different. In the other pictures there is something above the chair. In the second picture the doll is below the chair.
3 The last picture is different. In the other pictures people are shopping. In the last picture the boy is drinking (water).
4 The last picture is different. A bee, a parrot and a bat can fly. A rabbit can't fly.

Page 93

1

Learners work in groups. They need a dice, and a counter each. Learners move around the board according to the number they roll on the dice. On each square, they say what the people and animals did, using the past tense (e.g. *They washed the dishes.*). If they say it correctly, they stay where they are. If not, they return to their last square. The game finishes when one learner gets to the final square, or when all learners finish.

Unit 8

Page 94

See page TB94

Page 95

1 **Key:** 2 funfair 3 ticket 4 train station 5 car park 6 ride 7 road 8 map

2 4.34

snow station rainbow grown-up road car park coat

Key: yes: snow, rainbow, grown-up, road, coat
no: station, car park

3 4.35

snow rainbow grown-up road coat

Key: 1 (sn<u>ow</u>,) rainb<u>ow</u>, gr<u>ow</u>n-up 2 r<u>oa</u>d, c<u>oa</u>t

Page 96

1 3.24

See Pupil's Book page 96

Key: 2 ✓ 3 ✗ (they sat in the back) 4 ✓ 5 ✓ 6 ✗ (Harry took his hat)

2 **Key:** 2 bought 3 wore 4 chose 5 told 6 gave 7 took

Page 97

1 **Key:** 2 They gave me some skates. (orange) 3 It slept in the garden. (yellow) 4 She chose chocolate. (pink) 5 He fed them at eight o'clock. (blue) 6 They bought her a new sweater. (purple)

2 **Key:** 2 found 3 lost 4 bought 5 wore 6 drove 7 hid 8 gave 9 took 10 went

Page 98

1 **Key:** 2 bus station 3 shopping centre 4 cinema 5 sports centre 6 swimming pool 7 café 8 library 9 car park 10 market 11 hospital
Secret word: supermarket

2 **Key:** 2 library 3 market/supermarket 4 shopping centre 5 hospital 6 café 7 cinema 8 bus station

Page 99

1 **Key:** 2 get up 3 café 4 rides

2 **Key:** 2 Mary doesn't have to get up at seven o'clock.
3 Sally has to wear a helmet on her bike.
4 My parents don't have to do homework.
5 Do you have to study for tests?

Page 100

1 **Key:** 2 traffic lights 3 litter bin 4 pedestrian crossing 5 street lamp 6 pavement 7 road

2 **Key:** 2 e 3 b 4 c 5 f 6 a

Page 101

3 **Key:** 2 pavement – picture a 3 pedestrian crossing – picture b 4 look – picture d

Page 102

1 **Key:** 2 (Her name was) Brenda. 3 Bruno (was Tom's bus buddy). 4 It could fly. 5 (He could see) his town. 6 He saw Brenda and Bruno.

2 **Key:** b

Page 103

3 **Key:** 2 feed 3 wild 4 sandwich 5 jumped 6 didn't

Page 104

1 4.36

Where is Peter going with his mother?

Mum: Come on, Peter. We're going out now.
Peter: To the river? I love fishing there.
Mum: I thought we could walk in the forest and there are lots of things to see. So we're doing that today.
Peter: Oh, but that's boring. What about the lake? We can go on the boats there.
Mum: No, we did that last week, but we can go there again next weekend.

Can you see the tick? Now you listen and tick the box.

1 Which girl is Mr Ball's granddaughter?
Boy: Which girl is your granddaughter, Mr Ball?
Mr Ball: She's coming out of the bus station now. Can you see her?
Boy: Is she holding a map?
Mr Ball: No, that's her cousin. My granddaughter's holding her ticket.
Boy: Oh, yes, there she is!

2 Which sweater does Sam want to wear for the party?
Sam: I'd like to put on my favourite party sweater … you know … the one with the penguin on it.
Mum: Sorry, Sam. It's very small for you now! How about this one, with a panda on it?
Sam: All right. But Bill's sweater is nicer.
Mum: What's he got on his sweater?
Sam: A big whale!
Mum: Well, I think yours is really nice too!

3 Where was Zoe on Monday?
Zoe: Sorry I wasn't at school on Monday, Miss Hall.
Miss Hall: Were you at the hospital, Zoe?
Zoe: Yes. I cut my leg at the swimming pool.
Miss Hall: Oh, dear! Are you all right now?
Zoe: Yes, thanks … but this afternoon I have to go to the doctor's.
Miss Hall: That's fine. Thank you for telling me.

4 What is Fred doing now?
Man: Is Fred walking to the bus stop?
Woman: No, he isn't! Because he was asleep at eight o'clock!
Man: Oh, no! How's he going to school then? By bike?
Woman: Mrs Short's taking him and Mary in the car.
Man: Oh, that's good. Fred's lessons start at nine o'clock.

5 Which is the new building in the city?
Girl: Mum, did you see the new building in the city?
Mum: Do you mean the supermarket? The one opposite the library?
Girl: Yes! It's huge! I think it's bigger than the hospital!
Mum: Really? Well … I need to get some things. Let's go there today.
Girl: OK, Mum!

Key: 1 c 2 b 3 b 4 a 5 c

Page 105

1

Learners work in groups. They need a dice, and a counter each. Learners move around the board according to the number they roll on the dice. On each square, they change the sentence so it is negative (e.g. *He didn't buy a ticket online.*). If they say it correctly, they stay where they are. If not, they return to their last square. The game finishes when one learner gets to the final square, or when all learners finish.

Unit 9

Page 106

See page TB106

Page 107

1 **Key:** 2 easy 3 exciting 4 difficult 5 frightened 6 boring 7 tired 8 thirsty 9 dangerous 10 surprised 11 hungry

2 4.37

'ing' 'ing'
'in' 'in'
1 exciting exciting
2 wind wind
3 boring boring
4 penguin penguin
5 dolphin dolphin
6 swimming swimming

3 4.37

Key: 2 wind 3 boring 4 penguin 5 dolphin 6 swimming

Page 108

1 3.41

See Pupil's Book page 108

Key: 2 exciting 3 dangerous 4 beautiful 5 afraid 6 frightened

2 **Key:** 2 surprised 3 exciting 4 dangerous 5 circus 6 rode

Page 109

1 **Key:** 2 Bears are more dangerous than rabbits.
3 Daisy thinks that lions are more beautiful than bats.
4 At the funfair, Jim was more frightened than Jenny.
5 Jack thinks climbing's more difficult than riding a bike.

Page 110

1 **Key:** 2 cinema – hospital – library 3 letter – text – email 4 journey – travel – trip

2 **Key:** 2 for 3 maps 4 their 5 easiest 6 emails

Page 111

1 **Key:** 2 no 3 yes 4 no 5 no 6 no 7 yes 8 yes

2 4.38

1 Woman: Did you enjoy your school trip last week, Jack?
Jack: Oh, yes – it was the most exciting journey ever.
Woman: Did you fly?
Jack: No, we went by train.
2 Woman: Oh, yes. I like travelling by train too. Where did you go?
Jack: We went to the Bluegrass Mountains.
Woman: Bluegrass Mountains? Is that B-L-U-E-G-R-A-S-S?
Jack: Yes, that's right. Look, I can show them to you on the map.
Woman: Oh. They aren't near here.
3 Jack: No, they aren't. We had to catch the train at eight o'clock in the morning and we got off at four o'clock in the afternoon.
Woman: Eight hours! What did you do on the train?
Jack: Well, I looked at the countryside out of the window and listened to music, but a lot of my friends slept because they were tired.
Woman: How many children went on the trip?
Jack: There were 28 of us.
4 Woman: What did you see from the window?
Jack: The most beautiful thing was a rainbow above a forest. It was fantastic.
Woman: Hmm. Did you see any animals in the forest?
Jack: Yes, I did. I was really surprised to see a big, grey rabbit in the grass. It was near the train.
5 Woman: Were you hungry on the train?
Jack: No, I wasn't. We all had a picnic lunch. We brought our food from home.
Woman: What did you eat?
Jack: My dad made me a big chicken sandwich. I gave part of it to my friend because it was so big.
6 Woman: Oh, that's nice. Did your friend give you any food?
Jack: No, he didn't, but I was really thirsty and he gave me some fruit juice.
Woman: So, what did he drink?
Jack: He drank fruit juice too. He had two bottles.
Woman: What kind of juice was it?
Jack: It was my favourite. It was pineapple. It was great!

Key: 2 Bluegrass 3 28 4 rabbit 5 sandwich 6 fruit/pineapple

Page 112

2 **Key:** 2 Machu Picchu – South America 3 Stonehenge – Europe 4 Taj Mahal – Asia 5 Great Barrier Reef – Australia

Page 113

3 **Key:** 2 manmade 3 manmade 4 natural 5 natural 6 manmade

4 **Key:** 2 The Grand Canyon / North America 3 The Great Pyramid / Africa

Page 114

1 **Key:** 2 Richard hid the clues. 3 Some of the clues were in the trees (and some were on the ground). 4 There was a tree like a giraffe in the wood. 5 The last clue was one hundred steps from the picnic.

2 **Key:** 2 good 3 everyone 4 around 5 behind 6 Ben 7 giraffe 8 tree 9 news 10 know 11 shiver 12 eat

Page 115

4 4.39

1 What is the book about?
Girl: This book's great.
Boy: What's it about?
Girl: It's about Africa.
Boy: What – elephants and lions?
Girl: No. It's a story about giraffes.
2 Whose party is it?
Woman: Whose party are you going to?
Boy: Diana's.
Woman: Is Diana the girl with short, blonde hair?
Boy: No, she's the girl with long, red hair.
3 Where's the picnic?
Man: There's a school picnic today.
Boy: Yes, it's in the school playground, I think.
Girl: No, it isn't.
Man: Where is it then?
Girl: It's in the wood behind the school.
4 Which competition is Ana in?
Man: Where's Ana?
Woman: It's sports day at school today.
Man: Is she running or doing the high jump?
Woman: No, she's in the long jump competition.
Man: Well, let's go. The competition starts at two.

Key: 2 c 3 b 4 a

Page 116

1 **Key:** 1 vegetables 2 pictures 3 lizard 4 tail 5 downstairs

2 **Key:** Lily's Uncle Pat

Page 117

1

Learners work in groups. They need a dice, and a counter each. Each learner chooses one of the four buildings in the corners to start from. They tick four places from the list in the centre – they must visit these places on the board. Learners move around the board according to the number they roll on the dice. If they land on a blue square, they have to read the sentence aloud and move their counter to the corresponding picture square. The game finishes when one learner has visited all four places they ticked on their list.

Review Units 7–9

Page 118

1 4.40

Girl: I had an exciting day yesterday! First I went to the train station to buy a ticket for my trip next week. I went to the library and chose a book about travelling the world. I went to a café to buy some lunch because I was hungry. I ate a bowl of pasta and drank a glass of orange juice. I looked at a map to find my friend's house. I didn't get lost! Sally's dad took us to the funfair. The rides were more exciting than last year! We bought a bottle of water because we were thirsty. I sent a text to my dad and he drove us home. I slept in the car because I was tired!

Key: a 5 b 2 (c 1) d 8 e 7 f 4 g 3 h 6

2 **Key:** 2 station 3 email 4 map 5 trip 6 text 7 travel 8 world

Page 119

5 **Key:** (possible sentences) She's frightened because she's at the funfair. He's surprised because his parents gave him a bike for his birthday. He's thirsty because it's a hot day. She's tired because she ran a race at sports day today.

Numbers 21–100 (Pupil's Book page 120)

2 4.05

The bus to the funfair.	[47]
The bus to the train station.	[58]
The bus to the school.	[92]
The bus to the beach.	[35]
The bus to the city centre.	[86]
The bus to the library.	[74]
The bus to the hospital.	[29]
The bus to the sports centre.	[100]
The bus to the lake.	[63]

Key: See numbers in audioscript